NEW ROGET'S THESAURUS

1989 Edition

Published by

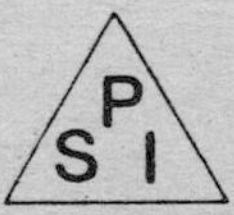

P.S.I. & Associates, Inc.
13322 S.W. 128th Street
Miami, Florida 33186

ISBN 0-938261-40-1

PLAN OF CLASSIFICATION.

Class.	Sect.	Nos.
I. ABSTRACT RELATIONS	1. Existence,	1–8
	2. Relation,	9–24
	3. Quantity,	25–57
	4. Order,	58–83
	5. Number,	84–105
	6. Time,	106–139
	7. Change,	140–152
	8. Causation,	153–179
II. SPACE,	1. Generally,	180–191
	2. Dimensions,	192–239
	3. Form,	240–263
	4. Motion,	264–315
III. MATTER,	1. Generally,	316–320
	2. Inorganic,	321–356
	3. Organic,	357–449
IV. INTELLECT,	1. Formation of Ideas,	450–515
	2. Communication of Ideas,	516–599
V. VOLITION,	1. Individual,	600–736
	2. Intersocial,	737–819
VI. AFFECTIONS,	1. Generally,	820–826
	2. Personal,	827–887
	3. Sympathetic,	888–921
	4. Moral,	922–975
	5. Religious,	976–1000

TABULAR SYNOPSIS OF CATEGORIES.

CLASS I. ABSTRACT RELATIONS.

EXISTENCE.

1. ABSTRACT, . . .	1. Existence.	2 Inexistence.
2. CONCRETE, . . .	3. Substantiality.	4. Unsubstantiality
3. FORMAL, ...	*Internal.*	*External.*
	5. Intrinsicality.	6. Extrinsicality.
4. MODAL, ...	*Absolute.*	*Relative.*
	7. State.	8. Circumstance.

II. RELATION.

1. ABSOLUTE, . . .	9. Relation.	10. Irrelation.
	11. Consanguinity.	
	12. Reciprocality.	
	13. Identity.	14. Contrariety.
		15. Difference.
2. CONTINUOUS, . .	16. Uniformity.	
3. PARTIAL, . . .	17. Similarity.	18. Dissimilarity.
	19. Imitation.	20. { Non-imitation. Variation.
	21. Copy.	22. Prototype.
4. GENERAL, . . .	23. Agreement.	24. Disagreement.

III QUANTITY.

	Absolute.	*Relative.*
1. SIMPLE, ...	25. Quantity.	26. Degree.
2. COMPARATIVE, .	27. Equality.	28. Inequality.
	29. Mean.	
	30. Compensation.	
	By comparison with a Standard.	
	31. Greatness.	32. Smallness.
	By comparison with a similar Object.	
	33 Superiority.	34. Inferiority.
	Changes in Quantity.	
	35. Increase.	36. Decrease.
3 CONJUNCTIVE, .	37. Addition.	38. { Non-addition. Subduction.
	39. Adjunct.	40. Remainder.
	41. Mixture.	42. Simpleness.
	43. Junction.	44. Disjunction.
	45. Vinculum.	
	46. Coherence.	47. Incoherence
	48. Combination.	49. Decomposition.

4. CONCRETE,		50. Whole.	51. Part.
		52. Completeness.	53. Incompleteness.
		54. Composition.	55. Exclusion.
		56. Component.	57. Extraneousness.
IV ORDER.			
1. GENERAL, . .		58. Order.	59. Disorder.
		60. Arrangement.	61. Derangement.
2 CONSECUTIVE, .		62. Precedence.	63. Sequence.
		64. Precursor.	65. Sequel.
		66. Beginning.	67. End.
		68. Middle.	
		69. Continuity.	70. Discontinuity.
		71. Term.	
3. COLLECTIVE, . .		72. Assemblage.	73. Non-assemblage. Dispersion.
		74. Focus.	
4. DISTRIBUTIVE, .		75. Class.	
		76. Inclusion.	77. Exclusion.
		78. Generality.	79. Speciality.
5. CATEGORICAL, .		80. Rule.	81. Multiformity.
		82. Conformity.	83. Unconformity.
V. NUMBER.			
1. ABSTRACT, . . .		84. Number.	
		85. Numeration.	
		86. List.	
2. DETERMINATE, .		87. Unity.	88. Accompaniment.
		89. Duality.	
		90. Duplication.	91. Bisection.
		92. Triality.	
		93. Triplication.	94. Trisection.
		95. Quaternity.	
		96. Quadruplication.	97 Quadrisection.
		98. Five, &c.	99. Quinquesection, &c
3. INDETERMINATE,		100. Plurality.	101. Zero.
		102. Multitude	103. Fewness.
		104. Repetition	
		105. Infinity.	
VI. TIME.			
1. ABSOLUTE, . .		106. Duration.	107. Non-duration.
		Definite.	*Indefinite.*
		108. Period.	109. Course.
		110. Diuturnity.	111. Transientness
		112. Perpetuity.	113. Instantaneity.
		114. Chronometry	115. Anachronism.
2. RELATIVE,	*to Succession*	116. Priority.	117. Posteriority.
		118. Present time.	119. Different time
		120. Synchronism	
		121. Futurity.	122 Preterition.
	to a Period	123. Newness.	124. Oldness.
		125. Morning.	126. Evening.
		127. Youth.	128. Age.
		129. Infant.	130. Veteran.
		131. Adolescence.	
	to an Effect or Purpose,	132 Earliness.	
		134 Occasion.	

3. RECURRENT, . .	136. Frequency.	137. Infrequency.
	138. Periodicity.	139. Irregularity.

VII. CHANGE.

1 SIMPLE, . . .	140. Change.	140.*a*. Absence of change.
	141. Cessation.	142. Permanence.
		143. Continuance.
	144. Conversion.	145. Reversion.
	146. Revolution.	
	147. Substitution.	148. Interchange.
2. COMPLEX, . . .	149. Changeableness	150. Stability.
	Present.	*Future.*
	151. Eventuality.	152. Destiny.

VIII. CAUSATION.

1. CONSTANCY OF SEQUENCE, . . .	153. *Constant Antecedent.* Cause.	154. *Constant Sequent.* Effect.
	155. *Assignment of Cause.* Attribution.	156. *Absence of Assignment.* Chance.
2. CONNECTION BETWEEN CAUSE AND EFFECT, . . .	157. Power.	158. Impotence.
	Degrees of Power.	
	159. Strength.	160. Weakness.
3. POWER IN OPERATION, ...	161. Production.	162. Destruction.
	163. Reproduction.	
	164. Producer.	165. Destroyer.
	166. Paternity.	167. Posterity.
	168. Productiveness.	169. Unproductiveness.
	170. Agency.	
	171. Energy.	172. Inertness.
	173. Violence.	174. Moderation.
4. INDIRECT POWER,	175. Influence.	
	176. Tendency.	177. Liability.
5. COMBINATIONS OF CAUSES, . . .	178. Concurrence.	179. Counteraction

---

CLASS II. SPACE

I SPACE IN GENERAL.

1. ABSTRACT SPACE,	180 *Indefinite.* Space.	181. *Definite.* Region.
		182. *Limited.* Place.
2. RELATIVE SPACE,	183. Situation.	
	184. Location.	185. Displacement.
3. EXISTENCE IN SPACE . . .	186. Presence.	187. Absence.
	188. Inhabitant.	189. Abode.
	190. Contents.	191. Receptacle.

II DIMENSIONS.

1. General, . . .		192. Size.	193. Littleness.
		194. Expansion.	195. Contraction.
		196. Distance.	197. Nearness.
		198. Interval.	199. Contiguity.
2 Linear, . . .		200. Length.	201. Shortness.
		202. { Breadth. Thickness.	203. { Narrowness Thinness.
		204. Layer.	205. Filament.
		206. Height.	207. Lowness.
		208. Depth.	209. Shallowness.
		210. Summit.	211. Base.
		212. Verticality	213. Horizontality
		214. Pendency.	215. Support.
		216. Parallelism.	217. Obliquity
		218. Inversion.	
		219. Crossing.	
3. Centrical,	*General,*	220. Exteriority.	221. Interiority.
		222. Centrality.	
		223. Covering.	224. Lining.
		225. Investment.	226. Divestment.
		227. Circumjacence.	228. Interjacence.
		229. Circumscription.	
		230. Outline.	
		231. Edge.	
		232. Enclosure.	
		233. Limit.	
	Special,	234. Front.	235. Rear.
		236. Laterality.	237. Anteposition.
		238. Dextrality.	239. Sinistrality.

III. FORM.

1. General, . . .	240. Form.	241. Amorphism.
	242. Symmetry.	243. Distortion.
2. Special, . . .	244. Angularity.	
	245. Curvature.	246. Straightness.
	247. Circularity.	248. Convolution.
	249. Rotundity.	
3. Superficial, .	250. Convexity.	251. Flatness.
		252. Concavity.
	253. Sharpness.	254. Bluntness.
	255. Smoothness.	256. Roughness.
	257. Notch.	
	258. Fold.	
	259. Furrow.	
	260. Opening.	261. Closure.
	262. Perforator.	263. Stopper.

IV MOTION.

1. Motion in general, . . .	264. Motion.	265. Quiescence.
	266. Journey.	267. Navigation.
	268. Traveller.	269. Mariner.
	270. Transferrence.	
	271. Carrier.	
	272. Vehicle.	273. Ship.

2. DEGREES OF MOTION, ...	274. Velocity.	275. Slowness.
3. CONJOINED WITH FORCE, . . .	276. Impulse.	277. Recoil.
4 WITH REFERENCE TO DIRECTION, .	278. Direction.	279. Deviation.
	280. Precession.	281. Sequence.
	282. Progression.	283. Regression.
	284. Propulsion.	285. Traction.
	286. Approach.	287. Recession.
	288. Attraction.	289. Repulsion.
	290. Convergence.	291. Divergence
	292. Arrival.	293. Departure.
	294. Ingress.	295. Egress.
	296. Reception.	297. Ejection.
	298. Food.	299. Excretion.
	300. Insertion.	301. Extraction.
	302. Passage.	
	303. Transcursion	304. Shortcoming
	305. Ascent.	306. Descent.
	307. Elevation.	308. Depression.
	309. Leap.	310. Plunge.
	311. Circuition.	
	312. Rotation.	313. Evolution.
	314. Oscillation.	
	315. Agitation.	

CLASS III. MATTER.

I. MATTER IN GENERAL, ...	316. Materiality.	317. Immateriality
	318. World.	
	319. Gravity.	320. Levity.

II INORGANIC MATTER.

1 SOLIDS, ...		321. Density.	322. Rarity.
		323. Hardness.	324. Softness.
		325. Elasticity.	326. Inelasticity.
		327. Tenacity.	328. Brittleness.
		329. Texture.	
		330. Pulverulence	
		331. Friction.	332. Lubrication.
2. FLUIDS.	1. *In general,*	333. Fluidity. Liquidity.	334. Gaseity.
		335. Liquefaction.	336. Vaporization
	2. *Specific,*	337. Water.	338. Air.
		339. Moisture.	340. Dryness.
		341. Ocean.	342. Land.
		343. Gulf. Lake.	344. Plain.
		345. Marsh.	346. Island.
	3. *In Motion,*	347. Stream.	
		348. River.	349 Wind.
		350. Conduit.	351 Airpipe

3. **Imperfect Fluids.**

352. Semiliquidity.	353. Bubble.
354. Pulpiness.	355. Unctuousness.
	356. Oil.

III. ORGANIC MATTER.

1. **Vitality,**

In general,

357. Organization	358. Inorganization.
359 Life.	360. Death.
	361. Killing.
	362. Corpse.
	363. Interment.

Special,

364. Animality.	365. Vegetability.
366. Animal.	367. Vegetable.
368 Zoölogy.	369. Botany.
370. Cicuration	371. Agriculture.
372. Mankind.	
373. Man.	374. Woman.

2. **Sensation**

(1) *General,* . . . .

375. Sensibility.	376. Insensibility.
377. Pleasure.	378. Pain.

(2) *Special,*

1. *Touch,*

379. Touch.	
380. Perceptions of Touch.	381. Numbness.

2. *Heat,*

382. Heat.	383. Cold.
384. Calefaction.	385. Refrigeration.
386. Furnace.	387. Refrigeratory.
388. Fuel.	
389. Thermometer.	

3. *Taste,*

390. Taste.	391. Insipidity.
392. Pungency.	
393. Condiment.	
394. Savoriness.	395. Unsavoriness.
396. Sweetness.	397. Sourness.

4. *Odor,*

398. Odor.	399. Inodorousness.
400. Fragrance.	401. Fetor.

5. *Sound,*

1. *Sound in general.*

402. Sound.	403. Silence.
404. Loudness.	405. Faintness.

2. *Specific Sounds.*

406. Snap.	407. Roll.
408. Resonance.	409. Sibilation.
410. Stridor.	
411. Cry.	412. Ululation.

3. *Musical Sounds.*

413. Melody. Concord.	414. Discord.
415. Music.	
416. Musician.	
417. Musical Instruments.	

4. *Perception of Sound.*

418. Hearing.	419. Deafness.

6. *Light*

1. *Light in general.*

420. Light.	421. Darkness.
	422. Dimness.
423. Luminary.	424. Shade.
425. Transparency.	426. Opacity.
	427. Semitransparency.

6. *Light, continued,*	*2. Specific Light.*	
	428 Color.	429. Achromatism.
	430. Whiteness.	431. Blackness.
	432. Gray.	433. Brown.
	434. Redness.	435. Greenness.
	436. Yellowness.	437. Purple.
	438. Blueness.	439. Orange.
	440. Variegation.	
	3. Perceptions of Light.	
	441. Vision.	442. Blindness.
		443. Dimsightedness
	444. Spectator.	
	445. Optical Instruments.	
	446. Visibility.	447. Invisibility.
	448. Appearance.	449. Disappearance.

Class IV. INTELLECT.

Division I. Formation of Ideas.

I. Operations of Intellect in general, .	450. Intellect.	450. *a.* Absence of Intellect
	451. Thought.	452. Incogitancy.
	453. Idea.	454. Topic.
II. Precursory Conditions and Operations, ...	455. Curiosity.	456. Incuriosity.
	457. Attention.	458. Inattention.
	459. Care.	460. Neglect.
	461. Inquiry.	462. Answer.
	463. Experiment.	464. Comparison.
	465. Discrimination.	465. *a.* Indiscrimination
	466. Measurement.	
III. Materials for Reasoning, ...	467. Evidence.	468. Counter evidence
		469. Qualification.
	Degrees of Evidence.	
	470. Possibility.	471. Impossibility.
	472. Probability	473. Improbability.
	474. Certainty.	475. Uncertainty.
IV. Reasoning Processes,	476. Reasoning.	477. { Intuition. / Sophistry.
	478. Demonstration.	479. Confutation.
V Results of Reasoning, ...	480. Judgment.	481. Misjudgment.
	482. Over-estimation.	483. Under-estimation
	484. Belief.	485. { Unbelief / Doubt.
	486. Credulity.	487. Incredulity.
	488. Assent.	489. Dissent.
	490. Knowledge.	491. Ignorance.
	492. Scholar.	493. Ignoramus.
	494. Truth.	495. Error
	496. Maxim.	497. Absurdity.
	Faculties.	
	498. { Intelligence. / Wisdom.	499. { Imbecility. / Folly.

V. RESULTS OF REASONING — *continued*,		500. Sage.	501. Fool.
		502. Sanity.	503. Insanity.
			504. Madman.
VI. EXTENSION OF THOUGHT,	1. *To the Past*,	505. Memory.	506. Oblivion.
	2. *To the Future*, .	507. Expectation.	508. Inexpectation.
			509. Disappointment.
		510. Foresight.	
		511. Prediction.	
		512. Omen.	
		513. Oracle.	
VII. CREATIVE THOUGHT,		514. Supposition.	
		515. Imagination.	

Division II. COMMUNICATION OF IDEAS.

I. NATURE OF IDEAS COMMUNICATED, . . .		516. Meaning.	517. Unmeaningness.
		518. Intelligibility.	519. Unintelligibility.
		520. Equivocalness.	
		521. Metaphor.	
		522. Interpretation.	523. Misinterpretation.
		524. Interpreter.	
II. MODES OF COMMUNICATION, ...		525. Manifestation.	526. Latency.
		527. Information.	528. Concealment.
		529. Disclosure.	530. Ambush.
		531. Publication.	
		532. News.	533. Secret.
		534. Messenger.	
		535. Affirmation.	536. Negation.
		537. Teaching.	538. Misteaching.
			539. Learning.
		540. Teacher.	541. Learner.
		542. School.	
		543. Veracity.	544. Falsehood.
			545. Deception.
			546. Untruth.
		547. Dupe.	548. Deceiver.
			549. Exaggeration.

III. MEANS OF COMMUNICATION.

1. *Natural Means*, . .		550. Indication.	
		551. Record.	552. Obliteration.
		553. Recorder.	
		554. Representation.	555. Misrepresentation
		556. Painting.	
		557. Sculpture.	
		558. Engraving.	
		559. Artist.	
2. *Conventional Means*,	1. *Language generally*,	560. Language.	
		561. Letter.	
		562. Word.	563. Neology.
		564. Nomenclature.	565. Misnomer.
		566. Phrase.	
		567. Grammar.	568. Solecism.
		569. Style.	
		Qualities of Style.	
		570. Perspicuity.	571. Obscurity.
		572. Conciseness	573. Diffuseness.

2. *Conventional Means, continued,*		574. Vigor.	575. Feebleness.
		576. Plainness.	577. Ornament.
		578. Elegance.	579. Inelegance.
	2. *Spoken Language,*	580. Voice.	581. Aphony.
		582. Speech.	583. Stammering
		584. Loquacity.	585. Taciturnity
		586. Allocution.	587. Response.
		588. Interlocution.	589. Soliloquy.
	3. *Written Language,*	590. Writing.	591. Printing.
		592. Correspondence.	593. Book.
		594. Description.	
		595. Dissertation.	
		596. Compendium.	
		597. Poetry.	598. Prose.
		599. The Drama.	

CLASS V. VOLITION.

Division I. INDIVIDUAL VOLITION.

I. VOLITION IN GENERAL,	1. *Acts,*	600. Will.	601. Necessity.
		602. Willingness.	603. Unwillingness
		604. Resolution.	605. Irresolution.
		606. Obstinacy	607. Tergiversation
			608. Caprice.
		609. Choice.	610. Rejection
		611. Predetermination.	612. Impulse.
		613. Habit.	614. Desuetude.
	2. *Causes,*	615. Motive.	616. Dissuasion.
		617. Plea.	
	3. *Objects,*	618. Good.	619. Evil.
II. PROSPECTIVE VOLITION,	1. *Conceptional,*	620. Intention.	621. Chance.
		622. Pursuit.	623. Avoidance.
			624. Relinquishment
		625. Business.	
		626. Plan.	
		627. Method.	
		628. Mid course.	629. Circuit.
		630. Requirement.	
	2 *Subservience to Ends,*	*1. Actual Subservience*	
		631. Instrumentality.	
		632. Means.	
		633. Instrument.	
		634. Substitute.	
		635. Materials.	
		636. Store.	
		637. Provision.	638. Waste.
		639. Sufficiency.	640. Insufficiency.
		641. Redundance.	
		2. Degree of Subservience.	
		642. Importance.	643. Unimportance

II. **Prospective Volition**—*continued*,	2. *Subservience to Ends*—*continued*,	644. Utility.	645. Inutility.
		646. Expedience.	647. Inexpedience.
		648. Goodness.	649. Badness.
		650. Perfection.	651. Imperfection.
		652. Cleanness.	653. Uncleanness.
		654. Health.	655. Disease.
		656. Salubrity.	657. Insalubrity.
		658. Improvement.	659. Deterioration.
		660. Restoration.	661. Relapse.
		662. Remedy.	663. Bane.
		3. *Contingent Subservience.*	
		664. Safety.	665. Danger,
		666. Refuge.	667. Pitfall.
		668. Warning.	
		669. Alarm.	
		670. Preservation.	
		671. Escape.	
		672. Deliverance.	
	3. *Precursory Measures*,	673. Preparation.	674. Non-preparation.
		675. Essay.	
		676. Undertaking.	
		677. Use.	678. Disuse.
			679. Misuse.
III. **Action**,	1. *Simple*,	680. Action.	681. Inaction.
		682. Activity.	683. Inactivity.
		684. Haste.	685. Leisure.
		686. Exertion.	687. Repose.
		688. Fatigue.	689. Refreshment.
		690. Agent.	
		691. Workshop.	
	2. *Complex*,	692. Conduct.	
		693. Direction.	
		694. Director.	
		695. Advice.	
		696. Council.	
		697. Precept.	
		698. Skill.	699. Unskilfulness.
		700. Proficient.	701. Bungler.
		702. Cunning.	703. Artlessness.
IV. **Antagonism**,	1. *Conditional*,	704. Difficulty.	705. Facility.
		706. Hinderance.	707. Aid.
		708. Opposition.	709. Coöperation.
		710. Opponent.	711. Auxiliary.
		712. Party.	
		713. Discord.	714. Concord.
	2 *Active*,	715. Defiance.	
		716. Attack.	717. Defence.
		718. Retaliation.	719. Resistance.
		720. Contention,	721. Peace.
		722. Warfare.	723. Pacification.
		724. Mediation.	
		725. Submission.	
		726. Combatant.	
		727. Arms.	
		728. Arena.	

V RESULTS OF ACTION, .	729. Completion,	730. Non-completion.
	731. Success.	732. Failure.
	733. Trophy.	
	734. Prosperity.	735. Adversity.
	736. Mediocrity.	

Division II. INTERSOCIAL VOLITION

I. GENERAL, ...	737. Authority.	738 Laxity.
	739. Severity.	740. Lenity.
	741. Command.	
	742. Disobedience.	743. Obedience.
	744 Compulsion.	
	745. Master.	746. Servant.
	747. Sceptre.	
	748. Freedom.	749. Subjection.
	750. Liberation.	751. Restraint.
		752. Prison.
	753. Keeper.	754. Prisoner.
	755. Commission.	756. Abrogation.
		757. Resignation.
	758. Consignee.	
	759. Deputy.	
II. SPECIAL, ...	760. Permission	761. Prohibition.
	762. Consent.	
	763. Offer.	764. Refusal.
	765. Request.	766. Deprecation.
	767. Petitioner.	
III. CONDITIONAL, . .	768. Promise.	768. *a.* Release.
	769. Compact.	
	770. Conditions.	
	771. Security.	
	772. Observance.	773. Non-observance
	774. Compromise.	

IV. POSSESSIVE RELATIONS.

1. *Property in general*, .	775. Acquisition.	776. Loss.
	777. Possession.	778. Participation.
	779. Possessor.	
	780. Property.	
	781. Retention.	782. Relinquishment
2 *Transfer of Property*,	783. Transfer.	
	784. Giving.	785. Receiving.
	786. Apportionment.	
	787. Lending.	788. Borrowing.
	789. Taking.	790. Restitution
	791. Stealing.	
	792. Thief.	
	793. Booty	
3 *Interchange of Property*, ...	794. Barter.	
	795. Purchase.	796. Sale.
	797 Merchant.	
	798. Merchandise.	
	799 Mart.	

4. Monetary Relations,	800. Money.	
	801. Treasurer.	
	802. Treasury.	
	803. Wealth.	804. Poverty.
	805. Credit.	806. Debt.
	807. Payment.	808. Non-payment.
	809. Expenditure.	810. Receipt.
	811. Accounts.	
	812. Price.	813. Discount.
	814. Dearness.	815. Cheapness.
	816. Liberality.	817. Economy.
	818. Prodigality.	819. Parsimony.

Class VI. AFFECTIONS.

I AFFECTIONS GENERALLY	820. Affections.	
	821. Feeling.	
	822. Sensibility.	823. Insensibility.
	824. Excitation.	
	825. Excitability.	826. Inexcitability
II PERSONAL.		
1. Passive, .	827. Pleasure.	828. Pain.
	829. Pleasurableness.	830. Painfulness.
	831. Content.	832. Discontent.
		833. Regret.
	834. Relief.	835. Aggravation.
	836. Cheerfulness.	837. Dejection.
	838. Rejoicing.	839. Lamentation
	840. Amusement.	841. Weariness.
	842. Wit.	843. Dulness.
	844. Humorist.	
2 Discriminative	845. Beauty.	846. Ugliness.
	847. Ornament	848. Blemish.
		849. Simplicity.
	850. Taste.	851. Vulgarity.
	852. Fashion.	853. Ridiculousness
		854. Fop.
		855. Affectation.
		856. Ridicule.
		857. Laughing stock
3 Prospective, .	858. Hope.	859. Hopelessness.
		860. Fear.
	861. Courage.	862. Cowardice.
	863. Rashness.	864. Caution.
	865. Desire.	866. Indifference.
		867. Dislike.
		868. Fastidiousness
		869. Satiety.

4. CONTEMPLATIVE, .	870. Wonder.	871. Expectance.
	872. Prodigy.	
5. EXTRINSIC, . . .	873. Repute.	874. Disrepute.
	875. Nobility.	876. Commonalty.
	877. Title.	
	878. Pride.	879. Humility.
	880. Vanity.	881. Modesty.
	882. Ostentation.	
	883. Celebration.	
	884. Boasting.	
	885. Insolence.	886. Servility
	887. Blusterer.	
III. SYMPATHETIC.		
1. SOCIAL, . . .	888. Friendship.	889. Enmity.
	890. Friend.	891. Enemy.
	892. Sociality	893. Seclusion.
	894. Courtesy.	895. Discourtesy.
	896. Congratulation.	
	897. Love.	898. Hate.
	899. Favorite.	
		900. Resentment.
		901. Irascibility.
	902. Endearment.	
	903. Marriage.	904. Celibacy.
		905. Divorce.
2. DIFFUSIVE . .	906. Benevolence.	907. Malevolence.
		908. Malediction.
		909. Threat.
	910. Philanthropy.	911. Misanthropy.
	912. Benefactor.	913. Evil doer.
3. SPECIAL . . .	914. Pity.	914. *a.* Pitilessness.
	915. Condolence.	
4. RETROSPECTIVE,	916. Gratitude.	917. Ingratitude.
	918. Forgiveness	919. Revenge.
		920. Jealousy.
		921. Envy.
IV. MORAL.		
1. OBLIGATIONS, .	922. Right.	923. Wrong.
	924. Dueness.	925. Undueness.
	926. Duty.	927. Exemption.
2. SENTIMENTS, . .	928. Respect.	929. Disrespect.
		930. Contempt.
	931. Approbation.	932. Disapprobation.
	933. Flattery.	934. Detraction.
	935. Flatterer.	936. Detractor.
	937. Vindication.	938. Accusation.
3. CONDITIONS, . .	939. Probity.	940. Improbity.
		941. Knave.
	942. Disinterestedness.	943. Selfishness.
	944. Virtue.	945. Vice.
	946. Innocence.	947. Guilt.
	948. Saint.	949. Sinner.
	950. Penitence.	951 Impenitence.
	952. Atonement.	

4. PRACTICE, . . .	953. Temperance.	954. Intemperance.
	955. Asceticism.	
	956. Fasting.	957. Gluttony.
	958. Sobriety.	959. Drunkenness.
	960. Purity.	961. Impurity.
		962. Libertine.
5. INSTITUTIONS, .	963. Legality.	964. Illegality.
	965. Jurisprudence.	
	966. Tribunal.	
	967. Judge.	
	968. Lawyer.	
	969. Lawsuit.	
	970. Acquittal.	971. Condemnation.
		972. Punishment.
	973. Reward.	974. Penalty.
		975. Scourge.

V RELIGIOUS

1. SUPERHUMAN BEINGS AND REGIONS,	976. Deity.	
	977. Angel.	978. Satan.
	979. Jupiter.	980. Demon.
	981. Heaven.	982. Hell.
2. DOCTRINES, . . .	983. Theology.	984. Heterodoxy.
	985. Revelation.	986. Pseudo-revelation
3. SENTIMENTS, . .	987. Piety.	988. Irreligion.
		989. Impiety.
4. ACTS, ...	990. Worship.	991. Idolatry.
		992. Sorcery.
		993. Spell.
		994. Sorcerer.
5. INSTITUTIONS, . .	995. Churchdom	
	996. Clergy.	997. Laity.
	998. Rite.	
	999. Canonicals.	
	1000. Temple.	

ABBREVIATIONS.

Adj. Adjectives, Participles, and words having the power of Adjectives.
Adv Adverbs and adverbial expressions.
V. Verbs.

THESAURUS

OF

ENGLISH WORDS AND PHRASES.

CLASS I.

WORDS EXPRESSING ABSTRACT RELATIONS.

Section I. EXISTENCE.

1. Being, in the Abstract.

1 Existence, being, entity, subsistence: — coexistence, *see* 120.

Reality, actuality, positiveness, absoluteness, fact, matter of fact; *see* Truth, 494.

Science of existence, Ontology.

Existence in space; *see* 186.

V. To be, to exist, have being, subsist, live, breathe, stand, obtain, occur.

To consist in, lie in.

To come into existence, 141, to arise, come out, come forth, appear, 448.

To bring into existence; 161.

Adj. Existing, being, subsisting, in being, in existence, ex-

2. Inexistence, non-existence, nonentity, no such thing negativeness; vacuity, 4.

Annihilation, abeyance, extinction, *see* Destruction, 162, and Disappearance, 449.

V. Not to be, not to exist, &c., to have no existence.

To cease to be, pass away vanish, fade, dissolve, melt away perish, disappear, 449, to be annihilated, extinct, &c., to be no more, to die, 360.

Adj. Inexistent, non-existent, non-existing, (that which does not exist, has no existence, or is without existence,) &c., negative blank.

* The heavy figures indicate the articles to which the figures in the index refer.

tant, living, breathing, obtaining, current, undestroyed.

Real, actual, positive, absolute, virtual, substantial, substantive, self-existing, self-existent, — not ideal, not imagined, unimagined, not supposititious, not potential, true, 494.

Adv. Actually, really, absolutely, positively, &c., in fact, in reality.

Unreal, potential, virtual, baseless, unsubstantial, 4, imaginary, ideal, vain, supposititious, shadowy, (imagined, dreamy.)

Unborn, uncreated, unbegotten

Annihilated, destroyed, extinct, gone, lost, perished, (passed away, abolished, nullified, done away with,) melted, dissolved, faded, exhausted, vanished, missing, disappeared, departed, defunct, 360.

Absence, 187, removal, 185.

Adv. Negatively, virtually, &c.

2. Being, in the Concrete.

3. Substantiality, thing, something, a being, an existence, creature, a body, substance, object, article, matter, material, stuff, 316.

Totality of existences, *see* World, 318.

Adj. Substantive, substantial, bodily, material.

Adv. Substantially, bodily, &c., essentially.

---

4. Unsubstantiality, nothingness, nothing, nought, nullity, zero; nothing at all; nothing whatever; nothing on earth.

Nobody, 187.

A shadow, phantom, phantasm, vision, dream, air, thin air.

Void, vacuum, vacuity, vacancy, inanity, emptiness, hollowness, blank, chasm, gap, hiatus, &c., 198.

Adj. Unsubstantial, void, vacuous, blank, null, inane, vacant, hollow.

3. Formal Existence.

Internal conditions.

5. Intrinsicality, inbeing, inherence, inhesion, essence, essentialness, essential (nature, character, or) part, quintessence, gist, pith, marrow.

Constitution, character, quality, 157, temperament, temper, spirit, humor, grain, endowment, capacity, capability, mood, features, aspects, specialities, peculiarities, 79, (characteristics,) idiosyncrasy.

Adj. Derived from within; subjective, intrinsic, intrinsical, inherent, essential, natural, internal, innate, inborn, inbred

External conditions.

6. Extrinsicality, extraneousness, objectiveness, accident

Adj. Derived from without, objective, extrinsic, extrinsical, extraneous, modal, adventitious adscititious, incidental, accidental, non-essential, 220.

Implanted, ingrafted.

Adv. Extrinsically, &c.

---

ingrained, inherited, immanent, congenital, indigenous, in the grain, bred in the bone, instinctive, 221.

Characteristic, peculiar, special, diagnostic, 79.

Adv. Intrinsically, &c.

4. Modal Existence.

Absolute.

7. State, condition, category, estate, case, constitution, habitude, mood, plight.

Frame, fabric, structure, texture, contexture, 329, conformation.

Mode, modality, form, shape, figure, cut, cast, mould, stamp, set, fit, tone, tenor, turn, trim, guise, fashion, aspect, complexion, character.

V. To be in a state, condition, &c., on a footing.

To fare; to have, possess, enjoy, &c., a state, &c.

To bring into a state, &c., 144.

Adj. Conditional, modal, formal, structural, textural.

Adv. Conditionally, &c.

Relative.

8. Circumstance, situation, phase, position, posture, attitude, place, point, terms, fare, footing, standing, predicament, contingency, occasion, juncture, conjuncture, emergence, emergency, exigency, crisis, pinch, pass, push.

Adj. Circumstantial, — given, conditional, provisional, critical, contingent, incidental, 6, 151.

Adv. In, or under the circumstances, conditions, &c. — Thus, accordingly, being so, such being the case, since, seeing that, as matters stand, as things go.

Conditionally, provided, if, if so, if so be, if it be so; if it so happen, or turn out, provisionally, unless, without.

Section II. RELATION.

1. Absolute Relation.

9. Relation, bearing, reference, concern, cognation, correlation, analogy, affinity, alliance, homogeneousness, association, approximation, filiation, &c., 166, interest, habitude.

Relevancy, pertinency, fitness, &c., 23, 646.

Aspect, point of view, comparison, 464, — ratio, proportion.

V To be related, have a relation, &c.; to relate to, refer to, bear upon, regard, concern, touch; to have to do with, pertain to, belong to, appertain to, answer to, interest.

10. Irrelation, want, or absence of relation, disconnection, dissociation, independence, isolation 44, disproportion; — incommensurability, irrelevancy; — heterogeneousness, irreconcilableness, 24, impertinence.

V. To have no relation, &c. to; to have nothing to do with; not to concern, &c.

To isolate, separate, detach, segregate, 44.

Adj. Irrelative, irrespective, unrelated, without reference, &c. to, arbitrary, remote, out of place, irrelevant, foreign to, alien, imper-

To bring into relation with, connect, affiliate, link, 43, bring together, bring near, approximate; to bring to bear upon.

Adj. Relative, correlative, cognate, relating to, relative to, relevant, in relation with, referable (or referrible) to, pertinent, 23; belonging, pertaining, or appertaining to.

Implicated, associated, connected, affiliated.

Approximative, approximating, proportional, proportionate, proportionable; comparable, &c., 23.

tinent, extraneous to, stranger to, independent, outlandish, exotic, unallied, unconnected, disconnected, adrift, isolated, insular.

Not comparable, incommensurable, inapplicable, 24, irreconcilable, heterogeneous.

Foreign to the purpose, nothing to the purpose, neither here nor there; beside the mark.

Adv. Parenthetically, by the way, by the by, incidentally.

Adv. Relatively, thereof, as to, as for, about, concerning, touching, as relates to, with relation to, relating to; as respects, with respect to, in respect of, respecting; as regards, with regard to, regarding, with reference to, while speaking of, in connection with, inasmuch as, in point of, as far as, on the part of, on the score of, pertinently, &c.

In various ways, in all manner of ways, under the head, category, class, &c. of, 75.

11. Relations of kindred.

CONSANGUINITY, relationship, kindred, blood, parentage, filiation, lineage, connection, alliance, family connection, family tie; *see* Paternity, 166.

A kinsman, relation, relative, connection, cousin, brother, sister, &c., &c.; — a near relation, a distant relation.

Family, fraternity, brotherhood, sisterhood, cousinhood, &c.; — race, stock, generation, &c.

V. To claim relationship with.

Adj. Related, akin, (germane), consanguineous, family, allied, collateral, fraternal, &c., nearly or closely related, remotely or distantly related.

12. Double relation.

RECIPROCALNESS, reciprocity, correlation, (mutual) dependence, interchange, reciprocation, &c., 148, interchangeableness, 149.

V. To reciprocate, alternate, interchange, exchange, counterchange.

Adj. Reciprocal, mutual, correlative, alternate.

International, interchangeable.

13. IDENTITY, sameness, coincidence, coalescence, convertibility; self, one's self, number one; identification.

V. To be identical; to be the same, &c. to coincide, coalesce.

To render the same; to identify.

14. Non-coincidence.

CONTRARIETY, contrast, antithesis, contradiction, opposition, antagonism, 708, inversion, reversion, 218.

The opposite, the reverse, inverse, converse, antipodes, 237, counterpart.

To recognize the identity of; to identify; *see* to compare, 464.

Adj. Identical, same, self, very same, selfsame, no other, one and the same, unaltered, coincident, coinciding, coalescing, coalescent, indistinguishable, equivalent, convertible.

Adv. All one, all the same, identically, &c.

V. To be contrary, opposite, &c., to contrast with, contradict, contravene, oppose, antagonize, invert, reverse.

Adj. Contrary, opposite, counter, converse, reverse, diametrically opposite, opposed, antagonistic, opposing, inconsistent, contradictory.

Adv. Contrarily, contrariwise, oppositely, on the contrary, quite the contrary.

15. DIFFERENCE, variance, variation, variety, diversity, modification, shade of difference, deviation, divergence, divarication, 290, disagreement, 24.

Distinction, discrimination, 465, contradistiction. A nice, fine, or subtle distinction.

V. To be different, &c.; to differ, vary, mismatch, contrast.

To render different, &c., to vary, change, modify, &c., 140.

To distinguish, 465.

Adj. Different, differing, heterogeneous, varying, distinguishable, discriminative, varied, modified, diversified, deviating, diverging, devious, disagreeing, 24, various, divers, all manner of, multifarious, multiform, &c., 81.

Other, another, not the same, quite another thing, unmatched, widely apart, changed, 140.

Adv. Differently, variously, &c., otherwise.

2. CONTINUOUS RELATION.

16. UNIFORMITY, homogeneousness, consistency, conformity, 82, accordance, *see* Agreement, 23, and Regularity, 80.

Absence or want of uniformity, 83.

V. To be uniform, &c., to accord with.

To become uniform, to conform to.

To render uniform, to assimilate, level, smooth, &c., 255.

Adj. Uniform, homogeneous, homologous, of a piece, consistent, connatural.

Adv. Uniformly, uniformly with, conformably, consistently with, in unison with, in conformity with, according to, 23.

3. PARTIAL RELATION.

17. SIMILARITY, resemblance, likeness, similitude, affinity, semblance, approximation, paral-

18. DISSIMILARITY, unlikeness, dissimilitude, diversity novelty, 123, originality, 515.

lelism, 216, analogy, brotherhood, family likeness; alliteration, repetition, 104.

The like, match, fellow, pair, mate, twin, parallel, counterpart, brother, sister; simile, metaphor, 521.

V. To be similar, like, resembling, &c.; to resemble, bear resemblance, approximate, parallel, match, imitate, 19, represent, simulate, personate.

V. To be unlike, &c., to vary 20.

To render unlike, to diversify, vary, &c.

Adj. Dissimilar, unlike, of a different kind, class, &c., 75; diversified, novel, new, unmatched, 123, cast in a different mould.

To render similar, assimilate, approximate, bring near, &c.

Adj. Similar, like, alike, resembling, twin, analogous, analogical, parallel, allied to, of a piece, such as, matching.

Near, something like, a show of, mock, simulating, representing, approximating.

Exact, accurate, true, faithful, close, speaking.

Adv. As if, so to speak, as it were, as if it were.

19. Imitation, assimilation, copying, transcribing, transcription, repetition, 104, duplication, reduplication, quotation, reproduction.

Mockery, mocking, mimicry, echoing, simulation, counterfeiting, acting, personation, representation, parody, (travesty.)

Result of imitation, *see* Copy, 21.

An imitator, echo, cuckoo, parrot, ape, monkey, mocking bird.

V. To imitate, copy, repeat, 104, do like, echo, reëcho, transcribe, match, parallel, emulate; to take off, hit off; to model after.

20. Non-imitation.

Adj. Unimitated, uncopied, unmatched, unparalleled, inimitable, 648.

Variation, alteration, modification, *see* Difference, 15, Change, 140, Deviation, 279, Divergence, 281.

V. To vary, modify, diversify, change, &c., 140.

Adj. Varied, modified, diversified, &c.

To mock, mimic, ape, simulate, personate, 554, act, represent, adumbrate, counterfeit, parody, travesty, caricature, burlesque.

To take after; to follow, or tread in the steps, or footsteps of; to follow in the wake of; to follow the footsteps, strike in with.

Adj. Imitated, copied, matched, repeated, paralleled, mimic, parodied, &c., modelled after, moulded on, paraphrastic, imitative, second-hand, imitable.

Adv. Literally, verbatim, word for word, 562.

21. Result of imitation.
COPY, fac-simile, counterpart, form, likeness, similitude, semblance, cast, imitation, representation, 554, adumbration.

Duplicate, transcript, repetition, 104, reflection, shadow.

Rough copy, rough cast, draught, proof, reprint.

Counterfeit, parody, caricature, burlesque, (travesty,) paraphrase.

22. Thing copied.
PROTOTYPE, original, model, pattern, type, archetype, antitype, exemplar, example.

Text, copy, design; keynote.

Mould, matrice, last, mint.

---

4. GENERAL RELATION.

23. AGREEMENT, accord, accordance, unison, harmony, union, concord, concert, concordance, 714, conformity, consonance, consentaneousness, consistency, congruity, congruence, congeniality, correspondence, parallelism.

Fitness, (concinnity,) pertinence, suitableness, adaptation, relevancy, aptitude, propriety, appositeness, reconcilableness, applicability, applicableness, admissibility, commensurability, compatibility.

Adaptation, adjustment, graduation, accommodation, reconciliation, reconcilement.

V. To be accordant, to agree, accord, correspond, tally, respond, harmonize, fall in with, chime in with, square with, quadrate with, comport with, dovetail, assimilate, unite with.

To render accordant; to fit, suit, adapt, accommodate, adjust, reconcile, dovetail, square, regulate, accord, comport, graduate.

Adj. Agreeing, accordant, concordant, consonant, congruous, consentaneous, corresponding, correspondent, harmonizing, harmonious with, tallying with, conformable with, in harmony with, in unison with, in keeping with, squaring with, falling in with,

24. DISAGREEMENT, discord, discordance, dissonance, discrepancy, unconformity, disconformity, non-conformity, incongruity, incongruence, jarring, clashing, jostling, 713, inconsistency, disparity, disproportion, disproportionateness, variance.

Unfitness, repugnance, unsuitableness, unaptness, inaptitude inaptness, impropriety, inapplicability, inadmissibility, irreconcilableness, incommensurability, inconcinnity, incompatibility, interference, intrusion; *see* Irrelation, 10.

V. To disagree, belie, clash, jar, oppose, 708, interfere, jostle 713, intrude.

Adj. Disagreeing, discordant, discrepant, at variance, clashing, repugnant, incompatible, irreconcilable, inconsistent with, unconformable, incongruous, disproportionate, (disproportioned,) unproportioned, unharmonious, misjoined, unconsonant, unconformable, incommensurable, divergent, 291.

Unapt, inappropriate, improper, unsuited, unsuitable, inapposite, inapplicable, irrelevant, not pertinent, impertinent, out of place, (not in keeping,) ill-timed, intrusive, unfit, unfitting, unbefitting

consistent with, compatible, reconcilable with.

Apt, apposite, pertinent, germane, to the purpose, to the point, bearing upon, 9; applicable, relevant, fit, fitting, suitable, proper, meet, appropriate, suiting, befitting, seasonable, accommodating.

unbecoming, forced, unseasonable, far-fetched, inadmissible, uncongenial, ill-sorted, repugnant to, unaccommodating, irreducible.

Adj. At variance with, in defiance of, in contempt of, in spite of.

Section III. QUANTITY.

1. Simple Quantity.

25. Absolute Quantity.

Quantity, magnitude, 192, amplitude, mass, amount, measure.

Science of quantity; Mathematics.

Adj. Quantitative.

---

26. Relative quantity.

Degree, grade, extent, measure, ratio, standard, height, pitch, reach, amplitude, range, scope, gradation, shade, compass, sphere, rank, standing, rate.

Point, mark, stage, step, position, peg; term, 71.

Intensity, might, fulness, (maximum.)

Adj. Comparative, gradual, shading off.

Adv. By degrees, gradually, step by step, little by little, by inches, by slow degrees.

2. Comparative Quantity.

27. Sameness of quantity or degree.

Equality, parity, coextension, evenness, level, balance, poise.

Equivalence, equipoise, equilibrium, equiponderance, par, tie.

Equalization, equation, equilibration, coördination, adjustment.

A match, peer, compeer, (equal,) mate, fellow, brother, &c., 17, a makeweight.

V. To be equal, &c.; to equal, match, come up to, come to, amount to; be or lie on a level with, to balance, to cope with.

To render equal, equalize, level, balance, equate, trim, adjust, poise; to strike a balance,

28. Difference of quantity or degree.

Inequality, disparity, odds, difference, 15, unevenness.

Preponderance, preponderation, inclination of the balance, advantage, prevalence; — superiority, 33; a casting weight.

Shortcoming, 304.

V. To be unequal, &c., to preponderate, outweigh, outbalance, overbalance, prevail, countervail, predominate, overmatch, 33.

To fall short of, to want, 304, not to come up to, 34.

Adj. Unequal, uneven, unbalanced, overbalanced, topheavy preponderating, prevailing, &c.

to establish or restore equality, to readjust.

Adj. Equal, even, level, co-equal, coördinate, on a par with, on a level with, up to the mark.

Equivalent, tantamount, as broad as long, as good as, equiponderant, equiponderous.

Rendered equal, equalized, equated, drawn, poised, levelled, balanced, trimmed, &c.

more than a match for; above par; below par.

---

29. Mean, medium, average, balance, middle, 68, the golden mean. Neutrality, middle course, 628.

V. To split the difference, take the average, reduce to a mean, strike a balance.

Adj. Mean, intermediate, middle, average.

Adj. On an average; in the long run; half way; taking the one with the other, taking all things together, taking all in all.

30. Compensation, equation, indemnification, neutralization, counteraction.

A setoff, offset, (equivalent,) makeweight, casting weight, counterpoise, amends. *See* Counteraction, 179, Recoil, 277, Atonement, 952.

V. To compensate, 973, indemnify, countervail, counterpoise, balance, outbalance, overbalance, counterbalance, set off, recompense, make up for, cover, fill up, redeem, make amends, neutralize; 28.

Adj. Compensating, compensatory, countervailing, &c., in the opposite scale.

Quantity by Comparison with a Standard.

31. Greatness, largeness, magnitude, size, 192, fulness, vastness, immensity, enormity, infinity, 105, intensity, 26.

A large quantity, deal, world, mass, heap, 72, pile, cartload, cargo, shipload, flood or spring tide, abundance, 639, wholesale, store, 636.

The greater part, 52.

V. To be great, &c., run high, soar, tower, transcend, rise, or carry to a great height, &c., 305.

Adj. Great, large, considerable, big, huge, ample, full, saturated, plenary, deep, extensive, goodly, heavy, mighty, 157, arrant, downright, utter, gross, arch, consummate, rank, thorough-going, sov-

32. Smallness, littleness, minuteness, 193, tenuity, scantiness slenderness, meanness, mediocrity.

A small quantity, atom, particle, molecule, corpuscle, jot, iota, minutiæ, whit, tittle, shade, shadow, touch, cast, grain, scruple, spice, drop, sprinkling, dash, scantling, scrap, mite, bit, morsel, crum, trifle, 51.

Finiteness, a finite (or limited) quantity.

V. To be small, &c., to run low, diminish, shrink, dwindle, &c., 195.

Adj. Small, little, inconsiderable, diminutive, minute, 193, tiny, puny, petty, sorry, misera-

ereign, above par, unparalleled, extraordinary, unapproached.

Vast, immense, enormous, towering, inordinate, excessive, extravagant, outrageous, preposterous, egregious, monstrous, overgrown, stupendous, prodigious, astonishing, 870, incredible, marvellous, transcendent, incomparable, tremendous.

Indefinite, boundless, unbounded, unlimited, incalculable, illimitable, immeasurable, infinite, 105, unapproachable, unutterable, unspeakable, inexpressible, beyond expression, unconscionable.

Undiminished, unabated, unreduced, unrestricted.

Absolute, positive, decided, unequivocal, serious, essential, perfect, finished, abundant, 639.

Adv. In a great degree; much, well, considerably, largely, greatly, very, very much, a deal, not a little, pretty, pretty well, enough, to a large or great extent, mainly, ever so, ever so much, insomuch, wholesale, in all conscience.

In a positive degree; truly, 494, purely, positively, verily, really, indeed, actually, in fact, fairly, assuredly, decidedly, unequivocally, absolutely, seriously, essentially, fundamentally, radically, downright.

In a comparative degree; comparatively, as good as; to say the least of, above all, most, preëminently.

In a complete degree; altogether, quite, entirely, wholly, totally, *in toto*, utterly, thoroughly, out and out, completely, outright, to the full, in every respect, in all respects, on all accounts, nicely, perfectly, fully, amply, richly, wholesale, abundantly, consummately, widely, as .... as can be every nce, far and wide.

ble, wretched, paltry, 643, weak, 160, slender, feeble, faint, slight, trivial, scanty, light, trifling, moderate, mean, passable, sparing.

Below par, below the mark, under the mark, at a low ebb, imperfect, 651.

Inappreciable, evanescent, infinitesimal, atomic.

Mere, simple, sheer, stark, bare.

Adv. In a small degree; something, somewhat, next to nothing, little, inconsiderably, slightly, so-so, minutely, faintly, feebly, lightly, imperfectly, perceptibly, moderately, scantily, miserably, sparingly, tolerably, passably, weakly, pretty well, well enough, slenderly, modestly.

In a limited degree; partially, in part; in a certain degree, to a certain degree or extent, some, somewhat, rather, in some degree, in some measure, something, simply, purely, merely, in a manner, at the most, at least, at the least, at most, as little as may be, next to nothing, in ever so small a degree.

Almost, nearly well nigh, all but, short of, not quite, scarcely, hardly, barely, near the mark.

In an uncertain degree; about, thereabouts, somewhere about, nearly.

In no degree; not at all, not in the least, not a bit, not a whit, not a jot, by no means, nowise in nowise, in no respect, by no manner of means, on no account

In a greater degree; even, yea still more.

In a high degree; highly, deeply, strongly, mightily, powerfully, 157, profoundly, superlatively, ultra, in the extreme, extremely, exceedingly, excessively, intensely, exquisitely, acutely, soundly, vastly, hugely, immensely, enormously, stupendously, surpassingly, supremely, beyond measure, immoderately, monstrously, inordinately, extraordinarily, exorbitantly, indefinitely, immeasurably, unspeakably, inexpressibly, ineffably, unutterably, incalculably, infinitely.

In a marked degree; particularly, remarkably, singularly, uncommonly, unusually, peculiarly, notably, signally, egregiously, prominently, glaringly, emphatically, strangely, wonderfully, amazingly, surprisingly, astonishingly, incredibly, marvellously, awfully, stupendously.

In a violent degree; violently, furiously, desperately, tremendously, outrageously, extravagantly, confoundedly, with a vengeance; 173.

In a painful degree; sadly, grossly, sorely, bitterly, grievously, cruelly, wofully, lamentably, shockingly, frightfully, dreadfully, fearfully, terribly, horribly.

Quantity by Comparison with a Similar Object.

33. Superiority, majority, supremacy, advantage, excess, 641.

Maximum, acme, climax, zenith, summit, utmost height, culminating point, 210, the height of.

V. To be superior, &c.; to exceed, excel, outweigh, surpass, overtop, cap, beat, cut out, override, (outdo,) out-Herod, overbalance, 30, overweigh; to render larger, 194.

Adj. Superior, greater, major, higher, exceeding, excelling, surpassing, ultra, vaulting, transcending, (transcendent,) unequalled, 648.

Supreme, greatest, utmost, paramount, preëminent, culminating, superlative, topmost, highest.

Adv. Beyond; over or above the mark; above par, over and above; at its height.

In a superior degree; eminently, egregiously, preeminently, prominently, superlatively, supremely, above all, principally, especially, particularly, peculiarly, &c.

34. Inferiority, minority, subordinacy, shortcoming, **304.**

Minimum.

V. To be less, inferior, &c., to fall, or come short of; not to surpass, 304.

To become smaller, (36), to render smaller, 195.

Adj. Inferior, smaller, minor, less, lesser, lower, subordinate, subaltern.

Least, smallest, minutest, &c., 193; lowest.

Adv. Less; under or below the mark; below par; at the bottom of the scale; at a low ebb.

At a disadvantage.

Changes in Quantity.

35. Increase, augmentation, enlargement, extension, dilatation, 194, increment, accretion, development, growth, swell, swelling, aggrandizement, aggravation, rise, spread, diffusion, 73, flood tide, accession, 37.

V. To increase, augment, enlarge, amplify, extend, dilate, swell, expand, grow, stretch, shoot up, rise, run up, sprout, advance, spread, aggrandize, add, raise, heighten, strengthen, exalt, enhance, magnify, redouble, aggravate, exaggerate, exasperate, exacerbate.

Adj. Increased, augmented, enlarged, bloated, &c.; undiminished.

36. Non-increase.

Decrease, diminution, lessening, reduction, abatement, bating, declension, falling off, dwindling, contraction, 195, shrinking, attenuation, extenuation, abridgment, curtailment, 201, narrowing.

Subsidence, wane, ebb, decrement.

V. To decrease, diminish, lessen, dwindle, shrink, contract, shrivel, fall away, waste, wane, ebb, decline, wear off.

To abridge, reduce, curtail, cut down, pare down, cut short, dock, &c., 201, bate, abate, extenuate, lower, weaken, dwarf; to mitigate, &c., 174.

Adj. Unincreased, decreased, diminished, lessened, &c., shorn, short by; decreasing, on the wane.

3. Conjunctive Quantity.

37. Addition, annexation, (adjunction,) superposition, superaddition, accession, supplement, accompaniment, 88.

V. To add, annex, affix, superadd, subjoin, clap on, tack to, append, saddle on, tag, ingraft, saddle with.

To become added, to accrue.

Adj. Added, annexed, &c., additional, supplementary, suppletory, (subjoined,) adscititious, additive, accessory.

Adv. In addition, more, plus, extra.

And, also, likewise, too, furthermore, and also, besides, to boot, et cætera, and so forth, into the bargain, over and above, moreover.

With, together with, withal, along with, including, inclusive, as well as; not to mention; conjointly 43.

38. Non-addition, subtraction, deduction, retrenchment, removal, curtailment, &c., 36, garbling, mutilation, truncation, abscission, excision, amputation, 789.

V. To subduct, deduct, subtract, retrench, remove, withdraw, bate, detract, deduce, take away, deprive of, curtail, &c., 36, garble, truncate, mutilate, amputate, cut off, cut out, dock, lop, prune, pare, clip, thin, shear, decimate; to abrade, &c., 330.

Adj. Subtracted, deducted, &c.; subtractive.

Adv. In deduction, &c., less, *minus*, without, except, excepting, with the exception of, barring, save, exclusive of. 83

---

39. Thing added.

ADJUNCT, addition, affix, appendage, suffix, augment, increment, augmentation, accessory, supplement, complement, continuation.

Sequel, postscript, codicil, rider, trappings, tail, train, suite, accompaniment, 88.

---

40. Thing remaining.

REMAINDER, residue, remains, remnant, the rest, relic, leavings, odds and ends.

Residuum, ashes, cinders, slay, sediment, alluvium, stubble, result.

Surplus, overplus, surplusage, superfluity, excess, 641, balance, complement, fag-end, ruins. wreck.

V. To remain, be left, be left behind, to survive, to exceed.

Adj. Remaining, left, left behind, residual, residuary, outstanding, unconsumed.

Superfluous, over and above, exceeding, redundant, supernumerary.

41. Forming a whole without coherence.

MIXTURE, admixture, commixture, admixtion, commixtion, mixtion, intermixture, alloyage.

Impregnation, infusion, diffusion, suffusion, interspersion, transfusion, seasoning, sprinkling, interlarding, interpolation, interposition, 228, intrusion, adulteration, sophistication.

Thing mixed. A touch, spice, tinge, tincture, dash, smack, sprinkling, seasoning, infusion, &c.

Compound resulting from mixture. Alloy, amalgam, miscellany, medley, patchwork, odds and ends: — farrago, jumble, 59, mess, salad, sauce, hash, hodgepodge, salmagundi, mosaic, 440.

V. To mix, commix, intermix, mingle, commingle, intermingle, interlard, intersperse, interpolate, shuffle together, huddle together, pound together, stir up, knead, brew, jumble, 59.

To be mixed, to get among, to be entangled with.

To instil, imbue, infuse, infiltrate, dash, tinge, tincture, season, sprinkle, besprinkle, suffuse, transfuse, attemper, medicate, blend, alloy, amalgamate, compound, 48, adulterate, sophisticate.

Adj. Mixed, mingled, intermixed, &c.; composite, mixed

42. Freedom from mixture.

SIMPLENESS, singleness, purity, clearness, homogenousness.

Purification, 652, elimination sifting, winnowing.

V. To render simple, simplify sift, winnow, eliminate; to separate, disjoin, 44.

To purify, 652.

Adj. Simple, uniform, of a piece, homogeneous, single, pure, clear, sheer, neat, elementary: — unmixed, unmingled, untinged, unblended, uncombined, uncompounded, undecomposed, unadulterated, unsophisticated.

Free from, exempt from, exclusive.

---

up with, half and half, linsey-woolsey, hybrid, mongrel, heterogeneous.

Adv. Among, amongst, amid, amidst, with, in the midst of, in the crowd.

43. Junction, joining, connection, connecting, conjunction, conjugation, annexation, annexment, attachment, compagination, alligation, fastening, linking, coupling, matrimony, 903, grafting, infibulation; inosculation, confluence, association, 72, communication, approach, 197.

Joint, joining, juncture, pivot, hinge, articulation, commissure, seam, stitch, suture, meeting, reunion, mortise.

Closeness, firmness, tightness, compactness.

V. To join, conjoin, connect, associate, imbody, reimbody, hold together, pack, fix together, attach, affix, saddle on, fasten, bind, secure, make fast, tie, pinion, strap, sew, lace, stitch, tack, knit, button, buckle, hitch, lash, truss, bandage, braid, splice, swathe, gird, tether, picket, harness

Chain, enchain, shackle, pinion, manacle, handcuff, lock, leash, couple, link, yoke; hang together, pin, nail, bolt, hasp, clasp, clamp, screw, rivet, mortise, dovetail, enchase, ingraft, interlink, inosculate, intwine, interlace, intertwine, intertwist, interweave.

To be joined, &c., to hang together.

Adj. Joined, conjoined, coupled, &c., bound up together, conjunct, (joint,) corporate, compact.

Firm, fast, close, tight, secure, set, impacted, locked, &c., intervolved, inseparable, indissoluble, insecable, inseverable.

Adv. Conjointly, jointly, &c.

With, along with, together with, in conjunction with.

Fast, firmly, closely &c.

---

44. Disjunction, disconnection, disunity, disunion, disassociation, disengagement, abstractedness, isolation, insularity, separateness.

Separation, parting, detachment, discerption, division, subdivision, dismemberment, disintegration, dislocation, laxation, severance, disseverance, severing, scission, rescission, abscission, laceration, dilaceration, wrenching, disruption, avulsion, divulsion, tearing asunder, section, cutting, resection, cleavage, fissure, breach, rent, split, crack, slit, dispersion, 73, dissection, anatomy.

V. To be disjoined, separated, &c.

To disjoin, disconnect, disunite, dispart, detach, separate, segregate, dissociate, isolate, disengage, set apart, loose, set free, unloose, unfasten, untie, unbind, unfix, unlace, unclasp, undo, unbuckle, unchain, unfetter, untack, unharness, ungird, unbolt, unlatch, unlock, unlink, uncouple, unpin, unclinch, unscrew, unhook, unrivet, untwist, unshackle. unyoke, unsolder, unravel, disentangle, unglue.

Sunder, divide, sever, dissever, abscind, cut, incise, cleave, rive, rend, slit, split, splinter, chip, crack, snap, rend, break, or tear asunder, shiver, chop, cut up, rip up, hack, hew, slash, whittle, hackle, tear, lacerate, mangle.

Dissect, anatomize; take, pull, or pick to pieces; tear to tatters; tear piecemeal, divellicate, disintegrate; dismember, dislocate, disjoint, mince, break up

Adj. Disjoined, disconnected,

disjointed, &c., multipartite; abstract, disjunctive, isolated, separate, apart, asunder, loose, free, liberated, disengaged, unattached, unannexed, distinct, unassociated, adrift, straggling, dispersed, segregated.

Cut off, &c., rift.

Adv. Separately, one by one, severally, &c., apart, adrift; in the abstract, abstractedly.

45. Connecting medium.

VINCULUM, link, connective, copula.

Bond, filament, fibre, 205, hair, cordage, cord, thread, strings, packthread, twine, twist, tape, line, ribbon, rope, cable, hawser, wire, chain.

Fastening, tie, ligament, ligature, strap, tackle, rigging, traces, harness, band, brace, bandage, fillet, thong, braid, girder, girth, halter, noose, lasso, surcingle.

Pin, corking pin, nail, brad, skewer, staple, clamp, cramp, screw, button, clasp, hasp, hinge, latch, latchet, tag, hook, tooth, hook and eye, lock, locket, padlock, rivet, grappling iron, stake, post, shackle, &c., 752.

Cement, glue, gum, paste, size, solder, lute, putty, birdlime, mortar, stucco, plaster, grout.

46. COHERENCE, cohesion, adherence, adhesion, concretion, agglutination, conglutination, aggregation, consolidation, cementation, soldering, welding.

Sticking, clinging, adhesiveness, stickiness, gumminess, glutinousness, cohesiveness, density, 321, inseparability, inseparableness.

Clot, concrete, cake, lump, solid, conglomerate, 321.

V. To cohere, adhere, stick, cling, cleave, hold, take hold of, hold fast, grow or hang together, twine round.

To concrete, curdle, cake.

To glue, agglutinate, conglutinate, consolidate, solidify, 321, cement, lute, paste, gum, glue, solder, weld.

Adj. Cohesive, adhesive, cohering, &c.; inseparable, infrangible.

Sticky, glutinous, gluey, gummy, viscous, 352.

United, unseparated, inseparable, 321.

47. Want of adhesion, non-adhesion, immiscibility.

INCOHERENCE, looseness, laxity, slackness, relaxation, freedom

V. To loosen, slacken, relax, unglue, unsolder, &c., detach, untwist, unravel, unroll, &c., 44, 313

To comminute, &c., 330.

Adj. Incoherent, detached, non-adhesive, loose, slack, lax, relaxed.

Segregated, flapping, streaming, dishevelled, unincorporated, unconsolidated, uncombined, &c.

---

48. COMBINATION, union, synthesis, incorporation, amalgamation, coalescence, fusion, blending, absorption, centralization.

49. DECOMPOSITION, analysis, resolution, dissolution, corruption.

V. To decompose, analyze, de

Compound. amalgam, impregnation.

V. To combine, unite, incorporate, amalgamate, imbody, absorb, reimbody, blend, merge, fuse, melt into one, consolidate, coalesce, centralize, to impregnate, to put together, to lump together.

Adj. Combined, &c., impregnated with, ingrained.

compound, resolve, take to pieces, separate into its elements, dissect, unravel, &c., break up.

Adj. Decomposed, &c.

---

4. Concrete Quantity.

50. Whole, totality, integrity, totalness, collectiveness, individuality, unity, 87, indivisibility, indiscerptibility, indissolvableness; — integration.

All, the whole, total, aggregate, integer, gross, amount, sum, sum total, upshot, root and branch, trunk, hull, skeleton, lump, heap, 72.

The principal part, bulk, mass, tissue, staple, body, the main, the greater part, major part, essential part, best part, the marrow, soul, pith, nucleus.

V. To form, or constitute a whole, to integrate, imbody, aggregate, amass, 72; to amount to, come to.

Adj. Whole, total, integral, entire, one, unbroken, uncut, undivided, unsevered, unclipped, uncropped, unshorn, undiminished, undemolished, undissolved, unbruised, undestroyed, indivisible, indissoluble, indissolvable, indiscerptible.

Wholesale, sweeping.

Adv. Wholly, altogether, totally, entirely, all, all in all, wholesale, in the mass, in the lump, on the whole, in toto, in the gross, to the full, throughout, every inch, in the long run, in the main

51. Part, portion, division, subdivision, section, segment, fraction, fragment, detachment, piece, bit, scrap, whit, morsel, mouthful, scantling, slip, crum, fritter, tatter, splinter, cutting, slice, shiver, sliver, driblet, clipping, scale, lamina.

Part and parcel, share, dividend, particular, article, chapter, clause, count, paragraph.

Member, limb, lobe, lobule, arm, branch, bough, joint, link, ramification, twig, bush, spray, sprig, leaf, leaflet, stump.

V. To part, divide, subdivide, break, &c., 44; to partition, parcel out, portion, apportion, 786.

Adj. Fractional, fragmentary, lobular, sectional, aliquot, divided, partitioned, &c.

Adv. Partly, in part, partially, piecemeal, in detail, part by part, by driblets, by inches; inch by inch.

---

52. COMPLETENESS, fulness, completion, 729, perfection, 650, solidity, filling up, integration, absoluteness.

Complement, supplement, 39.

V. To be complete, &c.

To render complete, or whole, to complete, perfect, finish, make up, fill up, make good, piece out, eke out.

Adj. Complete, entire, perfect, full, thorough, plenary, solid, undivided, with all its parts.

53. INCOMPLETENESS, deficiency, defectiveness, failure, imperfection, 651, hollowness.

Part wanting, defect, deficit, caret.

V. To be incomplete, &c., to fail, fall short, 304.

Adj. Incomplete, imperfect, defective, deficient, wanting, failing, short by, hollow.

Mutilated, garbled, docked.

Adv. Completely, entirely, to the full, thoroughly.

54. COMPOSITION, constitution.

Inclusion, admission, comprehension, reception, (receptivity.)

Inclusion in a class, 76.

V. To be composed of, to consist of, be made of, formed of, made up of, be resolved into.

To contain, include, hold, comprehend, take in, admit, embrace, involve, implicate.

To compose, constitute, form, make, make up, fill up, build up, put together, imbody.

To enter into the composition of, to be, or form part of, 51, to merge in, be merged in.

Adj. Comprehending, containing, including, comprising, &c.

Forming, constituting, composing, &c., entering into, being or forming part of, &c., belonging to, appertaining to, inclusive.

55. EXCLUSION, non-admission, exception, rejection, repudiation, exile, banishment, excommunication.

Separation, segregation.

Exclusion from a class, 77.

V. to be excluded from, &c.

To exclude, shut out, bar, leave out, omit, reject, repudiate, neglect; lay, put, or set apart, or aside; segregate, pass over, throw overboard, slur over, neglect, 460, excommunicate, banish, expatriate, ostracize, relegate.

To eliminate, weed, winnow, garble, bar, separate, 44, strike off.

Adj. Excluding, omitting, &c., exclusive.

Excluded, omitted, &c.

Adv. Exclusive of, barring, &c.

56. COMPONENT, component part, element, constituent, ingredient, member, limb, 51, part and parcel, contents, appurtenance.

57. EXTRANEOUSNESS, foreign body, alien, stranger, intruder, interloper, foreigner.

SECTION IV. ORDER.

1. ORDER IN GENERAL.

58. ORDER, regularity, orderliness, uniformity, even tenor, symmetry

59. Absence, or want of order, &c.

DISORDER, irregularity, anoma

Gradation, progression, subordination, course, array, routine.

Method, disposition, (arrangement, combination,) system, economy, discipline.

Rank, station, place, stand, scale, step, stage, period, term, footing; rank and file, 71.

V. To be, or become in order, to form, fall in, draw up, arrange itself, place itself, range itself, fall into its place, fall into rank.

Adj. Orderly, regular, in order, arranged, &c., 60, in its proper place, well regulated, methodical, uniform, symmetrical, systematic, unconfused, undisturbed, untangled, unruffled, unravelled, &c., 265.

Adv. Orderly, &c., in turn, in its turn.

Step by step, by regular (gradation,) steps, stages, periods,

At stated periods, 138.

---

ly, confusion, confusedness, dis array, jumble, litter, lumber, farrago, mess, hodgepodge, anarchy chaos, 41.

Complexedness, complexity, complexness, complication, intricacy, intricateness, implication, perplexity, involution, ravelling, entanglement, knot, coil, Gordian knot.

Turmoil, tumult, ferment, fermentation, pother, riot, rumpus, scramble, vortex, whirlpool, hurly burly, Babel.

Tumultuousness, riotousness, inquietude, 173.

Derangement, 61, inversion of order.

Topsyturvy, 218.

V. To be out of order, irregular, disorderly, &c., to ferment.

To put out of order, 61.

Adj. Disorderly, out of order, deranged, 61, irregular, anomalous, unarranged, immethodical, unsymmetric, unsystematic, unmethodical, undigested, unsorted, unclassified, unclassed.

Disjointed, out of joint, confused, tangled, (disarranged,) involved, inextricable, irreducible.

Mixed, scattered, promiscuous, indiscriminate, straggling.

Tumultuous, turbulent, riotous, troublous, tumultuary, 173

Adv. Irregularly, &c., pellmell; at sixes and sevens; helter skelter; in a ferment.

60. Reduction to order.

ARRANGEMENT, disposal, disposition, collocation, distribution, sorting, assortment, allotment, apportionment, marshalling, gradation, organization.

Analysis, sifting, classification.

Result of arrangement, digest, synopsis, analysis, table, register, 551.

Instrument for sorting; sieve, riddle, screen.

V. To reduce to order, bring into order, introduce order into.

To arrange, dispose, place, form; to put, set, place, &c., in

61. Subversion of order, bringing into disorder.

DERANGEMENT, disarrangement, misarrangement, displacement, misplacement, discomposure, disturbance, disorganization, perturbation, shuffling, embroilment, corrugation, 258, inversion, 218.

V. To derange, disarrange, misplace, mislay, discompose, disorder, embroil, unsettle, disturb, confuse, perturb, jumble, tumble, bring, put, or throw into disorder, confusion, &c., to break the ranks

To unhinge, put out of joint

order, to set out, collocate, pack, marshal, range, rank, group, parcel out, allot, distribute, assort, sort, sift, riddle; to put or set to rights; to assign places to.

To class, classify, file, string, tabulate.

To methodize, digest, regulate, graduate, organize, settle.

To unravel, disentangle, disembroil.

Adj. Arranged, methodical, &c., *see* 58.

turn over, invert, turn topsyturvy; turn inside out, 218.

To complicate, involve, perplex, tangle, entangle, ravel, ruffle, dishevel, litter, scatter.

Adj. Deranged, &c., *see* 59.

Irreducible, &c.

---

2. Consecutive Order.

62. Precedence, coming before, antecedence, priority, anteriority, antecedency.

Superiority, 33, precession, 280.

V. To precede, come before, introduce, usher in; to lead, to get the start.

To place before; to prefix, affix, premise, prelude, preface.

To prepare, 673.

Adj. Preceding, precedent, antecedent, anterior, prior, previous, before, ahead of.

Former, foregoing; coming or going before; precursory, precursive, preliminary, prefatory, introductory, prelusive, prelusory, proemial, preparatory.

Adv. In advance, ahead, &c., in front of, *see* 234.

63. Sequence, coming after, consecution, succession, posteriority, secondariness.

Continuation, order of succession, successiveness.

Subordination, inferiority, 34.

Alternation, 138.

V. To succeed, come after, follow, come next, ensue, tread close upon; to alternate.

Adj. Succeeding, coming after, following, subsequent, ensuing, sequent, consequent, next; consecutive; alternate, 138.

Latter, posterior.

Adv. After, subsequently, since, behind, in the wake of, in the train of, in the rear of, *see* 235

64. Precursor, antecedent, predecessor, forerunner, (harbinger,) vancourier, outrider.

Prelude, preamble, preface, prologue, prolusion, proem, prolegomena, prefix, introduction, frontispiece, groundwork, 673.

65. Sequel, afterpart, suffix, successor, train, wake, trail, rear, retinue, suite, appendix, 39, postscript, epilogue, afterpiece, afterthought, codicil.

66. Beginning, commencement, outset, incipience, inception, initiative, overture, exordium, inauguration, onset.

Origin, source, rise, birth, bud, embryo, rudiment, start, cradle,

67. End, close, termination, conclusion, finish, finale, period, term, terminus, last, extreme, extremity, turning point, but-end, tag, fag-end, tail, tip, nib, after-part, rear, 235, peroration.

starting point *see* Departure, **293.**

Van, vanguard, titlepage, heading, front, 234, fore part, head, 210.

Dawn, morning, 125.

Opening, entrance, entry, inlet, orifice, porch, portal, gateway, door, gate, postern, wicket, threshold, vestibule, mouth.

V. To begin, commence, rise, arise, originate, initiate, open, dawn, set in, take its rise, enter upon, set out, 293, to recommence.

To usher in, lead off, lead the way, take the lead, or the initiative; head, stand at the head, stand first; broach, set on foot, 676, set a-going, set up, institute, launch, break ground, break the ice.

Completion, 729, winding-up catastrophe, consummation, finishing stroke, upshot, issue.

V. To end, close, finish, terminate, conclude; come, or draw to an end, close or stop.

To bring to an end, close, &c., to put a period, &c., to; to close, finish, seal, &c., to wind up, complete, achieve, 729, crown, determine.

Adj. Ending, closing, &c., final, terminal, definitive, crowning.

Last, ultimate, hindermost, rear, caudal, conterminous.

Ended, closed, terminated, &c.

Unbegun, fresh, uncommenced.

Adv. Once for all.

Adj. Beginning, commencing, arising, initial, initiatory, initiative, incipient, proemial, inaugural, inchoative, primogenial, aboriginal, rudimental, nascent, opening, dawning, entering.

First, foremost, leading, heading.

Begun, commenced, &c.

Adv. At, or in the beginning, (at the outset;) first, in the first place, first and foremost, in the bud.

From the beginning.

68. Middle, mean, medium, middle term, centre, 222, nave, nucleus.

Equidistance, midst; bisection, 91.

Interjacence, intervention, 228, mid-course, 628.

Adj. Middle, medial, mean, mid, middlemost, midmost, mediate, intermediate, 29, intervening, interjacent, 228, central, 222, equidistant, imbosomed, merged.

Mediterranean, equatorial.

Adv. In the middle, mid-way, half-way, in the thick of.

69. Uninterrupted sequence.

Continuity, consecution, succession, suite, progression, series, train, chain, catenation, concatenation, scale, gradation, course, procession, column, retinue, cavalcade, rank and file, line of battle, array, pedigree, genealogy, lineage, race.

File, line, row, range, tier, string, thread, suit, colonnade.

70. Interrupted sequence.

Discontinuity, interruption, break, interval, (cut,) gap, chasm, hiatus, 198.

Intermission, alternation, *see* Periodicity, 138.

V. To be discontinuous, &c.; to alternate, intermit.

To discontinue, pause, interrupt, break, interpose, 228; to break in upon, disconnect, 44

V. To follow in a series, &c.; to form a series, &c.; to fall in.

To arrange in a series, to marshal, &c., 60; to string together, file, graduate, tabulate.

Adj. Continuous, consecutive, serial, successive, continued, uninterrupted, unbroken, entire, linear, in a line, in a row, &c., gradual, unintermitting, 110.

Adv. Continuously, consecutively, &c.; in a line, in a string, in a row, series, &c., in succession, &c., running, gradually, step by step.

Adj. Discontinuous, unsuccessive, broken, interrupted, desultory, disconnected, unconnected, rhapsodical.

Alternate, every other, intermitting, alternating, 138.

Adv. At intervals, by snatches.

---

71. Term, rank, station, stage, step, degree, 26, remove, grade, link, place, point, period, pitch, stand, standing, footing, range.

V. To hold, occupy, find, fall into a place, station, &c.

3. Collective Order.

72. Assemblage, collection, collocation, levy, gathering, ingathering, muster, colligation, association, concourse, conflux, meeting, assembly, congregation, levee, club, array, accumulation, cumulation.

Congress, convocation, convention, quorum, conclave, synod, caucus, conventicle.

Miscellany, museum, menagery, portfolio.

A multitude, 102, crowd, throng, rabble, mob, press, horde, body, tribe, crew, gang, knot, band, party, bevy, galaxy, drove, corps, troop, squad, squadron, phalanx, platoon, company, regiment, battalion, legion, host, army, myrmidons.

Clan, brotherhood, (fraternity,) sisterhood, party, 712.

Volley, shower, storm, cloud, &c.

Group, cluster, clump, set, batch, lot, pack, budget, assortment, bunch, parcel, packet, package, bundle, pencil, fagot, truss, tuft, shock, rick, fardel, stack, sheaf.

Accumulation, congeries, heap, lump, pile, tissue, mass, bale, drift, acervation, agglomeration, conglomeration, conglomerate, coagmentation, aggregation, concentration.

V. To assemble, collect, muster, meet, unite, cluster, flock, herd, crowd, throng, associate, congregate, rendezvous, resort, flock together, reassemble.

To bring, or gather together, collect, draw together, group,

73. Non-assemblage. Dispersion, scattering, dissemination, diffusion, dissipation, spreading, distribution, sprinkling, circumfusion, interspersion, divergence, 290.

V. To disperse, scatter, sow, disseminate, diffuse, shed, spread, overspread, disperse, disband, distribute, dispel; strew, sprinkle, issue, deal out, retail, intersperse.

Adj. Unassembled, uncollected, dispersed, scattered, diffused, sparse, spread, broadcast, &c., adrift, dishevelled, streaming, &c

---

convene, convocate, (convoke,) scrape together, rake up, dredge, bring into a focus, amass, accumulate, heap up, pile, pack, stack, truss, pack together, agglomerate, garner up, lump together.

Adj. Assembled, collected, &c., unscattered, met together, closely packed, dense, crowded, huddled together, teeming, swarming, populous.

74. Place of meeting.

FOCUS, point of convergence, rendezvous, head quarters, centre 222, gathering, resort, museum, repository, depot, 636.

4. DISTRIBUTIVE ORDER.

75. CLASS, division, category, head, order, section, department, province.

Kind, sort, genus, species, family, race, tribe, caste, clan, breed, sect, set, assortment, suit, range.

Gender, sex, kin, manner, description, denomination, designation.

76. INCLUSION, comprehension under a class, reference to a class.

Inclusion in a compound, 54.

V. To be included in, to come under, to fall under, to range under; to belong, or pertain to; to range with, to merge in.

To include, comprise, comprehend, contain, admit, embrace, enumerate among, reckon among, number among, refer to, place under, arrange under, or with.

Adj. Including, &c., inclusive, congener, congenerous, of the same class, &c.

Included, merged, &c.

77. EXCLUSION from a class,* rejection, &c., proscription, nobody.

Exclusion from a compound, 55.

V. To be excluded from, &c.; to exclude, proscribe, &c.

Adj. Exclusive, excluding, &c.

---

78. GENERALITY, universality, catholicism, (bulk.)

Miscellaneousness, miscellany, generalization, prevalence,.

V. To be general, &c., to prevail.

To render general, to generalize.

Adj. General, generic, collective, comprehensive, sweeping, universal, catholic, common, ecumenical, prevalent, prevailing.

Every, every one, all, to a man, whatever, whatsoever, unspecified, impersonal

79. SPECIALITY, particularity, individuality, peculiarity, (specific difference,) personality, characteristic, mannerism, indiosyncrasy, specificness, singularity, 83.

Particulars, details, items, counts.

V. To specify, particularize, individualize, specialize, designate, determine, to descend to particulars, to enter into detail.

Adj. Special, particular, individual, specific, proper, personal,

* The same set of words are used to express *exclusion from a class* and *exclusion from compound.* Reference is therefore here made to the former at 55. This identity does not occur with regard to *inclusion*, which, therefore, required to be made a separate heading.

private, respective, definite, determinate, especial, certain, esoteric, endemic, partial, party, peculiar, characteristic, diagnostic, exclusive, singular, exceptional, 83.

Adv. Specially, specifically, &c., in particular, respectively, personally.

Each, apiece, one by one, severally.

5. Order as regards Categories.

80. Rule, regularity, uniformity, constancy, standard, model, nature, the order of things, routine, prevalence, practice, usage, custom, use, habit, 613, regulation.

Form, formula, law, canon, principle.

Type, pattern, precedent; the normal, natural, ordinary, or model state or condition.

81. Multiformity, variety diversity, multifariousness.

Adj. Multiform, manifold, multifarious, heterogeneous, motley, of all sorts and kinds, desultory, irregular, diversified.

82. Conformity, conformance, observance, naturalization.

Example, instance, specimen, sample, exemplar, exemplification, illustration, case in point, quotation — the rule.

V. To conform to rule, be regular, &c., to follow, observe, go by, bend to, obey rules, to be regulated (or guided) by, be wont, &c., 613, to naturalize.

To exemplify, illustrate, cite, quote, put a case, produce an instance, &c.

Adj. Conformable to rule, regular, uniform, constant, steady, according to rule, normal, formal, canonical, strict, rigid, positive, uncompromising.

Ordinary, natural, usual, common, wonted, accustomed, habitual, every day, current, prevailing, prevalent, established, received, acknowledged, recognized, hackneyed, well-known, familiar, vernacular, commonplace, trite, of daily or everyday occurrence, in the order of things, naturalized.

Exemplary, illustrative, in point.

83. Unconformity, informality, arbitrariness, abnormity, anomaly, anomalousness, lawlessness, peculiarity, exclusiveness; infraction, breach, violation, &c., of law, or rule; eccentricity, aberration, irregularity, singularity, exemption, salvo.

Exception, nondescript, nonesuch, monster, prodigy, 872, mongrel, half caste, cross breed, hybrid, mule, mulatto, hermaphrodite.

Phœnix, chimera, hydra, sphinx, minotaur, griffin, centaur, hippocentaur, sagittary, hippogriff, kraken, dragon, sea serpent, mermaid, unicorn, &c.

V. To be unconformable to rule, to be exceptional; to stretch a point.

Adj. Unconformable, exceptional, abnormal, anomalous, anomalistic, out of order, irregular, arbitrary, informal, aberrant, stray, peculiar, exclusive, unnatural, eccentric; desultory.

Unusual, unaccustomed, unwonted, uncommon, rare, singular, unique, curious, odd, extraordinary, strange, out of the way,

Adv. Conformably, by rule, regularly, &c., agreeably to.

Usually, generally, ordinarily, commonly, as usual.

Of course, as a matter of course.

For example, for instance, to wit, namely, that is to say.

unheard of, queer, quaint, nondescript, undescribed, none such, unprecedented, unparalleled, unfamiliar, fantastic, new-fangled, grotesque, outlandish, exotic, preternatural, denaturalized.

Heterogeneous, heteroclite, amorphous, out of the pale of, mongrel, amphibious, epicene, half-blood, hybrid.

Adv. Except, unless, save, barring, beside, without, and except.

However, yet, but, unusually, &c.

Section V. NUMBER.

1. Number in the Abstract.

84. Number, symbol, numeral, figure, cipher, digit, integer, counter, a round number, a formula; notation.

Sum, difference, complement, product, multiplicand, multiplier, multiplicator, coefficient, multiple, dividend, divisor, factor, quotient, submultiple, fraction, numerator, denominator, decimal, circulating decimal, repetend, common measure, aliquot part, reciprocal, prime number, permutation, combination, election.

Ratio, proportion, progression, (arithmetical, geometrical, harmonical,) figurate, pyramidal, and polygonal numbers.

Power, root, exponent, index, logarithm, antilogarithm; — differential, integral, fluxion, fluent.

Adj. Numeral, complementary, divisible, aliquot, reciprocal, prime, fractional, decimal, figurate, &c., fractional, mixed, incommensurable.

Proportional, series, exponential, logarithmic, logometric, differential, fluxional, integral.

Positive, negative, rational, irrational, surd, radical, real, imaginary, impossible.

85. Numeration, numbering, counting, tale, telling, calling over, recension, enumeration, summation, reckoning, computation, supputation, calculation, calculus, algorithm.

Arithmetic, analysis, algebra, fluxions, differential and integral calculus.

Statistics; dead reckoning, muster, poll, census, capitation, roll call, muster roll, account, score, recapitulation.

Operations; addition, subtraction, multiplication, division, reduction, involution, evolution, approximation, interpolation, differentiation, integration.

Instruments; abacus, swan-pan, logometer, sliding rule, tallies, Napier's bones, &c.

V. To number, count, tell, call over, take an account of, enumerate, muster, poll, run over, recite, recapitulate,—sum, sum up, tell off, score, compute, calculate, suppute,—add, subtract, &c., to amount to.

To check, prove, demonstrate, balance, audit.

Adj. Numerical, arithmetical, numeral, analytic, algebraic, statistical, computable, calculable, commensurable, incommensurate.

86. LIST, catalogue, inventory, schedule, register, record, 551, registry, syllabus, roll, file, muster roll, calendar, index, table, book, synopsis, contents, invoice, bill of lading, red book, prospectus, programme. Registration, &c., 551.

2. DETERMINATE NUMBER.

87. UNITY, oneness, individuality, singleness, solitariness, solitude, 893, isolation, abstraction.

One, unit, ace.

Some one, somebody, no other, none else, an individual.

V. To be one, to be alone, &c.; to isolate, insulate.

Adj. One, sole, single, individual, apart, alone, lone, isolated, solitary, lonely, lonesome, dreary, insular, insulated, disparate, discrete, detached, 44.

Unaccompanied, unattended, singular, odd, unique, unrepeated.

Insecable, inseverable, irresolvable, indiscerptible.

Adv. Singly, &c., alone, by itself, only, apart, in the singular number, in the abstract; one by one.

One and a half.

88. ACCOMPANIMENT, coexistence, concomitance, company, association, companionship, partnership, copartnership, coefficiency.

Concomitant, accessory, coefficient, 39, companion, attendant, fellow, associate, consort, spouse, colleague, partner, copartner, satellite, escort, hanger on.

V. To accompany, coexist, attend, be associated with, hang on, wait on, go hand in hand with, to join, tie together, &c., 43.

Adj. Accompanying, coexisting, attending, &c., concomitant, fellow, joint, associated with, accessory.

Adv. With, together with, along with, in company with, hand in hand, side by side, cheek by jowl, &c.; therewith, herewith.—And, &c., *see* 37.

89. DUALITY, dualism, duplicity, biformity.

Two, deuce, couple, brace, pair, twins, fellows, yoke, conjugation, polarity.

V. To unite in pairs, to pair, couple, bracket, yoke.

Adj. Two, dual, binary, dualistic, duplex, twofold, bifold, biform bifarious, duplicate, binomial, twin.

Coupled, bracketed, paired, &c., conjugate.

Both, the one and the other.

90. DUPLICATION, doubling, gemination, reduplication, ingemination, repetition, iteration, 104, renewal.

V. To double, redouble, gemi-

91. Division into two parts.

BISECTION, bipartition, dichotomy, halving, dimidiation, bifurcation, forking, branching, ramification, divarication splitting cleaving, fork, prong.

nate, reduplicate, repeat, iterate, reëcho, renew.

Adj. Doubled, redoubled, biform, bifold, bifacial, ingeminate, &c.

Adv. Twice, once more, over again, anew, as much again, twofold, 104, 136.

Secondly, in the second place, again.

Half, moiety, semi-, demi-, hemi-.

To bisect, halve, divide, cut in two.

To separate, fork, bifurcate, branch out, ramify, to split, cleave.

Adj. Bisected, halved, divided, &c., bipartite, biconjugate, bicuspid, bifurcated, bifid, bifurcous, bifurcate, cloven, cleft, split, &c.

92. TRIALTY, trinity.*

Three, triad, triplet, trey, trio, ternion, trinominal, leash.

Third power, cube.

Adj. Three, triform, trinal, trinominal, tertiary.

93. TRIPLICATION, triplicity, trebleness, trine.

V. To treble, triple, triplicate.

Adj. Treble, triple, tern, ternary, triplicate, threefold, trilogistic.

Adv. Three times, thrice, threefold, in the third place, thirdly.

94. Division into three parts.

TRISECTION, tripartition, trichotomy; third part, third.

V. To trisect, divide into three parts.

Adj. Trifid, trisected, tripartite.

95. QUATERNITY, four, quartet, quaternion, square, quadrature quarter.

V. To reduce to a square, to square.

Adj. Four, quaternary, quaternal, quadratic, quartile.

96. QUADRUPLICATION.

V. To multiply by four, quadruplicate, biquadrate.

Adj. Fourfold, quadruple, quadruplicate, quadrible.

Adv. Four times, in the fourth place, fourthly.

97. Division into four parts.

QUADRISECTION, quadripartition, quartering, a fourth, a quarter.

V. To quarter, to divide into four parts, &c.

Adj. Quartered, &c., quadripartite.

98. FIVE, cinque, quint, quincunx.

Adj. Five, quinary, quintuple.

SIX.

Adj. Senary, sextuple.

EIGHT, octuple.

TEN, a decade.

Adj. Decimal, denary, decuple.

TWELVE, a dozen.

Adj. Duodenary.

TWENTY, a score.

SIXTY.

EIGHTY, fourscore.

HUNDRED, centenary, heca-

99. QUINQUESECTION, &c.

Adj. Quinquepartite.

Octofid.

DECIMATION.

V. To decimate.

Adj. Decimal, tenth, tithe.

DUODECIMAL, twelfth.

Sexagesimal, sexagenary.

HUNDREDTH, centesimal.

* *Trinity* is hardly ever used, except in a theological sense, 976.

omb, century. — One hundred and forty-four, gross

V. To centuriate.

Adj. Centuple, centuplicate, centennial, centenary, centurial.

THOUSAND.

MYRIAD.

MILLION, billion, trillion, &c.

Millesimal, &c.

3. INDETERMINATE NUMBER.

100. More than one.

PLURALITY, a number, a certain number, a round number.

Adj. Plural, more than one, some, certain, some one, somebody.

101. ZERO, nothing, 4, nought, cipher, a solitude, a desert.

Adj. None, not one, not any nobody, not a soul.

102. MULTITUDE, numerousness, numerosity, multiplicity, legion, host, a great or large number, numbers, army, sea.

A shoal, swarm, draught, bevy, flock, herd, drove, covey, hive, brood, litter, teem, fry, nest, crowd, &c., 72.

Increase of number, multiplication.

V. To be numerous, &c., to swarm, teem, crowd, come thick upon, outnumber, multiply.

Adj. Many, several, sundry, divers, various, full many, ever so many, numerous, manifold, multiplied, multitudinous, multiple, multinominal, endless, 105.

Frequent, repeated, reiterated, outnumbering, thick, crowding, thickcoming, many more.

103. FEWNESS, paucity, a small number, scantiness, rareness, rarity, thinness.

Diminution of number, reduction, weeding, elimination, thinning.

V. To be few, &c.

To render few, reduce, diminish the number, weed, eliminate, thin, decimate.

Adj. Few, scanty, rare, thinly scattered, hardly or scarcely any reduced, thinned, weeded, &c. unrepeated.

---

104. REPETITION, iteration, reiteration, recurrence, 136, tautology, monotony, chimes, repetend, echo, burden of a song, refrain, renewal, rehearsal.

Cuckoo, mocking bird.

Periodicity, 138. Frequency, 136.

V. To repeat, iterate, reiterate, renew, reproduce, echo, reëcho, drum, rehearse, redouble.

Adj. Repeated, 136, repetitional, repetitionary, recurrent, recurring, reiterated, renewed, ever-recurring, thickcoming, monotonous harping, mocking, chiming, aforesaid.

Adv. Repeatedly, often, 136, again, anew, over again,

again and again, in quick succession, over and over again, ditto See Twice 90.

105. Infinity, infinitude.

Adj. Infinite numberless, innumerable, countless, sumless, untold, unnumbered, incalculable, unlimited, limitless, illimited, illimitable, immeasurable, unmeasured, measureless, unbounded, boundless, endless, interminable, unfathomable, exhaustless, termless, indefinite.

Adv. Infinitely, &c., without measure, limit, &c.

Section VI. TIME.

1. Absolute Time.

106. Duration, period, term, space, span, spell, season, era.

Intermediate time, the while, interval, interim, pendency, intervention, intermission, interregnum, interlude, intermittence, respite.

Long duration, 110.

V. To continue, last, endure, remain, to take, take up, fill or occupy time, to persist, to intervene.

To pass, spend, employ, (while away,) or consume time

Adj. Continuing, lasting, enduring, remaining, persistent, permanent, 150.

Adv. While, whilst, during or pending, till, until, during the time or interval; the whole time or period; all the time, in the long run, all along, throughout.

Pending, meantime, meanwhile, in the mean time, in the interim, from day to day, for a time, for a season, for good.

107. Non-duration, absence, of time, no time.

Short duration, 111.

Adv. Never, at no time, on no occasion, at no period, nevermore.

Hardly ever, scarcely ever.

---

108. Definite duration or portion of time.

Period, second, minute, hour, day, week, month, quarter, year, lifetime, (generation.)

Century, age, millennium.

Adj. Hourly, horary; diurnal, quotidian; (weekly,) hebdomadal, menstrual, monthly, annual, secular, (centennial, semi-centennial.)

Adv. From day to day, from hour to hour, &c., till, until, up to.

109. Indefinite duration.

Course, progress, process, succession, lapse, flow, flux, stream tract, current, tide, march, step, flight, &c., of time.

Indefinite time, aorist.

V. To elapse, lapse, flow, run, proceed, roll on, advance, pass, slide, press on, flit, fly, slip, glide.

Adj. Elapsing, passing, &c., aoristic.

Adv. In course of time; in due time or season; in process of time; in the fulness of time.

110. Long duration.

111. Short duration.

Diuturnity, a long time, an age, a century, an eternity.

Durableness, durability, persistence, continuance, permanence, 150, longevity.

Survival, survivance.

Distance of time, protraction, extension or prolongation of time, 133.

V. To last, endure, stand, &c.; tarry, protract, prolong, outlast, outlive, survive; spin out, draw out, eke out, linger, loiter, lounge, wait.

Adj. Durable, of long duration, permanent, enduring, chronic, lasting, persistent; livelong, longeval, longlived, diuturnal, evergreen, perennial, unintermitting, unremitting.

Protracted, prolonged, spun out, longwinded, surviving, &c.

Adv. Long, a long time, all the day long, all the year round, the livelong day, permanently, for good, till doomsday, for many a long day.

112. **Perpetuity**, eternity, aye, sempiternity, immortality, everlastingness, perpetuation.

V. To last or endure forever, to have no end, to eternize, perpetuate.

Adj. Perpetual, eternal, everlasting, (everduring, unending,) sempiternal, coeternal; endless, ceaseless, incessant, indesinent, unceasing, interminable, having no end, unfading, evergreen, never fading, deathless, immortal, undying, never dying, imperishable.

Adv. Always, ever, evermore, aye, forever, for aye, forevermore, perpetually, eternally, &c., in (or to) all ages, from age to age, to the end of time, every day.

114. Estimation, measurement and record of time

Transientness, transitoriness, evanescence, transitiveness, fugitiveness, caducity, mortality, span, shortness, brevity.

Quickness, promptness, 132, suddenness, abruptness.

V. To be transient, &c., to flit, pass away, fly, gallop, vanish, intromit.

Adj. Transitory, transient, passing, evanescent, fleeting, fugacious, fugitive, flitting, shifting, flying, temporary, provisional, provisory, temporal, cursory, galloping, shortlived, ephemeral, deciduous, vanishing.

Brief, sudden, quick, prompt, brisk, abrupt, extemporaneous, summary, hasty, precipitate.

Adv. Temporarily, &c.

In a short time, soon, a while, anon, by and by, briefly, apace, straight, straightway, quickly, speedily, promptly, directly, immediately, incontinently, presently, forthwith.

113. Point of time.

Instantaneity, instantaneousness, moment, instant, second, minute, twinkling, trice, flash, breath, span, jiffy, flash of lightning, stroke of time, epoch, the twinkling of an eye, suddenness, *see* 111.

V. To twinkle, flash, to be instantaneous, &c.

Adj. Instantaneous, momentary, extempore.

Adv. Instantly, momentarily, suddenly, in a moment, in an instant, in a second, in no time, in a trice, in a twinkling, at one jump, in a breath, extempore, on the spur of the moment; on the spot; on the instant.

115. False estimate of time.

Anachronism, prolepsis, me

CHRONOMETRY, chronology, horology, horometry, registry, date, epoch, style

Almanac, calendar, ephemeris, chronicle, annals, register, journal, diary, chronogram.

Instruments for the measurement of time; clock, watch, chronometer, timepiece, dial, sundial, horologe, pendulum, hourglass, clepsydra.

Chronographer, chronologer, chronologist, annalist.

V. To fix or mark the time, date, register, &c., to bear date, to measure time, to beat time, to mark time.

Adj. Chronological, chronometrical.

tachronism, prochronism, parachronism, misdate.

Anticipation, antichronism.

V. To misdate, antedate, postdate, overdate, anticipate.

Adj. Misdated, &c., undated, overdue.

2. Relative Time.

1. *Time with Reference to Succession.*

116. PRIORITY, antecedence, anteriority, precedence, preëxistence.

Precursor, predecessor, prelude, forerunner, &c., 64, harbinger, dawn, introduction.

V. To precede, come before, preëxist, prelude, usher in, dawn, forerun, announce, &c., 511.

Adj. Prior, previous, preceding, anterior, antecedent, preëxisting, former, foregoing.

Precursory, prelusive, prelusory, proemial, introductory, prefatory.

Adv. Before, prior to, previously, anteriorly, antecedently, afore, ere, erewhile, ere now, before now, already, yet.

117. POSTERIORITY, succession, sequence, subsequence, supervention, sequel, successor, 65.

V. To follow, come or go after, succeed, supervene.

Adj. Subsequent, posterior, following, after, later, succeeding, postliminious, postdiluvial, postdiluvian, posthumous.

Adv. Subsequently, (at a later period,) after, afterwards, since, later, next, in the sequel, close upon, thereafter, thereupon, upon which.

118 The PRESENT TIME, the existing time, the time being, the present moment, the present juncture, the nonce, crisis, epoch, day, hour.

Adj. Present, actual, instant, current, existing, that is.

Adv. At this time, moment, &c., now, at present, at this time of day, at the present time, day,

119. Time different from the present.

DIFFERENT TIME, other time.

Indefinite time, aorist.

Adj. Aoristic.

Adv. At that time, moment, &c., then, at which time, &c., on that occasion, upon.

When, whenever, whensoever upon which. on which occasions

&c., to-day, nowadays, already, even now, but now, just now, upon which.

at another or a different time, &c., at various times.

120. Synchronism, coexistence, coincidence, simultaneousness, contemporaneousness, concurrence, concomitance, contemporariness.

Having equal times, isochronism.

A contemporary, coetanian.

V. To coexist, concur, accompany.

Adj. Synchronous, synchronal, synchronical, synchronistical, simultaneous, coexisting, coincident, concomitant, concurrent, coeval, contemporary, coetaneous, contemporaneous, coeternal, isochronous.

Adv. At the same time, simultaneously, &c., together, during the same time, &c., in the same breath, meantime, 106. While, whilst.

121. Prospective time.

Futurity, the future, futurition, hereafter, the time to come, after time, after age, the coming time, the morrow, after days, hours, years, &c., after life, millennium, doomsday, the day of judgment.

The approach of time, advent, time drawing on, the womb of time.

Prospection, anticipation, prospect, perspective, expectation, 507, heritage, heirs, posterity, descendants, heir apparent, heir presumptive.

Future existence, future state, post-existence.

V. To look forwards, anticipate, have in prospect, keep in view, wait, 133, expect.

To impend, hang over, lie over, approach, await, threaten, draw near, prepare.

Adj. Future, to come, coming, going to happen, approaching, impending, instant, at hand, about to be or happen, next, hanging, awaiting, forthcoming, near, near at hand, imminent, threatening, brewing, preparing, in store, eventual, ulterior, in view, in prospect, prospective, in perspective, in the horizon, in the wind, that will be.

122. Retrospective time.

Preterition, the past, past time, days of yore, time gone by, former times, old times, the olden time, ancient times, antiquity antiqueness, time immemorial.

Archæology, paleology, archaism, retrospection, looking back.

Ancestry, 166, preëxistence.

V. To pass, lapse, go by elapse, run out, expire, blow over to look back, cast the eyes back

Adj Past, gone, gone by, over by-gone, foregone, pristine, quondam, lapsed, preterlapsed, expired, late, run out, blown over, that has been.

Former, foregoing, late, last, latter, recent, overnight, forgotten, irrecoverable, out of date.

Looking back, retrospective, retroactive.

Preëxisting, preëxistent.

Adv. Formerly, of old, erst, whilom, erewhile, before now, time was, ago, over, in the olden time, anciently, in days of yore, long since, retrospectively, ere now, before now, till now, once, hitherto, heretofore.

The other day, yesterday just now, recently, lately, of late (latterly.)

Long ago, a long while or time ago, some time ago; from time

Unborn, in embryo, in the womb of time.

Adv. Prospectively, hereafter, by and by, anon, in future, to-morrow, in course of time, in process of time, sooner or later.

immemorial, in the memory of man, time out of mind.

Already, yet, a length, at last.

On the eve of, soon, ere long, on the point of, beforehand, against the time.

After a time, from this time, henceforth, henceforwards, thence, thenceforth, thenceforward, whereupon, upon which.

2. *Time with Reference to a particular Period.*

123. NEWNESS, novelty, recentness, recency, freshness, greenness, immaturity, rawness.

Innovation, renovation, (renewal.)

Adj. New, novel, recent, fresh, green, raw, immature, untrodden, late, modern, new-fangled, vernal, renovated.

Adv. Newly, recently, &c., afresh, anew.

---

124. OLDNESS, age, antiquity, primitiveness, maturity, decline, decay, seniority, first-born, eldest, eldership, primogeniture.

Adj. Old, ancient, antique, after-age, antiquated, out of date, of long standing, time-honored, primitive, diluvian, antediluvian, primeval, primordial, primordinate, prime, preadamite.

Immemorial, inveterate, rooted.

Mediæval.

Senior, elder, eldest, oldest, first-born.

Obsolete, stale, time-worn, faded, decayed, effete, declining, &c., crumbling, decrepit, 128.

125. MORNING, morn, forenoon, prime, dawn, daybreak, peep of day, break of day, aurora, first blush of the morning, prime of the morning, twilight, crepuscule, sunrise, cockcrow.

Noon, noontide, meridian, noonday, prime, spring, (summer.)

Adj. Matutinal, vernal.

126. EVENING, eve, decline of day, fall of day, eventide, nightfall, curfew, dusk, twilight, eleventh hour, sunset, afternoon, going down of the sun.

Midnight, the dead of night.

Autumn, the fall, (winter.)

Adj. Nocturnal, autumnal.

127. YOUTH, infancy, babyhood, juvenility, childhood, juniority, minority, nonage, teens, tender age, bloom.

Cradle, nursery, leading strings, puberty, (juvenescence.)

Adj. Young, youthful, juvenile, sappy, beardless, under age, in one's teens.

---

128. AGE, old age, senility, senescence, oldness, years, anility, gray hairs, climacteric, decrepitude, hoary age, caducity superannuation, dotage, seniority green old age, eldership, elders.

Adj. Aged, old, elderly, senile, matronly, anile, in years, advanced in life or in years, stricken in years, ripe, mellow, gray, gray-headed, hoary, hoar, venerable, timeworn, declining, antiquated, rusty, effete, decrepit, superannuated.

Patriarchal, ancestral, primitive, preadamite, antediluvian, diluvian.

Older, elder, senior, turned of.

Eldest, oldest, first-born, firstling.

(Junior, younger.)

129. INFANT, babe, baby, nursling, suckling.

Child, little one, brat, chit, urchin, bantling, elf.

Youth, boy, lad, stripling, youngster, younker, whipster, schoolboy, cadet, minor.

Scion, sapling, seedling, tendril, mushroom, nestling, chicken, larva, chrysalis, tadpole, whelp, cub, pullet, fry, callow, codling, calf, colt, pup, foal, kitten.

Girl, lass, lassie, miss, damsel, maid, maiden, virgin.

Adj. Infantine, infantile, puerile, boyish, girlish, childish, baby, babyish, unfledged, new fledged, kittenish, callow.

130. VETERAN, old man, seer, patriarch, graybeard, grandsire, grandam, crone, sexagenarian, octogenarian, centenarian.

Preadamite, Methuselah, Nestor.

Elders, forefathers, fathers, ancestors, ancestry.

---

131. ADOLESCENCE, majority, adultness, manhood, virility, maturity.

Years of discretion; man's estate; the flower of age; the prime of life; the meridian of life.

A man, adult, 373, a woman, matron, 374.

Adj. Adolescent, of age, out of one's teens, grown up, mature, middle-aged, manly, virile, adult. Womanly, matronly.

3. *Time with Reference to an Effect or Purpose.*

132. EARLINESS, timeliness, punctuality, readiness, promptness, promptitude, expedition, quickness, haste, acceleration, hastening, 684, anticipation.

Suddenness, abruptness, 111.

V. To be early, to be in time, &c., to keep time.

To anticipate, forestall.

To expedite, hasten, haste, quicken, press, despatch, accelerate, precipitate, hurry, bustle.

Adj. Early, prime, timely, punctual, matutinal, forward, ready, quick, expeditious, precipitate, summary, prompt, premature, precocious, prevenient, anticipatory.

Sudden, abrupt, 111, unexpect-

133. LATENESS, tardiness, slowness, delay, procrastination, deferring, postponement, adjournment, prorogation, the Fabian policy.

Protraction, prolongation, leeway.

V. To be late, &c., tarry, wait, stay, bide, take time, dally, dawdle, linger, loiter, bide one's time; to take one's time, 275.

To stand over, lie over.

To put off, defer, delay, lay over, suspend, shift off, stave off, waive, remand, postpone, adjourn, procrastinate, prolong, protract, draw out, prorogue.

Adj. Late, tardy, slow, behind

ed, (unanticipated, unlooked for,) 508, subitaneous, extempore.

Adv. Early, soon, anon, betimes, apace, in time, ere long, punctually.

Beforehand, prematurely, before one's time, in anticipation.

Suddenly, abruptly, (hastily, precipitately,) on the point of, at short notice, extempore; on the spur of the moment.

hand, postliminous, posthumous, backward, unpunctual, belated.

Delayed, &c., suspended, in abeyance.

Adv. Late, after time, too late.

At length, at last, backward.

Slowly, leisurely, deliberately.

134. Occasion, opportunity, opening, room, suitable or proper time or season, high time, the nick of time, opportuneness, seasonableness, crisis, turn, juncture, conjuncture, golden opportunity, well-timed opportunity.

Spare time, leisure, holiday, 685, spare moments, hours, &c., time on one's hands.

V. To take the opportunity, to temporize, to time well.

To use, make use of, employ, profit by, avail one's self of, lay hold of, embrace, catch, seize, snatch, clutch, pounce upon, grasp, &c., the opportunity, 677.

To give, offer, present, afford, &c., the opportunity.

To spend or consume time.

Adj. Opportune, timely, well-timed, seasonable, happy, lucky, fortunate, favorable, propitious, auspicious, critical.

Adv. Opportunely, &c., on the spot, in proper or due time or season, high time; all in good time.

By the way, by the by.

135. Intempestivity, unsuitable time, improper time, unseasonableness, inopportuneness, evil hour.

V. To be ill-timed, out of time, &c., to mistime, intrude.

To lose, omit, let slip, let go, neglect, pretermit, allow or suffer the opportunity or occasion to pass, slip, go by, escape, lapse, slip through the fingers, lose time, 683, to fritter away time.

Adj. Ill-timed, untimely, intrusive, mistimed, unseasonable, out of season, unpunctual, (tardy,) inopportune, intrusive, too late, 133, unlucky, inauspicious, unpropitious, unfortunate, unfavorable.

Adv. Inopportunely, &c.

---

3. Recurrent Time.

136. Frequency, oftness, recurrence, repetition, 104, reiteration, iteration, run, reappearance, renewal, burden.

V. To recur, revert, return, repeat, reiterate, reappear, renew.

Adj Frequent, many times, not rare, repeated, reiterated, thick-coming, recurring, recurrent, &c.

137. Infrequency, rareness, seldomness.

V. To be rare, &c.

Adj. Infrequent, rare, unfrequent.

Adv. Seldom, rarely, scarcely, hardly ever; not often, unfrequently, scarcely ever, hardly ever.

Adv. Often, oft, ofttimes, frequently, oftentimes, repeatedly, not unfrequently, (not seldom,) many times, several times.

Again, anew, afresh, ditto, over again, again and again, over and over; ever and anon; many times over; time after time; repeatedly, 104.

Perpetually, continually, constantly, (incessantly, unceasingly, without cessation.)

Sometimes, occasionally, at times, now and then, from time to time, there are times when, &c.

Most often, for the most part, (most frequently.)

Once, once for all, once in a way.

---

138. Regularity of recurrence, punctuality.

Periodicity, intermittance, beat, alternation, alternity, pulsation, alternateness, alternativeness, bout, round, revolution, rotation, turn.

Anniversary, centenary.

Regularity of return, cycle, period, stated time, routine.

V. To recur in regular order or succession, to come round, return, revolve, alternate, come in its turn, beat, pulsate, intermit.

Adj. Periodic, periodical, recurrent, cyclical, revolving, intermittent, remittent, alternate, alternating, diurnal, quotidian, annual, &c., regular, steady, (stated, settled, established,) punctual.

Adv. Periodically, at regular intervals, at stated times, at fixed periods, punctually; from day to day.

By turns, in turn, in rotation, alternately.

139. Irregularity of recurrence, uncertainty, &c.

Adj. Irregular, uncertain, unpunctual, capricious, desultory, fitful, flickering.

Adv. Irregularly, &c., by fits, by snatches, by starts, by catches, skippingly, by skips.

Section VII. CHANGE.

1. Simple Change.

140. Difference at different times.

Change, alteration, mutation, permutation, variation, modification, modulation, mood, qualification, innovation, deviation, turn, inversion, reversion, reversal, eversion, subversion, organic change, revolution, 146, transit, transition, 144.

Transformation, transmutation, transfiguration, metamorphosis, transmigration, transubstantiation, metempsychosis.

Vicissitude, flux, unrest, 149.

V. To change, alter, vary, modify, modulate, qualify, tam-

140. *a.* Absence of change, see 265.

V. To let alone, to let be.

per with, turn, shift, veer, tack, chop, shuffle, swerve, warp, deviate, turn aside, turn topsyturvy, invert, reverse, subvert, evert, turn inside out.

Form, fashion, mould, model, vamp, warp, work a change, superinduce, disturb, 61, innovate, reform, remodel, refound, new model, revolutionize.

Transform, transmute, transfigure, metamorphose, to ring the changes, pass to, leap to, transfer, 270.

Adj. Changed, altered, new fangled, warped, &c.

141. Change from action to rest.

CESSATION, discontinuance, desistance, desinence, quiescence, 265.

Intermission, remission, suspension, interruption, suspense, stop, stoppage, pause, rest, respite, truce, drop, interregnum, abeyance.

Comma, colon, semicolon, &c.

V. To discontinue, cease, desist, stay, break off, leave off, hold, stop, pause, rest, drop, give over, relinquish, 624, surcease, intermit, remit.

To come to a stand or standstill, suspend, cut short, cast off, go out, be at an end; intromit, interrupt; put an end or stop to.

To pass away, go off, pass off, die away, wear away, wear off.

142. PERMANENCE, persistence endurance, maintenance, preservation, conservation, rest, sleep &c., 265, establishment, fixture.

V. To remain, stay, stop, tarry hold, last, endure, bide, abide maintain, keep, hold on, stand, subsist, live, stand still, outlive, survive.

Adj. Persisting, &c., unchanged, unmodified, unrenewed, unaltered, fixed, settled, unvaried, intact, persistent, stagnant, rooted, monotonous, conservative, undestroyed, unrepealed, unsuppressed, unfailing.

---

143. CONTINUANCE in action, continuation, perseverance, repetition, 104, persistence, run.

V. To continue, persist, go on, keep on, abide, keep, pursue, hold on, run on, carry on, keep up, uphold, hold up, persevere keep it up, maintain, maintain one's ground, harp upon, repeat, 104

Adj. Continuing, &c., uninterrupted, unintermitting, unreversed, unstopped, unrevoked, unvaried, unshifting.

144. Gradual change to something different.

CONVERSION, reduction, transmutation, resolution, assimilation; chemistry, alchemy; progress, growth, lapse.

Passage, transit, transition, transmigration, flux, shifting, sliding, running into, &c.; phase, conjugation; convertibility.

Laboratory, alembic, &c., 691.

V. To be converted into; to become, to wax, come to, turn to, assume the form of, pass into, slide into, glide into, lapse, shift, run into, fall into, merge into, melt, grow, grow into, open into, resolve itself into, settle into, mature, mellow; assume the form, shape, state, nature, character, &c., of.

To convert into, make, render, form, mould, reduce, resolve into fashion, model, remodel, reorganize, shape, mould, modify; assimilate to; reduce to; bring to

Adj. Converted into, become, &c., convertible.

Adv. Gradually, by degrees, step by step, by inches, inch by inch, by little and little, by slow degrees, consecutively.

145. REVERSION, reversal, return, reconversion, relapse, reaction recoil, rebound, revulsion, alternation, 138, inversion.

Reinstatement, reëstablishment, &c., 660.

V. To revert, return to, relapse, recoil, rebound, react; to restore, &c., 660, to undo, unmake.

Adj. Reverting, &c., restored, &c., placed (back,) revulsive.

146 Sudden or violent change.

REVOLUTION, counter-revolution, transilience, jump, leap, plunge, start, spasm, convulsion, throe, storm, earthquake, cataclysm, 173.

Legerdemain, conjuration, sleight of hand, hocus-pocus, harlequinade, witchcraft, &c., 992.

V. To revolutionize, new model.

147. Change of one thing for another.

SUBSTITUTION, commutation, enallage, metonymy, supplanting, synecdoche.

Thing substituted. Substitute, 634, makeshift, representative, proxy; deputy, 759, vice, double, dummy, changeling, stopgap, jurymast, palimpsest, metaphor, 521.

V. To substitute, commute, supplant, supersede, change for.

To give place to; to replace, supersede, cut out, serve as a substitute, &c., take the place of, supply the place of.

Adj. Substituted, &c., vicarious, subdititious.

Adv. Instead, in place of, in lieu of, in the room of.

148. Double and mutual change.

INTERCHANGE, exchange, commutation, reciprocation, transposition, permutation, intermutation, shuffling, interchangeableness.

Reciprocity, 12, retaliation, 719, barter, 794.

V. To interchange, exchange, bandy, transpose, shuffle, change hands, swap, permute, reciprocate, commute, counterchange.

Adj. Interchanged, &c., reciprocal, mutual, commutative, interchangeable, intercurrent.

Adv. In exchange.

2. COMPLEX CHANGES.

149. CHANGEABLENESS, inconstancy, variableness, mobility, instability, unsteadiness, vacillation, unrest, restlessness, slipperiness, impermanence, fragility, fluctuation, vicissitude, alternation, vibration, oscillation, 314 flux, ebbing and

150. STABILITY, immutability, unchangeableness, constancy, permanence, persistence, 106, invariableness, durability, steadiness, immobility, fixedness, stableness, stabiliment, firmness stiffness, solidity, incommutability insusceptibility, irrevocableness.

flowing, ebbs and flows, ups and downs, fidgets, fugitiveness, disquiet, disquietude.

A Proteus, chameleon, quicksilver, weathercock, a harlequin, *see* Tergiversation, 607.

Alternation, the times being changed.

V. To fluctuate, vary, waver, flounder, vibrate, flicker, flitter, shuffle, shake, totter, tremble, ebb and flow, turn and turn about, change and change about.

To fade; pass away like a cloud, shadow, or dream.

Adj. Mutable, changeable, variable, checkered, ever-changing, inconstant, unsteady, unstable, unfixed, fluctuating, vacillating, versatile, restless, erratic, unsettled, mobile, fickle, wavering, flickering, flitting, flittering, fluttering, oscillating, vibratory, vagrant, wayward, desultory, afloat, alternating, disquiet, alterable, plastic.

Frail, tottering, shaking, trembling, fugitive, ephemeral, transient, 111, fading, fragile, deciduous, slippery, unsettled, irresolute, 605.

Rock, pillar, tower, foundation

V. To be permanent, &c., 265 to stand, remain.

To settle, establish, stablish, fix, set, stabilitate, retain, keep, hold, make sure, nail, clinch rivet, fasten, 43, settle down.

Adj. Immutable, unchangeable, unaltered, unalterable, not to be changed, constant, permanent, invariable, undeviating, stable, durable, 265, perennial, 110.

Fixed, steadfast, firm, fast, steady, confirmed, immovable, irremovable, rooted, stablished, established, inconvertible, stereotyped, indeclinable, settled, &c., stationary, stagnant.

Indefeasible, irretrievable, intransmutable, irresoluble, irrevocable, irreversible, inextinguishable, irreducible, indissoluble, indissolvable, indestructible, undying, imperishable, indelible, indeciduous, insusceptible of change.

Present Events.

151. Eventuality, event, occurrence, incident, affair, transaction, proceeding, fact, matter of fact, phenomenon, advent.

Business, concern, circumstance, particular, casualty, accident, adventure, passage, crisis, pass, emergency, contingency, consequence.

The world, life, things, doings, course of things; the course, tide, stream, current, run, &c., of events.

V. To happen, occur, take place, take effect, come, come of, become of, come about, pass, come to pass, fall, fall out, run, be on foot, fall in, befall, betide.

Future Events.

152. Destiny, fatality, fate, doom, destination, lot, fortune, star, planet, stars, preordination, foreordination, predestination, fatalism, inevitableness, *see* Futurity, 121, and Necessity, 601.

V. To impend, hang over, be in store, await, come on, approach, stare one in the face, foreordain, preordain, predestine, doom, must be.

Adj. About to happen, impending, coming, &c., inevitable, (unavoidable,) inexorable fate doomed, devoted, spellbound.

---

chance turn out, prove, eventuate, draw on, turn up, cast up, supervene, issue, arrive, ensue, arise, spring, start, come into existence.

Pass off, wear off, blow over.

To experience, meet with, go through, endure, 821, suffer, fare.

Adj. Happening, occurring, &c., current, incidental, eventful, stirring, bustling.

Adv. Eventually, in the event of, or foot, as it may happen; happen what may; at all events; sink or swim.

SECTION VIII. CAUSATION.

1. CONSTANCY OF SEQUENCE IN EVENTS.

153. Constant antecedent.

CAUSE, origin, source, principle, element, occasioner, prime mover, spring, mainspring, agent, seed, leaven, groundwork, fountain, well, font, fountain head, spring head.

Pivot, hinge, turning point, key, lever.

Final cause, ground, reason, the reason why, the why and the wherefore, rationale, occasion, derivation.

Rudiment, germ, embryo, bud, root, radical, etymon, nucleus, seed, stem, stock, trunk.

Nest, cradle, nursery, womb, birthplace, hotbed.

Causality, origination, causation, production, 161.

V. To be the cause of, to originate, give origin to, cause, occasion, give rise to, kindle, suscitate, bring on, bring to pass, give occasion to, bring about, found, lay the foundation of, lie at the root of, procure, induce, draw down, realize, entail, develop, *see* 161.

To conduce, contribute, tend to, 176.

Adj. Caused, occasioned, &c., causal, original, primary, primordial, having a common origin, connate, radical, embryonic, embryotic.

154. Constant sequent.

EFFECT, consequence, product, result, resultant, resultance, issue, end, 67, fruit, crop, harvest, development.

Production, produce, work, performance, creature, creation, fabric, first fruits, firstlings, derivation.

V. To be the effect, work, fruit, result, &c., of, to be owing to, originate in or from, rise from, to take its rise from, arise, spring, proceed, come of, emanate, come, grow, bud, sprout, issue, flow, result, follow, accrue, &c., from, come to, to come out of, be derived from, be caused by, depend upon, hinge upon, turn upon, result from, to be dependent upon, hang upon.

Adj. Owing to, resulting from, through, &c., derivative, hereditary.

Adv. Of course, consequently, necessarily.

---

155 Assignment of cause.

ATTRIBUTION, theory, ætiology,

156. Absence of assignable cause.

ascription, reference to, rationale, accounting for, imputation, derivation from, filiation, genealogy, pedigree, paternity, maternity.

V. To attribute, ascribe, impute, refer to, derive from, lay to, point to, charge on, ground on, invest with, assign as cause, trace to, father upon, account for, theorize.

Adj. Attributable, imputable, ascribable, (assignable,) referable, (or referrible,) owing to, derivable from, &c.

Putative, attributed, imputed, &c.

Adv. Hence, thence, therefore, because, from that cause, for that reason, on that account, owing to, forasmuch as, whence.

Why? wherefore? whence? how comes it? how is it? how happens it? how does it happen?

In some way, somehow, somehow or other; in some such way.

CHANCE,* indetermination, accident, fortune, hazard, haphazard, chance medley, random, lot, fate, 152, casualty, contingence, adventure, venture, hit.

A lottery, toss up; game of chance; a cast, a throw of the dice, hazard; heads or tails, &c.

Possibility, contingency, odds.

V. To chance, happen, to fall to one's lot, to be one's fate, &c., 152, to light upon.

To take one's chance, to game, gamble, cast lots, toss up for, raffle, play for.

Adj. Casual, fortuitous, random, accidental, adventitious, causeless, incidental, contingent, uncaused, undetermined, indeterminate, possible, 470.

Adv. By chance, by accident, perchance, peradventure, perhaps, may be, mayhap, haply, possibly.

Casually, &c., at random, at a venture, as it may be, as it may chance, as it may turn up, as it may happen, as chance, luck, fortune, &c., would have it.

2. CONNECTION BETWEEN CAUSE AND EFFECT.

157. POWER, potentiality, potency, puissance, might, force, metal, dint, right hand, ascendency, sway, control, ability, ableness, competency, efficiency, effectiveness, efficacy, efficaciousness, validity, cogency, agency, 170, causality, 153, influence, *see* 175.

Capability, capacity, faculty, quality, attribute, endowment, virtue, gift, property.

V. To be powerful, &c., to exercise power, sway, &c., to constrain

158. IMPOTENCE, inability, disability, disablement, imbecility, inaptitude, incapacity, incapability, invalidity, inefficacy, inefficiency, inefficaciousness, ineffectualness, disqualification, helplessness, incompetence.

V. To be impotent, powerless, &c.

To render powerless, &c., to deprive of power, disable, disenable, incapacitate, disqualify, invalidate, deaden, cripple, cramp, paralyze, muzzle, hamstring, clip the wings of. *See* Weaken, 160

* The word *Chance* has two distinct meanings: the first, the absence of assignable *cause* as above; and the second, the absence of *design*. For the latter, *see* 621.

To be the property, virtue, attribute, &c., of; to belong to, pertain to.

To give or confer power, to empower, enable, invest, indue, endow, arm, &c., *see* Strengthen, 159.

To gain power, to take root.

Adj. Productive, prolific; *see* 168, powerful, potent, puissant, potential, capable, able, cogent, forcible, valid, effective, effectual, efficient, efficacious, adequate, competent.

Forcible, energetic, vigorous, vivid, sturdy, all-powerful, resistless, irresistible, inextinguishable, sovereign, invincible, unconquerable.

Adv. Powerfully, &c.

Adj. Powerless, impotent, unable, incapable, incompetent, inadequate, unequal to, inefficient, inefficacious, ineffectual, ineffective, incapacitated, imbecile, disqualified, disabled, armless, disarmed, unarmed, weaponless, defenceless, unnerved, paralyzed, nerveless.

---

159. Degree of power.

STRENGTH, energy, 171, vigor, force, main force, physical force, brute force, spring, elasticity, tone, tension.

Stoutness, sturdiness, lustiness, stamina, nerve, muscle, sinews, pith, pithiness.

Adamant, steel, iron, oak, heart of oak.

Strengthening, invigoration, bracing, recruiting, refreshment, 689.

Science of forces; Dynamics, Statics.

V. To be strong, &c., to be stronger, to overmatch.

To render strong, &c., to give strength, tone, &c., to strengthen, invigorate, brace, nerve, fortify, harden, caseharden, steel, gird, screw up, wind up, set up.

To reënforce, refit, recruit, vivify, restore, 660, refect, 689.

Adj. Strong, mighty, vigorous, robust, sturdy, powerful, puissant, adamantine.

Able-bodied, athleti Herculean, Cyclopean, muscular, brawny, sinewy, made of iron, strapping, stalwart, gigantic.

Manly, manlike, masculine, male, virile, manful

160. WEAKNESS, feebleness, debility, atony, relaxation, helplessness, languor, slackness, enervation, nervousness, faintness, faintishness, infirmity, emasculation, effeminacy, feminality, softness, defencelessness.

Childhood, &c., 127, 129, an orphan.

Declension, loss, failure, &c., of strength, invalidation, decrepitude, palsy, paralysis, exhaustion, collapse, prostration, syncope, apoplexy.

V. To be weak, &c., to droop, fade, faint, swoon, languish, decline, fail, droop.

To render weak, &c., to weaken, enfeeble, debilitate, deprive of strength, relax, enervate, unbrace, unman, emasculate, castrate, geld, maim, lame, hamstring, disable, unhinge, cripple, cramp, paralyze, sprain, exhaust, prostrate, blunt the edge of, deaden.

Adj. Weak, feeble, strengthless, nerveless, imbecile, helpless, unnerved, relaxed, unstrung, unbraced, enervated, nervous, sinewless, effeminate, feminine, womanly, unmanned, &c., shattered, broken, halting, shaken, crazy, shaky paralyzed, palsied.

Unweakened, unallayed, unwithered, unshaken, unworn, unexhausted.

Adv. Strongly, forcibly, &c., by main force, by might and main, tooth and nail.

paralytic, decrepit, drooping, languid, faint, sickly, flagging, dull slack, spent, effete, weather-beaten, worn, seedy, exhausted, languishing, wasted, washy, untenable.

Unstrengthened, unsustained, unsupported, unaided, unassisted, unfortified, unfriended, fatherless, &c.

---

3. Power in Operation.

161. Production, creation, formation, construction, fabrication, manufacture, building, architecture, edification, coinage, organization, putting together, performance, 729, workmanship.

Development, genesis, generation, procreation, propagation, bringing forth, parturition; growth.

V. To produce, effect, perform, do, make, form, construct, fabricate, frame, manufacture, weave, forge, coin, carve, chisel, build, raise, edify, rear, erect, put together, set up, run up, establish.

To constitute, compose, organize, institute, work out, realize, bring to bear, bring to pass, accomplish.

To create, beget, generate, engender, bring into being, breed, bear, procreate, bring forth, give birth to, hatch, develop, bring up.

To induce, superinduce, suscitate, *see* Cause, 153.

Adj. Produced, &c., producing, productive of, &c., parturient.

163. Reproduction, renovation, revival, regeneration, revivification, resuscitation, reanimation, resurrection, reappearance, phœnix.

V. To reproduce, revive, renovate, regenerate, revivify, resuscitate, quicken; come again into life, reappear.

162. Non-production.

Destruction, waste, dissolution, breaking up, consumption, disorganization, falling to pieces, crumbling, &c.

Fall, downfall, ruin, perdition, crash, smash, havoc, desolation, wreck, shipwreck, extinction, annihilation; doom, destruction of life, *see* Death, 360.

Demolition, demolishment, overthrow, subversion, suppression, dismantling, cutting up, corrosion, erosion, crushing, upsetting, abolition, abolishment, sacrifice, immolation, holocaust, dilapidation, devastation, extermination, eradication, extirpation, rooting out, sweeping, &c., deathblow.

V. To be destroyed, &c., perish, fall to pieces, break up, crumble.

To destroy, do away with, nullify, demolish, overturn, upset, throw down, overthrow, overwhelm, subvert, put an end to uproot, eradicate, extirpate, root out, grub up, break up, pull down, crumble, smash, crash, crush, quell, quash, cut up, shatter, shiver, batter, tear or shake to pieces, nip, tear to tatters, pick to pieces, put down, suppress, strike out, throw or knock down, cut down, knock on the head, stifle, dispel, fell, sink, swamp, scuttle ingulf, corrode, erode, consume

Adj. Reproduced, &c., renascent, reappearing.

---

sacrifice, immolate, blow down, sweep away, erase, expunge, mow down.

To waste, lay waste, ravage, dilapidate, dismantle, disorganize, devour, swallow up, desolate, devastate, sap, mine, stifle, blast, despatch, extinguish, quench, annihilate, kill, 361, unroot, root out.

Adj. Unproduced, unproductive, destroyed, &c., done for, dished, &c.

164. PRODUCER, originator, author, founder, workman, (maker,) doer, performer, &c., forger, agent, 690, builder, architect.

165. DESTROYER, extinguisher exterminator, assassin, 361, executioner, 975, ravager, annihilator, subverter, &c.

166. PATERNITY, parentage, parent, father, sire; procreator, progenitor, ancestor, ancestry, forefathers, grandsire; house, parent, stem, trunk, stock, pedigree.

Motherhood, maternity; mother, dam.

167. POSTERITY, progeny, breed, issue, offspring, brood, seed, spawn, scion, offset, child, son, daughter, bantling, shoot, sprout, branch, offshoot, ramification, descendant.

Straight descent, sonship, line, lineage, filiation, primogeniture.

168. PRODUCTIVENESS, fecundity, fruitfulness, fertility, prolificness.

Pregnancy, pullulation, fructification, multiplication, propagation, procreation.

V. To procreate, multiply, pullulate, fructify, generate.

Adj. Productive, prolific, teeming, teemful, fertile, fruitful, fecund, pregnant.

Procreant, procreative, generative, propagable, lifegiving.

169. UNPRODUCTIVENESS, infertility, barrenness, sterility, unfruitfulness, unprofitableness, infecundity, *see* Inutility, 645, non-agency.

V. To be unproductive, &c., arid.

Adj. Unproductive, inoperative, barren, addle, unfertile, unprolific, sterile, unfruitful, teemless, infecund, issueless, unprofitable, 645.

170. AGENCY, operation, force, working, function, office, hand, intervention, exercise, work, swing, play, interworking, causation, 153, mediation, 631.

Quickening power, maintaining power, home stroke.

V. To be in action, to operate, work, act, perform, play, support, sustain, strain, maintain, take effect, quicken, strike, strike hard, strike home.

Adj. Acting, operating, &c., operative, efficient, efficacious, effectual.

Acted upon, wrought upon.

171. Physical ENERGY, activity, keenness, intensity, sharpness, pungency, vigor, strength, elasticity, acrimony, causticity, virulence, corrosiveness, acritude,

172. Physical INERTNESS, inertia, passiveness, inertion, inactivity, 683, torpor, latency, torpidity, dulness, deadness, heaviness, flatness, slackness, tameness,

poignancy, harshness, severity, edge, point, raciness, metal.

Seasoning, mordant, pepper, mustard, cayenne, caviare, 392, cantharides.

Mental energy, *see* 604, mental excitation, 824, voluntary energy, 682.

Exertion, activity, stir, bustle, agitation, effervescence, fermentation, ferment, ebullition, splutter, pertubation, briskness, voluntary activity, 682, quicksilver.

Adj. Strong, energetic, active, keen, vivid, intense, severe, sharp, acute, irritating, pungent, poignant, mordant, acrid, acrimonious, virulent, caustic, corrosive, racy, brisk, harsh, stringent, double-edged, drastic.

V. To give energy, energize, stimulate, excite, exert, 173.

slowness, languor, quiescence 265, sleep, 683; suspense, intermission, 141.

V. To be inert, inactive, passive, &c.; to hang fire, to let alone.

Adj. Inert, inactive, passive, torpid, sluggish, dull, heavy, flat, slack, tame, slow, blunt, lifeless, &c.

Latent, dormant, smouldering, unexerted, uninfluential

Adv. Inactively, &c., in suspense, in abeyance.

---

173. VIOLENCE, inclemency, vehemence, might, impetuosity, boisterousness, abruptness, ebullition, turbulence, bluster, uproar, riot, fierceness, rage, wildness, fury, heat, exacerbation, exasperation, malignity, fit, paroxysm, orgasm, force, brute force, strain, shock, spasm, convulsion, throe.

Outbreak, burst, dissilience, discharge, volley, explosion, blow up, blast, detonation, eruption, displosion, torrent.

Turmoil, storm, tempest, squall, hurricane, tornado, earthquake, volcano, thunder storm, typhoon.

V. To be violent, &c., to run high, ferment, effervesce, run wild, run riot, rush, tear, rush headlong, bluster, rage, riot, storm, boil, fume, foam, wreak, bear down.

To break out, fly out, bounce, explode, displode, fly, detonate, blow up, flash, flare, burst, burst out, outburst, shock, strain.

To render violent, sharpen, stir up, quicken, excite, incite, stimulate, inflame, kindle, lash, suscitate, urge, accelerate, foment, ag-

174. MODERATION, gentleness, temperateness, calmness, mildness, softness, sobriety, slowness, tameness, quiet, 740, reason.

Relaxation, remission, measure, mitigation, tranquilization, assuagement, soothing, allaying, &c., contemperation, pacification, 723, restraint, check, 751, lullaby

Sedative, lenitive, demulcent, opiate, anodyne, milk, opium.

V. To be moderate, &c., to keep within bounds or within compass, to settle down, to keep the peace, to sober down, remit, relent.

To moderate, soften, soothe, mitigate, appease, temper, attemper, contemper, mollify, tame, dull, take off the edge, blunt, obtund, sheathe.

To tranquillize, assuage, appease, lull, smooth, compose, still, calm, quiet, hush, quell, sober, pacify, damp, lay, allay, rebate, slacken, smooth, soften, alleviate, rock to sleep, deaden, check, restrain, slake, curb, bridle, rein in, hold in, repress, smother, counteract 179.

gravate, exasperate, exarcerbate, infuriate, madden, lash into fury, explode, let off, discharge.

Adj. Violent, vehement, warm, acute, rough, rude, boisterous, impetuous, ungentle, abrupt, rampant, bluff, turbulent, blustering, riotous, thundering, obstreperous, uproarious.

Savage, fierce, ferocious, fiery, fuming, excited, unquelled, unquenched, unextinguished, unrepressed, boiling, boiling over, furious, outrageous, frantic, raging, running riot, storming, hysteric, wild, headstrong, running wild, ungovernable, unappeasable, unmitigable, uncontrollable, insuppressible, irrepressible, raging, desperate, mad, infuriate, exasperated.

Tempestuous, stormy, squally, spasmodic, convulsive, bursting explosive, detonating, &c., volcanic, meteoric.

Adv. Violently, &c., by force, by main force, &c.

Adj. Moderate, gentle, mild, sober, temperate, reasonable, tempered, calm, unruffled, tranquil, smooth, untroubled, unirritating, (unexciting,) soft, bland, oily, demulcent, lenitive, cool, quiet, anodyne, sedative, peaceful, peaceable, pacific, lenient, tame, halcyon.

Adv. Moderately, gently, softly, &c.

---

4. Indirect Power.

175. Influence, weight, pressure, prevalence, sway, predominance, predominancy, dominance, reign, ableness, capability, &c., 157.

Footing, hold, purchase, leverage, vantage ground, ascendence.

Independence, voluntary influence, 737, protection, patronage, auspices.

V. To have influence, &c., to have a hold upon, &c., to gain a footing, work upon, take root, take hold, prevail, dominate, predominate, outweigh, overweigh, to bear upon, to be in the ascendant.

Adj. Influential, valid, weighty, prevailing, prevalent, rife, dominant, regnant, predominating, predominant, in the ascendant.

176. Tendency, aptness, proneness, proclivity, conduciveness, bent, bias, quality, inclination, propensity, conducement, subservience, 631.

V. To tend, contribute, conduce, lead, dispose, incline, verge, bend to, affect, carry, promote, redound to, subserve to, 644, to bid fair to.

Adj. Tending, contributing, conducing, conducive, working towards, calculated to, disposing, inclining, bending, leading, carrying to, subservient, subsidiary, 644, 707.

Adj. Unconducing, unconducive, unconducting.

---

177. Liability, liableness, subjection to, dependence on, exposure to, contingency, *see* Chance, 156, susceptivity, susceptibility, obnoxiousness.

V. To be liable, &c., incur, to lay one's self open to, lie under, expose one's self, &c., stand a chance, to open a door to.

Adj. Liable, subject, open to, incident to, exposed to, dependent on, obnoxious to.

Contingent, incidental, guardless, 665.

5. Combinations of Causes.

178. Concurrence coöperation, (harmony of action, combined action,) union, agreement, pulling together, alliance.

Voluntary concurrence, 709.

V. To concur, coöperate, conspire, agree, conduce, contribute, unite; to pull together, to join forces.

Adj. Concurring, concurrent, coöperating, conspiring, agreeing, pulling together, &c., in alliance with; with one consent.

179. Counteraction, opposition, antagonism, (contravention,) polarity, clashing, &c., collision, resistance, interference, friction.

Neutralization, nullification, compensation, 30.

Reaction, retroaction, 277, repercussion, rebound, recoil, counterblast.

Check, obstacle, hinderance, 706.

Voluntary counteraction, 708.

V. To counteract, oppose, contravene, antagonize, interfere with, run counter, clash, neutralize, nullify, render null, withstand, resist, hinder, &c., 706, repress, control, curb, check, rein in, 174.

To react, 277, countervail, counterpoise, &c., 30, overpoise.

Adj. Counteracting, opposing, &c., antagonistic, opposite, conflicting, retroactive, cohibitive, counter, contrary, 14.

Adv. Counter, notwithstanding, nevertheless, yet, still, although, though, albeit, howbeit, maugre, at all events.

But, even, however, in spite of, in defiance of, in the teeth of, in despite of, against, *see* 708.

CLASS II.

WORDS RELATING TO SPACE.

Section I. SPACE IN GENERAL.

1. Abstract Space.

180. Indefinite space.

Space, extension. extent, expanse, room, scope, range, lati-

180. *a.* Inextension.

181. Definite space.

Region, sphere, ground, area

tude, field, way, expansion, compass, sweep, play, swing, spread, spare room, freedom, house room, stowage, roomage.

Open space, void space, vacuity, 2, opening, waste, wildness, moor, moorland.

Abyss, unlimited space, the four winds, *see* Infinity, 105, Ubiquity, 186.

Adj. Spacious, roomy, extensive, expansive, capacious, ample.

Boundless, unlimited, unbounded, limitless, infinite, ubiquitous, shoreless, trackless, pathless.

Adv. Extensively, &c., wherever, every where.

realm, hemisphere, quarter, district, orb, circuit, circle, compartment, domain, tract, department, territory, country, canton, county shire, province, parish, township, principality, duchy, kingdom.

Arena, precincts, walk, patch, plot.

Clime, climate, zone, meridian.

182. Limited space, locality.

Place, lieu, spot, point, dot, nook, corner, angle, recess, hole, niche, compartment, premises, precinct, station, venue, latitude and longitude, abode, 189.

Adv. Somewhere, in some place.

2. Relative Space.

183. Situation, position, locality, latitude and longitude, footing, standing, post, stage, bearings, aspect, attitude, posture.

Place, sight, station, seat, venue, the whereabouts, direction, azimuth, &c., 278.

Topography, Geography, Chorography.

A map, chart, plan, 554.

V. To be situated, to lie; to have its seat in.

Adj. Local, topical.

184. Location, localization, lodgment, deposition, reposition, stowage, package, collocation, packing, lading, establishment, grafting, insertion, 301, encampment, installation.

A colony, settlement, cantonment.

A habitation, residence, dwelling, cohabitation, 189.

V. To place, situate, locate, put, lay, set, seat, station, lodge, post, install, house, stow, establish, fix, root, plant, graft, stick in, insert, wedge in, shelve, pitch, camp, deposit, reposit, cradle, encamp, moor, pack, tuck in, embed, or imbed, vest.

To billet on, quarter upon.

To pocket, put up; to load, lade, freight, pack.

To inhabit, reside, 186, colonize, replace, reinstate, restore, 660.

185. Displacement, (dislocation,) dislodgment, ejectment, 297, deportation, exile.

Removal, remotion, transposition, &c., relegation, *see* Transference, 270, and Exhaustion, 638.

V. To displace, dislodge, displant, unkennel, break bulk, take off, eject, expel, &c., 297, exile, relegate, oust, ablegate, ostracize, remove, transfer, transplant, transport, transpose, 270, sweep off, sweep away; do away with, root out, unpeople, depopulate.

To vacate, leave, to get out, heave out, bale, lade, pour out.

Adj. Displaced, &c., unhoused houseless.

Adj. Placed located, &c., situate, situated, posted, nestled, imbosomed, housed, moored, rooted, unremoved.

3. Existence in Space.

186. Presence, occupancy, occupation, attendance.

Diffusion, permeation, pervasion, dissemination, 73.

Ubiquity, omnipresence.

V. To exist in space, to be present, attend.

To occur in a place, lie, stand, occupy.

To inhabit, dwell, reside, stay, sojourn, live, abide, lodge, nestle, perch, roost, put up at, squat, plant one's self, hive, burrow, camp, encamp, bivouac, anchor, settle, take up one's quarters, pitch one's tent, get a footing, resort to, frequent, haunt, tenant, take root, strike root, revisit.

To fill, pervade, permeate, be diffused through, be disseminated through, overspread, run through.

Adj. Present, occupying, inhabiting, &c., moored, at anchor, resident, residentiary.

Ubiquitous, omnipresent.

Adv. Here, there, where? every where, aboard, on board, at home, a-field, &c.

187. Absence, non-existence 2, non-residence, non-attendance absenteeism.

Void, vacuum, voidness, vacuity, vacancy, vacuousness.

An absentee, nobody.

V. To be absent, not present, &c., to keep away, to keep out of the way, absent one's self, take one's self off, vacate.

Adj. Absent, not present, away, gone, from home, missing, lost non-resident.

Vacant, untenanted, tenantless empty, uninhabited, deserted, void, devoid, unoccupied, unhabitable.

Adv. Without, nowhere, elsewhere.

---

188. Inhabitant, resident, residentiary, dweller, indweller, occupier, occupant, lodger, inmate, tenant, sojourner, commorant, settler, squatter, colonist, denizen, citizen, cit, townsman, burgess, villager, cotter, compatriot.

Native, indigene, aborigines.

Garrison, crew, population, colony, settlement; household.

Adj. Indigenous, native, domestic, (domiciled,) domiciliated, domesticated.

---

189. Place of habitation or resort.

Abode, dwelling, lodging, domicile, residence, address, habitation, local habitation, berth, seat, lap, sojourn, housing, quarters, head quarters, tabernacle.

Nest, lair, haunt, eyry, den, hole, aerie, rookery, hive, resort, retreat, perch, roost; — nidification.

Bivouac, camp, encampment, cantonment, castrametation, tent, wigwam, awning.

Cave, cavern, cell, grove, grot, grotto, alcove, bower, arbor, cove chamber, &c., 191.

Home, fatherland, country, homestead, homestall, fireside, snuggery, hearth, household gods, roof, household, housing

Building, structure, edifice, fabric, erection, pile, tenement, messuage, farm, farm house, grange.

Cot, cabin, hut, shed, booth, stall, hovel, outhouse, barn, hole, kennel, sty, coot, stable.

House, mansion, villa, cottage, box, lodge, bungalow, hermitage, folly, rotunda, tower, temple, castle, pavilion, hotel, court, hall, palace.

Inn, hotel, tavern, (public house,) caravansary, hospice, barrack.

Hamlet, village, borough, burgh, town, city, metropolis.

Street, place, terrace, parade, road, row, lane, alley, court, close, yard, passage, square, polygon, circus, crescent, mall, piazza, arcade.

Anchorage, roadstead, dock, basin, wharf, quay, port.

190. Things contained.

CONTENTS, cargo, lading, freight, load, burden, ware, 798.

191. RECEPTACLE, recipient, receiver, reservatory, compartment.

Cell, cellule, hole, corner, niche, recess, nook, crypt, stall, pigeon hole, lodging *see* 189, bed, berth, &c., 215, pew; store room.

Capsule, vesicle, cyst, utricle, bladder, utensil, alembic.

Stomach, paunch, ventricle, crop, craw, maw, gizzard.

Pocket, pouch, fob, sheath, scabbard, socket, bag, sac, (or sack,) wallet, porte monnaie, scrip, knapsack, haversack, sachel, reticule, budget.

Chest, box, coffer, caddy, case, casket, pyx, or (pix,) desk, bureau, cabinet, reliquary, trunk, portmanteau, carpet bag, bandbox, valise, boot, imperial, creel, crate, cage, portfolio.

Vessel, vase, bushel, barrel, canister, jar, can, pottle, basket, pannier, corbeille, hamper, dosser.

For liquids; cistern, tank, vat, caldron, barrel, cask, keg, rundlet, firkin, kilderkin, carboy, amphora, bottle, jar, decanter, ewer, cruise, crock, canteen, flagon, flask, flasket, noggin, vial, (or phial,) cruet, caster, urn.

Tub, bucket, pail, pot, tankard, jug, pitcher, mug, pipkin, galipot, (or gallipot,) matrass, receiver, alembic, bolthead, capsule, retort.

Bowl, basin, jorum, punch bowl, cup, goblet, chalice, tumbler, glass, can, pan, plate, platter, dish, trencher, patera, calabash, porringer, saucepan, skillet, tureen, potager, saucer, hod, scuttle, shovel, trowel, spoon, spatula, ladle.

Closet, commode, cupboard, cellaret, chiffonnier, locker, bin, buffet, press, safe, sideboard, drawer, chest of drawers, till.

Chamber, story, apartment, room, cabin, bower, office, court, hall, saloon, parlor, (dining room, sitting room,) state room, presence chamber, drawing room, gallery, cabinet, closet, boudoir, lumber room, dormitory, refectory.

Attic, loft, garret, cockloft, cellar, vault, hold, cockpit, ground floor basement, kitchen, pantry, scullery.

Portico, porch, veranda, balcony, lobby, court, hall, vestibule, corridor, passage, anteroom, antechamber.

Adj. Capsular, recipient, ventricular, cystic, vascular, cellular camerated, locular, multilocular.

SECTION II. DIMENSIONS.

1. GENERAL DIMENSIONS.

192. SIZE, magnitude, dimension, bulk, volume, largeness, greatness, 31, expanse, amplitude, mass, massiveness.

Capacity, capaciousness, tonnage, (or tunnage,) calibre, scantling.

Turgidity, turgidness, expansion, 194, corpulence, obesity, plumpness, stoutness, brawniness.

Hugeness, vastness, enormousness, enormity, immensity, monstrousness, monstrosity; infinity, 105.

A mountain, mound, heap, 72.

V. To be large, &c., to become large, *see* Expansion, 194.

Adj. Large, big, great, considerable, bulky, voluminous, ample, massive, massy, capacious, comprehensive.

Corpulent, stout, fat, plump, lusty, strapping, bouncing, portly, burly, brawny, fleshy, goodly, in good case, chopping, jolly, chubby, full-grown, chubfaced, lubberly, hulky, unwieldy, lumpish, gaunt, stalwart.

Overgrown, bloated, tumid, turgid, hypertrophied, swoln, potbellied, puffy, distended, dropsical.

Squab, dumpy, squat, squabby, pursy, blowzy.

Huge, immense, enormous, mighty, unbounded, vast, stupendous, inordinate, monstrous, monster; gigantic, giant-like, colossal, Cyclopean; indefinite, infinite.

194. EXPANSION, enlargement, extension, augmentation, increase of size, amplification, aggrandizement, spread, incre-

193. LITTLENESS, smallness, minuteness, diminutiveness, inextension, puniness, dwarfishness, undersize, epitome, rudiment, microcosm.

Leanness, emaciation, thinness, macilency, flaccidity.

Animalcule, mite, insect, emmet, fly, gnat, shrimp, minnow, worm, grub, tit, tomtit, small fry, mushroom, millet seed, mustard seed, grain of sand.

Atom, point, speck, dot, mote, ace, jot, iota, tittle, whit, particle, corpuscule, molecule, monad, granule, grain, crum, globule, nutshell, minim, drop, bit, thimbleful, sprinkling, dash, minimum, powder, 330, driblet, patch, scrap, chip, inch, mathematical point; minutiae.

V. To be small, &c., to become small, *see* Contraction, 195.

Adj. Little, small, minute, diminutive, inconsiderable, puny, tiny, petty, miniature, pygmy, undersized, dwarf, stunted, dwarfed, dwarfish, Liliputian; pocket, portative, portable.

Microscopic, evanescent, impalpable, imperceptible, invisible, inappreciable, infinitesimal, homœopathic, atomic, corpuscular, molecular, rudimentary, rudimental.

Lean, thin, meagre, emaciated, lank, macilent, fallen away, scrubby, reduced, shrunk, extenuated, shrivelled, flaccid, starved, skinny, stunted.

195. CONTRACTION, reduction, diminution or decrease of size, defalcation, lessening, decrement, shrinking, collapse, emaci-

ment, growth, development, pullulation, swell, dilatation, rarefaction, turgescence, turgidity, tumefaction, intumescence, swelling, distension, puffing, inflalation.

Overgrowth, over-distension, tympany.

Bulb, knot, knob, 249.

Superiority of size.

V. To become larger, to expand, enlarge, extend, grow, increase, swell, gather, fill out, deploy, dilate, stretch, spread, mantle, bud, shoot, (put forth,) spring up, sprout, germinate, vegetate, pullulate, open, burst forth, gather flesh, outgrow.

To render larger, to expand, aggrandize, &c., distend, develop, amplify, magnify, rarefy, inflate, puff, blow up, stuff, pad, cram.

To be larger than, to surpass, exceed, be beyond, cap, overtop, *see* Height, 206, and Superiority, 33.

Adj. Expanded, enlarged, increased, &c., swelled out, bulbous; exaggerated, bloated, &c., full-blown, full-grown, full-formed.

196. Distance, remoteness, farness, longinquity, elongation, offing, parallax, reach, span.

Antipodes, outpost, outskirt, aphelion, horizon.

Separation, 44, transferrence, 270.

Diffusion, dispersion, 73.

V. To be distant, &c.; to extend to, stretch to, reach to, spread to, go to, get to, stretch away to; outgo, outstep, to go great lengths.

To remain at a distance, keep away, stand off, keep off, stand aloof.

Adj. Distant, far, far off, remote, wide of, stretching to, yonder, at arm's length, apart, asunder, ulterior, ultramontane, transmontane, transalpine, ultramundane, hyperborean.

ation, attenuation, tabefaction, consumption, marasmus, atrophy.

Condensation, compression, squeezing, cramping; friction, 331, corrugation; contractility; astringency.

Inferiority of size.

V. To become smaller, to lessen, diminish, decrease, grow less, dwindle, shrink, contract, shrivel, collapse, wither, lose flesh, fall away, decay, waste, wane, ebb.

To render smaller, to contract, lessen, &c., to draw in, condense, reduce, clip, compress, squeeze, cramp, attenuate, chip, dwarf, bedwarf, cut short, 201, corrugate.

To be smaller than, to fall short of, not to come up to.

Adj. Contracting, &c., astringent, contracted, &c., stunted, waning, ebbing, &c., neap, condensed, compact.

Unexpanded, contractile, compressible.

197. Nearness, nighness, propinquity, vicinity, vicinage, neighborhood, adjacency, closeness; perihelion.

A short distance, a step, an earshot, close quarters, a stone's throw, a hair's breadth, a span, bowshot, gunshot.

Purlieus. neighborhood, vicinage, environs, suburbs, border land, the whereabouts.

A bystander, neighbor.

Approach, approximation, appropinquation, appulse, 286, junction, 43, concentration.

Meeting, (encounter.)

V. To be near, &c., to adjoin, hang about, trench on, border upon, stand by, approximate, tread on the heels of, cling to

Inaccessible, out of the way, unapproachable; incontiguous.

Adv. Far, away, far away, afar, off, a long way off, afar off, wide away, aloof, wide of, clear of, out of the way, a great way off, out of reach, abroad, yonder, farther, beyond.

Apart, asunder, wide apart, wide asunder.

---

clasp, hug, get near, approach, 286, to meet, 290.

To bring near, to crowd, pack, huddle together.

Adj. Near, nigh, close at hand, neighboring, proximate, adjacent, adjoining, bordering upon, close upon, hard upon, trenching on, treading on the heels of, verging to, at hand, handy, near the mark, home, intimate.

Adv. Near, nigh, hard by, fast by, close to, close upon, within call, within hearing, within an ace of, but a step, at hand, on the verge of, near the mark, in the environs, &c., a stone's throw, &c., cheek by jole, (or jowl,) beside, alongside, at he heels of.

About, hereabouts, thereabouts, in the way, in presence of, in round numbers, approximatively.

198. Interval, interspace, *see* Discontinuity, 70, break, gap, opening, 260, chasm, hiatus, interstice, cleft, foss, mesh, crevice, chink, cranny, crack, chap, slit, fissure, scissure, rift, flaw, gash, cut, leak, dike, fracture, solution of continuity, breach, rent, rime, oscitation, gaping, yawning, pandiculation, insertion, 300.

Gorge, defile, ravine, inlet, frith, furrow, *see* 259.

Thing interposed, a go-between, *see* Interjacence, 228.

V. To separate, 44, gape, 260.

199. Contiguity contact, proximity, apposition, no interval, juxtaposition, touching, abutment, osculation, meeting, 294, coincidence, coexistence, adhesion, 46.

Confine, frontier, demarcation, 233.

V. To be contiguous, &c., to touch, meet, adhere, 46, osculate, coincide, coexist, abut on, graze.

Adj. Contiguous, touching, meeting, in contact, conterminous, osculating, osculatory, proximate.

2. Linear Dimensions.

200. Length, longitude, span.

A line, bar, rule, stripe, streak, spoke, radius.

Lengthening, elongation, prolongation, production, producing, protraction, extension, stretching.

V. To be long, &c., to extend to, reach, stretch to.

To render long, lengthen, extend elongate, prolong, produce, stretch, draw out, protract, spin out, drawl.

201. Shortness, brevity, briefness, a span, &c., *see* Smallness, 193.

Shortening, abbreviation, abbreviature, abridgment, epitome, curtailment, decurtation, reduction, contraction, compression, 195, retrenchment, elision, ellipsis, compendium, 596, conciseness in style, 572.

V. To be short, brief, &c.

To render short, to shorten, curtail, abridge, abbreviate, epito-

Adj. Long, lengthy, wiredrawn, outstretched, lengthened, produced, &c., Alexandrine, sesquipedalian, interminable.

Linear, lineal, longitudinal, oblong.

Adv. Lengthwise, longitudinally, in a line, along, from end to end, fore and aft, from head to foot, from top to toe.

202. Breadth, width, latitude, amplitude, diameter, bore, calibre, superficial extent, expanse.

Thickness, crassitude, 192, expansion, dilatation, &c., 194.

V. To be broad, thick, &c.

To become broad, to render broad, to swell, dilate, expand, outspread, &c., 194, to incrassate.

Adj. Broad, wide, ample, extended, fan-like, outstretched, &c.

Thick, dumpy, squab, squat.

mize, reduce, contract, compress scrimp.

To retrench, cut short, cu down, pare down, clip, dock, lop, prune, crop, snub, truncate, cut, hack, hew, &c.; (in drawing,) to foreshorten.

Adj. Short, brief, curt, (truncated,) compendious, compact, stubby, scrimp, stumpy, thickset, pug, oblate, elliptical, concise, 572, summary.

203. Narrowness, slenderness, closeness, scantiness, exility, lankness, incapaciousness.

A line, 205, a hair's breadth, a finger's breadth, streak, vein.

Thinness, tenuity, leanness, meagreness, emaciation.

A shaving, a slip, 205, a mere skeleton, a shadow.

A middle constriction, stricture, neck, waist, isthmus, wasp, hourglass, ridge, ravine, defile, gorge, pass.

Narrowing, tapering, compression, squeezing, &c., 195.

V. To be narrow, &c., to taper, contract, shrink.

To render narrow, &c., to narrow, contract, coarctate, attenuate, constrict, constringe, cramp, pinch, squeeze, compress, corrugate.

To shave, shear, &c., *see* 195.

Adj. Narrow, slender, thin, fine, (thread-like,) filiform, filamentous, fibrous, funicular, capillary, stringy, wire drawn, finespun, anguilliform, taper, dapper, slim, slight-made, scant, spare, delicate, unenlarged, incapacious.

Meagre, lean, macilent, emaciated, lank, starveling, attenuated, skinny, scraggy, gaunt, raw-boned.

204. Layer, stratum, bed, zone, substratum, floor, flag, stage, story, tier.

Plate, lamina, lamella, sheet, flake, scale, coat, pellicle, membrane, film, leaf, slice, shive, cut, shaving, board, plank.

Stratification, scaliness, a nest of boxes, coats of an onion.

V. To slice, shave, &c.

Adj. Lamellar, laminated, lam-

205. Filament, line, fibre, fibril, hair, capillament, gossamer, wire, thread, cord, rope, yarn, &c., *see* 45.

Strip, shred, slip, spill, list, string, band, fillet, ribbon, (or rib-band;) roll, lath, splinter, shiver, shaving; arborescence, *see* 256.

ellated, lamelliform, scaly, filmy, membranous, flaky, foliated, foliaceous, stratified, stratiform, tabular.

206. HEIGHT, altitude, elevation, eminence, pitch, loftiness, sublimity.

Stature, tallness, procerity, culmination, *see* Summit, 210.

A giant, grenadier, giraffe.

Alps, mountain, mount, hill, hillock, monticle, fell, moorland, hummock, knap, knoll, cape, headland, foreland, promontory, ridge, pike, uplands, highlands, rising ground, downs, mound, mole, steeps, bluff, cliff, crag, vantage ground.

Tower, pillar, column, obelisk, monument, steeple, spire, minaret, turret, dome, cupola, pilaster.

Pole, pikestaff, maypole, (liberty pole,) flag staff, topmast, topgallant mast, housetop.

Ceiling, roof, awning, canopy, *see* 210, attic, loft, garret.

Growth, upgrowth, 194.

V. To be high, &c., to tower, soar, ride, beetle, hover, cap, overtop, culminate, overhang, hang over, impend, bestride, mount, surmount, to cover, 223.

To become high, grow, upgrow, soar, tower, rise, 305.

To render high, to heighten, exalt, *see* Elevate, 307, to perch up, to perk up.

Adj. High, elevated, eminent, exalted, lofty, supernal, tall, topping, towering, beetling, soaring, stalwart, colossal, gigantic, Patagonian, culminating, raised, &c., perched up, hanging (gardens,) crowning.

Upland, moorland, hilly, mountainous, alpine, cloud-touching, cloud-topped, cloud-capped, aerial.

Upper, uppermost.

Overhanging, impending, incumbent, superincumbent, (overlying,) superimposed, hovering.

Adv. On high, high up, aloft, above, aloof, overhead, in the clouds, on tiptoe, on stilts, on the shoulders of.

Over, upwards, from top to bottom, from top to toe, from head to foot.

207. LOWNESS, lowlands, (flats,) depression, recumbency, prostration, *see* Horizontality, 213, a molehill.

A ground floor, 191, basement floor.

V. To be low, &c., crouch, slouch, lie flat; to lie low; to underlie.

To lower, depress, 306.

Adj. Low, neap, debased, nether, prostrate, flat, level with the ground, grovelling, crouched, crouching, subjacent, underlying, squat.

Adv. Under, beneath, underneath, below, down, adown, down wards, underfoot, at the foot of, underground.

---

208. DEPTH, deepness, profundity, profoundness, depression, bathos, anti-climax, depth of water, draught.

A pit, shaft, well, crater, gulf, abyss.

209. SHALLOWNESS, shoaliness, shoals.

Adj. Shallow, skin-deep, superficial, shoaly.

Soundings, submersion, plunge, dive, 210.

V. To be deep, &c.

To render deep, &c., to deepen.

To sink, submerge, plunge, dip, dive, 310.

To dig, scoop out, hollow, sink, delve, 252.

Adj. Deep, deep-seated, profound, sunk, buried, submerged, &c., subaqueous, submarine, subterranean, underground, subterrene.

Bottomless, soundless, fathomless, unfathomed, unfathomable.

Adv. Beyond one's depth, out of one's depth, underground.

210. SUMMIT, top, vertex, apex, zenith, pinnacle, acme, climax, culminating point, pitch, water shed, meridian, sky, pole.

Tip, tiptop, crest, peak, turning point, crown, brow.

Head, pate.

Capital, cornice, sconce, pediment, entablature, frieze.

Roof, ceiling, thatch, tiling, slating, awning, canopy, *see* Cover, 223.

Adj. Top, topmost, uppermost, tiptop, culminating, meridian, capital, head, polar, supreme, crowning.

211. BASE, basement, plinth, foundation, substratum, ground, earth, pavement, floor, paving, flag, ground floor, deck, substructure, footing, groundwork.

The bottom, nadir, foot, sole, toe, root, keel.

Adj. Bottom, undermost, nethermost, fundamental.

212. VERTICALITY, erectness, uprightness, perpendicularity; right angle, normal.

Wall, precipice, cliff.

Erection, raising, rearing.

V. To be vertical, &c., to stand up, to stand on end, to stand erect, to stand upright, to stick up.

To render vertical, to set up, stick up, erect, rear, raise up, cock up, raise on its legs.

Adj. Vertical, upright, erect, perpendicular, straight, standing up, &c., up on end, bolt upright, rampant.

Rectangular, normal, orthogonal.

Adv. Up, vertically, &c., on end, endwise.

213. HORIZONTALITY, a level, plane, dead level, flatness, 251.

Recumbency, lying, lying down, reclination, decumbence, decumbency, discumbency, accubation, prostration.

A plain, floor, platform, bowling green, plateau, terrace, estrade, esplanade, offset, parterre, table land.

V. To be horizontal, recumbent, &c., to lie, recline, lie down, couch, lie flat, lie prostrate, sprawl, loll.

To render horizontal, &c., to lay, lay down, level, flatten, prostrate, knock down, floor.

Adj. Horizontal, level, plane, flat, even.

Recumbent, decumbent, procumbent, accumbent, lying, prone, supine, couchant, couching, jacent, prostrate, sitting, reclining.

Adv. Horizontally, &c.

214. Pendency, dependency, suspension, hanging.

A pedicle, peduncle, tail, flap, skirt, pendulum.

A peg, knob, button, hook, nail, ring, staple, knot, 45, tenterhook.

V. To be pendent, &c., to hang, swing, dangle, swag, daggle, flap, trail.

To suspend, hang, sling, hook up, hitch, fasten to.

Adj. Pendent, pendulous, pensile, hanging, swinging, &c., suspended, &c., loose, flowing.

Having a peduncle, &c., pedunculate, tailed, caudate.

---

215. Support, ground, foundation, base, basis, fulcrum, landing, landing-place, resting-place, groundwork, substratum, floor, bed, stall, berth.

A supporter, prop, stand, stay shore, truss, sleeper, staff, stick, crutch, stilts.

Post, pillar, shaft, column, pediment, pedicle, pedestal, plinth, 211.

A frame, framework, scaffold skeleton, beam, rafter, joist, travis, trave, shaft, corner stone stanchion, girder, tiebeam, 45, keystone, axletree, axle; axis.

A board, form, ledge, platform, stage, shelf, hob, bracket, arbor, rack, mantel, counter, dresser flange, corbel, lintel, table, trestle, shoulder, perch, truss, horse, easel, desk.

A seat, throne, divan, chair, bench, sofa, settee, couch woolsack, ottoman, settle, bench.

Bed, pillow, bolster, mattress, shakedown, tester, pallet hammock, crib, cradle.

Cushion, stool, footstool, hassock, tabouret, tripod, trevet.

V. To be supported, &c.; to lie, sit, recline, lean, abut, bear, rest, repose, &c., on; be based on, to bestride, straddle.

To support, bear, carry, hold, sustain, shoulder, uphold, hold up, prop, underprop, shore up, underpin.

To give, furnish, afford, supply, lend, &c., support; to bottom, to found.

Adj. Supported, &c., fundamental.

216. Parellelism, coextension.

V. To be parallel, &c.

Adj. Parallel, coextensive.

Adv. Alongside, abreast, beside.

---

217. Obliquity, inclination, slope, leaning, slant, crookedness, bias, bend, bevel, tilt, swag, cant, lurch.

Acclivity, uphill, rise, ascent, rising ground, bank. Declivity, downhill, dip, fall, a gentle or rapid slope, an easy ascent or descent.

Steepness, precipitousness, cliff, precipice, escarpment.

Measure of inclination, clinometer.

Diagonal, zigzag, distortion, hypothenuse, *see* Angle, 244.

V. To be oblique, &c., to slope, slant, lean, incline, shelve, stoop, bend, sag, slouch, cant.

To render oblique, &c., to slope, tilt, bend, incline, &c., distort.

Adj. Oblique, inclined, leaning, recumbent, sloping, shelving, askew, aslant, slanting, indirect, distorted, wry, awry, crooked, canted, tilted, biased, swagging, bevel, slouched, slouching, &c.

Uphill, rising, ascending.

Downhill, falling, descending, declining.

Steep, abrupt, precipitous, breakneck.

Diagonal, transverse, athwart, transversal, anti-parallel.

Adv. Obliquely, &c., on one side, askew, askant.

Sidewise, slopewise, all on one side.

218. Inversion, contraposition, overturn, overset, somerset, retroversion, reversion, eversion, transposition, supination, antipodes, 237.

V. To be inverted, &c.

To render inverted, &c., to invert, reverse, upset, overset, overturn, turn over, upturn, subvert, retrovert, transpose, turn topsyturvy, tilt over, topple over, capsize.

Adj. Inverted, inverse, upside down, topsyturvy, topheavy.

Adv. Inversely, topsyturvy, hurdy gurdy, &c.

219. Crossing, intersection, decussation, transversion.

Reticulation, network, interweaving, twining, intertwining, matting, plaiting.

Net, web, mesh, twill, skein, felt, lace, wicker, trellis, lattice, grating, tracery, fretwork, filigree.

Cross, chain, wreath, braid, St. Andrew's cross.

V. To cross, intersect, decussate, interlace, intertwine, intertwist, intwine, weave, interweave, inweave, twine, twist, wreathe, inosculate.

To mat, plait, plat, braid, felt, twill, tangle, entangle, ravel, net, knot, dishevel.

Adj. Crossing, intersecting, &c., crossed, intersected, matted, &c., crucial, cruciform.

Retiform, reticulated, cancellated, grated, barred, streaked.

Adv. Across, thwart, athwart, transversely.

3. Centrical Dimensions.*

1. *General.*

220. Exteriority, the outside, the exterior, surface, superficies, superstratum, eccentricity, extremity.

Disk, face, facet, front, 234, skin, &c., *see* 223.

V. To be exterior, &c.

To place exteriorly or outwardly, to turn out.

Adj. Exterior, external, outer,

221. Interiority, the inside, interior, interspace, substratum, subsoil.

Vitals, viscera, pith, marrow, heart, bosom, breast, entrails, bowels, intestines, lap, backbone, inmost recesses, cave, cavern, &c., 191.

V. To be interior, internal, within, &c.

* That is, dimensions having reference to a centre.

outward, outlying outside, superficial, skin-deep, frontal, eccentric.

Adv. Externally, &c., out, without, outwards.

To place or keep within, to enclose, circumscribe, *see* 231, 232.

Adj. Interior, internal, inner, inside, inward, inmost, innermost, deep-seated, intestine, intestinal, inland, interstitial, subcutaneous.

Home, domestic, in-door, 191.

Adv. Internally, inwards, inwardly, within, inly, therein, withinside, in-doors, within doors, at home,

222. CENTRALITY, 68, centre, middle, focus, core, kernel, nucleus, heart, pole, axis, nave, concentration.

V. To be central, &c.

To render central, centralize, concentrate; bring to a focus.

Adj. Central, centrical, middle, median, focal, umbilical, concentric.

Adv. Midst, centrally, &c.

223. COVERING, cover, roof, canopy, awning, tilt, tent, lid, covercle, 263.

Integument, skin, tegument, pellicle, fleece, cuticle, scarfskin, hide, pelt, peel, crust, bark, rind, cortex, busk, scale, shell, capsule, coat, tunic, tunicle, sheath, case, sheathing, wrapping, wrapper, envelope, vesicle, veneer.

Superposition, coating, paint, varnish, anointing, incrustation, plaster, stucco.

V. To cover, superpose, overspread, wrap, lap, overlap, case, incase, veneer.

To coat, paint, varnish, daub, bedaub, incrust, stucco, dab, smear, anoint, do over, gild, plate, japan, lacquer.

Adj. Covering, &c., cutaneous, dermal, cortical, cuticular, tegumentary, skinny, scaly, squamous, imbricated.

224. LINING, coating, facing, internal, incrustation, stalactite, stalagmite.

Wainscot, wall.

V. To line, stuff, incrust, face.

Adj. Lined, stuffed, incrusted.

---

225. INVESTMENT, dress, clothing, raiment, drapery, costume, attire, trim, habiliment, vesture, apparel, wardrobe, fancy dress, accoutrement, outfit, uniform, regimentals, equipment, livery, gear, harness, turnout, caparison, suit, rigging, trappings, frippery.

Dishabille, morning dress, undress, rags, tatters, old clothes.

Clothes, garment, garb, robe, tunic, habit, gown, coat, frock, stole, blowze, bodice, dreadnaught, &c.

Mourning, weeds

226. DIVESTMENT, nudity, bareness, nakedness, baldness, undress, dishabille, threadbareness.

Denuding, nudation, denudation, stripping, uncovering, decortication, peeling, flaying, excoriation, moulting, exfoliation.

V. To divest, uncover, denude, bare, strip, unclothe, undress, unrobe, disrobe, disarray, take off, doff, cast off, peel, pare, excoriate, skin, flay, expose, exfoliate, lay open, unroof, uncase, moult.

Adj. Bare, naked, nude, stripped

Cloak, mantle, mantlet, shawl, wrapper, veil, tippet, kirtle, plaid, chlamys, mantilla, tabard, bornouse, greatcoat, surtout, spencer, surplice, cassock, pallium, &c., mask, domino, cardinal, pelerine.

Jacket, vest, jerkin, waistcoat, doublet, gabardine, stays, corslet, corset, cestus, petticoat, farthingale, kilt, stomacher, kirtle, apron.

Trousers, breeches, pantaloons, overalls, inexpressibles, smalls, tights,

Headdress; cap, hat, beaver, castor, bonnet, hood, kerchief, scarf, coiffure, coif, tartan, skullcap, cowl, capote, calash, pelt, wig, peruke, periwig, turban, helmet.

Body clothes; shirt, chemise, drawers, (flannels,) collar, cravat, neckcloth, stock, handkerchief, scarf.

Shoe, boot, jackboot, slipper, legging, buskin, greaves, galligaskins, moccason, gaiter, spatterdash, stocking, sock, sandal.

Glove, gauntlet, mitten.

V. To invest, cover, envelop, lap, involve, inwrap, wrap up, sheathe, vest, clothe, array, enrobe, dress, attire, apparel, accoutre, trick out, rig, fit out,

To wear, caparison, don, put on, slip on, roll up in, muffle, mantle, swathe, swaddle, circumvest, equip, harness.

Adj. Invested, clothed, habited, arrayed, &c., clad, shod, &c.

denuded, undressed, unclothed, uncovered, exposed, in dishabille, in buff, bald, threadbare, roofless.

---

227. Circumjacence, circumambiance, encompassment, atmosphere, medium. outpost, skirt, outskirts, suburbs, purlieus, precinct, faubourgs, environs.

V. To lie around, surround, beset, compass, encompass, environ, enclose, encircle, embrace, circumvent, lap, gird, begird, engird, skirt, twine, round.

Adj. Circumjacent, circumambient, surrounding, &c., circumfluent, circumferential, suburban, begirt, buried in, 363, immersed in, 301, imbosomed, in the bosom of, landlocked.

Adv. Around, about, without, on every side, on all sides, right and left

---

228. Interjacence, intervention, intervenience, interlocation, insertion, interposition, interdigitation, interpolation, interlineation, intercurrence, intrusion, obtrusion, insinuation, intercalation, interference, permeation, infiltration.

An intermedium, a go-between, intruder, interloper, flyleaf, *see* Mean, 68, a partition, diaphragm, midriff, party wall, panel, veil.

V. To lie, come, or get between, intervene, intrude, slide in, permeate, to put between, interpose, interject, throw in, wedge in, thrust in, foist in, insert, intercalate, interpolate, interline, interleave, interlard, interdigitate, dovetail, worm in, insinuate, obtrude 301, intersperse, infiltrate

Adj Interjacent, intervening, &c., intermediate, intercalary, interstitial, parenthetical, mediterranean.

Adv. Between, betwixt, among, amongst, amid, amidst midst; betwixt and between.

229. CIRCUMSCRIPTION, limitation, enclosure, confinement, shutting up, circumvallation, intombment. Imprisonment, incarceration, 751.

V. To circumscribe, limit, bound, confine, enclose, surround, 227, compass about, impound, restrict, restrain, imprison, &c., *see* 751, shut in, shut up, lock up, bottle up, hem in, hedge in, wall in, rail in, fence, picket, pen, infold, coop, incage, cage, intomb, bury, immure, incase, pack up, box up, seal up, wrap up, 223, &c.

Adj. Circumscribed, &c., imprisoned, pent up, 754, landlocked.

230. OUTLINE, circumference, perimeter, periphery, ambit, circuit, lines, contour, profile, silhouette.

Zone, belt, girth, band, baldric, zodiac, girdle, cingle, clasp, girt.

231. EDGE, verge, brink, brow, brim, margin, border, skirt, rim, side, mouth, jaws, lip, muzzle, door, porch, portal, 260.

Frame, flounce, frill, list, fringe, edging, hem, selvage, welt, furbelow.

232. ENCLOSURE, envelope, case, box, &c., 191, pen, penfold, paddock, pound, wall, hedge.

Barrier, bar, gate, door, barricade, cordonet.

Dike, ditch, foss, moat.

Fence, pale, paling, balustrade, rail, railing, palisade, battlement, rampart, &c., 717, circumvallation, contravallation.

233. LIMIT, boundary, bounds, confine, term, bourn, curbstone, line of demarcation, termination, frontier, precinct, marches, line of circumvallation, the pillars of Hercules, the Rubicon, the turning point.

Adj. Definite, conterminate, conterminable.

2. *Special.*

234. FRONT, forepart, face, anteriority, forerank, foreground, van, vanguard, advanced guard, outpost, frontispiece, disk.

Forehead, visage, physiognomy, countenance, beak, bow, stem, prow.

In a medal, the obverse.

V. To be in front, &c., to front, face, confront, bend forwards, &c.

Adj. Fore, anterior, front.

Adv. Before, in front, ahead, right ahead, in the van, foremost, in the foreground, face to face, before one's eyes.

235. REAR, back, posteriority, the rearrank, rearguard, the background, heels, tail, rump, croup, breech, dorsal region, stern, poop, afterpart.

In a medal, the reverse.

V. To be in the rear, behind, &c., to fall astern, to bend backwards, turn the back upon

Adj. Back, rear, postern, hind, hinder, hindermost, posterior, dorsal, after.

Adv. Behind, in the rear, in the background, behind one's back, at the back of, after, aft, abaft astern, sternmost, aback, rearward

236. LATERALITY, side, flank, quarter, hand, cheek, wing, profile, temple, loin, haunch, hip, broadside, leeside.

East, orient; west.

V. To be on one side, &c., to flank, outflank, to sidle.

Adj. Lateral, sidelong, collateral, sideling, many-sided.

Eastern, orient, oriental.

Western, occidental.

Adv Sidewise, side by side, 216, abreast, alongside, aside, by the side of, to windward, or to leeward.

237. ANTI-POSITION, opposite side, contraposition, reverse, inverse, antipodes, opposition, inversion, 218.

Polarity, opposite poles, north, south.

V. To be opposite, &c., to subtend.

Adj. Opposite, (over against,) reverse, inverse, antipodal, subcontrary.

Fronting, facing, diametrically opposite.

Boreal, arctic; austral, antarctic.

Adv. Over, over the way, over against, facing, against, fronting, 234, subtending.

238. DEXTRALITY, right, right hand, off side, starboard.

Adj. Dextral, right-handed, ambidextral.

239. SINISTRALITY, left, left hand, sinister, near side, larboard, port.

Adj. Sinistral, left-handed.

SECTION III. FORM.

1. GENERAL FORM.

240. FORM, figure, shape, configuration, make, formation, frame, construction, conformation, cut, set, build, trim, stamp, cast, mould, fashion, *see* Structure, 329.

Feature, lineament, phase, turn, attitude. Outline, 229.

Formation, figuration, sculpture.

V. To form, shape, figure, fashion, carve, cut, chisel, hew, roughhew, cast, roughcast, hammer out, trim, lick into shape, mould, sculpture, cast, stamp.

Adj. Formed, &c., receiving form, plastic, fictile.

Giving form, plasmatic.

241. Absence of form.

AMORPHISM, disfigurement, defacement, mutilation, informity, *see* Deformity, 846.

V. To destroy form, deface, deform, disfigure, mutilate.

Adj. Shapeless, amorphous, formless, unhewn, rough, unfashioned, unshapen.

---

242. Regularity of form.

SYMMETRY, (proportion,) shapeliness, uniformity, finish, *see* Beauty, 845, arborescence, 256.

243. Irregularity of form.

DISTORTION, twist, wryness, detortion, contortion, *see* Ugliness 846.

Adj. Symmetrical, regular, shapely, well set, uniform, finished, &c., arborescent, 256.

V. To distort, twist, wrest, writhe, contort.

Adj. Irregular, unsymmetric distorted, twisted, awry, askew, crooked, on one side, hunchbacked.

2. Special Form.

244. Angularity, angularness, angle, cusp, bend, elbow, knee, knuckle, groin, crinkle, crotch, crutch, crane, fluke, scythe, sickle, zigzag, kimbo. Fold, *see* 258.

Fork, bifurcation, dichotomy.

A right angle, *see* Perpendicularity, 212, salient and reëntering angles.

A polygon, square, triangle, &c., lozenge, diamond, rhomb, &c., wedge.

V. To bend, fork, bifurcate, crinkle.

Adj. Angular, bent, aduncous, aquiline, jagged, serrated, falciform, furcated, forked, bifurcate, zigzag; dovetailed, crinkled, kimbo, geniculated, polygonal, &c., fusiform, wedge-shaped, cuneiform.

245. Curvature, curvation, incurvation, bend, flexure, flexion, crook, bending, deflexion, inflexion, arcuation, turn, deviation, sweep, sinuosity, curl, curling, winding, recurvity, recurvation, flexibility, 324.

A curve, arc, arch, arcade, vault, bow, crescent, half moon, lunule, horseshoe, loop, crane-neck, conchoid, &c.

V. To be curved, &c., to decline, turn, trend, deviate, reenter, sweep.

To render curved; to bend, curve, incurvate, deflect, inflect, crook, turn, arch, arcuate, bow, curl, recurve, frizzle.

Adj. Curved, bent, &c., curvilinear, (or curvilineal,) recurved, bowed, crooked, arched, vaulted, arcuated, hooked, falciform, falcated, semicircular, luniform, lunular, semilunar, conchoidal, cordiform, cardioid, heart-shaped, lenticular, reniform; devious.

246. Straightness, rectilinearity, directness.

A straight line, a right line a direct line; inflexibility, 324.

V. To be straight, &c.

To render straight, to straighten, rectify, unbend, unfold, uncurl, uncoil, unroll, unwind, unravel, untwist, untwine, unwreathe, unwrap.

Adj. Straight, rectilinear, (or rectilineal,) direct, even, right, in a line; not inclining, bending, turning, or deviating to either side; undeviating, unturned, undistorted, unswerving.

---

247. Simple circularity.

Circularity, roundness

A circle, circlet, ring, hoop, roundlet, annulet, bracelet, ringlet, eye, loop, wheel, cycle, orb,

248. Complex circularity.

Convolution, winding, wave, undulation, circuit, tortuosity, sinuosity, involution, sinuation, circumvolution. meandering, twist

orbit, rundle, zone, belt, band, sash, girdle, cestus, cincture, baldric, fillet, fascia, wreath, garland, crown, corona, coronet, chaplet, necklace; noose, lasso.

An ellipse, oval, ellipsoid, cycloid, epicycloid, epicycle, &c.

V. To encircle, environ, &c., 227.

Adj. Round, circular, annular, orbicular.

Oval, elliptical, elliptic, ovate, egg-shaped; cycloidal, &c., moniliform.

---

twirl, windings and turnings, inosculation, reticulation, *see* 219.

A coil, spiral, helix, corkscrew, worm, volute, rundle, scallop.

Maze, labyrinth.

V. To be convoluted, &c.

To wind, twine, turn and twist, twirl, wave, undulate, meander, scallop, inosculate, intwine, twist together, 219.

Adj. Convoluted, winding, twisting, contorted, waving, waved, wavy, undulating, serpentine, anguilliform, mazy, tortuous, sinuous, flexuous, involved, sigmoidal, snaky, vermiform, vermicular, meandering; scalloped, wreathed, wreathy, crisped, ravelled, twisted, dishevelled.

Spiral, coiled, heliacal, turbinated.

249. Rotundity; cylinder, barrel, drum, cylindroid, roll, roller, rouleau, column.

Cone, conoid; pear-shape, bell-shape.

Sphericity, spheroidity; a sphere, globe, ball, spheroid, ellipsoid, drop, spherule, globule, vesicle, bulb, bullet, pellet, pill, clew, marble, knob, pommel.

V. To form into a sphere, (to render spherical,) to roll into a ball, give rotundity, &c.

Adj. Rotund, cylindric, cylindrical, columnar; conic, conical.

Spherical, globular, globated, globous, globose, ovoid, egg-shaped, oviform, gibbous, bell-shaped, campanulate, fungiform.

3. Superficial Form.

250. Convexity, prominence, projection, swelling, (swell,) gibbosity, bulge, protuberance, intumescence, tumor, tuberosity, tubercle, tooth, knob, excrescence, process, bulb, node, nodule, nodosity, boss, embossment, clump, sugar loaf, point, 253.

Pimple, wen, wheal, pustule, caruncle, (boil,) corn, wart, furuncle, fungus, fungosity, blister, blain.

Papilla, nipple, teat, pap, mammilla, proboscis, nose, neb, beak, snout, nozzle, belly, back, shoulder, elbow, lip, flange.

251. Flatness, plane; *see* Horizontality, 213, Layer, 204, and Smoothness, 255, plate, platter.

V. To render flat, flatten, smooth, level.

Adj. Flat, plane, level, &c., flush, scutiform.

252. Concavity, depression, hollow, hollowness, indentation, cavity, dent, dint, dimple, follicle, pit, honeycomb, excavation, trough, 259.

Cup, basin, crater, chalice, &c., 191, bowl, socket.

Valley, vale, dale, dell, dingle,

Peg, button, stud, ridge, rib, snag, eaves.

Cupola, dome, balcony.

Mount, hill, &c., 206; cape, promontory, foreland, headland, point of land, mole, jetty, hummock.

V. To be prominent, &c., to project, bulge, jut out, protrude, barrow, stand out, start up, shoot up, swell, to hang over, beetle, bend over.

glade, glen, cave, cell, cavern, cove, grotto, alcove, gully.

V. To be depressed, &c., to retire.

To depress, hollow, scoop, dig, delve, excavate, dent, mine, undermine, burrow, tunnel.

Adj. Depressed, concave, hollow, stove in, retiring, retreating, cavernous, honeycombed, funnel-shaped, bell-shaped.

To render prominent: to raise, *see* 307.

Adj. Prominent, projecting, salient, in relief, bulging, &c., bowed, arched, bold, tuberous, bellied, tuberculous, tumerous, bossed, bossy, embossed, gibbous, mammiform.

253. SHARPNESS, pointedness, acuteness, acumination, spinosity, prickliness.

A point, spike, spine, needle, pin, prickle, prick, spear, bayonet, spur, rowel, barb, spit, cusp, horn, barb, snag, tag, thorn, brier, bramble, thistle, nib, tooth, tusk, spoke, cog, staple, bristle, beard, crag, crest, cone, peak, spire, pyramid, steeple, porcupine, hedgehog.

Cutting edge, wedge, edge tool, knife, razor, scalpel, axe, adze, &c.

V. To be sharp, &c., to taper to a point, to bristle with.

To render sharp, &c., to sharpen, point, aculeate, whet, barb, speculate, bristle up.

Adj. Sharp, pointed, conical, acute, aculeated, needle-shaped, spiked, spiky, ensiform, peaked, acuminated, salient, cusped, cornuted, prickly, spiny, spinous, thorny, bristling, pectinated, studded, thistly, briery, cragged, craggy, snaggy, digitated, barbed, spurred, twoedged, tapering, fusiform, denticulated, toothed, cutting, sharpedged.

Starlike, stellated, stelliform.

254. BLUNTNESS, obtuseness, dullness.

V. To be blunt, &c., to render blunt, &c., to obtund, dull, take off the point or edge, turn.

Adj. Blunt, obtuse, dull, bluff.

---

255. SMOOTHNESS, evenness, level, &c., 213, polish, glassiness, sleekness, slipperiness, lubricity, lubrication, down, velvet.

V. To smooth, plane, polish, burnish, calender, glaze, iron, file, lubricate, 332.

Adj. Smooth, even, level, plane, sleek, polished, glazed, glossy, silken, silky, velvety, glabrous,

256. ROUGHNESS, unevenness, asperity, rugosity, ruggedness, scabrousness, scragginess, cragginess, craggedness, corrugation, nodosity, crispness.

Arborescence, branching, ramification.

Brush, hair, hairiness, beard, shag, mane, whisker, mustache, tress, lock, curl, ringlet.

slippery, oily, soft, lubricated, unwrinkled.

———

Plumage, plumosity, plume, crest; feather, tuft, fringe, wool, velvet, plush, nap, pile, floss, down; byssus, moss, burr.

V. To be rough, &c.

To render rough, to roughen, crisp, crumple, corrugate, rumple.

Adj. Rough, uneven, scabrous, rugged, rugose, rugous, unsmooth, roughhewn, craggy, cragged, scraggy, prickly, 253.

Arborescent, dendriform, arboriform, branching, dendroid.

Feathery, plumose, tufted, hairy, ciliated, hirsute, bushy, hispid, downy, velvety, villous, bearded, pilous, shaggy, fringed, befringed.

257. Notch, dent, nick, indent, indentation, dimple.

Embrasure, battlement, saw, tooth.

V. To notch, nick, cut, dent, indent, jag.

Adj. Notched, &c., jagged, crenate, dented, dentated, denticulated, toothed, palmated, indented, serrated.

258. Fold, plicature, plait, ply, crease, flexion, flexure, joint, elbow, doubling, duplicature, gather, wrinkle, rivel, ruffle, corrugation.

V. To fold, double, plait, crease, wrinkle, curl, frizzle, rivel, twill, corrugate.

Adj. Folded, &c.

259. Furrow, groove, rut, scratch, streak, crack, score, rib.

Channel, gutter, trench, ditch, dike, foss, trough, ravine, *see* 198.

V. To furrow, &c., flute, plough.

Adj. Furrowed, &c., ribbed, striated, sulcated, bisulcate, trisulcate, &c., corduroy.

260. Opening, hole, perforation, window, eye, eyelet, keyhole, loophole, porthole, pigeonhole, pinhole, puncture.

Aperture, yawning, oscitancy, dehiscence, patefaction, pandiculation, *see* Interval, 198.

Orifice, mouth, throat, inlet, muzzle, throat, gullet, nozzle, portal, porch, gate, gateway, door, doorway, arcade.

Channel, passage, tube, pipe, vessel, canal, thoroughfare, gut, ajutage, chimney, flue, funnel, gully, tunnel, pit, adit, shaft, gallery, alley, aisle, glade, vista, bore, mine, calibre, pore, follicle, porousness.

Sieve, cullender, cribble, riddle, screen.

261. Closure, occlusion, blockade, shutting up, filling up, plugging, sealing, obstruction, impassableness, blocking up, obstipation, blind alley, blind corner.

Imperforation, imperviousness, impermeability.

V. To close, occlude, plug, block up, fill up, blockade, obstruct, stop, bung up, seal, plumb, cork up, shut up, choke, throttle, dam up, cram.

Adj. Closed, shut, unopened, occluded, &c., impervious, imperforate, impassable, pathless, untrodden, (impenetrable), impermeable, imporous, operculated air-tight.

———

Apertion, perforation, piercing, boring, mining, drilling, &c., impalement, pertusion, puncture, penetration, 302.

V. To open, gape, yawn.

To perforate, lay open, pierce, bore, mine, drill, scoop out, tunnel, transpierce, transfix, enfilade, impale, spike, spear, gore, stab, pink, puncture, stick, prick, riddle; punch.

To uncover, rip, stave in.

Adj. Open, pierced, perforated, &c., wide open, unclosed, unstopped, oscitant, gaping, yawning, patent.

Tubular, cannular, fistulous, pervious, permeable, foraminous, follicular, honeycombed.

262. Perforator, borer, auger, gimlet, stylet, drill, wimble, awl, scoop, corkscrew, dibble, trepan, probe, bodkin, needle, stiletto, warder, lancet, punch.

263. Stopper, stopple, plug, cork, bung, spigot, spike, stop cock, tap, rammer, ramrod, piston, wadding.

Cover, lid, covering, covercle, door, &c., *see* 223, valve.

A janitor, doorkeeper, porter, warder, beadle.

Section IV. MOTION.

1. Motion in General.

264. Successive change of place.

Motion, movement, transit, transition, move, going, &c., passage, course, stir, evolution.

Step, gait, post, footfall, carriage, transferrence, 270, locomotion, 266.

Mobility, restlessness, unrest, movableness, inquietude, flux.

V. To be moving, &c., to move, go, hie, budge, stir, pass, flit, shift, roll, roll on, flow, 347, 348, sweep along, wander, 279, change or shift one's place or quarters, dodge.

Adj. Moving, in motion, on the move, going, &c., transitional.

Shifting, movable, 270, mobile, restless, nomadic, wandering, vagrant, discursive, excursive, erratic, 279, mercurial.

265. Quiescence, rest, stillness, stagnation, stagnancy, fixedness, immobility.

Quiet, tranquillity, calm, calmness, sedentariness.

Pause, suspension, suspense, lull, stop, stoppage, interruption, stopping, stand, standstill, standing still, lying to, repose, 687, respite.

Lock, dead lock, dead stop, embargo.

Resting-place, anchorage, post, 189, 666, bed, pillow, &c., 215.

V. To be quiescent, &c., to remain, stand, stand still, lie to, pull up, hold, halt, stop, stop short, rest, pause, repose, keep quiet, take breath.

To stay, tarry, sojourn, dwell, 186, pitch one's tent, cast anchor, settle, encamp, bivouac, moor, tether, picket, plant one's self, alight, land &c., 292, ride at anchor

To stop, suspend, arrest, interrupt, intermit, discontinue, 142, put a stop to, quell, becalm, hush.

Adj. Quiescent, still, motionless, moveless, at rest, stationary, untravelled, at a stand, stock still, standing still, sedentary, undisturbed, unruffled, fast, stuck fast, rooted, moored, aground, at anchor, tethered, becalmed, stagnant, quiet, unmoved, immovable, restful, irremovable, stable, steady, steadfast.

Adv. At a stand, at a stand still, &c.; at anchor.

266. Locomotion by land.

JOURNEY, travel, travelling, excursion, expedition, tour, trip, circuit, peregrination, discursion, ramble, pilgrimage, course, ambulation, march, marching, walk, walking, promenade, stroll, saunter, perambulation, ride, equitation, drive, airing, jaunt.

Roving, vagrancy, flit, flitting, migration, emigration, immigration.

Plan, itinerary, road book, guide.

Procession, cavalcade, caravan.

Organs and instruments of locomotion; legs, feet, pegs, pins; arms; locomotive.

V. To travel, journey, ramble, roam, rove, course, wander, stroll, range, straggle, expatiate, gad about; to go or take a walk, journey, tour, turn, trip, &c.; to prowl, stray, saunter, make a tour, emigrate, flit, migrate.

To walk, march, step, tread, pace, wend, wend one's way, promenade, perambulate, circumambulate, take a walk, take the air, trudge, stalk, stride, strut, tramp, traverse, bend one's steps, thread one's way, make one's way, find one's way, take a course.

Ride, jog on, trot, amble, canter, gallop, take horse, prance, frisk.

To drive, slide, glide, skim, skate.

To go to, repair to, resort to, hie to.

To march in procession, to file off, defile.

Adj. Travelling, &c., ambulatory, itinerant, peripatetic, discursive, migratory, nomadic, on the wing, &c.

267. Locomotion by water or air.

NAVIGATION, voyage, sail, cruise, boating, circumnavigation.

Natation, swimming, drifting.

Flight, volitation, aeronautics, aerostatics, balloonry.

Wing, pinion, fin; oar, sail, paddle, screw.

V. To sail, make sale, put to sea, navigate, take ship, get under way, spread sail, spread canvas, carry sail, plough the waves, plough the deep, scud, boom, drift, course, cruise, coast, circumnavigate.

To row, paddle, scull.

To swim, float, buffet the waves, skim, dive, wade.

To fly, be wafted, hover, soar.

Adj. Sailing, &c., seafaring, nautical, volant, aerostatic.

Adv. Under way, under sail, on the wing.

---

268. TRAVELLER, wayfarer, voyager, itinerant, passenger, tourist, wanderer, rover, straggler, rambler, bird of passage, vagrant, vagabond, nomad, pilgrim, palmer,

269. MARINER, navigator, seaman, sailor, seafarer, shipman, tar, bluejacket, marine, jolly, boatman, ferryman, midshipman, &c.

runner, courier, pedestrian, peripatetic, emigrant, fugitive.

Rider, horseman, equestrian, cavalier, jockey, postilion.

An aerial navigator, aeronaut balloonist.

---

270. Transferrence, displacement, transposition, 148, removal, 185, relegation, deportation, extradition, conveyance, carriage, carrying.

Transmission, passage, transit, ferry, transport, portage, porterage, cartage, carting, shipment, freight, transportation, transplantation, translation, shifting, dispersion, 73, traction, 285.

V. To transfer, convey, transmit, transport, carry, bear, carry over, pass, remove, &c., 185, transpose, shift, convey, conduct, convoy, send, relegate, turn over to, deliver, waft, ship, embark, ferry over.

To bring, fetch, reach, draft.

To load, lade, ship, charge.

To unload, (unlade,) decant, empty.

Adj. Transferred, &c., movable, portable, portative.

271. Carrier, porter, bearer, conveyor, conductor.

Beast of burden, cattle, horse, steed, nag, palfry, galloway, charger, courser, racer, racehorse, pony, colt, roan, jade, hack, packhorse, drafthorse, carthorse, posthorse, bayard, mare, stallion, gelding, stud.

Pegasus, Bucephalus, Rozinante.

Ass, donkey, jackass, mule, sumpter mule.

Camel, dromedary, lama, elephant; carrier pigeon.

272. Vehicle, conveyance.

Carriage, wagon, baggage wagon, cariole, wain, dray, cart, sledge, sled, truck, tumbrel, barrow, wheelbarrow, hand barrow.

Equipage, turnout, carriage, coach, chariot, chaise, phaeton, curricle, post chaise, diligence, stage, stage coach, car, omnibus, gig, cabriolet, cab, calash, buggy, tandem, sedan chair, palanquin, litter, velocipede.

Shovel, spoon, spatula, ladle, hod.

---

273. Ship, vessel, shipping, marine, craft, bottom.

Navy, fleet, flotilla, squadron, armada.

Man-of-war, ship of the line or line-of-battle-ship, first rate, flag ship, frigate, sloop of war, transport, fire ship, bomb vessel, store ship, tender.

Ship, bark, brig, brigantine, schooner, sloop, cutter, corvette, clipper, skiff, yawl, smack, lugger, barge, lighter. Sailer, steamer, steamboat, (steamship,) tug.

Merchant ship, merchantman, packet, whaler, slaver, collier, coaster, lighter.

Boat, longboat, pinnace, launch, shallop, jollyboat, flyboat, wherry, cockboat, fishing boat, lifeboat, gondola, felucca, canoe, float, raft.

Galley, brigantine, galleon, galliot, junk.

Balloon, air balloon aerostat, pilot balloon, kite.

Adv. Afloat, aboard

2. Degrees of Motion.

274. Velocity, speed, celerity, swiftness, rapidity, fleetness, expedition, speediness, quickness, nimbleness, briskness, agility, promptness, promptitude, despatch, acceleration.

Haste, precipitation, posthaste, hurry scurry, precipitancy, &c., 684, forced march, race.

Rate, pace, step, gait, course, progress.

Gallop, canter, trot, run, rush, scamper, amble; flight, dart, bolt, flying, &c.

Lightning, light, rocket, arrow, dart, telegraph, express train.

An eagle, antelope, courser, racehorse, gazelle, greyhound, hare, squirrel.

V. To move quickly; to trip, speed, haste, hie, hasten, press, press on, press forward, post, push on, scamper, run, scud, scour, shoot, tear, whisk, sweep, skim, brush, glance, cut along, dash on, dash forwards, trot, gallop, amble, troll, rush, bound, bolt, flit, spring, dart, boom.

To haste, hurry, scramble, hasten, accelerate, expedite, urge, whip forward, hurry, precipitate, quicken pace, ride hard.

To keep up with, keep pace with, outrun, outstrip, gain ground.

Adj. Fast, speedy, swift, rapid, full drive, quick, fleet, nimble, agile, expeditious, prompt, brisk, frisky, hasty, hurried, flying, &c., lightfooted, nimble footed, winged, electric, telegraphic.

Adv. Swiftly, with speed, speedily, trippingly, &c., apace, posthaste, by express, by telegraph, headlong.

275. Slowness, tardiness, dilatoriness, slackness, languor, drawl, *see* Inactivity, 683.

Retardation, slackening.

Hobbling, creeping, lounging, &c., claudication, halting, jog trot, dog trot, mincing steps.

A slow goer, lingerer, slow coach, drone, tortoise, snail, slug.

V. To move slowly, to creep, crawl, lag, drawl, dawdle, linger, loiter, plod, trudge, flag, saunter, lounge, lumber, trail, grovel, glide, steal along, jog on, rub on, halt, hobble, limp, shamble, mince, falter, totter, stagger.

To retard, slacken, relax, check, rein in, curb, strike sail, reef.

Adj. Slow, slack, tardy, dilatory, easy, lazy, languid, drowsy, sleepy, heavy, drawling, sluggish, snail-like, creeping, crawling, &c., lumbering, hobbling.

Adv. Slowly, &c., gingerly, softly, gently, leisurely, deliberately, gradually, &c., 144, lamely, &c.; at a foot's pace; at a snail's pace.

---

3. Motion conjoined with Force.

276. Impulse, momentum, impetus, push, impulsion, thrust, shove, jog, jolt, brunt, booming, throw; volley, explosion, 173.

Percussion, collision, concus-

277. Recoil, retroaction, revulsion, reaction, rebound, repercussion, rebuff, reverberation, reflux, springing back, &c.

A spring, &c., *see* Elasticity, 325

sion, clash, encounter, appulsē, shock, bump.

Blow, stroke, knock, pat, rap, hit, thump, pelt, kick, lunge, calcitration, recalcitration, beating, 972.

Hammer, mallet, flail, cudgel, bludgeon, cane, stick, club, &c., ram, battering ram, catapult, balistes, rammer, sledge hammer.

Propulsion, 284; Science of mechanic forces, Dynamics.

V. To impel, push, give impetus, &c., drive, urge, thrust, elbow, shoulder, jostle, justle, hustle, jolt, encounter, clash, fall foul of.

To strike, knock, tap, pat, smite, butt against, impinge, thump, beat, batter, pelt, patter, drub, buffet, belabor, whip, &c., *see* 972, lunge, kick, calcitrate, recalcitrate.

To throw, &c., *see* Propel, 284, to shy.

Adj. Impelling, &c., impulsive, impellent, impelled, &c., booming.

V. To recoil, react, spring back, fly back, bound back, rebound, reverberate, repercuss.

Adj. Recoiling, &c., on the recoil, &c., refluent, repercussive.

---

4. Motion with Reference to Direction.

278. Direction, bearing, course, bent, inclination, drift, tenor, tendency, incidence, set, leaning, bending, trending, dip, steerage, tack, steering, aim.

A line, path, road, aim, range, quarter, point of the compass, 236, 237, rhomb, azimuth.

V. To tend towards, go to, point to or at; trend, verge, incline, dip, conduct to.

To make for or towards, aim at, take aim, level at, steer for, keep or hold a course, be bound for, bend one's steps towards, direct one's course.

Adj. Directed, &c., direct, straight, undeviating.

Adv. Towards, to, thither, directly, straight, straightforwards, 628, point blank, before the wind, near the wind, close to the wind, whither, in a line with.

279. Deviation, swerving, aberration, bending, refraction, sweep, sideling, straying, straggling, warping, &c., digression, circuit, departure from, divergence, 291, desultory motion.

Motion sidewise, sidling.

V. To alter one's course, deviate, depart from, turn, bend, curve, 311, swerve, shift, warp, stray, straggle, sidle, diverge, 291, digress, wander, meander, veer, tack, turn aside, turn a corner, turn away from, face about, wheel, wheel about, steer clear of, ramble, rove, go astray, step aside.

Adj. Deviating, &c., aberrant, discursive, devious, desultory, erratic, vagrant, undirected, circuitous, crab-like.

Adv. Astray from.

280. Going before.

Precession, leading, heading.

Precedence in order, 62.

281. Going after.

Sequence, following, pursuit chase, hunt.

V. To precede, lead, go ahead, to go in the van, take the lead.

Adj. Preceding, leading, &c.

Adv. In advance; before, in the van, ahead, 62.

A follower, pursuer, attendant, satellite, shadow.

Sequence in order, *see* 63.

V. To follow, pursue, chase, hunt, go after, to fly after, to go in the rear or in the wake of, tread in the steps of, tread on the heels of, to follow as a shadow, to lag behind.

Adj. Following, &c.

Adv. Behind, in the rear, &c., *see* 63, in the wake of, on the heels of.

282. Motion forwards.

PROGRESSION, advance, progress, progressiveness, progressive motion, floodtide, headway, advancing, &c., pursuit, *see* 622.

V. To advance, proceed, progress; go, move, bend or pass forwards; go on, pass on, get on, push on, go one's way, go ahead, make head, make way, make headway, work one's way, press forward, get over the ground, gain ground, make progress, keep or hold on one's course, keep up with, get forward, distance.

Adj. Advancing, &c., progressive, profluent, undeviating, unbending.

Adv. Forward, onward, forth, on, in advance, ahead, under way, straight forwards.

283. Motion backwards.

REGRESSION, regress, (retrocession,) retrogression, retrogradation, crab-like motion, refluence, reflux, return, ebb, tergiversation, countermotion, countermarch, veering, regurgitation.

V. To recede, retrograde, return, rebound, fall back, fall or drop astern, lose ground, put about, go back, turn back, double, wheel, countermarch, draw back, get back, regurgitate.

Adj. Receding, &c., retrograde, retrogressive, regressive, refluent, reflex, crab-like.

Adv. Backwards, reflexively, to the right about.

284. Motion given to an object situated in front.

PROPULSION, push, pushing, projection, jaculation, throw, fling, toss, shot, discharge.

Things thrown; a missile, projectile, shot, ball, bolt, dart, arrow, bullet, stone, shaft, brickbat.

Bow, sling, catapult, &c., 727.

V. To propel, project, throw, fling, cast, pitch, toss, jerk, lance, tilt, ejaculate, hurl, bolt, drive, sling, dart, send, roll, send off, let off, discharge, fire off, shoot, launch, let fly.

Bowl, trundle, roll along, 312.

To put in motion, start, give an impulse, impel, 276, expel, 296.

Adj. Propelling, &c., propulsive, projectile, &c.

285. Motion given to an object situated behind.

TRACTION, drawing, draught, pull, pulling.

V. To draw, pull, haul, lug, drag, tug, tow, trail, train, wrench, jerk, twitch; to take in tow.

Adj. Drawing, &c., tractile.

---

286. Motion towards.

APPROACH, approximation, appropinquation, appulse, afflux, affluxion, pursuit, 622, collision, 276.

V. To approach, draw near, approximate, to near, drift, come, get, go, draw near, &c., to set in towards, make up to, gain upon.

Adj. Approaching, &c., approximative.

287 Motion from.

RECESSION, retirement, withdrawal, retreat, retrocession, *see* 283, departure, 293, recoil, 277, decampment, flight.

A runaway, a fugitive.

V. To recede, go, move or fly from, retire, retreat, withdraw, come away, go or get away, draw back, shrink, move away.

To move off, stand off, fall back, march off, decamp, sheer off, bolt, slip away, run away, pack off, fly, remove, abscond, sneak off slink away.

Adj. Receding, &c., fugitive, run away, 671.

288. Motion towards, actively.

ATTRACTION, drawing to, pulling towards, adduction, attractiveness.

A loadstone, magnet.

V. To attract, draw, pull, drag, &c., towards, adduce.

Adj. Attracting, &c., attrahent, adductive, attractive.

289. Motion from, actively.

REPULSION, (repellency,) push, driving from, repulse, abduction, *see* Impulse, 276.

V. To repel, push, drive, &c., from, (carry off,) abduct.

Adj. Repelling, &c., repellent, repulsive, abducent, abductive.

Int. Begone! be off! &c., 293.

290. Motion nearer to.

CONVERGENCE, appulse, meeting, confluence, concourse, conflux, congress, concurrence, concentration.

Resort, assemblage, 72, focus, 74.

V. To converge, come together, unite, meet, fall in with, close in upon, close with, centre in, enter in, to meet, come across.

To gather together, unite, concentrate, &c.

Adj. Converging, &c., convergent, confluent, concurring, concurrent, centripetal.

291. Motion farther off.

DIVERGENCE, aberration, divarication, radiation, separation, 44, dispersion, diffusion, dissemination, 73.

Oblique motion, sidling, deviation, 279.

V. To diverge, divaricate, wander, radiate, branch off, file off, draw aside.

To spread, disperse, scatter, distribute, diffuse, disseminate, shed, sow broadcast, sprinkle.

To sidle, swerve, heel.

To part, part company, turn away from, wander from.

Adj. Diverging, &c., divergent, radiant, wandering, aberring, aberrant, centrifugal.

Adv. Broadcast.

292. Terminal motion at.

ARRIVAL, advent, reception, welcome, return.

Home, goal, resting-place, des-

293. Initial motion from.

DEPARTURE, outset, removal, exit, exodus, decampment, embarkation, flight.

tination, harbor haven, port, landing-place.

Meeting, rencounter, encounter.

V. To arrive, get to, come, come to, reach, attain, come up with, come up to, make, fetch, overtake.

To light, alight, dismount, land, disembark, debark, put in, put into, visit, cast anchor.

To come upon, light upon, pitch upon, hit, drop in, close with.

To come back, return.

To meet, encounter, rencounter, come in contact, 199.

Adj. Arriving, &c., here, hither.

294. Motion into.

Ingress, entrance, entry, introgression, admission, admittance, intromission, introduction, insinuation, insertion, 300, intrusion, inroad, incursion, influx, irruption, invasion, penetration, interpenetration, infiltration, import, importation, immigration.

A mouth, door, &c., *see* Opening, 260.

V. To enter, go into, come into, set foot in, intrude, break in, invade, flow into, insinuate itself, penetrate, interpenetrate, infiltrate, to put into, &c., bring in, insert, drive in, run in, wedge in, 300, intromit, introduce, import, smuggle.

Valediction, adieu, farewell.

A starting point or post, place of departure or embarkation.

V. To depart, go, set out, set off, start, start off, issue, go forth, sally, sally forth, set forward, be off, move off, pack off, begone get off, sheer off.

To leave a place, quit, retire withdraw, go one's way, take wing, take flight, flit, embark, go on board, set sail, put to sea, weigh anchor, slip cable, decamp 671.

Adj. Departing, &c., valedictory.

Adv. Whence, hence, thence.

295. Motion out of.

Egress, exit, issue, emersion, emergence.

Exudation, 348, leakage, percolation, distillation, oozing, effluence, efflux, effusion, drain dropping, dripping, filtering, defluxion, gush, trickling, eruption.

Export, expatriation, emigration.

An outlet, vent, spout, flue, chimney, pore, drain, sewer, 350.

V. To emerge, emanate, issue, go, come, move, pass, pour, flow, &c., out of, pass off.

To transude, (exude,) leak, percolate, strain, distil, drain, ooze, filter, filtrate, dribble, trickle, drizzle, drip, gush, spout, run, flow out, effuse, disembogue, 348.

296. Motion into, actively.

Reception, admission, importation, immission, absorption, ingurgitation, inhalation; *see* Insertion, 300

Eating, swallowing, deglutition, devouring, gorging.

Drinking, potation, sipping, suction, sucking, draught, libation.

Mastication. manducation,

297. Motion out of, actively.

Ejection, emission, effusion rejection, expulsion, detrusion, extrusion.

Discharge, ejection, evacuation.

Deportation, exile, banishment, relegation, extradition.

V. To be let out, &c., to ooze, percolate, fall out, to emit, eject, expel, reject, discharge, give out, let out, cast out, clear out, sweep

V. To admit, receive intromit, import, absorb, imbibe, inhale, let in, take in, readmit, resorb, reabsorb, snuff up, suck in, swallow, ingurgitate, ingulf.

To eat, fare, feed, devour, lay in, gorge, engorge, fall to, stuff, cram, eat heartily, do justice to, gormandize, 957.

To feed upon, live on, feast upon, carouse, batten upon, fatten upon, dine, &c., browse, graze, crop, chew, champ, gnaw, nibble, masticate.

To drink, quaff, sip, lap, drain the cup, tipple, 959.

Adj Admitting, &c., admitted, &c., admissible; omnivorous.

out, clean out, turn out, drive out, root out, pour out, shed, void, evacuate, disgorge, empty, drain, extrude, detrude, throw off, spit, spill.

To vomit, spew, puke, cast up, eructate, belch, give vent to, tap, open the sluices, heave out, bale out, shake off.

To unpack, unlade, unload, 270.

To banish, exile, deport.

Adj. Emitting, &c., emitted, &c.

---

298. FOOD, pabulum, aliment, nourishment, nutriment, sustenance, nurture, subsistence, provender, provision, prey, forage, pasture, pasturage, fare, cheer, diet, regimen.

Comestibles, eatables, victuals, meat, bread, breadstuffs, viands, delicacy, creature comforts, contents of the larder, pottage, pudding, ragout.

Table, board, commons, good cheer, bill of fare, commissariat, ordinary.

Meal, repast, mess, dish, plate, course, regale, regalement, refreshment, refection, picnic, entertainment, feast, banquet; breakfast, luncheon, lunch, dinner, supper, dessert.

Drink, beverage, liquor, broth, soups, &c.

Adj. Eatable, edible, esculent, alimentary, cereal, culinary, nutritive, succulent, potable.

299. EXCRETION, emanation, exhalation, exudation, secretion, evacuation. fæces, excrement, 653, prespiration, &c., discharge.

V. To emanate, exhale, excrete, exude, effuse, secrete, evacuate, discharge, &c., 297.

---

300. Forcible ingress.

INSERTION, putting in, implantation, introduction, interjection, insinuation, planting, intercalation, injection, inoculation, importation, intervention, 228, dovetailing, wedge.

Immersion, dip, plunge, bath, submersion, duck, soak.

Interment, burying, burial, &c., 363.

V. To insert, introduce, put into, import, throw in, interlard, in-

301. Forcible egress.

EXTRACTION, taking out, removal, elimination, extrication, evulsion, avulsion, wrench.

Expression, squeezing.

V. To extract, take out, draw, draw out, pull out, tear out, pluck out, wring from, wrench, rake up, grub up, root up, dredge, remove, get out, 185, educe, elicit, extricate, eliminate.

To express, squeeze out.

Adj. Extracted, &c.

-ect, interject, intercalate, infuse, instil, inoculate, impregnate, imbue, imbrue, graft, ingraft, bud, plant, implant, obtrude, worm in, thrust in, let in, dovetail, mortise, insinuate, wedge in, press in, impact, drive in, run in, 260.

To immerse, dip, steep, immerge, merge, submerge, bathe, plunge, drop in, soak, duck.

To inter, bury, &c., 363.

Adj. Inserting, inserted, &c.

302. Motion through.

PASSAGE, transmission, permeation, penetration, interpenetration, infiltration, 294.

Terebration, impalement, &c., 260.

V. To pass, pass through, traverse, perforate, &c., *see* 260; pierce, impale, spear, spike, penetrate, permeate, thread, enfilade, go through, go across, go over, pass over, cut across, pass and repass, work, thread or worm one's way, force a passage.

Adj. Passing, intercurrent, &c.

303. Motion beyond.

TRANSCURSION, transilience, transgression, trespass, encroachment, infringement, transcendence.

V. To transgress, overstep, surpass, overpass, overgo, outgo, outstep, outrun, overleap, outleap, pass, go by, strain, overshoot the mark, overlap, go beyond, transcend, encroach, exceed, trespass, infringe, trench upon.

304. Motion short of.

SHORTCOMING, failure, falling, short, 732, defalcation, leeway, incompleteness, 53.

V. To fall short of, not to reach, keep within bounds, keep within compass; to stop short.

Adj. Unreached, deficient, 53, short, minus.

Adv. Within the mark, within compass, within bounds, &c., behindhand.

305. Motion upwards.

ASCENT, rise, ascension, upgrowth, leap, 309.

A rocket, skyrocket, lark, skylark.

V. To ascend, rise, mount, arise, uprise, go up, get up, climb, clamber, scale, scramble, escalade, surmount, aspire, override, overreach, start up.

To tower, soar, hover, swim, float, surge.

To leap, jump, hop, skip vault, bound, dance, bob, curvet, romp, caracole, caper.

Adj. Rising, &c., buoyant, floating, supernatant, leaping, &c., saltatory, frisky, rampant.

Adv. Uphill.

306. Motion downwards.

DESCENT, fall, descension, declension, declination, drop, cadence, subsidence, lapse, downfall, tumble, slip, tilt, toppling, trip, lurch.

Titubation, shambling, stumble.

V. To descend, go down, fall, sink, drop, drop down, droop, come down, dismount, alight, settle, slide, slip.

To stoop, bend, bow, courtesy, bob, bend the head or knee, dip, crouch, cower.

To recline, lie, lie down, sit, sit down, couch, squat.

To tumble, slip, trip, stumble, lurch, swag, topple, topple over, swoop, tilt, sprawl, plump down.

To alight, dismount, get down.

Adj. Descending, &c., descendent.

307. Elevation, raising, lifting, erection, lift, sublevation, sublimation.

V. To elevate, raise, lift, uplift, upraise, set up, erect, stick up, rear, uprear, upbear, upcast, hoist, uphoist, heave, upheave, weigh, exalt, sublimate.

To drag up, fish up, dredge.

Adj. Elevated, &c.

308. Depression, lowering abasement, detrusion, reduction

Overthrow, upset, prostration, subversion, overset, overturn, precipitation.

V. To depress, lower, let down, let fall, sink, debase, abase, reduce, detrude, cast down.

Overthrow, overturn, upset, overset, subvert, prostrate, level, fell; cast, take, throw, fling, dash, pull, cut, knock, hew, &c., down.

Adj. Depressed, sunk, prostrate, &c.

309. Leap, jump, hop, spring, bound, vault, saltation.

Dance, caper, curvet, caracole.

310. Plunge, dip, dive, ducking.

V. To plunge, dip, duck, dive.

To submerge, submerse, sink, ingulf.

---

311. Curvilinear motion.

Circuition, turn, wind, circuit, curvet, excursion, circumvention, circumnavigation, circulation.

Turning, winding, twist, twisting, wrench, evolution, twining, coil, circumambulation, meandering.

V. To turn, bend, wheel, put about, go round, or round about, to turn or round a corner, double a point, wind, whisk, twirl, twist.

Adj. Turning, &c., circuitous.

Adv. Round about.

312. Motion in a continued circle.

Rotation, revolution, gyration, roll, circumrotation, circumgyration, volutation, circumvolution, convolution, whirl, eddy, vortex, whirlpool, gurge, a dizzy round; Maelstrom, Charybdis.

A wheel, screw, whirligig, rolling stone, windmill; top.

313. Motion in a reverse circle

Evolution, unfolding, &c., development, introversion, reversion; eversion, 218.

V. To evolve, unfold, unroll, unwind, uncoil, untwist, unfurl, develop, introvert, reverse.

Adj. Evolving, &c., evolved, &c.

Axis, spindle, pivot, pin, hinge, pole, swivel.

V. To rotate, roll, revolve, spin, turn, turn round, circumvolve, circulate, gyrate, wheel, whirl, twirl, trundle, troll, roll up, furl, wallow, welter.

Adj. Rotating, &c., rotatory, rotary, vertiginous, gyratory.

314. Reciprocating motion, motion to and fro.

Oscillation, vibration, undulation, pulsation, libration, nutation, swing, beat, shake, wag, seesaw, going and coming.

Fluctuation, vacillation, dance, lurch, rolling, pitching, tossing &c

V. To oscillate, vibrate, undulate, librate, wave, rock, swing, pulsate, beat, wag, nod, tick, play, dangle.

To fluctuate, vacillate, dance, curvet, reel, quake, roll, pitch, flounder, stagger, totter, brandish, shake, flourish; to move up and down, to and fro, backwards and forwards; to pass and repass.

Adj. Oscillating, &c., oscillatory, vibratory, undulatory, pulsatory libratory, pendulous.

Adv. To and fro, up and down, backwards and forwards, seesaw zigzag.

315. Irregular motion.

AGITATION, stir, tremor, shake, ripple, jog, jolt, jar, trepidation, quiver, dance, restlessness, flicker, flutter.

Disturbance, perturbation, commotion, turmoil, turbulence, tumult, tumultuation, jerk, throe, convulsion, staggers, epilepsy, writhing, ferment, fermentation, effervescence, hurly burly.

V. To be agitated, to shake, tremble, quiver, quaver, shiver, writhe, toss about, tumble, stagger, reel, wag, dance, wriggle, stumble, flounder, shuffle, totter, flounce, curvet, prance, throb, pulsate, beat, palpitate, flutter, flitter, flicker.

To agitate, shake, toss, tumble, bandy, wield, brandish, flap, flourish, whisk, jerk, hitch, jolt, jostle, disturb, shake up, churn, ferment, effervesce, boil.

Adj. Shaking, &c., agitated, tremulous, desultory, shambling, saltatory.

CLASS III.

WORDS RELATING TO MATTER.

SECTION I. MATTER IN GENERAL.

316. MATERIALITY, corporeity, corporality, materialness, substantiality, physical condition.

Matter, body, substance, brute matter, stuff, element, principle, material, substratum, frame.

Science of matter; Physics, Somatology, Somatics, Natural Philosophy, Physical Science, Experimental Philosophy, Materialism.

317. IMMATERIALITY, spirituality, spirit, &c., 450, immaterialness.

Personality, spiritualism.

V. To disimbody.

Adj. Immaterial, incorporeal immateriate, unextended, incorporal, unbodied, disimbodied, spiritual, extramundane, unearthly; spiritualist.

Personal, subjective.

Adj. Material, bodily, corporeal or corporal, physical, sensible, tangible, ponderable; objective, materialistic.

318. World, nature, universe; earth, globe; the wide world, sphere, macrocosm.

The heavens, sky, welkin, empyrean, starry heaven, firmament; the vault or canopy of heaven; the celestial spaces, the starry host, the heavenly bodies, stars, asteroids, constellations, galaxy, milky way, nebulæ, &c. Sun, planets, satellites.

Science of the heavenly bodies: Astronomy, Uranography, Cosmography, Cosmogony; orrery.

An astronomer, stargazer.

Adj. Cosmical, mundane, terrestrial, terraqueous, terrene, sublunary, under the sun.

Celestial, heavenly, starry, stellar, nebular, &c., sidereal, astral.

319. Gravity, weight, heaviness, gravitation, ponderosity, ponderousness, pressure, load, burden, ballast, a lump, mass.

Science of gravity, Statics.

V. To be heavy, to gravitate, weigh, press, cumber, load.

Adj. Weighty, heavy, ponderous, gravitating, weighing, &c., ponderable, cumbersome, massive, unwieldy, incumbent, superincumbent.

320. Levity, lightness, imponderability, buoyancy, airiness, portableness.

A feather, dust, mote, down, thistledown, flue, cobweb, gossamer, straw, cork, bubble; a float, buoy.

V. To be light, to float, swim, be buoyed up.

Adj. Light, subtile, airy, imponderable, etherial, sublimated, floating, swimming, buoyant, portable.

Section II. INORGANIC MATTER.

1. Solid Matter.

321. Density, solidity, solidness, impenetrability, incompressibility, cohesion, coherence, cohesiveness, 46, imporosity, impermeability, closeness, compactness, constipation, consistence, spissitude, thickness.

Specific gravity; hydrometer, areometer.

Condensation, consolidation, solidification, concretion, coagulation, petrifaction, lapidification, lapidescence, vitrification, crystallization, precipitation, inspissation, thickening.

Indivisibility, indiscerptibility, indissolvableness.

322. Rarity, tenuity, absence of solidity, subtility, sponginess, (porosity,) compressibility; hollowness, 252.

Rarefaction, expansion, dilatation, inflation, subtillization.

Ether, vapor, air, gas, 334.

V. To rarefy, expand, dilate, subtillize.

Adj. Rare, subtile, thin, fine, compressible.

Porous, cavernous, spongy.

Rarefied, expanded, dilated, subtillized, unsubstantial, uncompact, uncompressed; hollow, 252.

A solid body, mass, block, lump, concretion, cake, clot, stone, curd, coagulum.

V. To be dense, &c.

To become or render solid; solidify, concrete, consolidate, congeal, coagulate, curdle, curd, fix, clot, cake, cohere, crystallize, petrify, vitrify, condense, thicken, inspissate, compress, squeeze, constipate.

Adj. Dense, solid, solidified, consolidated, &c., coherent, cohesive, compact, close, thickset, substantial, massive, lumpish, impenetrable, incompressible, impermeable, imporous, constipated, concrete, crystalline, crystallizable, vitreous, coagulated, thick, incrassated, inspissated, curdled, clotted.

Undissolved, unmelted, unliquefied, unthawed.

Indivisible, indiscerptible, infrangible, indissolvable, indissoluble, insoluble.

323. Hardness, rigidity, firmness, inflexibility, stiffness, starchness, starchedness, temper, callosity, induration, grittiness, petrifaction, &c., 321, ossification.

A stone, pebble, flint, marble, rock, granite, iron, steel, adamant.

Tenseness, stretching, tension, 200.

V. To render hard, harden, stiffen, indurate, petrify, temper, ossify.

Adj. Hard, horny, corneous, rigid, stiff, firm, starch, unbending, unyielding, inflexible, tense, indurate, indurated, gritty, &c., proof, adamantean, adamantine.

324. Softness, tenderness, flexibility, pliancy, pliableness pliantness, pliability, suppleness, ductility, malleability, tractility, extensibility, plasticity.

Mollification, softening, &c.

V. To render soft, soften, mollify, relax, temper, mash, knead.

To bend, yield, relent, relax.

Adj. Soft, tender, supple, pliable, limber, flexible, flexile. lithe, pliant, plastic, ductile, tractile, tractable, malleable, extensile.

Yielding, bending, flabby, flocculent, downy, flimsy, spongy, argillaceous, mellow.

325. Elasticity, springiness, spring, resilience, contractility, 195, compressibility.

V. To be elastic, &c., to spring back, fly back, rebound, recoil, 277.

Adj. Elastic, tensile, springy, resilient, buoyant.

326. Inelasticity, want of absence of elasticity, *see* 324

327. Tenacity, toughness, strength, cohesion, 46, stubbornness.

V. To be tenacious, &c., to resist, fracture.

Adj. Tenacious, tough, stubborn, cohesive, strong, resisting.

328. Brittleness, fragility, crispness, friability, frangibility.

V. To be brittle, break, crack, snap, split, shiver, splinter, crumble, fly, break short.

Adj. Brittle, frangible, fragile, frail, shivery, fissile, (shaky,) splitting, splintery, crisp, crumbling.

---

329. Texture, structure, organization, anatomy, frame, mould, fabric, framework, architecture, substance, constitution, intertexture, contexture, tissue, grain, web, woof, nap, 256, fineness or coarseness of grain.

Adj. Textural, structural, organic, anatomical.

Fine, delicate, subtile.—Coarse, rough-grained.

Flimsy, unsubstantial, gossamery.

330. PULVERULENCE, state of powder, dust, sand, shingle, sawdust, grit, meal, bran, flour, limature, filings, flocculence, efflorescence, sandiness, friability.

Reduction to powder, pulverization, comminution, granulation, disintegration, contusion, trituration, levigation, abrasion, filing, &c., 331.

Instruments for pulverization; a mill, grater, rasp, file, pestle and mortar.

V. To reduce to powder, to pulverize, comminute, granulate, triturate, levigate, scrape, file, abrade, rub down, grind, grate, rasp, pound, bray, beat, crush, crumble, disintegrate.

Adj. Powdery, granular, mealy, floury, farinaceous, branny, flocculent, dusty, sandy, gritty, efflorescent, impalpable, pulverizable, pulverulent, friable, crumbly, shivery, pulverized, &c., attrite.

331. FRICTION, attrition, confrication, rubbing, abrasion, contrition, rub, &c., scouring, limature, filing, rasping.

V. To rub, abrade, &c., 330, scrape, fray, rasp, pare, scour, polish, rub out.

332. Absence of friction.

LUBRICATION, prevention of friction, oiling.

V. To lubricate, smooth, 255.

Adj. Lubricated, &c.

---

2. FLUID MATTER.

1. *Fluids in general.*

333. FLUIDITY, fluid, (including both inelastic and elastic fluids.)

Inelastic fluid.

LIQUIDITY, liquidness, a liquid, liquor, lymph, humor, juice, sap, serum, serosity. Solubility, solubleness.

Science of liquids at rest; Hydrology, Hydrostatics.

V. To be fluid or liquid, to flow, run, 348.

Adj. Liquid, fluid, serous, juicy, succulent, sappy, fluent, running.

Liquefied, uncongealed, melted, &c., 335.

334. Elastic fluid.

GASEOUSNESS, vaporousness, gas, air, vapor, ether, steam, fume, effluvium.

Smoke, cloud, 353.

Science of elastic fluids; Pneumatics, Aerostatics.

V. To emit vapor, *see* 336.

Adj. Gaseous, aeriform, ethereal, aerial, airy, vaporous, volatile, evaporable.

335. LIQUEFACTION fusion, melting, thaw.

Solution, dissolution, decoction, infusion, &c., liquescence.

336. VAPORIZATION, volatilization, vaporation, evaporation, distillation, sublimation, exhalation, volatility.

V. To render liquid, to liquefy, run, melt, thaw, fuse, solve, dissolve, resolve; to hold in solution.

Adj. Liquefied, &c., molten, liquescent, liquefiable, soluble.

V. To render gaseous, vaporize, volatilize, evaporate, exhale, smoke, fume, steam, distil, sublimate.

Adj. Volatilized, &c., volatile, evaporable.

2. *Specific Fluids.*

337 WATER, serum, lymph, rheum.

Dilution, immersion, maceration, humectation, infiltration, sprinkling, affusion, irrigation, balneation, bath, inundation, deluge, *see* 348, a diluent.

V. To be watery, &c., to reek.

To add water, to water, wet, moisten, 339, dilute, dip, immerse, plunge, merge, immerge, steep, duck, submerge, drown, soak, macerate, pickle, wash, sprinkle, affuse, splash, drench, slop, irrigate, inundate, deluge.

To syringe, inject.

Adj. Watery, aqueous, wet, aquatic, lymphatic, diluted, &c., reeking, dripping, soaking, washy, sloppy, diluent.

338. AIR, common air, atmospheric air.

The atmosphere, the sky, the open air, weather, climate.

Science of air; Aerology.

Exposure to the air or weather

Adj. Containing air, windy flatulent, effervescent.

Atmospheric, airy, aerial, aeriform.

---

339. MOISTURE, moistness, humidity, dampness, wetness, madefaction, dew, muddiness.

V. To be moist, &c.

To moisten, wet, damp, bedew, imbue, infiltrate, imbrue.

Adj. Moist, damp, watery, undried, humid, wet, dank, muggy, dewy, roral, (roriferous,) juicy; swampy.

340. DRYNESS, aridity, drought.

Exsiccation, desiccation, arefaction, drainage.

V. To be dry, &c.

To render dry, to dry, dry up, exsiccate, desiccate, drain, parch.

Adj. Dry, arid, dried, &c., undamped, husky, waterproof, juiceless, sapless.

341. OCEAN, sea, main, the deep, brine, salt water, tide, wave, surge, &c., 348.

Neptune, Thetis, Tritons, Naiads, &c., trident.

Adj. Oceanic, marine, maritime, pelagic.

Adv. At sea, on sea.

---

342. LAND, earth, ground, continent, oasis, mainland, peninsular, delta, isthmus, tongue of land

Cape, promontory, &c., 25[illegible], headland, point of land, highland. Coast, shore, seaboard, seaside, seabank, strand, beach, bank, lea.

Soil, glebe, clay, loam, marl, clod, rock, crag, &c., 206, mould, subsoil.

Adj. Terrene, earthy, continental.

Littoral, midland.

Adv. Ashore, on shore, on land.

343. Gulf, bay, inlet bight, estuary, arm of the sea, armlet, sound, frith, lagoon, cove, creek, strait.

Lake, loch, mere, tarn, pond, pool, puddle, well, standing water, dead water, a sheet of water; fishpond, ditch, dike, &c.

344. Plain, table land, (plateau,) open country, the face of the country, champaign country, basin, downs, waste, steppe, pampas, savanna, prairie, heath, common, moor, moorland.

Meadow, mead, pasturage, park, field, lawn, terrace, esplanade, sward, turf, sod, heather; lea, grounds, pleasure grounds.

Adj. Campestrian, alluvial, champaign.

345. Marsh, swamp, morass, fen, bog, quagmire, slough.

Adj. Marshy, swampy, boggy, paludal.

346. Island, isle, islet, reef, breaker.

Adj. Insular.

3. *Fluids in Motion.*

347. Fluid in motion.

Stream, flow, current, jet, undercurrent.

V. To flow, stream, issue.

348. Water in motion.

River, running water, jet, spirt, spout, splash, gush, waterspout, sluice, waterfall, fall, cascade, cataract, inundation.

Rain, shower, driving rain, drizzle, dripping, flux, flow, profluence, effluence, efflux, effluxion, effusion, defluxion.

Spring, fountain, rill, rivulet, streamlet, runnel, brook, stream, torrent, rapids, flood, tide, spring tide, high tide, freshet, current, eddy, gurge, whirlpool, regurgitation.

Confluence.

Wave, billow, surge, swell, ripple, ground swell, surf, breakers.

Science of fluids in motion; Hydrodynamics, Hydraulics.

V. To flow, run, gush, spout, roll, jet, well, drop, drip, trickle, ooze, 295, percolate, distil, transude, stream, sweat, perspire, overflow, flow over, splash, gurgle, spurt, regurgitate.

To rain, rain hard, pour with rain, drizzle, set in.

To flow into, fall into, open into, discharge itself, disembogue, disgorge, meander.

To cause a flow, to pour, drop, distil, splash, squirt, spill

349. Air in motion.

Wind, draught, breath, air breath of air, puff, zephyr, blow.

Gust, blast, breeze, squall, gale, storm, tempest, hurricane, whirlwind, tornado, simoom, monsoon, trade wind, sirocco, windiness.

Sufflation, blowing, fanning. ventilation, blowing up, inflation, afflation, sneezing, sternutation.

Bellows, fan, ventilator.

V. To blow, waft, blow hard, blow a hurricane.

To breathe, puff, whiffle, wheeze, snuffle, sneeze, cough.

To fan, ventilate, inflate, perflate, blow up.

Adj. Blowing, &c., windy breezy, gusty, squally, stormy tempestuous, blustering.

---

drain, empty, discharge, pour out, open the sluices or floodgates; shower down, 297.

To stop a flow, to stanch, dam, dam up, 261, intercept.

Adj. Fluent, profluent, affluent, tidal, flowing, &c., babbling, bubbling, purling, gurgling, meandering.

Fluvial, fluviatile, streamy, showery, rainy, pluvial.

350. Channel for the passage of water.

CONDUIT, channel, duct, watercourse, race, adit, aqueduct, canal, sluice, gully, moat, ditch, trough, gutter, drain, sewer, culvert, siphon, pipe, gullyhole, artery, pore, spout, ajutage, waste pipe.

Floodgate, dam, watergate, lock, valve.

351. Channel for the passage of air.

AIRPIPE, airtube, shaft, flue, chimney, vent, blowhole, nostril, throat, weasand, trachea, windpipe, spiracle, ventiduct.

---

3. IMPERFECT FLUIDS.

352. SEMILIQUIDITY, viscidity, ropiness, sliminess, gumminess, siziness, clamminess, mucosity, spissitude, lentor, thickness, crassitude.

Inspissation, thickening, incrassation.

Jelly, mucilage, gelatin, mucus, gum, albumen, size, milk, cream, soup, mud, slush.

V. To inspissate, thicken, incrassate, mash, squash, churn, beat up.

Adj. Semi-fluid, semi-liquid, milky, emulsive, creamy, curdy, thick, succulent.

Gelatinous, albuminous, gummy, mucilaginous, slimy, ropy, clammy, glutinous, 46, viscid, viscous, sticky, slabby, sizy.

353. Mixture of air and water.

BUBBLE, foam, froth, spume, lather, spray, surf, yeast, suds.

Cloud, vapor, fog, mist, haze, scud, nimbus, cumulus, &c.

Effervescence, foaming, mantling, fermentation, frothing, &c.

V. To bubble, boil, foam, froth, mantle, sparkle, gurgle, effervesce, ferment.

Adj. Bubbling, &c., frothy, nappy, effervescent, sparkling.

354. PULPINESS, pulp, paste, dough, curd, pap, jam, pudding, poultice.

Adj. Pappy, pasty, pulpy, grumous, doughy.

---

355. UNCTUOUSNESS, unctuosity, oiliness, greasiness, slipperiness, lubricity.

Lubrication, anointment.

V. To oil, grease, anoint, wax, lubricate.

Adj. Unctuous, oily, oleaginous, adipose, sebaceous, fat, fatty, greasy, waxy, soapy, saponaceous, pinguid.

356. OIL, fat, butter, cream, grease, tallow, suet, lard, dripping, blubber, pomatum, oleagine, soap, wax, spermaceti, ointment, unguent, liniment.

SECTION III. ORGANIC MATTER.

1. VITALITY.

1. *Vitality in general.*

357. ORGANIZATION, the organized world, organized nature, living nature, animated nature, living beings.

358. INORGANIZATION, the mineral world or kingdom, unorganized, inorganic, brute, or inanimate matter.

359. LIFE,* vitality, animation, the vital spark or flame; the breath of life.

Vivification, revivification.

The science of life; Physiology, the animal economy.

V. To be living, alive, &c., to live, breathe, respire, draw breath, to be born.

To come to life, to revive, to come to.

To bring, restore, or recall to life, to vivify, revive, revivify.

Adj. Living, alive, in life, above ground, breathing.

Vital, vivifying, vivified, Promethean.

---

360. DEATH, decease, dissolution, demise, departure, expiration, termination, close or extinction of life, existence, &c., mortality, fall, doom, fate, release, rest, loss, bereavement.

Last breath, last gasp, last agonies, the death rattle, dying breath, agonies of death, dying agonies.

V. To die, expire, breathe one's last, cease to live, depart this life, be no more, go off, drop off, lose one's life, drop down dead, resign, relinquish, or surrender one's life, drop or sink into the grave, close one's eyes.

Adj. Dead, lifeless, deceased, gone, departed, defunct, exanimate, inanimate, out of the world, mortuary.

Dying, expiring, in the agony of death, &c., going, life-ebbing, going off, life-failing.

361. Destruction of life, violent death.

KILLING, homicide, murder, assassination, blood, gore, bloodshed, slaughter, carnage, butchery, massacre.

Suicide, execution, *see* 972, deathblow.

Slaughter house, shambles.

A butcher, slayer, murderer, assassin, cutthroat, executioner *see* 975.

V. To kill, put to death, slay, murder, assassinate, slaughter butcher, immolate, massacre, take away life, make away with, despatch.

To strangle, throttle, choak, stifle, suffocate, smother, drown, hang, to commit suicide; to make away with one's self.

To cut down, sabre, cut to pieces, cut off, cut the throat, stab, shoot, behead, decapitate, execute, *see* 972.

Adj. Killing, &c., murderous, slaughterous, bloodstained.

Mortal, fatal, deadly, mortiferous, suicidal, 657.

* Including the life both of *plants* and *animals*.

362. Corpse, corse, carcass, bones, skeleton, carrion, relic, remains, ashes, earth, clay, mummy, food for worms.

Shade, ghost.

363. Interment, burial, sepulture, inhumation, obsequies, exequies, funeral, wake, pyre, funeral pile.

Funeral solemnity, knell, passing bell, tolling, dirge, requiem.

A shroud, graveclothes, winding sheet, pall, hearse, urn, coffin, bier.

Grave, pit, vault, sepulchre, sarcophagus, tomb, shrine, crypt, cenotaph, mausoleum, house of death, (the narrow house,) mortuary, cemetery, churchyard, graveyard, burial ground, burial-place, tumulus, catacomb, necropolis, ossuary, charnel house.

Exhumation, disinterment.

V. To inter, bury, lay in the grave, consign to the grave or tomb inhume, lay out.

To exhume, disinter.

Adj. Buried, &c., funereal, mortuary, sepulchral.

2. *Special Vitality.*

364. Animality, animal life, animation, breath, animalization.

366. Animal, the animal kingdom, fauna.

A beast, brute, creature; created being; creeping or living thing; dumb creature; the beasts of the field; fowls of the air; denizens of the deep; flock, fold, hord, flight.

Mammal, quadruped, bird, reptile, fish, mollusk, worm, insect, zoöphyte, animalcule, &c., menagerie, fossil remains.

Adj. Animal, zoölogical, piscatory, fishy, molluscous, vermicular, &c.

368. The science of animals: Zoölogy, Anatomy, Comparative Anatomy, Animal or Comparative Physiology.

370. The economy or management of animals:

Domestication, (training.)

V. To tame, domesticate, train, tend, &c.

365. Vegetability, vegetable life, vegetation.

367. Vegetable, plant, the vegetable kingdom, flora, herbage.

Tree, fruit tree, shrub, bush, creeper, herb, grass; a perennial, an annual, biennial, &c., an exotic.

Forest, wood, greenwood, bush, grove, copse, plantation, thicket, underwood, brushwood, jungle; clump of trees; garden, parterre.

Herbarium, herbal.

Adj. Vegetable, herbaceous, herbal, botanic, sylvan, woody, rural, verdant.

369. The science of plants: Botany, Vegetable Physiology,

371. The economy or management of plants:

Agriculture, cultivation, husbandry, farming, tillage, gardening, horticulture, vintage, &c., arboriculture, floriculture.

Vineyard, garden, bed, nursery, arboretum, hothouse, orchard, conservatory.

A husbandman, horticulturist, gardener, florist, agriculturist, farmer

Adj. Agricultural, agrarian, arable, pastoral, bucolic (agrestic.)

372. MANKIND; the human race or species; man, human nature (humankind,) humanity, mortality, flesh, generation.

The science of man: Anthropology, Ethnology, Ethnography.

Human being, person, individual, creature, fellow-creature mortal, body, somebody, one, some one, a soul, living soul; party personage; inhabitant, *see* 188.

People, persons, population, the public, society, the world, community, nation, state, realm, commonwealth, republic, common weal, nationality.

Adj. Human, mortal, personal, individual, cosmopolitan; national, civic, public, social.

373. MAN, manhood, virility.

A gentleman, sir, master, yeoman, citizen, cit, denizen, burgess, cosmopolite, wight, swain, fellow, blade.

Adj. Male, masculine, manly, virile.

374. WOMAN, female, feminality, womanhood, muliebrity.

Womankind, the sex, the fair, the fair sex, the softer (or gentler) sex.

Dame, madam, mistress, lady. belle, matron, dowager.

Damsel, girl, lass, lassie, maid, maiden, (young lady,) nymph.

Adj. Female, feminine, womanly, ladylike, matronly. maidenly, girlish.

2. SENSATION.

(1.) *Sensation in general.*

375. PHYSICAL SENSIBILITY, sensitiveness, feeling, perceptivity, acuteness, &c.

Sensation, impression, consciousness, 490.

The external senses, sensation.

V. To be sensible of, to feel, perceive, be conscious of.

To render sensible, to sharpen.

To cause sensation, to impress, excite, produce an impression.

Adj. Sensible, conscious, sensitive, sensuous, æsthetic, perceptive.

Acute, keen, vivid, lively, impressive.

376. PHYSICAL INSENSIBILITY, obtuseness, dulness, apathy, callousness, 823, paralysis.

V. To be insensible, &c.

To render insensible, to blunt, dull, benumb, paralyze.

Adj. Insensible, unfeeling, senseless, apathetic, callous, obtuse, dull, paralytic, &c., unaffected, untouched, &c.

377. PHYSICAL PLEASURE, bodily enjoyment, animal gratification, luxury, sensuality, voluptuousness.

V To feel, experience, receive,

378. PHYSICAL PAIN, bodily pain, suffering, sufferance, dolor, ache, aching, smart, smarting, shooting pain, twinge, twitch, gripe, griping, headache, &c.

&c., pleasure; to enjoy, relish, luxuriate, revel, riot, bask, wallow in.

To cause or give physical pleasure, to gratify, tickle, regale, &c., *see* 829.

Adj. Enjoying, &c.

Spasm, cramp, nightmare, crick, convulsion, throe.

Pang, anguish, agony, torment, torture, rack, cruciation, crucifixion, martyrdom.

V. To feel, experience, suffer, &c., pain; to suffer, ache, smart, bleed, tingle, gripe, shoot, twinge, wince, writhe.

To give pain; to pain, hurt, chafe, sting, bite, gnaw, pinch, grate, gall, fret, prick, pierce, &c., wring, torment, torture, rack, agonize, excruciate, break on the wheel, &c., convulse

Adj. In pain, in a state of pain, &c., pained, &c.

Painful, aching, &c., sore, raw, agonizing, excruciating, &c

(2.) *Special Sensation.*

1. *Touch.*

379. Sensation of pressure.

Touch, tact, taction, tactility, feeling, palpation, manipulation palpability.

V. To touch, feel, handle, finger, thumb, fumble, pass or run the fingers over, manipulate.

Adj. Tactual, tangible, palpable, tactile.

380. Perceptions of Touch.

Itching, titillation, formication, &c., creeping, tingling, thrilling.

V. To itch, tingle, creep, thrill; to tickle, titillate,

Adj. Itching, &c

381. Insensibility to touch.

Numbness, deadness.

V. To benumb, paralyze, to put under the influence of chloroform (or ether.)

Adj. Numb, benumbed, intangible, impalpable.

2. *Heat.*

382. Heat, (caloric,) temperature, warmth, calidity, incalescence, incandescence, (fervor, ardor,) glow, flush, fever, hectic.

Fire, spark, scintillation, flash, flame, blaze, bonfire, firework, wildfire, pyrotechny, ignition, 384.

Insolation, summer, dog days, tropical heat, sirocco, simoom.

V. To be hot, to glow, flush, sweat, swelter, bask, smoke, reek, stew, simmer, seethe, boil, burn, broil, blaze, smoulder; to be in a

383. Cold, frigidity, (frigidness,) coolness, gelidness, chilliness, freshness, inclemency.

Frost, ice, snow, sleet, hail, hailstone, rime, hoarfrost, icicle, iceberg, glazier, winter.

Incombustibility, incombustibleness.

Sensation of cold, (chill,) chilliness, shivering, shuddering, chattering of teeth, &c.

V. To be cold, &c., to shiver quake, shake, tremble, shudder quiver.

heat, in a glow, in a fever, in a blaze &c.

Adj Hot, warm mild, unfrozen, genial, tepid, lukewarm, blood (warm,) thermal, calorific, sunny, close, sultry, baking, boiling, broiling, torrid, tropical, canicular, glowing, piping, scalding, reeking, &c., on fire, afire, fervid, fervent, ardent, unquenched.

Igneous fiery, incandescent, red-hot, white-hot, incalescent, smoking, blazing.

Unextinguished, smouldering.

Adj. Cold, cool, chill, gelid, frigid, bleak, raw, inclement, bitter, biting, cutting, nipping, piercing, fresh, pinched, shivering, &c., aguish, frostbitten, frostnipped, frostbound, unthawed, unwarmed.

Icy, glacial, frosty, freezing, wintry, brumal, hibernal, boreal, arctic, hyemal, hyperboreal, ice bound.

384. Calefaction, increase of temperature, heating.

Melting, fusion, liquefaction, thaw, liquescence.

Burning, combustion, cremation, cautery, roasting, broiling, frying, torrefaction, scorification, branding, incineration, cineration, carbonization.

Boiling, coction, ebullition, simmering, scalding, decoction, smelting, incineration.

Ignition, inflammation, setting fire to, deflagration, arson, conflagration, (incendiarism.)

385. Refrigeration, infrigidation, reduction of temperature, cooling, freezing, congealing, congelation, conglaciation.

V. To cool, refrigerate, congeal, freeze, benumb, refresh, damp, slack, quench, put out, blow out, extinguish, starve, pinch, cut, pierce.

Adj. Cooled, frozen, benumbed. &c. frigorific.

Inflammability, combustibility. Incendiary.

V. To heat, warm, fire, set fire to, set on fire, kindle, enkindle, light, ignite.

To melt, thaw, fuse, liquefy.

To burn, inflame, roast, toast, broil, fry, singe, parch, scorch, brand, scorify, torrify, bake, cauterize, sear, char, calcine, incinerate, smelt, reduce to ashes.

To boil, stew, cook, seethe, scald, parboil, simmer.

To take fire, catch fire, kindle, light, ignite.

Adj. Combustible, heating, &c.

386. Furnace, stove, kiln, oven, bakehouse, hothouse, conservatory, focus, fireplace, grate, (range,) salamander, heater, warming pan, stew pan, boiler, caldron, kettle, chafing dish, gridiron, frying pan, sudatory.

387. Refrigeratory, icehouse, freezing mixture, cooler.

---

388. Fuel, firing, coal, charcoal, peat, firewood, fagot, combustible, tinder, touchwood, lucifer, brand, match, firebrand, incendiary. embers.

389. Thermometer pyrometer, calorimeter, thermoscope; (isothermal.)

3. *Taste.*

390. TASTE, flavor, gust, savor, sapor, twang, smack, aftertaste, sapidity.

Tasting, gustation, degustation.

Palate, tongue, tooth, stomach.

V. To taste, savor, smack, flavor.

Adj. Sapid, gustable, gustatory, saporific.

391. INSIPIDITY, tastelessness, insipidness, vapidness, mawkishness, mildness.

V. To be void of taste, to be tasteless, &c.

Adj. Insipid, tasteless, gustless, savorless, ingustible, mawkish, flat, vapid, mild; untasted.

392. PUNGENCY, strong taste, raciness, saltness, sharpness, roughness.

V. To be pungent, &c.

To render pungent, to season, spice, salt, pepper, pickle.

Adj. Pungent, high-flavored, sharp, piquent, racy, biting, mordant, spicy, seasoned, high-seasoned, hot, peppery.

Salt, saline, brackish.

393. CONDIMENT, salt, mustard, pepper, cayenne, curry, (catchup, sauce,) seasoning, spice.

394. SAVORINESS, palatableness, daintiness, delicacy, relish, zest.

A tidbit, dainty, delicacy, ambrosia, nectar.

V. To be savory, &c.

To render palatable, &c.

To relish, like.

Adj. Savory, well-tasted, palatable, nice, dainty, delectable, delicate, delicious, exquisite, rich, luscious, ambrosial.

395. UNSAVORINESS, unpalatableness, bitterness, acrimony, acritude, roughness, acerbity, gall and wormwood.

V. To be unpalatable, &c.

To sicken, disgust, nauseate, pall.

Adj. Unsavory, unpalatable, ill-flavored, bitter, acrid, acrimonious, rough.

Offensive, repulsive, nasty sickening, nauseous, nauseating, disgusting, loathsome, palling.

396. SWEETNESS, nectar, sugar, sirup, treacle, molasses, honey, manna, confection, conserve, jam, julep, sugar candy, plum, sugar plum, comfit, sweetmeat, nectar, honeysuckle.

V. To be sweet, &c.

To render sweet, to sweeten, candy, dulcify.

Adj. Sweet, saccharine, dulcet, candied, honeyed, luscious, nectarious.

397. SOURNESS, acid, acidity, tartness, crabbedness, hardness, roughness, the acetous fermentation.

Vinegar, verjuice, crab.

V. To be sour, &c., set the teeth on edge.

To render sour, turn sour, acidify, acidulate.

Adj. Sour, acid, acidulous, sourish, tart, crabbed, acetous, acetose, hard, rough.

4. *Odor.*

398. ODOR, smell, scent, effluvium, fume, exhalation, essence.

399. INODOROUSNESS, absence or want of smell.

The sense of smell, act of smelling.

V. To have an odor, to smell of, to exhale, to give out a smell, &c.

To smell, scent, snuff.

V. To be inodorous, &c.

Adj. Inodorous, scentless, wanting smell, inodorate.

Adj. Odorous, odoriferous, smelling, strong-scented, pungent.

Relating to the sense of smell; olfactory; quick-scented.

400. Fragrance, aroma, redolence, perfume.

Incense, musk, frankincense, ottar, bergamot, balm, scentbag, nosegay.

V. To perfume, scent, embalm.

Adj. Fragrant, aromatic, redolent, balmy, scented, sweet-smelling, sweet-scented, perfumed, muscadine.

401. Fetor, strong smell, stench, stink, mustiness, fustiness, rancidity, foulness, putrescence, putridity.

V. To smell, to stink.

Adj. Fetid, strong-smelling, noisome, offensive, rank, rancid, mouldy, musty, foul, frowzy, stinking, rotten, putrescent, putrid, putrefying, mephitic.

5. *Sound.*

(1.) Sound in general.

402. Sound, noise, strain, voice, 580, accent, twang, intonation, resonance; sonorousness, audibleness.

Science of Sound; Acoustics, Phonics, Phonetics, Phonology, Diacoustics.

V. To produce sound; to sound; make a noise; give out or emit sound, to resound.

Adj. Sonorous, sounding, sonorific, sonoriferous, resonant, audible.

403. Silence, stillness, quiet, peace, calm, hush, lull; muteness, 581.

V. To be silent, &c.

To render silent, to silence, still, hush, stifle, muffle, gag.

Adj. Silent, still, noiseless, soundless, inaudible, hushed, &c., mute, mum, solemn, awful, deathlike.

Adv. Silently, softly, &c.

404. Loudness, din, clangor, clang, roar, uproar, racket, hubbub, flourish of trumpets, peal, blast, echo, chorus, clamor, hue and cry, larum, whoop, vociferation, lungs.

Stentor.

Artillery, cannon, thunder.

V. To be loud, &c., to resound, echo, reëcho, peal, clang, boom, thunder, fulminate, roar, whoop, shout, 411, deafen, stun, pierce, split or rend the ears or head.

405. Faintness, lowness, faint sounds, whisper, undertone, breath, murmur, mutter, hum.

Hoarseness, huskiness, raucity.

V. To whisper, breathe, murmur, purl, hum, gurgle, ripple, babble, flow.

Adj. Inaudible, scarcely audible, low, dull, stifled, muffled, hoarse, husky, gentle, breathed, &c., soft, floating, purling, &c., liquid, mellifluous, dulcet, flowing, soothing.

Adj. Loud, resounding, &c., high-sounding, big-sounding, deep, full, clamorous, vociferous, stunning, piercing, splitting, rending, deafening, ear-deafening, ear-piercing, obstreperous, open mouthed, trumpet-tongued, uproarious, stentorian.

Adv. In a whisper, with bated breath, between the teeth, aside.

Adv. Loudly, aloud, at the top of one's voice, &c.

(2.) SPECIFIC SOUNDS.

406. Sudden and violent sounds.

SNAP, knock, click, clash, slam, crack, crackling, crepitation, decrepitation, report, pop, bang, clap, burst, explosion, discharge, crash, detonation, firing, salvo.

Squib, cracker, gun, popgun.

V. To snap, knock, &c., brustle.

Adj. Snapping, &c.

407. Repeated and protracted sounds.

ROLL, rumble, rumbling, hum, humming, shake, trill, chime, tick, beat, toll, tattoo, drumming, clatter, rattle, racket.

V. To roll, beat, tick, toll, drum.

Adj. Rolling, rumbling, &c.

408. RESONANCE, ring, ringing, jingle, chink, tinkle, chime.

Reverberation, echo.

V. To resound, ring, jingle, clink, &c.; echo, reverberate.

Adj. Resounding, resonant, ringing, &c.

BASS, low, flat or grave note, barytone, deep-toned, hollow, sepulchral.

409. Hissing sounds.

SIBILATION, hiss, buzz, whiz, rustle, wheeze, whistle, sneeze, sternutation.

V. To hiss, buzz, &c.

Adj. Sibilant, hissing, buzzing, &c.

HIGH notes, *see* 410.

---

410. Harsh sounds.

STRIDOR, jar, grating, creak, clank, twang, jangle, jarring, creaking, rustling, roughness, gruffness, sharpness.

High note, shrillness, acuteness, soprano, falsetto, treble.

V. To creak, grate, jar, pipe, twang, jangle, rustle, clank.

Adj. Stridulous, jarring, &c., harsh, hoarse, discordant, 414, cacophonous, rough, gruff, sepulchral.

Sharp, high, acute, shrill, piping, screaming.

411. Human sounds, *see* Voice, 580.

CRY, vociferation, outcry, roar, shout, bawl, brawl, halloo, whoop, yell, cheer, hoot, howl, chorus, scream, screech, shriek, squeak, squall, whine, pule, pipe, grumble, plaint, moan, groan, snore, snort.

V. To vociferate, roar, shout,

412. Animal sounds.

ULULATION, latration, cry, roar, bellow, bark, yelp, howl, bay, baying, growl, grunt, snort, neigh, bray, croak, snarl, howl, mew, purr, pule, bleat, low, caw, coo, cackle, gobble, quack, chuckle, cluck, clack, chirp, chirrup, crow, twitter.

Insect cry drone.

bawl, &c., raise or lift up the voice.
Adj. Vociferating, &c., *see* 404.

Cuckoo, screechowl.
V. To cry, bellow, rebellow, &c
Adj. Crying, &c., blatant, latrant.

(3.) Musical Sounds.

413. Melody, rhythm.
Pitch, note, tone, intonation, treble, tenor, bass; high or low, acute or grave notes, alto, soprano, barytone, falsetto.
Scale, interval, gamut; diatonic, chromatic and enharmonic scales; key, (or clef,) chords; modulation, temperament, syncopation.
Staff, lines, spaces, brace; bar, rest.

414. Discord, discordance dissonance, jar, jarring, cacophony.
Hoarseness, croaking, &c , 410
V. To be discordant, &c., to croak, grate, jar.
Adj. Discordant, dissonant, out of tune, unmusical, unharmonious, inharmonious, unmelodious.
Cacophonous, harsh, hoarse, croaking, grating, jarring, stridulous, &c., 410.

Concord, harmony, unison, unisonance, concent, consonance, chime; harmonics.
V. To harmonize, chime, symphonize; to be in unison, &c.
Adj. Harmonious, harmonical, in concord, in unison, in tune, in concert, in harmony, unisonant, symphonizing.
Measured, rhythmical, diatonic, chromatic, enharmonic.
Melodious, musical, tuneful, tunable, sweet, dulcet, canorous, mellow, mellifluous, silver-toned, euphonious, euphonic, euphonical, symphonious; enchanting, ravishing, &c.

415. Music, tune, air, overture, symphony, accompaniment variations; fugue, march, waltz, &c., serenade, opera, oratorio, &c., composition.
Instrumental music, solo, duet, trio, quartet, &c.; minstrelsy, band, orchestra.
Vocal music, chant, psalmody, psalm, hymn, song, sonnet, canticle, canzonet, lay, ballad, ditty, pastoral, recitative:—Solo, duet, trio, &c.; glee, choir, chorus.
Dirge, requiem, lullaby, knell, lament.
Performance, execution, touch, expression, cadence.
V. To play, pipe, fiddle, strike, strike up, thrum, touch, sound the trumpet, &c., execute, perform.
To compose, to set to music.
To sing, chant, hum, warble, carol, chirp, chirrup, purl, quaver, trill, shake, twitter, whistle.
To put in tune, to tune, attune, accord, string.
Adj. Musical, harmonious, &c., 413, instrumental, vocal, choral, operatic, performing, playing, singing, &c.

416. Musician, performer, player, minstrel.
Organist, pianist, harper, violinist, fiddler, flutist, fifer, trumpeter piper, drummer, &c.; band [illegible] chestra.

Vocalist, singer, songster, songstress, chanter, chantress, troubadour, minnesinger.

Chorus, choir.

417. Musical Instruments.

1. Stringed instruments; harp, lyre, lute, mandolin, guitar, cithern, rebec, &c.

Violin, fiddle, violoncello, bassviol, doublebass, psaltery, &c.

Piano forte, harpsichord, clavichord, spinet, virginal, dulcimer, Æolian harp, &c.

2. Wind instruments; organ, siren, pipe, pitchpipe, Pandean pipes, flute, fife, clarionet, cornet, clarion, flageolet, hautboy, bassoon, horn, bugle, trumpet, trombone, accordeon, seraphina, bag pipes.

3. Vibrating surfaces, cymbal, bell, gong, tabor, tambourine, drum, kettledrum, timbrel; castanet, harmonica, sounding-board, &c.

(4.) Perception of Sound.

418. Sense of sound.

Hearing, auscultation, listening, eavesdropping.

Acuteness, nicety, delicacy of ear.

Ear, acoustic organs, auditory apparatus, eardrum, tympanum.

A hearer, auditor, listener, eavesdropper, auditory, audience.

V. To hear, overhear, hark, listen, hearken, give or lend an ear, give a hearing or audience to.

To become audible, to catch the ear, to be heard.

Adj. Hearing, &c., auditory, auricular, acoustic.

419. Deafness, hardness of hearing, surdity.

V. To be deaf, to shut, stop, or close one's ears.

To render deaf, to stun, to deafen.

Phr. To turn a deaf ear to.

Adj. Deaf, hard of hearing, surd, dull of hearing, deafmute, stunned, deafened, having no ear.

---

6. *Light.*

(1.) Light in general.

420. Light, ray, beam, stream, gleam, streak, pencil, sunbeam.

Day, daylight, sunshine, sunlight, the light of day, the light of heaven, noontide, noonday, noontide light, broad daylight.

Glimmer, glimmering, phosphorescence, lambent flame, play of light.

Flush, halo, glory.

Meteor, northern lights, aurora borealis, ignis fatuus, will-o'-the-wisp.

421. Darkness, night, midnight, obscurity, dusk, duskiness, gloom, gloominess, shade, umbrage, shadiness.

Obscuration, adumbration, obfuscation, caligation, extinction, eclipse, penumbra, gathering of the clouds, dimness, 422.

V. To be dark, &c.

To darken, obscure, shade, dim, overcast, overshadow, obfuscate, obumbrate, adumbrate,

Spark, sparkling, emication, scintillation, flame, flash, blaze, coruscation, fulguration, lightning.

Lustre, shine, sheen, gloss, tinsel, spangle, brightness, brilliancy, refulgence, dazzlement, resplendence, (splendor,) luminousness, lucidity, lucidness, radiance, transplendency, illumination, irradiation, glare, flare, glow, effulgence.

V. To shine, glow, glitter, glisten, glister, twinkle, gleam, flare, glare, beam, irradiate, shoot out beams, shimmer, sparkle, scintillate, coruscate, flash, blaze, dazzle, hang out a light; to clear up, brighten.

To illuminate, illume, illumine, enlighten, light, light up, irradiate, shine upon, cast lustre upon, cast, throw or shed a light upon; to brighten, (relume.)

Adj. Luminous, shining, glowing, &c., sheen, glossy, lucid, lucent, luculent, lustrous, glassy, clear, bright, scintillant, unclouded, sunny, orient, noonday, noontide, beaming, vivid, splendent, radiant, radiating, cloudless, clear, unobscured.

Gairish, resplendent, transplendent, refulgent, effulgent, in a blaze, relucent, splendid, blazing, meteoric, burnished.

cast in the shade, **becloud**, bedim, put out, extinguish.

To cast, throw, or spread a shade or gloom.

Adj. Dark, unenlightened, obscure, darksome, tenebrious, rayless, beamless, sunless, pitch dark, pitchy, caliginous, Stygian, Cimmerian.

Sombre, dusky, unilluminated, nocturnal, dingy, lurid, overcast, cloudy, murky, shady, umbrageous.

422. Dimness, paleness, glimmer, glimmering, nebulousness, nebulosity, cloud, film, mist, haze, fog, smoke, haziness, eclipse, cloudiness, dawn, twilight, crepuscule, moonlight.

V. To be dim, &c., to glimmer, loom, lower, twinkle.

To grow dim, to render dim, to dim, obscure, pale.

Adj. Dim, dull, lacklustre, dingy, glassy, faint, confused.

Cloudy, misty, hazy, foggy, nebulous, lowering, **overcast, crepuscular**, lurid.

423. Source of light, self-luminous body.

Luminary, sun, Phœbus, (moon,) star, orb, meteor, galaxy, blazing star, glowworm, firefly.

Artificial light, flame, torch, candle, flambeau, light, taper, lamp, (gaslight,) lantern, rushlight, firework, rocket, bluelights, electric light.

Chandelier, candelabra, girandole, lustre, sconce.

Lighthouse, beacon, watchfire, cresset.

Adj Self-luminous, phosphoric, phosphorescent.

424. Shade, **screen, curtain, veil, mantle, mask; cloud, mist, gauze**, blind.

A shadow, penumbra.

Adj. Umbrageous, &c.

---

425. Transparency, (translucency,) pellucidness, lucidity, limpidity, water.

426. Opacity, **thickness, turbidness**, opaqueness, **muddiness**, cloud, film, haze.

Glass, crystal, lymph.

V. To be transparent, &c., to transmit light.

Adj. Transparent, pellucid, diaphanous, translucent, relucent, limpid, clear, crystalline, vitreous, transpicuous, glassy.

V. To be opaque, &c., to obstruct the passage of light.

Adj. Opaque, impervious to light, turbid, thick, muddy, obfuscated, fuliginous, cloudy, hazy, misty, foggy.

427. SEMI-TRANSPARENCY, opalescence, gauze, milkiness.

Adj. Semi-transparent, opaline, pearly, milky.

(2.) SPECIFIC LIGHT.

428. COLOR, hue, tint, tinge, dye, complexion, shade, tincture, cast, livery, coloration.

Science of color, Chromatics.

A pigment, coloring matter, paint, dye, wash, distemper, stain, mordant.

V. To color, dye, tinge, stain, paint, wash, illuminate, emblazon, imbue.

Adj. Colored, (tinted, tinged,) colorific, chromatic, prismatic, full-colored.

Bright, florid, fresh, high-colored, unfaded, gay, showy, gaudy, gairish, flaunting, vivid, gorgeous, glaring, flaring, flashy, double-dyed.

429. Absence of color.

ACHROMATISM, discoloration, paleness, pallidity, pallidness.— Neutral tint.

A spot, blot, &c., 846.

V. To lose color, to fade, become colorless.

To deprive of color, discolor, bleach, tarnish.

Adj. Colorless, uncolored, untinged, achromatic, hueless, undyed, pale, pallid, pale-faced, faint, faded, dull, wan, sallow, dead, dingy, ashy, cadaverous, glassy, lacklustre, tarnished, bleached, discolored.

430. WHITENESS, milkiness, hoariness.

Snow, paper, chalk, milk, lily, ivory, silver, alabaster.

V. To be white, &c.

To render white, whiten, bleach, whitewash, blanch.

Adj. White, milk-white, snow-white, hoary, hoar, silvery, argent, pearly, fair, blonde.

431. BLACKNESS, swarthiness, dinginess, lividness, inkiness, pitchiness.

Jet, ink, ebony, coal, pitch, charcoal, soot, smut, raven, negro

V. To be black, &c.

To render black, to blacken, infuscate, denigrate, blot, blotch.

Adj. Black, sable, swarthy, sombre, inky, ebon, atramentous, livid, coal-black, fuliginous, dingy, Ethiopic, nocturnal, nigrescent.

432. GRAY, dun, drab, dingy, sombre, tawny, mouse-colored, ash, cinereous, slate, stone

433. BROWN, bap, dapple, auburn, chestnut, nut-brown, fawn, russet, olive, hazle, tawny, choco-

late, liver-colored, maroon, foxy, brunette, sallow.
V. To render brown, to tan, &c.
Adj. Brown, &c.

Primitive Colors. *Complementary Colors.*

434. REDNESS, scarlet, vermilion, crimson, pink, carnation, damask, ruby, carbuncle, rose, rubescence, rosiness, ruddiness, rubicundity, blush, color, flesh-color.

V. To become red, to blush, flush, mantle, redden.

435. GREENNESS, verdure, (verdancy,) emerald, verdantique.

Adj. Green, verdant, pea-green grass-green, apple-green, sea green, olive-green, bottle-green, virescent.

To render red, redden, rouge, rubify.

Adj. Red ruby, crimson, pink, &c., ruddy, florid, roseate, rose-colored, blushing, mantling, &c., erubescent, rubicund, blood-red, claret, rubiform, sorrel.

436. YELLOWNESS, buff color, flesh color, crocus, saffron, &c.

Adj. Yellow, citron, gold-colored, aureate, citrine, fallow, fulvous, saffron, lemon, sulphur, amber, straw-colored, sandy-colored, cream-colored.

437. PURPLE, violet, plum, lavender, lilac, peach color; lividness.

Adj. Purple, violet, livid, &c.

438. BLUENESS, bluishness, azure, indigo, ultramarine, bloom.

Adj. Blue, cerulean, sky blue, sky-colored, azure, bluish, sapphire.

439. ORANGE, gold, flame, copper, brass, apricot color.

Adj. Orange, golden, &c.

440. VARIEGATION, iridescence, play of colors, variegatedness, patchwork, maculation, spottiness.

A rainbow, iris, tulip, peacock, chamelion, butterfly, tortoise shell, leopard, zebra, mother-of-pearl, opal, marble.

V. To be variegated, &c.

To variegate, speckle, stripe, streak, checker, bespeckle, inlay.

Adj. Variegated, many-colored, many-hued, divers-colored, party-colored, polychromatic.

Iridescent, prismatic, opaline, pearly, shot, pied, piebald, motley, mottled, veined, marbled, paned, dappled, clouded, all manner of colors.

Mosaic, inlaid, tesselated, checkered, tortoise shell.

Dotted, spotted, bespotted, spotty, speckled, bespeckled, maculated, freckled, studded.

Striped, striated, streaked, barred, veined, brinded, brindled, tabby, grizzled, listed.

(3.) PERCEPTIONS OF LIGHT.

441 VISION, sight, optics, eye-view, look espial, glance,

442. BLINDNESS, cataract, nictation, wink, blink.

glimpse, peep, gaze, stare, leer, perlustration, contemplation, regard, survey, introspection, inspection, speculation, watch, ocular demonstration.

A point of view, vista, loophole, field of view, theatre, amphitheatre, horizon, arena, commanding view, periscope.

The organ of vision; the eye; the naked or unassisted eye, retina, optics.

Perspicacity, lynx, eagle, Argus.

V. To see, behold, discern, have in sight, descry, catch a sight, glance, or glimpse of, spy, espy.

To look, view, eye; to open one's eyes, glance on; cast or set one's eyes on; look on or upon; turn or bend one's looks upon; turn the eyes to; peep, peer, scan, survey, glance round, reconnoitre, inspect, recognize, mark, regard, watch, contemplate, speculate, discover, distinguish, see through, speculate.

To look intently, strain one's eyes, stare, gaze, pore over, gloat on, leer; ogle, *see* 459.

Adj. Visual, ocular, optic, optical.

Seeing, &c., the eyes being directed to, fixed, riveted upon.

Sharpsighted, quicksighted, eagle-eyed, hawk-eyed, lynx-eyed, keen-eyed, Argus-eyed, piercing, penetrating.

Adv. Visibly, &c., in sight of, to one's face, before one's face, with one's eyes open; at sight, at first sight, at a glance.

V. To be blind, &c., not to see to lose sight of.

Not to look, to close or shut the eyes, to look another way, to turn away or avert the eyes, to wink, blink, nictate.

To render blind, &c., to put out the eyes, to blind, blindfold, hoodwink, dazzle.

Adj. Blind, purblind, eyeless, sightless, dark, stone-blind, sand-blind, stark-blind, dazzled, hoodwinked, blindfolded, undiscerning.

Adv. Blindly, &c., blindfold.

---

443. Imperfect vision.

DIMSIGHTEDNESS, confusion of vision, failing sight, shortsightedness, longsightedness, squint, strabism, cast of the eye.

Fallacies of vision; refraction, false light, phantasm, distortion, looming, mirage, ignis fatuus, phantasmagoria, dissolving views, &c.

V. To be dimsighted, &c., to see double, to squint, look askant or askance, to see through a prism, wink.

To glare, dazzle, loom.

Adj. Dimsighted, halfsighted, shortsighted, nearsighted, long sighted, blear-eyed, winking.

444. SPECTATOR, looker on, bystander, inspector, spy, beholder observer, stargazer, &c.

V. To witness, behold, &c., 441.

445. OPTICAL INSTRUMENTS, lens, magnifier, microscope, spectacles, glasses, goggles, eyeglass, (opera glass,) telescope, spy glass, glass.

Mirror, reflector, speculum, looking glass, pier glass, kaleidoscope Prism, camera obscura, magic lantern, phantasmagoria.

446. VISIBILITY, perceptibility, conspicuousness, distinctness, conspicuity, appearance.

V. To be visible, &c., to appear, come in sight, come into view, heave in sight, open to the view, catch the eye, show its face, present itself, show itself, manifest itself, produce itself, discover itself, reveal itself, expose itself, betray itself, come out, come to light, come forth, come forward, arise, peep out, peer out, start up, loom, glare, burst forth.

Adj. Visible, perceptible, discernible, in sight, apparent, plain, manifest, patent, obvious, clear, distinct, definite, well-defined, well-marked, recognizable, evident, unmistakable, palpable, naked, bare, barefaced, ostensible, conspicuous, prominent, staring, glaring, notable, notorious, overt, above-board, exposed to view, (phenomenal.)

Intelligible, &c., *see* 518.

447 INVISIBILITY, indistinctness, imperceptibility, non-appearance, concealment, latency, 526.

V. To be invisible, &c., to lie hidden, concealed, &c., to be in or under a cloud, in a mist, in a haze, &c.; to lurk, lie in ambush, skulk.

Not to see, &c., to be blind to.

To render invisible, to hide, conceal, &c., 528.

Adj. Invisible, imperceptible, unseen, unbeheld, undiscerned, viewless, undiscernible, indiscernible, sightless, unapparent, non-apparent, hid, hidden, concealed, &c., 528, covert.

Confused, dim, obscure, dark, misty, hazy, foggy, indistinct, shadowy, ill-defined, indefinite, ill-marked, blurred, shadowy, nebulous, hazy, clouded, misty, shaded, screened, veiled, masked.

Unintelligible, &c., *see* 519.

448. APPEARANCE, phenomenon, sight, spectacle, show, premonstration, scene, view, lookout, prospect, vista, perspective, bird's eye view, scenery, landscape, picture, display, exposure.

Pageant, spectacle, raree show, panorama, diorama.

Phantasm, phantom, apparition, spectre, mirage, &c., 443.

Aspect, phase, seeming, guise, look, complexion, shape, mien, air, cast, carriage, port, demeanor, presence, expression, first blush.

Lineament, feature, trait, lines, outline, face, countenance, physiognomy, visage, phiz, profile, (contour.)

V. To seem, look, appear, show; to present, wear, carry, have, bear, exhibit, take, take on, or assume the appearance of; to look like; to be visible, *see* 446.

To show, to manifest, &c., 525.

Adj. Apparent, seeming, &c.

Adv. Apparently, to all appearance, &c., on the face of it; at the first blush; in full view.

449. DISAPPEARANCE, evanescence, eclipse, occultation.

V. To disappear, vanish, dissolve, fade, melt away, pass, be lost, &c.

To efface, blot, blot out, erase, rub out, expunge, 552.

Adj. Disappearing, &c., lost, vanishing, evanescent, missing, unconspicuous, inconspicuous.

CLASS IV.

WORDS RELATING TO THE INTELLECTUAL FACULTIES.

Division I. FORMATION OF IDEAS.

Section I. Operations of Intellect in general.

450. Intellect, mind, understanding, reason, thinking principle, (intellectual powers or faculties,) sense, common sense, consciousness, capacity, intelligence, intellection, intuition, instinct, conception, judgment, genius, parts, wit, wits, shrewdness, archness, intellectuality; *see* Skill, 698, and Wisdom, 498.

Soul, spirit, ghost, inner man, heart, breast, bosom.

Organ or seat of thought; sensory, brain, head, skull.

Science of mind: Metaphysics, Psychology, Idealism, Ideality, Pneumatology.

Adj Relating to intellect; intellectual, mental, spiritual, (rational,) subjective, metaphysical, psychological, ghostly, immaterial, 317, cerebral.

450. *a.* Absence or want of intellect, *see* 499.

---

451. Thought, reflection, cogitation, consideration, meditation, study, lucubration, speculation, deliberation, pondering, headwork, application, attention, 457, contemplation, (mental activity.)

Abstraction, musing, revery, Platonism; depth of thought, workings of the mind, inmost thoughts, self-counsel, self-communing, self-consultation; succession, flow, train, current, &c., of thought or of ideas.

Afterthought, reconsideration, retrospection, retrospect, 505, examination, *see* Inquiry, 461.

Thoughtfulness, pensiveness, intentness, intentiveness.

452. Absence or want of thought.

Incogitancy, vacancy, (stupidity,) fatuity, *see* 499, thoughtlessness, *see* Inattention, 458.

V. Not to think, to take no thought of, not to trouble one's self about, to think little of, to put away thought, to dismiss, discard, or discharge from one's thoughts or from the mind; to drop the subject, set aside, turn aside, turn away from; divert or turn one's attention from, abstract one's self, dream; to indulge in revery.

To unbend, relax, divert the mind.

V. To think, reflect, cogitate, excogitate, consider, deliberate, speculate, contemplate, meditate, ponder, muse, ruminate, brood over, animadvert, con over, study, bend or apply the mind, digest, discuss, weigh, take into account, take into consideration.

To harbor, entertain, cherish, nurture, &c., an idea or a thought, a notion, a view, &c.

To enter the mind, come into the head, occur, present itself, pass in the mind, suggest itself; to fancy, trow, dream of.

To make an impression; to sink or penetrate into the mind; to fasten itself on the mind.

Adj. Thinking, &c., thoughtful, pensive, meditative, reflective, wistful, contemplative, speculative, (philosophical, abstract,) deliberative, studious, sedate, Platonic.

Close, active, diligent, mature, deliberate, labored, steadfast, deep, profound, intense, &c., thought, study, reflection, &c.

Intent, engrossed, absorbed, deep-musing, rapt, abstracted.

Adj. Vacant, unintellectual, unideal, 499, unoccupied, unthinking, inconsiderate, thoughtless, absent, inattentive, 458, diverted, distracted, (abstracted,) unbent, &c.

Unthought of, unconsidered, undreamed.

---

453. Object of thought.

Idea, notion, conception, thought, fancy, conceit, impression, perception, image, sentiment, *see* Opinion, 484, fantasy, flight of fancy.

Point of view, light, aspect, field of view.

454. Subject of thought.

Topic, subject, matter, theme, thesis, text, subject matter, point, proposition, theorem, business, affair, matter in hand, question, argument, motion, resolution, head, chapter; nice or subtile point, moot point, problem, *see* 461.

Adj. Thought of.

Section II. Precursory Conditions and Operations.

455. The desire of knowledge.

Curiosity, curiousness, inquisitiveness.

V. To be curious, &c., to take an interest in, to stare, gape; to see sights, to lionize.

Adj. Curious, inquisitive, inquiring, over-curious, staring, gaping, agape.

456. Absence of curiosity.

Incuriosity, incuriousness, want of interest.

V. To be incurious, &c., to have no curiosity, take no interest in, &c., not to care, not to mind, &c.

Adj. Incurious, uninquisitive.

457. Attention, advertence, advertency, observance, observation, notice, heed, look, regard,

458. Inattention, inconsideration, inconsiderateness, inadvertence, inadvertency, non-ob

view, remark, inspection, introspection, mindfulness, lookout, watch, vigilance, circumspection, consideration, revision, review, revise, particularity, *see* Care, 459.

Close, intense, deep, profound, &c., attention, application or study.

V. To be attentive, &c.; to attend, advert to, mind, observe, look, look at, see, view, look to, see to, remark, heed, notice, take heed, take notice, mark; give or pay attention to; give heed to, have an eye to; turn, (bend,) apply or direct the mind, the eye, or the attention to; look after, give a thought to, animadvert to, occupy one's self with.

To examine cursorily; to glance at, upon, or over; cast or pass the eyes over, run over, turn over the leaves, dip into, perstringe; to revert to.

To examine closely or intently, (scrutinize;) to consider, give one's mind to, overhaul, pore over, note, mark, inspect, review; to fix the eye, mind, thoughts, or attention on, keep in view, contemplate, &c., 451.

To fall under one's notice, observation, &c., to catch the eye; to catch, awaken, wake, invite, solicit, attract, claim, excite, engage, occupy, strike, arrest, fix, engross, absorb, rivet, &c., the attention, mind, or thoughts.

Adj. Attentive, mindful, heedful, regardful, alive to, bearing in mind, occupied with, engaged, taken up with, engrossed, rapt in, absorbed.

Awake, watchful, 459, broad awake, wide awake, intent on, with eyes fixed on, open-eyed, undistracted, upon the stretch.

servance, disregard, regardlessness, unmindfulness, giddiness, thoughtlessness, *see* Neglect, 460, wandering, distracted, &c., attention.

Absence of mind, abstraction, preoccupation, distraction, revery, brown study.

V. To be inattentive, &c., to overlook, disregard, pass by, slur over, pass over, gloss over, blink, miss, skim, skim the surface, 460.

To call off, draw off, call away, divert, &c., the attention; to distract; to disconcert, put out, discompose, confuse, perplex, bewilder.

Adj. Inattentive, mindless, unobservant, unmindful, inadvertent, heedless, regardless, careless, *see* 460, unwatchful, listless, cursory, percursory, blind, deaf, &c.

Absent, abstracted, lost, preoccupied, dreamy, napping.

Disconcerted, put out, &c., dizzy, *see* 460.

Adv. Inattentively, &c., cavalierly.

---

459. Care, caution, heed, heedfulness, wariness, prudence, discretion, 698, watch, vigil, watchfulness, vigilance, circumspection, watch and ward, deliberation, forethought, solicitude, precaution, 673, scruple, scrupulousness, scrupulosity, particularity.

460. Neglect, negligence, omission, heedlessness, carelessness, remissness, imprudence, secureness, indiscretion, incautiousness, indiscrimination, rashness, 863, recklessness.

V. To be negligent, &c., to neglect, pass over, omit, pre-

V. To be careful, &c., to take care, have a care, look to it, heed, take heed, keep watch, keep watch and ward, set watch, take precautions.

Adj. Careful, cautious, heedful, wary, guarded, on one's guard, on the alert, on the watch, watchful, on the lookout, awake, vigilant, circumspect, broad awake, having the eyes open, Argus-eyed.

Discreet, prudent, surefooted, provident, scrupulous, particular.

Adv. Carefully, &c., with care, &c.

---

termit, set aside, cast or put aside.

To overlook, disregard, pass by, slight, pay no regard to, make light of, trifle with, wink at, connive at; gloss over, slur over, slip over, skip, jump over.

To render neglectful, &c., to put or throw off one's guard.

Adj. Neglecting, &c., unmindful, heedless, careless, negligent, neglectful, slovenly, remiss, perfunctory, thoughtless, uncircumspect, off one's guard, unwary, incautious, unguarded, indiscreet inconsiderate, imprudent, improvident, rash, headlong, reckless, witless, hairbrained, giddy-brained, offhand, cursory.

Neglected, unheeded, unperceived, unseen, unobserved, unnoticed, unnoted, unmarked, unattended to, unthought of, overlooked, unmissed, unexamined, unstudied, unsearched, unscanned, unweighed, unsifted.

461. INQUIRY, search, research, quest, pursuit, examination, scrutiny, investigation, inquest, inquisition, exploration, sifting, calculation, analysis, dissection, resolution, induction; the (inductive or) Baconian method; a searching inquiry.

Questioning, asking, interrogation, interrogatory, examination, cross examination, cross questioning, catechism; the Socratic method.

Reconnoitring, prying, spying, espionage; the lantern of Diogenes.

Subject of inquiry; QUESTION, moot-point, query, difficulty, problem, desideratum, point to be solved; point or matter in dispute; question at issue, plain question, fair question, open question, knotty point, vexed question.

Enigma, riddle, conundrum, a bone to pick, Gordian knot.

An inquirer, (investigator,) querist, quidnunc, newsmonger

V. To inquire, seek, search, look for, look about for, look out for, cast about for, beat about, grope for, feel for, reconnoitre, explore, sound, rummage, ransack, pry, look round, look over, look through.

462. ANSWER, response. reply, replication, rejoinder, rebutter, retort, repartee, antiphony, acknowledgment.

Explanation, solution, resolution, exposition, rationale, interpretation, 522.

A key, master key, clew.

V. To answer, respond, reply, rebut, retort, rejoin, give or return for answer, acknowledge, echo.

To explain, solve, resolve, expound, decipher, spell, interpret, 522, to unriddle, unlock, cut the knot, unravel, discover; to find a clew to.

Adj. Answering, responding, &c., responsive, respondent.

To pursue, hunt, track, trail, mouse, trace.

To investigate, take up, follow up, institute, pursue, conduct, carry on, prosecute, &c., an inquiry, &c., to overhaul, to examine, study, consider, fathom, dip into, look into, calculate, preëxamine, dive into, delve into; to discuss, canvass, agitate, trace up, probe, fathom, sound, scrutinize, analyze, anatomize, dissect, sift, ventilate, winnow, torture, resolve.

To ask, question, demand, put, propose, propound, moot, raise, stir, suggest, put forth, start, pop, &c., a question, interrogate, catechize, pump, cross question, cross examine, require an answer, *see* 765.

To undergo examination; to be in course of inquiry, &c.

Adj. Inquiring, &c., inquisitive, catechetical, inquisitorial, analytic, in search of, in quest of, on the lookout for.

Undetermined, untried, undecided, in question, in dispute, moot, proposed.

463. EXPERIMENT, essay, trial, tentative method, verification, probation, proof, criterion, test, touchstone, assay, ordeal. Empiricism.

A feeler, a pilot balloon, a messenger balloon; a pilot engine.

V. To essay, try, explore, grope; to feel or grope one's way; to thread one's way; to make an experiment, make trial of.

To subject to trial, &c., to experiment upon, give a trial to; to put, bring, or submit to the test or proof; to prove, verify, test, touch, practise upon.

Adj. Experimental, tentative, probationary, empirical.

464. COMPARISON, collation, contrast, identification.

A comparison, simile, metaphor, allegory, 521.

V. To compare to or with; to collate, confront, place side by side or in juxtaposition; to draw a parallel, institute a comparison, contrast, identify.

Adj. Comparative, metaphorical, figurative, allegorical

Compared with, pitted against, 708.

465. DISCRIMINATION, distinction, perception or appreciation of difference, diagnosis, taste, 850, judgment, nice perception, tact, critique.

V. To discriminate, distinguish, to separate or winnow the chaff from the wheat

Adj. Discriminating, &c., discriminative, distinctive, diagnostic.

465. *a.* INDISCRIMINATION, indistinctness, indistinction, 460.

V. Not to distinguish or discriminate; to neglect, overlook, or lose sight of a distinction.

Adj. Indiscriminate, undistinguished, (undistinguishing,) undistinguishable, unmeasured.

---

466. MEASUREMENT, admeasurement, mensuration, survey, valuation, appraisement, assessment, assize, estimation, reckoning.

Geometry, geodetics, gauging, sounding, surveying, weighing, ponderation, dead reckoning.

A measure, standard, rule, compass, gauge, meter, line, rod, plumb line, plummet, log, log line, sounding rod, sounding line, sound, check; index, *see* 550, floodmark.

Scale, graduation, graduated scale, quadrant, theodolite, &c., balance, scales, steelyard, beam, weather glass, barometer, areometer, &c.

V. To measure, mete, value, assess, rate, appraise, estimate, form an estimate, set a value on, appreciate, span, pace, step, apply the compass, rule, scale, &c., gauge, plumb, probe, sound, fathom, survey, weigh, poise, balance, hold the scales, take an average, graduate, to place on the beam, to take into account.

Adj. Measuring, &c., metrical, ponderable, measurable.

Section III. MATERIALS FOR REASONING.

467. EVIDENCE on one side, premises, data, indication, 550.

Testimony, testimonial, deposition, declaration, attestation, testification, authority, warrant, warranty, surety, handwriting, autograph, signature, indorsement, seal, sigil, signet, superscription, entry.

Voucher, credential, certificate, deed, indenture, docket, probate, affidavit, attestation, diploma; admission, concession, allegation, deposition, citation, quotation, reference.

Criterion, test, touchstone, check, argument.

A witness, eye witness, indicator, ear witness, deponent, telltale, sponsor.

Reason, proof, *see* Demonstration, 478.

Ex parte evidence, one-sided view.

Secondary evidence, confirmation, corroboration, ratification, support, approval.

V. To be evidence, &c., to evince, show, indicate, 550, imply, involve, argue, admit, acknowledge, allow, concede, certify, testify, attest, bear testimony, depose, witness, vouch for, sign, seal, set one's hand and seal to, indorse, confirm, ratify, corroborate, support, bear upon, bear out, to speak volumes.

To adduce, attest, cite, quote,

468. Evidence on the other side, on the other hand.

COUNTER EVIDENCE, disproof, contradiction, rejoinder, answer, 462, weak point, conflicting evidence, *see* Refutation, 479, counter protest.

V. To countervail, oppose, rebut, (overthrow,) check, weaken, invalidate, contradict, contravene.

Adj. Countervailing, &c., contradictory. Unattested.

469. QUALIFICATION, limitation, modification, allowance, grains of allowance, consideration, extenuating circumstance, condition, proviso, exception, 83, assumption, 514.

V. To qualify, limit, modify, allow for, make allowance for, take into account, introduce new conditions, admit exceptions, take exception.

Adj. Qualifying, &c., conditional, exceptional, 83, postulatory, hypothetical, 514.

Adv. Provided, if, unless, but, yet, according as, conditionally, admitting, supposing; on the supposition, assumption, presumption, allegation, hypothesis, &c., of; with the understanding, even, although, for all that, after all.

refer to, call, bring forward, allege, plead, produce, bring into court, confront witnesses; to collect, bring together, or rake up evidence, to make out a case.

Adj. Showing, indicating, &c., indicative, indicatory, following, deducible, consequential, consectary collateral, corroborative, confirmatory; presumptive.

Sound, logical, strong, valid, cogent, persuasive, persuasory demonstrative, irrefragable, irresistible, &c., 478.

Adv. According to; witness; still more, still less, &c.

Degrees of Evidence.

470. Possibility, potentiality, contingency, *see* Chance, 156, what may be, what is possible, &c.

Practicability, feasibility, 705, compatibility, 23.

V. To be possible, &c., to admit of, to bear; may, may be.

To render possible, &c., to put into the way of.

Adj. Possible, contingent.

Practicable, feasible, achievable, attainable, obtainable, compatible.

Adv. Possibly, by possibility, may be, perhaps, 156.

471. Impossibility, what cannot be, what can never be, hopelessness, 859, a dead lift.

Impracticability, incompatibility, 704, incredibility.

V. To be impossible, &c., to have no chance whatever.

Adj. Impossible, contrary to reason, inconceivable, unreasonable, incredible, marvellous, desperate, hopeless, unheard of.

Impracticable, unattainable, unachievable, unfeasible, unobtainable, beyond control.

472. Probability, likelihood, verisimilitude, plausibility, a show of, credibility, reasonable chance, favorable chance, fair chance, presumptive evidence, circumstantial evidence.

V. To be probable, &c., to bid fair, to stand fair for, to stand a good chance, to stand to reason.

Adj. Probable, likely, likely to happen, in a fair way, hopeful, well founded; to be expected, 507.

Plausible, specious, ostensible, colorable, standing to reason, reasonable, credible, easy of belief, presumable, presumptive.

Adv. Probably, &c., in all probability or likelihood, apparently, to all appearance.

473. Improbability, unlikelihood, unfavorable chances, small chance, &c., incredibility.

V. To be improbable, &c., to have a small, little, poor, &c., chance.

Adj. Improbable, unlikely, incredible.

---

474. Certainty, certitude, positiveness, infallibleness, infallibility, gospel, scripture, surety assurance, indisputableness, *see* Truth, 494.

Fact, matter of fact.

475. Uncertainty, incertitude, hesitation, suspense, perplexity, *see* Doubt, 485.

Doubtfulness, dubiousness, indefiniteness, indetermination, ambiguity; vagueness, &c., pre-

V. To be certain, &c., to believe, 454.

To render certain, &c., to insure.

Adj Certain, sure, assured, solid, absolute, positive, determinate, categorical, unequivocal, inevitable, unavoidable, unerring, infallible, indubitable, indubious, indisputable, undisputed, uncontested, incontestable, incontrovertible, undoubted, doubtless, without doubt, beyond a doubt, past dispute, unanswerable, decided, unquestionable, beyond all question, unquestioned, questionless, demonstrable, 478, authoritative, official.

Adv. Certainly, assuredly, &c., for certain, sure, surely, sure enough, of course, as a matter of course, yes, *see* 488.

cariousness, slipperiness, fallibility.

V. To be uncertain, (to be a fault,) &c.

To render uncertain, &c., to perplex, embarrass, confuse, confound.

Adj. Uncertain, doubtful, dubious, precarious, casual, random, contingent, indecisive, dependent on circumstances, undecided, vague, indeterminate, indefinite, ambiguous, undefined, equivocal, undefinable, puzzling, enigmatic, questionable, apocryphal, problematical, hypothetical, controvertible, fallible, fallacious, suspicious, slippery, debatable.

Unauthentic, unconfirmed, undemonstrated, undemonstrable

Section IV. Reasoning Processes.

476. Reasoning, ratiocination, dialectics, induction, generalization.

Argumentation, discussion, controversy, polemics, debate, wrangling, logomachy, disputation.

The art of reasoning, logic, process, train or chain of reasoning, argument, 514, proposition, terms, premises, postulate, data, starting point, principle; result, conclusion.

Correctness, soundness, force, validity, cogency, conclusiveness.

A disputant, controversialist, controvertist, wrangler, arguer, debater.

V. To reason, argue, discuss, debate, dispute, wrangle; bandy words or arguments; hold or carry on an argument, controvert, contravene, comment upon, moralize upon, spiritualize.

To open a discussion or case;

477. The absence of reasoning. Intuition, instinct, presentiment.

False or vicious reasoning; show of reason.

Sophistry, paralogy, fallacy, perversion, casuistry, jesuitry, equivocation, evasion, chicanery, quiddity, mystification.

Misjudgment, miscalculation, 481.

Sophism, solecism, paralogism, quibble, fallacy, subterfuge; subtlety.

Speciousness, plausibility, illusiveness, irrelevancy, invalidity.

V. To judge intuitively, &c.

To reason ill, falsely, &c. To pervert, quibble, equivocate, mystify, evade, elude, gloss over, varnish, misjudge, miscalculate, 481.

To refine, subtilize, mislead &c., 538.

to moot, to join issue; to stir, agitate, torture or ventilate a question; to take up a side or case.

Adj. Reasoning, &c., argumentative, controversial, dialectic, polemical, discursory, discursive, debatable, controvertible; disputatious.

Correct, just, fair, sound, valid, cogent, logical, demonstrative, 478, relevant, pertinent, 9, to the point, to the purpose, subtile, fine spun.

Adj. Intuitive, instinctive, impulsive, independent of, or anterior to reason.

Sophistical, illogical, false, unsound, not following, inconsequent, unwarranted, untenable, inconclusive, incorrect, fallacious, groundless, fallible, unproved, deceptive, illusive, illusory, specious, plausible, evasive, irrelevant.

Weak, feeble, poor, flimsy, trivial, trumpery, trashy, puerile, childish, irrational, silly, foolish, imbecile, absurd, extravagant, far-fetched.

478. DEMONSTRATION, proof, conclusiveness, probation, comprobation, test, &c., 463.

V. To demonstrate, prove, establish, show, evince, verify, make good, substantiate, settle the question, reduce to demonstration.

Adj. Demonstrating, &c., demonstrative, demonstrable, unanswerable, conclusive, irrefutable, irrefragable, categorical.

Demonstrated, &c., unconfuted, unrefuted; evident, self-evident, axiomatic

479. CONFUTATION, refutation, disproof, conviction, invalidation, exposure, exposition; demolition of an argument, a clincher.

V. To confute, refute, disprove, expose, show the fallacy of, rebut, defeat, overthrow, demolish, overturn, invalidate, silence, reduce to silence.

Adj. Confuting, &c., confuted, &c., capable of refutation, refutable, confutable, &c., exhaustive; unproved, &c.

Section V. RESULTS OF REASONING.

480. JUDGMENT, conclusion, determination, deduction, inference, corollary.

Estimation, valuation, appreciation, dijudication, judication, arbitrament, arbitration, assessment, review; finding, detection, discovery, &c.

Decision, determination, sentence, verdict, moral, finding; estimate.

A judge, umpire, arbiter, arbitrator, assessor, censor, referee, reviewer.

V. To judge, deduce, conclude, draw a conclusion, infer, make a deduction, draw an inference;

481. MISJUDGMENT, obliquity of judgment, *see* Error, 495, presumption.

Prejudgment, prejudication, foregone conclusion, prejudice, preconception, prepossession, preapprehension, presentiment.

Bias, warp, twist, narrow mindedness, bigotry, dogmatism, intolerance, tenacity, obstinacy, 606, blind side; one-sided, partial, narrow or confined views, ideas, conceptions, or notions.

V. To misjudge, misestimate, misconceive, misreckon, &c., *see* 495.

To prejudge, forejudge, prejudi-

come to, arrive, or jump at a conclusion; to derive, gather, collect.

To estimate, appreciate, value, count, assess, rate, account, regard, review, settle, pass an opinion, decide, pronounce, pass judgment, arbitrate, *see* Investigate, 461.

To ascertain, determine, find, find out, make out, detect, discover, elicit, recognize, trace, get at; get or arrive at the truth; meet with, fall upon, light upon, hit upon, fix upon, fall in with, solve, resolve, unravel, fish out, worm out, ferret out, root out, fish up.

Adj. Judging, &c., deducible, 467.

Impartial, unbiased, unprejudiced, unwarped, unbigoted, equitable, fair, sound, rational, judicious.

482. OVER-ESTIMATION, exaggeration.

V. To over-estimate, overrate, overvalue, overprize, overweigh, outreckon; exaggerate, extol, make too much of, overstrain.

Adj. Over-estimated, &c.

---

483. UNDER-ESTIMATION, depreciation, disparagement, detraction, underrating, under-estimation, undervaluing, &c.

V. To depreciate, disparage, detract, underrate, under-estimate, undervalue, under-reckon, misprize, not to do justice to, make light of, slight; make little or make nothing of, hold cheap, disregard, to care nothing for, set at nought, derogate, decry, 932.

To scout, deride, mock, scoff at, laugh at, play with, trifle with, ridicule, 856.

Adj. Depreciating, &c., derogatory, detractory, cynical.

Depreciated, &c., unvalued, unprized.

484. BELIEF, credence, faith, trust, confidence, credit, dependence on, reliance, assurance.

Opinion, notion, idea, 453, conception, apprehension, impression, conceit, mind, view, persuasion, conviction, sentiment, voice, judgment, estimation, self-conviction.

System of opinions, creed, doctrine, tenet, dogma, principle, way of thinking, popular belief, public opinion.

Proselytism, propagandism, 537.

V. To believe, credit, give faith to, give credit to, rely upon, make no doubt, doubt not, confide in,

cate, dogmatize, have a bias, &c., presuppose, presume.

To give a bias, twist, &c., to bias, warp, twist, prejudice, &c.

Adj. Prejudging, &c., prejudiced, jaundiced, narrow-minded, dogmatic, besotted, positive, obstinate, tenacious, having a bias, twist, &c., warped, partial.

---

485. UNBELIEF, disbelief, misbelief, discredit, scepticism.

DOUBT, dubitation, misgiving, demur, suspense; shade or shadow of doubt, distrust, mistrust, suspicion, shyness, embarrassment, hesitation, uncertainty, 475, scruple, qualm, dilemma; casuistry, 489, incredulity, 487.

V. To disbelieve, discredit, not to believe, refuse to admit or believe, misbelieve, controvert; put or set aside; join issue, dispute, &c.

To doubt, be doubtful, &c., distrust, mistrust, suspect, have, har-

count upon, depend upon, calculate upon, take upon trust, swallow, take one's word for, take upon credit.

To think, hold, take, look upon, take it, consider, esteem.

To be of opinion, to opine, to have, hold, possess, entertain, adopt, imbibe, embrace, foster, nurture, cherish, &c., a notion, idea, opinion, &c.; to think, look upon, view, consider, take, take it, hold, ween, conceive, fancy, apprehend, regard, esteem, deem, account.

To cause to be believed, thought, or esteemed; to satisfy, persuade, assure, convince, convert, bring over, win over, indoctrinate; *see* Teach, 537.

Adj. Believing, &c., impressed with, imbued with, wedded to, unsuspecting, unsuspicious, void of suspicion, &c., credulous, 486, convinced, &c.

Believed, &c., credited, accredited, unsuspected, received, current, popular.

Worthy or deserving of belief, commanding belief, credible, *see* Probable, 472, fiducial, fiduciary; relating to belief, doctrinal.

Firm, implicit, steadfast, fixed, rooted, stanch, unshaken, inveterate;—calm, sober, dispassionate, impartial.

bor, entertain, &c., doubts; demur, stick at, pause, hesitate, scruple, question, call in question.

To cause, raise, suggest, or start a doubt; to pose, startle, stagger, embarrass, puzzle; shake, or stagger one's faith or belief.

Adj. Unbelieving, &c., sceptical, shy of belief, at sea, at a loss, 487.

Doubting, &c., doubtful, dubious, scrupulous, suspicious, *see* Uncertain, 475.

Unworthy or undeserving of belief, hard to believe, doubtful, dubious, staggering, puzzling, &c., paradoxical, incredible, inconceivable.

---

486. Credulity, credulousness, infatuation, self-delusion, self-deception, superstition, gross credulity, dogmatism, &c., 606.

A credulous person; dupe, 547.

V. To be credulous, &c., to follow implicitly, to swallow, &c.

To impose upon, practise upon, palm upon, cajole, &c., *see* Deceive, 545.

Adj. Credulous, easily deceived, cajoled, &c., superstitious, simple, unsuspicious, &c., 484, soft, childish, silly, stupid; over-credulous, over-confident.

487. Incredulity, scepticism, Pyrrhonism, suspicion, &c., *see* 485, suspiciousness, scrupulousness, scrupulosity.

An unbeliever, sceptic, misbeliever.

V. To be incredulous, &c., to distrust, *see* 485.

Adj. Incredulous, hard of belief, sceptical, unbelieving, inconvincible.

488. Assent, acquiescence, admission, nod, consent, concession, accord, accordance, agreement, concordance, concurrence, ratification, confirmation, recognition,

489. Dissent, discordance, denial, 536, dissonance, disagreement; difference or diversity of opinion, recusancy, contradiction, nonconformity, schism; secession, protest.

acknowledgment, acceptance, granting, avowal, confession.

Unanimity, chorus; *see* Affirmation, 535.

V. To assent, acquiesce, agree, accede, yield assent, accord, concur, consent, nod assent, accept, coincide, go with, go along with, chime in with, strike in with, close with, conform with, defer to.

To acknowledge, own, avow, confess, concede, subscribe to, admit, allow, recognize, grant.

Adj. Assenting, &c., acquiescent, willing; agreed; uncontradicted, unquestioned, uncontroverted.

Adv. Affirmatively, in the affirmative, 535.

A dissenter, nonconformist, recusant.

V. To dissent, demur, deny, disagree, secede, refuse assent, to ignore, to refuse to admit; to repudiate, protest, contradict.

Adj. Dissenting, &c., dissentient, discordant, protestant, recusant; unconvinced, unconverted, unavowed, unacknowledged.

Unwilling, reluctant, extorted, &c.

Adv. Negatively, in the negative, 536.

490. KNOWLEDGE, cognizance, cognition, acquaintance, privity, insight, familiarity, comprehension, understanding, recognition; discovery, 480.

Intuition, consciousness, conscience, light, enlightenment, glimpse, inkling, glimmer, scent, suspicion; conception, notion, idea, 453.

System or body of knowledge; science, philosophy, doctrine, theory, literature, 560.

Erudition, learning, lore, scholarship, book learning, bookishness, bibliomania, education, instruction, information, acquisitions, acquirements, accomplishments, proficiency; a liberal education, encyclopedical knowledge, omniscience, pantology.

Elements, rudiments, abecedary, cyclopædia, encyclopædia, school, &c.

Depth, extent, profoundness, profundity, stores, &c., solidity, accuracy, &c., of knowledge.

V. To know, be aware of, ween, have, possess, conceive, apprehend, understand, comprehend, make out, recognize, be master

491. IGNORANCE, unacquaintance, unconsciousness, darkness, blindness, incomprehension, inexperience, emptiness.

Imperfect knowledge, smattering, sciolism, glimmering; bewilderment, perplexity; incapacity.

Affectation of knowledge, pedantry.

V. To be ignorant, &c., not to know, to know not, to know not what, not to be aware of, to be at a loss, to be at fault, to ignore, to be blind to, &c., not to understand, &c.

Adj. Ignorant, unconscious, unaware, unwitting, witless, a stranger to, unacquainted, unconversant, unenlightened, unversed, uncultivated, in the dark.

Uninformed, uninstructed, untaught, unapprised, untutored, unschooled, unguided.

Shallow, superficial, green, rude, half-learned, illiterate, unread, uneducated, unlearned, unlettered, having a smattering, &c., pedantic.

Confused, puzzled, bewildered, lost, benighted, at a loss, at fault

of, know full we , possess the knowledge of, experience, discern, perceive, see through.

Adj. Knowing, aware of, &c., cognizant of, acquainted with, privy to, conscious of, no stranger to, versed in, conversant with, proficient in, read in, familiar with.

Apprised of, made acquainted with, led into, informed of; undeceived, unbeguiled, unbenighted, unbigoted.

Erudite, instructed, learned, (educated,) well-read, lettered, well-informed, bookish, scholastic, deep-read, book-learned; self-taught, well-grounded, well-conned.

Known, (ascertained,) &c., well-known, notorious, proverbial, familiar, cognoscible.

Extensive, vast, encyclopedical, deep, profound, accurate, solid.

posed, blinded, distracted, in a maze, hoodwinked, in the dark.

Unknown, unapprehended, unexplained, unascertained, uninvestigated, unexplored, unheard of, unperceived.

Adv. Ignorantly, unwittingly, unawares; for any thing one knows; for aught one knows.

---

492. Scholar, schoolman, graduate, doctor, (professor,) gownsman, philosopher, linguist.

Pedant, pedagogue, bookworm, bibliomaniac, bluestocking.

493. Ignoramus, sciolist, smatterer, novice, greenhorn, half scholar, booby, dunce, 501, bigot, 481.

Adj. Bookless, shallow, 499, ignorant, &c., 491.

494. Object of knowledge.

Truth, verity, actual existence, 1, reality, fact, matter of fact, actuality, nature, principle; substantialness, genuineness, authenticity.

Accuracy, exactness, exactitude, precision, preciseness, niceness, delicacy, fineness, strictness, rigor, punctuality.

V. To be true, real, &c., to hold good.

To render true, legitimatize, substantiate, to make good, establish.

To get at the truth, *see* 480.

Adj. True, real, veritable, actual, certain, 474, positive, absolute, existing, 1, substantial, categorical; unrefuted, unconfuted.

Exact, accurate, definite, precise, just, correct, well-defined, strict, rigid, rigorous, scrupulous, conscientious, religious, punctilio-

495. Untruth, *see* 546.

Error, mistake, fallacy, misconception, misapprehension, misunderstanding, inaccuracy, incorrectness, inexactness, vagueness, &c., misconstruction, 523, miscomputation, miscalculation.

Fault, blunder, bull, slip of the tongue, cross purposes, oversight, misprint, erratum, slip of the pen; heresy, misstatement, misreport.

Illusion, delusion, self-deceit, self-deception, hallucination, monomania, aberration; dream, shadow, bubble, false light, the mists of error, chimera.

V. To be erroneous, false, &c., to cause error, to mislead, lead astray, lead into error, delude, give a false impression, idea, &c., to falsify, misstate, misrepresent, deceive, 545, beguile.

To be in error, to mistake, to

ous, nice, mathematical, axiomatic, demonstrable, scientific, unerring, faithful, curious, delicate.

Genuine, authentic, legitimate, orthodox, pure, sound, sterling, unsophisticated, unadulterated, unvarnished; solid, substantial, undistorted, undisguised, unaffected, unexaggerated, unromantic.

Adv. Truly, verily, veritably, certainly, assuredly, in truth, in good truth, of a truth, really, indubitably, in sooth, forsooth, in reality, in fact, indeed, in effect, actually, positively, virtually, at bottom.

Precisely, accurately, &c., mathematically, to a nicety, to a hair.

In every respect, in all respects, at any rate, at all events, by all means.

496. MAXIM, aphorism, apothegm, dictum, saying, adage, saw, proverb, sentence, precept, 697, rule, formula, code, motto, word, by-word, moral, sentiment, conclusion, reflection, thought, golden rule, axiom, theorem, scholium, truism.

Catechism, creed, profession of faith.

Adj. Aphoristic, proverbial, axiomatic, conclusive.

Wise, sage, true, received, admitted, recognized; common, hackneyed, trite, commonplace.

receive a false impression; to be or labor under an error, mistake, &c., to blunder, be at fault, to misapprehend, misconceive, misunderstand, misconjecture, misreckon, miscalculate, miscount, misestimate, misjudge, flounder, trip.

Adj. Erroneous, untrue, false, unreal, unsubstantial, baseless, groundless, ungrounded.

Inexact, unexact, incorrect, illogical, partial, one-sided, unreasonable, indefinite, unscientific, inaccurate, aberrant.

In error, mistaken, &c., tripping, floundering, &c.

Illusive, illusory, ideal, fanciful, chimerical, visionary, shadowy, mock.

Spurious, illegitimate, bastard, meretricious, deceitful, sophisticated, adulterated.

497. ABSURDITY, absurdness, nonsense, paradox, inconsistency, quibble, sophism, 477, bull, Hibernicism. Folly in action, 699.

Jargon, gibberish, rigmarole, fustian, rant, bombast, bathos, rhapsody, extravagance, rhodomontade, romance.

Twaddle, fudge, verbiage, trash, stuff, balderdash, palaver, moonshine, wishwash, platitude, flummery, inanity.

Vagary, foolery, mummery, monkey trick.

Adj. Absurd, nonsensical, foolish, &c., *see* 499, sophistical, inconsistent, extravagant, quibbling, trashy, washy, twaddling, &c.

498. INTELLIGENCE, capacity, parts, sagacity, sagaciousness, wit, mother wit, quick parts.

Acuteness, acumen, shrewdness, astuteness, sharpness, cleverness, aptness, aptitude, quickness, subtlety, archness, penetra-

499. IMBECILITY, incapacity, vacancy of mind, poverty of intellect, shallowness, dulness, stupidity, obtuseness, stolidity, doltishness.

Silliness, simplicity, childishness, puerility; dotage, second

tion, perspicacity, perspicaciousness, clearsightedness, discrimination, discernment.

Head, brains, headpiece, a long head.

WISDOM sapience, sense, good sense, common sense, plain sense, reason, reasonableness, judgment, judiciousness, solidity, depth, profoundness, enlarged views; reach or compass of thought.

Genius, inspiration, the fire of genius.

Wisdom in action; prudence, discretion, 864, sobriety, tact, ballast, 698.

V. To be intelligent, wise, &c., to reason, 476, to discern, 441, discriminate, 465, to penetrate, to see far into.

Adj. (Applied to persons.) Intelligent, lougheaded, sagacious, quick, sharp, clever, apt, acute, shrewd, astute, sharpsighted, quicksighted, quickeyed, keen, keeneyed, keensighted, keenwitted, sharpwitted, penetrating, piercing, clearsighted, discerning.

Wise, sage, sapient, sagacious, reasonable, rational, sound, sensible, judicious, enlightened, impartial, unprejudiced, unbiased, unprepossessed, undazzled, unperplexed.

Cool, coolheaded, longheaded, calculating, thoughtful, reflecting, oracular, Heaven directed.

Prudent, discreet, sober, staid, solid, considerate, provident, politic.

(Applied to actions.) Wise, sensible, reasonable, judicious, well-judged, well-advised, prudent, politic, expedient, 646.

500. SAGE, wise man, expert, adept, authority.

childishness, fatuity, idiocy, idiotism, 503.

FOLLY, absurdity, irrationality, senselessness, foolishness, inconsistency, conceit, giddiness, extravagance, oddity, eccentricity, ridiculousness.

Act of folly, blunder, 497, imprudence, 699, rashness, 863.

V. To be imbecile, foolish, &c., to trifle, drivel, ramble.

Adj. (Applied to persons.) Unintelligent, unintellectual, shallow, weak, soft, sappy, weak-headed, weak-minded, feeble-minded, half-witted, short-witted, shallow-brained, dull, stupid, obtuse, blunt, stolid, doltish, asinine, dull-witted, blunt-witted.

Childish, infantine, infantile, babyish, childlike.

Fatuous, idiotic, imbecile, drivelling, brainless, witless, having no head or brains, thick-skulled, blockish, Bœotian, Bœotic.

Foolish, silly, senseless, irrational, insensate, nonsensical, muddy-headed, ungifted, undiscerning, unenlightened, unphilosophical; prejudiced, bigoted, purblind, narrow-minded, wrong-headed, crotchety, conceited, self-opinionated, mulish, besotted, infatuated.

Wild, giddy, thoughtless, eccentric, odd, extravagant, light headed, hairbrained, shatter-brained, 503, ridiculous.

(Applied to actions.) Foolish, unwise, injudicious, imprudent, unreasonable, nonsensical, absurd, ridiculous, silly, stupid, asinine, ill-advised, ill-judged, ill-devised, inconsistent, irrational, unphilosophical, extravagant, preposterous, egregious, imprudent, indiscreet, improvident, impolitic, improper, 645, 647.

501. FOOL, wiseacre, simpleton, witling, ninny, dolt, numskull

Oracle, a Solomon, a Nestor, a master mind, a shining light, schoolman, academician, academist.

Venerable, reverenced, authoritative.

502. SANITY, rationality, being in one's senses, in one's right mind, in one's sober senses; sobriety, lucidness, lucid interval.

V. To be sane, &c., to retain one's senses, reason, &c.

To become sane, come to one's senses, sober down.

To render sane, bring to one's senses, to sober.

Adj. Sane, rational, reasonable, sober, in one's sober senses, in one's right mind, sober-minded.

Adv. Sanely, soberly, &c.

half-wit, driveller, idiot; child, infant, baby, innocent, greenhorn, flat, dunce, lout, changeling, dotard, driveller.

503. INSANITY, lunacy, madness, derangement, alienation, aberration, mania, calenture of the brain, frenzy, raving, monomania, disordered intellect, incoherence, wandering, delirium, hallucination, fantasia; vertigo, dizziness, swimming, dementation

V. To be or become insane, &c., to lose one's senses, intellects, reason, faculties, &c., to run mad, rave, dote, ramble, wander, drivel.

To render or drive mad; to madden, dementate, turn the brain, turn one's head, befool, infatuate, derange the head.

Adj. Insane, mad, lunatic, crazy, crazed, out of one's mind, bereft of reason, insensate, beside one's self, demented, possessed, maniacal, delirious, incoherent, rambling, doting, wandering, frantic, raving, rabid, lightheaded, giddy, vertiginous, wild, haggard, flighty, distracted.

504. MADMAN, lunatic, maniac, bedlamite, raver, monomaniac, dreamer, insane, a highflier, madcap.

Section VI. EXTENSION OF THOUGHT.

1. *To the Past.*

505. MEMORY, remembrance, reminiscence, recognition, retention, retentiveness, tenacity, readiness.

Recurrence, recollection, retrospection, retrospect.

Suggestion, prompting, 514; hint.

Token of remembrance, memorial, memento, souvenir, keepsake, relic, reliquary, memorandum, remembrancer.

Art of memory, artificial memory; mnemonics.

V. To remember, retain, mind,

506. OBLIVION, forgetfulness, obliteration, 552, a short memory, the memory failing, being in fault, or deserting one.

V. To forget, lose, unlearn, discharge from the memory.

To slip, escape, fade, die away from the memory, to sink into oblivion.

Adj. Forgotten, &c., lost, effaced, blotted out, obliterated, discharged, past recollection, unremembered.

Forgetful, oblivious, mindless, out of mind.

bear or keep in mind; have or carry in the memory, know by heart or by rote.

To be deeply impressed, to live, remain, or dwell in the memory; to be stored up, to sink in the mind, to rankle, &c.

To occur to the mind, 514, to recollect, bethink one's self, recall, call up, retrace, look back, rake up, think upon.

To suggest, prompt, hint, recall to mind, put in mind, remind, call up, summon up, refresh the memory.

To commit to memory, get or learn by heart or rote, con, con over, repeat, to fix, imprint, impress, stamp, grave, engrave, store, treasure up, embalm, enshrine, &c., in the memory; to load, store, stuff, or burden the memory with.

Adj. Remembering, &c., mindful, remembered, &c., fresh, green, unforgotten; present to the mind; living in, being in or within one's memory; indelible, green in remembrance.

The memory being retentive, tenacious, ready, correct, exact, faithful, trustworthy, capacious.

Adv. By heart, by rote.

2. *To the Future.*

507. Expectation, expectance, anticipation, forestalling, foreseeing, reckoning, calculation.

Contemplation, prospect, perspective, hope, trust, 858, abeyance, waiting, &c., 121.

V. To expect, look for, look out for, look forward to, anticipate, contemplate, flatter one's self, to dare to say, foresee, 510, forestall, reckon upon, count upon, lay one's account to, to calculate upon, rely upon, build upon, make sure of, prepare one's self for.

To wait, tarry, lie in wait, watch for; abide.

To raise or excite expectation, to bid fair, to promise, to augur, &c., 511.

Adj. Expectant, expecting, &c., prepared for, ready for.

Expected, anticipated, foreseen, &c. long expected; in prospect, &c.

Anxious, ardent, eager, breathless, sanguine.

508. Inexpectation, non-expectation, *see* Surprise, 870.

False or vain expectation, miscalculation.

V. Not to expect, not to look for, &c., to be taken by surprise, to come upon, to fall upon; to miscalculate.

To be unexpected, &c., to pop, to come unawares, suddenly, abruptly; like a thunderbolt, burst upon.

Adj. Non-expectant, unexpected, unlooked for, unhoped for, unforeseen, beyond expectation, abrupt, sudden; happening contrary to or against expectation.

Surprised, taken by surprise, unwarned, startled, &c., taken aback.

Adv. Suddenly, abruptly, unexpectedly, unawares, without notice or warning, 113.

---

509. Failure of expectation.

Disappointment, surprise, astonishment, 870.

A balk, an afterclap.

V. To be disappointed, &c., to look blank; to look agnast.

To disappoint, balk, to crush or dash one's hope, 859.

Adj. Disappointed, aghast, blue.

510. Foresight, prescience, foreknowledge, forethought, forecast, prevision, precognition, second sight, clairvoyance.

Anticipation, foretaste, presentiment, foregone conclusion, providence.

Announcement, programme.

V. To foresee, foreknow, forejudge, forecast, anticipate, look forwards or beyond; look, peep, or pry into the future.

Adj. Foreseeing, &c., prescient, farseeing; farsighted; weatherwise.

Rational, sagacious, perspicacious

511. Prediction, announcement, prophecy, vaticination, prognostication, premonstration, auguration, augury, horoscope, nativity, fortune telling, ominousness; *see* Necromancy, 992.

V. To predict, prognosticate, prophesy, vaticinate, presage, augur, bode, forebode, foretell, soothsay.

To foretoken, betoken, prefigure, portend, foreshadow, foreshow, usher in, herald, signify, premise, announce, point to, admonish, warn, forewarn, advise.

Adj. Predicting, &c., predictive, prophetic, oracular, sibylline.

Ominous, portentous, auspicious, monitory, premonitory, significant of, pregnant with, weatherwise.

512. Omen, portent, presage, prognostic, augury, auspice, sign, forerunner, precursor, 64, harbinger, herald, monitor, warning.

513. Oracle, prophet, seer, soothsayer, fortune teller, witch, necromancer.

Section VII. Creative Thought.

514. Supposition, conjecture, surmise, guess, divination, conceit; assumption, postulation, presumption, presupposition, hypothesis, postulate, theory; suggestion, proposition, motion, proposal, allusion.

V. To suppose, conjecture, surmise, guess, divine, give a guess, hazard a conjecture, throw out a conjecture, &c., presuppose, fancy, take it, dare to say, take it into one's head, presume.

To suggest, hint, insinuate, put forth, propound, propose, start, prompt, put a case, move, make a motion, allude to.

To suggest itself, occur to one, come into one's head; to run in the head; to haunt, 505.

Adj. Supposing, &c., supposed, supposititious, suppositive, putative, suggestive, allusive, conjectural, presumptive, hypothetical, theoretical.

Warranted, authorized, fair, reasonable, just, natural.

Unwarranted, gratuitous, baseless, wild, hazarded, rash, untenable, extravagant, unreasonable, unsatisfactory, loose, vague, unconnected.

515. **Imagination**, fancy, conception, ideality, idealism, inspiration, dreaming, somnambulism, frenzy, ecstasy, excogitation; liveliness of fancy.

Invention, originality, fertility, conceit, figment, coinage, fiction, romance, novel, fairyland, myth, dream, daydream, vapor, phantom, fantasy, whim, whimsy, vagary, rhapsody.

A visionary, romancer, rhapsodist, highflier, enthusiast, dreamer seer, fanatic, knight errant, Don Quixote.

V. To imagine, fancy, conceive, idealize, realize; fancy or picture to one's self; create, devise, invent, coin, fabricate.

Adj. Imagining, imagined, &c.; ideal, unreal, imaginary, fictitious, fanciful, air-drawn, air-built, original, fantastic, unsubstantial, whimsical, high-flown.

Imaginative, inventive, creative, fertile, romantic, flighty, extravagant, fanatic, enthusiastic, Utopian, Quixotic.

Warm, heated, excited, sanguine, ardent, fiery, boiling, wild, bold, daring; playful, fertile, &c.

Division II. COMMUNICATION OF IDEAS.

Section I. Nature of Ideas communicated.

516. Idea to be conveyed.

Meaning, signification, sense, import, purport, significance, drift, gist, acceptation, bearing, interpretation, 522, reading, tenor, allusion, spirit, coloring, expression.

Literal meaning, obvious meaning, first blush; after acceptation.

Equivalent meaning, synonyme.

Thing signified; matter, substance, pith, marrow, argument, text.

V. To mean, signify, express, import, purport, convey, imply, bespeak, bear a sense, involve, declare, 527, insinuate, allude to, point to, drive at.

To take, understand, receive, or accept in a particular sense.

Adj. Meaning, &c., significant, significative, pithy, telling, striking, full of meaning, pregnant with meaning.

Synonymous, equivalent, tantamount; the same thing as.

517. Absence of meaning.

Unmeaningness, empty sound, a dead letter, inexpressiveness.

Nonsense, gibberish, empty babble, empty sound.

V. To mean nothing, to be unmeaning, &c.

Adj. Unmeaning, void of meaning, of sense, &c., senseless, not significant.

Undefinable, unmeant, unconceived.

Plain, simple, natural, obvious, explicit, precise, **518**, downright, definite, distinct, defined, literal, ostensible, overt broad, naked, unstrained, undisguised, positive, formal, honest, emphatic, true.

Implied, tacit, understood, implicit, inferred, latent.

Adv. Literally, &c., 522.

518. INTELLIGIBILITY, clearness, lucidness, perspicuity, explicitness, distinctness, plain speaking, expressiveness, legibleness, visibility, 446.

Intelligence, comprehension, understanding, learning, 539.

V. To be intelligible, &c.

To render intelligible, &c.; to throw light upon, to simplify.

To understand, comprehend, take, take in, catch, grasp, collect; to come to an understanding.

Adj. Intelligible, clear, lucid, explicit, expressive, significant, express, distinct, precise, definite, well-defined, perspicuous, plain, obvious, manifest, palpable, glaring, transparent, above board, unshaded, recognizable, unambiguous, unmistakable, legible, open, positive, unconfused, unequivocal, graphic.

519. UNINTELLIGIBILITY, incomprehensibleness, inconceivableness, darkness, 421, obscurity, confusion, indistinctness, indefiniteness, vagueness, (mistiness,) ambiguity, looseness, uncertainty, mysteriousness, 526, paradox, inexplicableness.

Jargon, gibberish, rhodomontade, &c., 497.

V. To be unintelligible, &c.

To render unintelligible, &c., 528, to perplex, confuse, confound, bewilder, darken.

Not to understand, &c., to lose, miss, &c., to lose the clew.

Adj. Unintelligible, inapprehensible, incomprehensible, inconceivable, above or past comprehension, inexplicable, illegible, undecipherable, inscrutable, beyond one's depth, paradoxical, insolvable, impenetrable,

Obscure, dark, confused, indistinct, indefinite, nebulous, undefined, ill-defined, crooked, indirect, perplexed, loose, vague, ambiguous, enigmatical, mysterious, mystic, mystical, intricate.

Hidden, sealed, recondite, abstruse, transcendental, far fetched.

520. Having a double sense.

EQUIVOCALNESS, double meaning, equivocation, prevarication slip of the tongue.

Having a doubtful meaning, ambiguity, *see* 475; homonymy.

Having a false meaning, *see* 544.

V. To be equivocal, &c., to have two senses, &c., to equivocate, prevaricate, palter to the understanding.

Adj. Equivocal, ambiguous, double-tongued, equivocating, &c.

521. METAPHOR, figure, metonymy, trope, figure of speech, figurativeness, image, imagery, type, 22.

Personification, allegory, apologue, parable.

Implication, inference, allusion, adumbration, hidden meaning.

V. To employ metaphor, &c., to personify, allegorize, adumbrate shadow forth, imply, understand, apply, allude to

Adj. Metaphorical, figurative, typical, parabolic, allegorical, allusive, implied, inferential, implicit, understood.

522. Interpretation, exegesis, explanation, explication, expounding, exposition, (paraphrase.)

Translation, version, (rendering,) construction, reading, restoration.

Comment, commentary, illustration, exemplification, definition, elucidation, dilucidation, gloss, glossary, annotation, scholium, note, key, master key, answer, 462.

V. To interpret, expound, explain, construe, translate, render, turn into, transfuse the sense of.

To read, spell, make out, decipher, unfold, disentangle, elicit the meaning of, find the key of, unriddle, unravel, resolve, 480, restore.

To elucidate, illustrate, exemplify, comment upon, define, unfold.

523. Misinterpretation, misapprehension, misunderstanding misconstruction, misspelling, misapplication, mistake.

Misrepresentation, perversion, falsification, misquotation, garbling, exaggeration, 549, false coloring, abuse of terms, parody, travesty, misstatement, &c., 544.

V. To misinterpret, misapprehend, misunderstand, misconceive, misspell, mistranslate, misconstrue, misapply, mistake, 495.

To misstate, &c., 544; to pervert, falsify, distort, travesty, stretch, strain, or wrest the sense or meaning; to misquote, garble, belie, explain away.

Adj. Misinterpreted, &c., untranslated, untranslatable.

Adj. Explanatory, expository, explicatory, exegetical.

Paraphrastic, metaphrastic, literal.

Adv. That is to say, in other words, in plain words, simply, in plain English.

Literally, verbatim, strictly speaking.

524. Interpreter, expositor, scholiast, commentator, (annotator,) speaker, mouthpiece, dragoman.

Section II. Modes of Communication.

525. Manifestation, expression, showing, &c., indication, exposition, demonstration, exhibition, production, display, showing off.

Openness, frankness, 543, publicity, 531.

V. To manifest, show, express, indicate, point out, bring forth, bring forward, set forth, exhibit, expose, produce, bring into view, set before one, hold up to view, lay open, lay bare, expose to

526. Latency, secrecy, secretness, privacy, invisibility, *see* 447, occultness, darkness, silence, closeness, reserve, inexpression. A sealed book.

Retirement, seclusion, 893.

V. To be latent, &c., to keep back, reserve, suppress, keep close, keep secret, keep to one's self, hold one's peace, leave in the dark, hush up.

Adj. Latent, secret, close, dormant, unapparent, unknown, 491

view, set before one's eyes, show up, shadow forth, bring to light, display, demonstrate, to unroll, unveil, unmask, disclose, *see* 529, to elicit, educe, draw out, bring out, disinter.

To be manifested, &c., to appear, transpire, come to light, to come out, *see* Visibility, 446.

Adj. Manifest, clear, apparent, evident, visible, 446, prominent, in the foreground, (in full view,) salient, open, conspicuous, palpable, glaring.

Manifested, shown, expressed &c., disclosed, *see* 529, frank, capable of being shown, producible.

in the background, occult, private, privy, sequestered.

Unconspicuous, indiscoverable, unperceived, invisible, 447, unseen, unwitnessed, impenetrable, unspied, unsuspected.

Untold, unpublished, unbreathed, untalked of, unsung, unpronounced, unreported, unexposed, unproclaimed, unexpressed, not expressed, tacit, implied, undeveloped, unsolved, unexplained undiscovered, untracked, unexplored, uninvented.

Adv. Openly, before one's eyes, face to face, above board, in open court, in open daylight, in the open streets.

527. Information, communication, intimation, notice, notification, enunciation, announcement, annunciation, statement, specification, report, advice, monition, mention, acquainting, &c., intercommunication, communicativeness.

An informant, teller, intelligencer, messenger, 534, authority.

Hint, suggestion, 514, insinuation, inuendo, wink, glance, leer, nod, shrug, gesture, whisper, implication, cue.

V. To inform, acquaint, tell, mention, express, intimate, communicate, apprise, make known, notify, signify to, let one know, advise, state, specify, give notice, announce, annunciate, report, set forth, bring word, send word, leave word, write word, declare, pronounce, explain, undeceive; to convey the knowledge of; to open the eyes of; to give an account of.

To say, &c., *see* 582.

To hint, give an inkling of; give, throw out, or drop a hint; insinuate, allude to, glance at, make allusion to; to wink, glance,

528. Concealment, hiding &c., secrecy, stealth, stealthiness slyness, disguise, masquerade mystery, mystification, freemasonry, reservation, suppression reserve, uncommunicativeness a secret path, a trap door.

A mask, visor, ambush, &c., *see* 530, enigma, riddle, &c. 533.

V. To conceal, hide, secrete, cover, screen, cloak, veil, shroud, shade, eclipse, ensconce, muffle, mask, disguise.

To keep from, lock up, seal up, bury, sink, suppress, hush up, keep snug or close, &c.

To keep in ignorance, blind, hoodwink, mystify, pose, puzzle, perplex, embarrass, bewilder, &c., 545.

To ignore; to shut one's eyes; to turn a deaf ear to.

To be concealed, &c., to lurk, skulk, smoulder, lie hid, lie in ambush, sneak, retire, steal into, steal along.

To conceal one's self, put on a veil, mask, &c., 530; to retire from sight.

Adj. Concealed, hid, hidden

leer, nod, shrug, give the cue, wave, whisper, suggest, prompt, whisper in the ear.

To be informed, &c., of; made acquainted with; to understand.

To hear of; to come to one's ears, to come to one's knowledge, to reach one's ears.

Adj. Informed, &c., of, made acquainted with; undeceived.

Reported, made known, bruited.

Expressive, significant, pregnant with meaning, &c., *see* 516, declaratory, enunciative, nuncupatory, expository, communicatory, communicative.

Adv. Expressively, significantly, &c.

By post, courier, express, telegraph, messenger, &c., 534.

&c., secret, auricular, clandestine, close, furtive, surreptitious, stealthy, underhand, sly, sneaking, skulking, undivulged, unrevealed, undisclosed, unmentioned.

Mysterious, mystic, mystical, enigmatical, problematical, paradoxical, occult, recondite, abstruse, unexplained, impenetrable, indiscoverable, inexplicable, in a maze, irrevealable, undiscovered.

Covered, closed, shrouded, veiled, masked, screened, shaded, disguised, under cover, under a cloud, veil, &c., in a fog, haze, mist, &c., under an eclipse.

Reserved, uncommunicative, mum, taciturn, 585.

Adv. Secretly, clandestinely, privily, in secret, incognito, with closed doors, under the rose, underhand, privately, in private, behind one's back; one's back being turned, behind the scenes, behind the curtain.

Confidentially, between ourselves, between you and me, in strict confidence; it must go no farther.

529. Disclosure, revealment, revelation, exposition.

Acknowledgment, avowal, confession.

V. To disclose, open, lay open, divulge, reveal, unfold, let drop, let out, lay open, acknowledge, allow, admit, concede, grant, own, confess, avow; to unburden or disburden one's mind or one's conscience, to unbosom one's self, to open one's mind.

To unfold, unseal, unveil, unmask.

To blab, let out, tell tales, speak out.

To make public, publish, *see* 531.

To make no secret of, to disabuse, undeceive.

To be disclosed, revealed, &c., to come out, to transpire, to ooze out, to creep out.

Adj. Disclosed, revealed, divulged, laid open, &c., unriddled, &c.

Open, public, exoteric.

530. Ambush, hiding-place, retreat, cover, lurking-hole, secret-place, recess, ambuscade, trap, gin, *see* 545.

A mask, veil, visor, cloak, screen, curtain, shade, cover, disguise, masquerade dress, domino.

V. To lie in ambush, lurk, lie in wait for, lay or set a trap for.

---

531. Publication, announcement, notification, enunciation, annunciation, advertisement, promulgation, circulation, propagation proclamation.

Publicity, notoriety, currency, flagrancy, cry, bruit, rumor, fame report, the town talk.

Notice, notification, manifesto, advertisement, (despatch,) placard bill, newspapers, gazette.

V. To publish, make known, announce, notify, annunciate, broach set forth, put forth, emit, give forth, give out, utter, advertise, placard circulate, propagate, spread, spread abroad, promulgate, edit, rumor diffuse, disseminate, blaze about; blaze or noise abroad; bandy, hawk about, trumpet, herald, give tongue, raise a cry, raise a hue and cry; to bring, lay, or drag before the public, give currency to.

To be published, &c., to become public, to go forth, to get abroad, to get wind, to get afloat, to acquire currency, to spread, to go the rounds.

Adj. Published, &c., made public, rumored, rife, current, floating, afloat, notorious, flagrant, whispered, disseminated, reported, trumpet-tongued, encyclical.

532. News, piece of information, intelligence, tidings, budget of news, word, advice, message, errand, embassy, despatch, bulletin.

Report, rumor, hearsay, fame, talk, gossip, scandal, bruit; the town talk.

533. Secret, profound secret, mystery, problem, enigma, riddle, puzzle, conundrum, charade, rebus, logograph, monogram, paradox, maze, labyrinth, perplexity.

Letters, mail, post, 592, letter bag, (telegraphic despatch.)

Glad tidings; fresh news, old news, stale news; a stale story.

534. Messenger, envoy, nuncio, internuncio, herald, ambassador, legate, emissary.

Marshal, crier, trumpeter, pursuivant, courier, runner.

Narrator, &c., talebearer, spy, scout.

535. Affirmation, predication, assertion, declaration, word, averment, asseveration, protestation, protest, profession, deposition, avouchment, assurance, allegation, acknowledgment, avowal, confession, oath.

Remark, observation, position, (ground,) thesis, proposition, saying, dictum, theorem.

Positiveness, dogmatism.

V. To assert, make an assertion, &c., say, affirm, predicate, declare, profess, aver, avouch, hold out, put forth, advance, allege, propose, propound, broach, set forth, maintain, contend, pronounce, pretend, pass or hazard an opinion, &c.; to reassert, reaffirm.

536. Negation, abnegation, denial, disavowal, disclaimer, abjuration, contradiction, contravention, retraction, retractation, recantation, renunciation, recusancy.

Qualification, modification, 469.

V. To deny, disown, contradict, negative, gainsay, contravene, disclaim, withdraw, eat one's words, recant, disavow, retract, revoke, abjure.

To dispute, impugn, question call in question, give the lie to rebut, belie.

Adj. Denying, &c., denied, &c contradictory, recusant.

Adv. No, nay, not, *see* 489.

To vouch, assure, vow, swear, take oath, recognize, avow, acknowledge, own, confess, announce.

To dogmatize, lay down, lay down the law; to call Heaven to witness, protest, depose, warrant.

Adj. Asserting, &c., dogmatic, positive, absolute, emphatic, predicable, pronunciative.

Positive, broad, round, express, explicit, pointed, marked, distinct, decided, formal, solemn, categorical, peremptory, emphatic.

Adv. Positively, broadly, roundly, flatly, emphatically, &c.

537. Teaching, instruction, direction, guidance, tuition, inculcation, indoctrination, explanation.

Education, initiation, preparation, training, schooling, discipline, exercise, drill, exercitation, breaking in, taming, drilling, &c., persuasion, edification, proselytism, propagandism.

A lesson, lecture, prolusion, prelection, exercise, task.

Rudiments, elements, text book, guide book, school book.

V. To teach, instruct, enlighten, edify, inculcate, indoctrinate, instil, imbue, inoculate, infuse, impregnate, graft, infix, ingraft, implant, sow the seeds of, infiltrate, give an idea of, cram.

To explain, expound, lecture, hold forth, read a lecture or sermon, give a lesson, preach; sermonize, moralize, point a moral.

To educate, train, discipline, school, form, ground, tutor, prepare, qualify, drill, exercise, bring up, nurture, break in, tame.

To direct, guide, put in the way of, put one up to, enlighten, set right; to give one new ideas.

To persuade, convince; bring over, bring round or win over to an opinion.

Adj. Teaching, &c., taught, &c. Didactic, academic, doctrinal, disciplinal, instructive, scholastic, persuasive.

538. Misteaching, misdirection, misinformation, misguidance, misinstruction, perversion, false teaching, (misleading.)

Indocility, incapacity, dulness.

V. To misinform, mislead, misdirect, misguide, misinstruct, miscorrect, pervert, lead into error, bewilder, mystify, 528, to unteach.

Adj. Misteaching, &c., unedifying.

539. Learning, acquisition of knowledge, acquirement, attainment, scholarship, erudition, instruction, study, &c., *see* Knowledge, 490, apprenticeship.

Docility, aptitude, aptness to be taught, persuasibility, capacity.

V. To learn; to acquire, gain, catch, receive, imbibe, pick up, gather; collect, glean, &c., knowledge or information.

To hear, overhear, catch hold of, take in, drink in, master.

Adj. Docile, apt, teachable, persuasible, studious.

---

540. Teacher, instructor, master, director, tutor, preceptor, institutor, Mentor, adviser, monitor, counsellor, disciplinarian, guide, cicerone, pioneer, governess.

541. Learner, scholar, student, disciple, pupil, schoolboy beginner, tyro, abecedarian, novice.

Proselyte, convert, catechu

Orator, speaker, mouthpiece, 582.

Professor, lecturer, reader, prelector, (principal, head master, assistant teacher, schoolmaster, schoolmistress, schooldame,) usher. pedagogue.

men, class, form, (division, section.)

Pupilage, apprenticeship, novitiate, matriculation.

---

542. School, university, college, seminary, lyceum, academy, institute, institution, gymnasium, (Latin school, high school, grammar school, secondary or intermediate school, primary school, infant school, charity school, public school, common school, law, medical, divinity school, theological seminary, scientific school, polytechnic school, normal school, young ladies' seminary, boarding school, family school, school of design, asylum for the deaf mutes, for the blind, for idiots.)

Horn book, rudiments, school book, manual.

Professorship, lectureship, chair, forum, stage, rostrum, platform, pulpit.

Adj. Scholastic, academic.

543. Veracity, truthfulness, truth, sincerity, frankness, straightforwardness, ingenuousness, candor, honesty, fidelity, openness, unreservedness, bluntness, plainness, plain speaking, plain dealing.

Simplicity, artlessness, 703, love of truth.

V. To speak the truth, speak one's mind, think aloud.

Adj. Truthful, true, veracious, sincere, candid, frank, open, free-spoken, open-hearted, honest, simple, simple-hearted, ingenuous, blunt, plain-spoken, straightforward, fair, artless, guileless, pure, natural, unaffected, simple-minded, undisguised, unfeigned, unflattering.

Adv. Truly, &c., 494, above board, broadly.

---

544. Falsehood, falseness, mendacity, falsification, perversion of truth, romance, forgery, prevarication, equivocation, shuffling, evasion, unfairness, dishonesty, misrepresentation.

Insincerity, duplicity, double dealing, dissimulation, dissembling, hypocrisy, cant, humbug, Jesuitry, mental reservation, disguise, simulation, acting, sham, pretending, &c., crocodile tears, false coloring, art, artfulness, 702, perjury, deceiver, *see* 548.

V. To be false, &c., to speak falsely, lie, fib, tell a lie or untruth, &c., 546, to mistake, misreport, misrepresent, falsify, prevaricate, equivocate, palter, shuffle, fence, mince the truth.

To forswear, swear false, perjure one's self, bear false witness.

To garble, gloss over, disguise, color, varnish, dress up, put a false coloring or construction upon, 523.

To invent, fabricate, trump up, forge, romance.

To dissemble, dissimulate, feign, assume, put on, act or play a part, simulate, pass off for, counterfeit, sham, make believe, cant.

Adj. False, dishonest, faithless, truthless, unfair, uncandid, disingenuous, hollow, insincere, canting, hypocritical, Jesuitical, pharisaical, double, double-tongued, double-faced, smooth tongued, plausible.

Artful, insidious, sly, designing, diplomatic, Machiavelian

Untrue, unfounded, fictitious, invented, forged, falsified, &c., counterfeit, spurious, sham, mock, disguised, simulated, &c., artificial, supposititious, colorable, catchpenny, illusory, elusory, surreptitious, ironical

Adv. Falsely, &c.

545. DECEPTION, fraud, deceit, guile, imposition, artifice, juggle, juggling, sleight of hand, legerdemain, conjuration, trickery, fraudulence, imposture, circumvention, collusion.

Quackery, charlatanism, charlatanry, empiricism, humbug, mummery.

Stratagem, trick, cheat, wile, artifice, fraud, deception, ruse, manœuvre, finesse, hoax, forgery, delusion.

Snare, trap, pitfall, decoy, gin, springe, noose, net, meshes, ambush, ambuscade, *see* 547.

V. To deceive, mislead, cheat, impose upon, practise upon, circumvent, play upon, put upon, dupe, mystify, blind, hoodwink, outreach, trick, hoax, befool, entrap, beguile, lure, inveigle, decoy, insnare, entangle, lay a snare for, trip up.

To defraud, cheat, take in, jockey, cozen, jilt, swindle, victimize, outwit, overreach, palm upon, foist upon, balk, trump up.

Adj. Deceiving, cheating, &c. Deceived, duped, &c.

Deceptive, deceitful, illusive, illusory, delusory, (delusive,) elusive, insidious.

546. UNTRUTH, falsehood, lie, falsity, fiction, fabrication, story, fable, novel, romance, humbug, white lie.

Falsification, perjury, forgery, false swearing, misstatement, misrepresentation.

Pretence, pretext, profession, subterfuge, evasion, disguise, irony, plea, 617, claptrap, shuffle, shift, mask, cloak, veil.

547. DUPE, gull, victim, puppet, *see* Credulity, 486.

---

548. DECEIVER, liar, hypocrite, shuffler, dissemble, Pharisee, Jesuit, Janus.

Pretender, imposter, knave, cheat, rogue, trickster, juggler, swindler, sharper, jockey, blackleg, sharp, gipsy.

Quack, charlatan, mountebank, empiric, quacksalver.

Actor, player, tumbler, posture master.

549. EXAGGERATION, hyperbole, stretch, strain, coloring, flourish, vagary, bombast, figure of speech, flight of fancy, extravagance, rhodomontade, *see* Boasting, 884.

V. To exaggerate, amplify, heighten, overcharge, overstate; overdraw, overcolor, puff, overlay, strain, stretch, flourish; to hyperbolize, aggravate.

Adj. Exaggerated, &c., hyperbolical, turgid, highly-colored, extravagant, bombastic.

Section III. Means of communicating Ideas.

1. *Natural Means.*

550. Indication, symbolization, notation, prefigurement, representation, 554, exposition, notice, 527, trace, 551.

A sign, symbol, index, point or exponent, indicator, mark, token, symptom, type, figure, emblem, cipher, device, motto.

Lineament, feature, line, stroke, dash, trait, score, stripe, streak, dot, point, notch, asterisk, red letter, Italics, print, impress, imprint, underlining, jotting.

For identification: Badge, criterion, check, countercheck, countersign, duplicate, tally, counterfoil, label, ticket, billet, card, bill, witness, voucher, signature, handwriting, sign-manual, cipher, seal, signet, autograph, superscription, indorsement, title, heading, watchword, password.

Insignia: Banner, banneret, flag, colors, streamer, standard, eagle, ensign, pennon, pennant, pendant, gonfalon; crest, arms, armorial bearings, shield, escutcheon, livery, cockade, epaulet.

Indication of locality: Beacon, post, staff, flagstaff, hand, pointer, vane, guidepost, handpost, finger post, directing post, signpost, landmark, seamark, lighthouse, polestar, loadstar, cynosure, guide, address, direction, signboard, watchfire.

Monitory indication: Signal, rocket, bluelight, nod, wink, beck, cue, gesture, gesticulation, dumb show, pantomime, telegraph.

Indication of danger: Alarm, alarum, alarm bell, tocsin, beat of drum, fire cross, sound of trumpet, war cry, war whoop.

Badge of authority, 747; of triumph, 733.

V. To indicate, point out, be the sign, &c., of, denote, betoken, represent, stand for, typify, shadow forth, argue, bear the impress of, witness, attest, testify.

To put an indication, mark, &c.; to note, mark, stamp, label, ticket, indorse, sign, countersign; put, append, or affix a seal or signature; set one's hand to, jot down, book, score, trace, chalk, underline, print, imprint, engrave, stereotype, make an impress of.

To make a sign, signal, &c., signalize; give or hang out a signal; give notice, beckon, beck, nod, wink, give the cue; wave, unfurl, hoist or hang out a banner, flag, &c., show one's colors; give or sound an alarm, beat the drum, sound the trumpets, raise a cry, &c.

Adj. Indicating, &c., indicatory, indicative, typical, symptomatic, exponential, emblematic, attesting, armorial.

Indicated, &c., typified, impressed, &c.

Capable of being denoted, denotable, indelible.

551. Record, trace, vestige, relic, remains, scar, footstep, footmark, footprint, footfall, wake, trail, scent.

Monument, trophy, obelisk, pillar, column, testimonial, memorial, medal.

552. Suppression of sign.

Obliteration, erasure, rasure, cancel, cancellation, deletion, application of the sponge.

V. To efface, obliterate, erase, raze, expunge, cancel, blot out, take out, rub out, scratch out,

Note, minute, register, registry, memorandum, document, voucher, protocol, inscription.

Paper, parchment, scroll, instrument, deed, 771, testament, will, roll, archive, schedule, tablet, cartulary, table, affidavit, certificate, attestation, entry, diploma, protest, muster roll, muster book, note book, commonplace book, portfolio.

Chronicle, annals, gazette, newspaper, gazetteer, state paper, almanac, calendar, ephemeris, diary, log, journal, *see* History, 594, and List, 86.

Registration, tabulation, enrolment, entry, booking.

V. To record, note, register, chronicle, calendar; to make an entry of, insert; to enter, book, take a note of, post, enroll, jot down, take down, mark, sign, &c., 550; to tabulate, catalogue, file.

Adj. Registered, &c.

strike out, wipe out, wash out, sponge, render illegible.

To be effaced, &c., to leave no trace.

Adj. Obliterated, effaced, &c., printless, leaving no trace.

Unrecorded, unregistered, intestate; unattested, unauthenticated.

---

553. Recorder, notary, clerk, registrar, registrary, prothonotary secretary, scribe, remembrancer, historian, annalist, &c., book keeper.

554. Representation, delineation.

Art, the fine arts, design, designing, illustration, imitation, 19, copy, 21.

An image, likeness, effigy, fac simile, imagery, figure, puppet, doll, manikin, model, 599, waxwork.

Hieroglyphic, anaglyph, inscription, diagram, monogram, draught.

Map, plan, chart, ground plan, projection, elevation, iconography, atlas, outline, scheme, schedule.

V. To represent, delineate, design, figure; to shadow out, copy, mould.

To imitate, impersonate, personate, personify, act, take off, hit off.

Adj. Representing, &c.; artistic, imitative.

555. Misrepresentation, distortion, 243, caricature, a bad likeness, daub, scratch, sign painting, anamorphosis; misprint, erratum

---

556. Painting, depicting, &c., photography, &c.

Drawing in pencil, crayons, chalk, water colors.

Painting in oils, in distemper, in fresco; encaustic painting, enamel painting, scene painting.

A picture, drawing, painting, sketch, outline, (group,) tableau, cartoon, fresco; pencil, &c., drawing; oil, &c., painting; daguerreotype, talbotype, photograph; mosaic, tapestry, &c., picture gallery

Portrait, portraiture, likeness, miniature, profile, silhouette.

Landscape, view, still-life.

V. To paint, depict, portray, draw, sketch, pencil, dash off, chalk out, shadow out, adumbrate; daguerreotype, &c., to take a portrait, o take a likeness.

Adj. Painted, &c.; pictorial, graphic, picturesque; like, &c., 17.

557. SCULPTURE, carving, modelling.

A statue, statuary, statuette, figure, model, bust, image, cast, marble, intaglio, anaglyph; medallion, cameo.

V. To sculpture, carve, cut, chisel, model, mould, cast.

Adj. Sculptured, &c.

558. ENGRAVING, etching, xylography, &c.

A print, engraving, impression, plate, cut, woodcut, vignette.

An etching, mezzotint, aquatint, stippling, lithograph.

V. To engrave, grave, etch, lithograph, print, &c.

559. ARTIST, painter, limner, draughtsman, drawer, sketcher, designer, engraver, copyist.

Academician; historical, landscape, portrait, miniature, scene, sign, &c., painter; engraver.

A sculptor, carver, modeller.

Implements of art: Pen, pencil, brush, chalk, crayon; stump, graver, style, burin, canvas, easel, pallet, &c.; studio.

2. *Conventional Means.*

1. *Language generally.*

560. LANGUAGE, tongue, vernacular, mother tongue, vulgar tongue, native tongue; the king's English; the genius of a language. Speech, *see* 582.

Literature, letters, polite literature, the belles lettres, the muses, the humanities; the republic of letters.

Scholarship, 490, scholar, 492.

V. To express by words.

Adj. Literary, linguistic, dialectic, vernacular, current, polyglot, pantomimic.

561. LETTER, alphabet; character, 591, hieroglyphic. Consonant, vowel, diphthong

Syllable, monosyllable, polysyllable.

562. WORD, term, vocable, monogram, cipher, terminology, etymon.

A dictionary, vocabulary, lexicon, index, polyglot, glossary, thesaurus; lexicography; a lexicographer.

Derivation, etymology.

Adj. Verbal, literal, titular.

Similarly derived, conjugate.

563. NEOLOGY, neologism, barbarism, slang, cant, by-word.

A pun, play upon words, conundrum, acrostic.

Dialect, brogue, provincialism, broken English.

Adj. Nominally, &c., verbatim, word for word, literally.

564. NOMENCLATURE.

A name, appellation, designation, appellative, denomination,

565. MISNOMER, missaying, antiphrasis, nickname, assumed name or title. alias.

erm, expression, epithet, style, title, cognomen, patronymic, surname.

Synonyme, namesake; euphemism.

Quotation, citation.

V. To name, call, term, denominate, designate, style, entitle, dub, christen, characterize, specify, define, distinguish.

To be called, &c., to take the name of, quote, cite.

Adj. Named, called, &c., known as; nuncupatory, nuncupative, cognominal, titular, nominal.

Literal, verbal.

V. To misname, missay, miscall, misterm, nickname.

To assume a name; to coin words.

Adj. Misnamed, pseudonymous, &c., self-called, self-styled, newfangled expressions.

Nameless, anonymous, without a name, having no name, innominate, unnamed.

---

566. PHRASE, expression, phraseology, paraphrase, periphrasis, circumlocution, set phrase, round terms; mode or turn of expression; idiom, wording, plain terms, plain English.

Sentence, paragraph, motto.

Figure, trope, metaphor, 521, antiphrasis.

V. To express, phrase, couch, clothe in words, to give expression to.

Adv. Expressed, &c., couched in; periphrastic, circumlocutory.

567. GRAMMAR, accidence, rudiments, syntax, punctuation, philology.

V. To parse, (analyze,) punctuate.

---

568. SOLECISM, bad or false grammar, slip of the pen or tongue, bull.

V. To use bad or faulty grammar, to commit a solecism.

Adj. Ungrammatical, incorrect, faulty, inaccurate.

569. STYLE, diction, phraseology, turn of expression, idiom, manner, strain, composition, authorship.

Various Qualities of Style.

570. PERSPICUITY, lucidness, clearness, plain speaking, intelligibility, 518.

Adj. Perspicuous, clear, lucid, intelligible, plain, transparent, correct.

571. OBSCURITY, ambiguity, &c., *see* Unintelligibility, 519, involution, vagueness.

Adj. Obscure, confused, ambiguous, vague, unintelligible, &c., involved.

572. CONCISENESS, brevity, briefness, terseness, compression, condensation, laconism, pithiness, succintness, quaintness, stiffness.

V. To be concise, &c., to condense, compress, abridge, abbreviate, cut short, curtail, abstract.

Adj. Concise, brief, short, terse, neat, compact, laconic, pithy,

573. DIFFUSENESS, prolixity, verbosity, pleonasm, tautology, copiousness, exuberance, laxity, looseness, verbiage, flow, pleonasm, digression, circumlocution, periphrasis. redundance, episode, expletive, *see* Length, 200.

V. To be diffuse, &c., to expatiate, enlarge, launch out, dilate.

nervous, succinct, quaint, stiff, close, cramped, elliptical.

Adv. In short, briefly, in a word, in a few words; to the point.

expand, spin out, dwell, harp on, insist upon, descant, digress, ramble, rant.

Adj. Diffuse, wordy, verbose, prolix, copious, exuberant, flowing, bombastic, lengthy, long-winded, spun out, long-spun, loose, lax, frothy, flatulent, digressive, discursive, excursive, rambling, pleonastic, periphrastic, episodic.

Minute, detailed, particular, circumstantial.

Adv. In detail.

574. VIGOR, power, force, spirit, point, raciness, liveliness, glow, warmth, piquancy, boldness, gravity, sententiousness, elevation, loftiness, sublimity, eloquence.

Adj. Vigorous, powerful, forcible, nervous, spirited, lively, glowing, sparkling, racy, bold, piquant, pointed, antithetical, sententious, lofty, elevated, sublime, eloquent, vehement, impassioned, full of point, poetic, &c.

575. FEEBLENESS, baldness, tameness, meagreness, coldness, frigidity, poverty, puerility, childishness, dulness.

Adj. Feeble, bald, tame, meagre, jejune, vapid, cold, frigid, poor, dull, languid, prosing, prosy, prosaic.

576. PLAINNESS, simplicity, homeliness, chasteness, neatness, dryness, monotony, severity.

Adj. Simple, unornamental, plain, unadorned, homespun, dry, unvaried, monotonous, severe, &c.

577. ORNAMENT, floridness, richness, flourish, flower of speech; well-rounded periods; high-sounding words; turgidity, pomposity, inflation, pretension, fustian, affectation, inversion, figurativeness, rant, bombast, frothiness.

V. To ornament, overcharge, overlay with ornament, to round a period.

Adj. Ornamented, &c., florid, rich, pedantic, affected, pompous, declamatory, fustian, high-sounding, sententious, inflated, bombastic, high-flowing, frothy, flowery, turgid, swelling, grandiose, grandiloquent, magniloquent; Johnsonian.

578. ELEGANCE, grace, ease, nature, purity, concinnity, readiness, euphony.

Adj. Elegant, polished, classical, attic, Ciceronian, graceful, easy, natural, unlabored, chaste, pure, flowing, mellifluous, euphonious, rhythmical.

579. INELEGANCE, stiffness, uncouthness, barbarism, rudeness, abruptness, artificialness, affectation, cacophony.

V. To be inelegant, &c.

Adj. Inelegant, dry, stiff, forced, harsh, cramped, rude, crude, uncouth, barbarous, affected, artificial, graceless, abrupt.

2. *Spoken Language.*

580. VOICE, vocality, vocalization, utterance, accent, cry, strain, articulate sound, articulation, enunciation, delivery pronunciation, orthoepy; euphony.

Cadence, accent, accentuation, emphasis, stress, intonation, exclamation, ejaculation, vociferation, ventriloquism, polyphonism.

A ventriloquist, polyphonist.

Science of voice; Phonetics, Phonology.

V. To utter, breathe, cry, exclaim, shout, ejaculate, vociferate; raise, lift, or strain the voice; to vocalize, articulate, enunciate, pronounce, accentuate, aspirate deliver, mouth.

Adj. Vocal, oral, articulate.

Silvery, euphonious, mellow, mellifluous, soft, (sonorous, clear, shrill,) *see* Melodious, 413.

581. APHONY, absence or want of voice, dumbness, muteness, speechlessness, hoarseness, vacuity.

V. To render mute, to muzzle, to gag, to strike dumb, dumbfounder.

Adj. (Voiceless,)dumb,speechless, mute, tongueless, muzzled, tongue-tied, inarticulate, inaudible, unspoken, lips closed or sealed, wordless, deaf-mute, raucous, hoarse.

(Dry, husky, sharp, screeching, hollow, sepulchral voice.)

582. SPEECH, talk, parlance, verbal intercourse, oral communication, word of mouth, palaver, prattle, effusion, oration, recitation, delivery, harangue, formal speech.

Oratory,elocution, rhetoric, declamation, eloquence, grandiloquence, magniloquence.

A speaker, spokesman; prolocutor, mouthpiece, orator.

V. To speak, break silence, say, tell, talk, discourse, hold forth, make or deliver a speech, harangue, declaim, flourish,spout, rant, recite, expatiate, lecture, sermonize, soliloquize, 589.

Adj. Speaking, &c., oral, spoken, unwritten, outspoken.

583. IMPERFECT speech, inarticulateness.

STAMMERING, stuttering, impediment in one's speech, faltering, hesitation, lisp, drawl, sputter, mumbling, mincing, muttering, mouthing, twang, a broken or cracked voice, broken accents or sentences, falsetto, a whisper.

V. To stammer, stutter, hesitate, falter, mumble, lisp, jabber, gibber, mutter, sputter, drawl, mouth, lisp, croak, speak through the nose, snuffle, clip one's words, mispronounce.

To speak aside, whisper.

Adj. Stammering, &c., inarticulate, guttural, nasal.

584. LOQUACITY, loquaciousness, talkativeness, garrulity, flow of words, prate, verbosity, chatter, prattle, rattle, twaddle.

Fluency, flippancy, volubility.

A chatterer, chatterbox, bab-

585. TACITURNITY, closeness, reserve, muteness, silence.

V. To be silent, &c., 403, keep silence, hold one's peace, say nothing, close one's mouth or lips.

bler, ranter, sermonizer, proser, gossip, driveller.

V. To be loquacious, &c., to prate, palaver, prose, chatter, prattle, babble, outtalk, descant, dilate, dwell on, expatiate, launch out.

Adj. Loquacious, talkative, garrulous, open-mouthed, chatty, cosy, chattering, &c.,

Fluent, voluble, glib, flippant, long-winded.

To render silent, silence, put to silence, seal one's lips, smother, suppress, stop one's mouth, gag, muffle, muzzle.

Adj. Taciturn, close, reserved, mute, sparing of words, uncommunicative, inconversable.

586. Allocution, address, apostrophe, appeal, invocation, salutation.

V. To speak to, address, accost, apostrophize, appeal to, invoke, hail, make up to, call to, halloo, salute.

Adj. Accosting, &c.

587. Response, answer, reply, &c., *see* 462.

V. To answer, respond, reply, &c.

Adj. Answering, responding, replying, &c., respondent, responsive, *see* 462.

588. Interlocution, collocution, colloquy, conversation, converse, confabulation, talk, discourse, verbal intercourse, dialogue, logomachy, communication, commerce.

Chat, chitchat, small talk, table talk, tattle, gossip, idle talk.

Conference, parley, interview, audience, reception, palaver, debate.

A talker, interlocutor, gossip, tattler, chatterer, babbler.

V. To talk together, converse, discourse with, engage in conversation; hold or carry on a conversation; chat, gossip, tattle, babble, prate, 584, prattle; to put in a word.

To confer with, hold conference, &c., to parley, palaver, hold intercourse with, be closeted with, commune with.

Adj. Conversing, &c., interlocutory, verbal, colloquial, cosy, chatty, gossiping, &c., conversible.

589. Soliloquy, monologue, apostrophe.

V. To soliloquize; to say or talk to one's self; to say aside, to think aloud, to apostrophize.

Adj. Soliloquizing, &c.

---

3. *Written Language.*

590. Writing, chirography, penmanship, caligraphy.

Scribble, scrawl, scratch, scribbling, &c., jotting, interlineation.

Transcription, inscription, superscription, minute.

Shorthand, stenography, tachigraphy

591. Printing, print, letterpress, text, context, note, page, &c.

Typography, &c., type, character, black letter, font, pie, &c., capitals, majuscules.

Folio, quarto, medium, octavo duodecimo, octodecimo, &c.

Secret writing, writing in cipher, cryptography.

Composition, authorship.

Manuscript, copy, transcript, rough copy, fair copy, handwriting, autograph, signature, sign manual.

V. To print, put to press, publish, edit, get out a work, &c.

Adj. Printed, &c.

A scribe, amanuensis, scrivener, secretary, clerk, penman, copyist, transcriber, penny-a-liner.

Writer, author, scribbler, pamphleteer, essayist, novelist, fabulist; reporter, editor, (critic, reviewer;) bookseller, bibliopole.

Pen, quill, pencil, style, paper, parchment, vellum, tablet, slate, &c.

V. To write, pen, write out, copy, engross, write out fair, transcribe, scribble, scrawl, scratch, interline; to sign, undersign, countersign, indorse, set one's hand to.

To compose, indite, draw up, minute, jot down, make or take a minute of, put or set down in writing; to indite, to dictate.

Adj. Writing, &c., written, in writing, penned, &c.

592. Correspondence, letter, epistle, note, billet, missive, circular, billet doux, despatch, bulletin.

Letter bag, mail, post.

V. To correspond, write to, send a letter to.

---

593. Book, writing, work, volume, tome, library, tract, codex, manual, pamphlet, circular, publication, part, number, journal, album.

Knowledge of books; bibliography.

Paper, bill, sheet, leaf, flyleaf, page.

Chapter, section, paragraph, head, article, passage, clause.

594. Description, historiography, account, statement, report, return delineation, monograph, sketch, representation, narration, narrative, relation, recital, rehearsal, annals, chronicle, journal, 551, itinerary, log book.

Story, history, memoir, tale, tradition, legend, anecdote, fable, novel, romance, apologue, parable.

Biography, necrology, obituary, life, personal narrative, adventures, autobiography.

An historian, historiographer, narrator, annalist, journalist, biographer, fabulist, novelist.

V. To describe, speak of, state, set forth, sketch, delineate, represent, portray, depict, paint, shadow forth, adumbrate.

To relate, recite, recount, sum up, run over, recapitulate, narrate, rehearse, tell, give or render an account of, report, draw up a statement, &c.

To take up or handle a subject; to descend to particulars; to enter into detail, particulars, &c., to detail, retail; to come to the point.

Adj. Descriptive, graphic, well-drawn, historic, traditional, traditionary, legendary, anecdotic, described, &c.

595. Dissertation, treatise, tract, tractate, essay, discourse memoir, disquisition, exposition, compilation, sermon, homily, pandect.

V. To descant, treat of, discuss, write, compile, touch upon, handle or ventilate a subject; to do justice to a subject.

Adj. Discursive, expository; compiled, &c.

596. Compendium, compend, summary, abstract, epitome, digest, sum and substance, draft, brief, recapitulation, abridgment, abbreviation, minute, note, synopsis, syllabus, contents, heads, prospectus, (circular.)

Scrap book, album, note book, commonplace book, extracts, text book, flowers, anthology.

V. To abridge, abstract, abbreviate, recapitulate, run over, skim, make or prepare an abstract, &c., *see* 201.

Adj. Compendius, &c., synoptic, abridged, &c.

597. Poetry, poetics, poesy, the Muse.

Verse, metre, measure, foot, numbers, strain, rhyme, blank verse, versification, doggerel rhyme, prosody.

Poem, epic, epic poem, ode, epode, idyl, lyrics, eclogue, pastoral, bucolic, Anacreontic, sonnet, lay, roundelay, madrigal, canzonet, opera, anthology, distich, stanza, canto, strophe, couplet, quartrain, cento; monody.

A poet, bard, poetess, rhymer, rhymist, versifier, rhymester, sonneteer, poetaster.

V. To rhyme, versify, sing, make verses.

Adj. Poetical, poetic, lyric, metrical, epic, &c.

598. Prose.

A proser, prosaist, (prose writer.)

V. To prose.

Adj. Prosaic, prosing, rhymeless, unpoetical, commonplace.

---

599. The Drama, stage, theatre, the histrionic art, acting, &c., the buskin, sock.

Play, stage play, piece, tragedy, comedy, melodrame, interlude, afterpiece, opera, farce, pantomine, dumb show, puppet show.

Theatre, playhouse, stage, scene, the boards, greenroom.

An actor, a player, stager, stage player, performer, mime, comedian, tragedian, Thespian, clown, harlequin, buffoon, star.

Dramatic writer, playwright; pantomimist.

V. To act, play, perform, personate, 554, play a part, rehearse, spout, rant; to star it.

Adj. Dramatic, theatric, theatrical, scenic, histronic, comic, tragic, buskined, farcical, tragi-comic.

CLASS V.

WORDS RELATING TO THE VOLUNTARY POWERS.

Division I. INDIVIDUAL VOLITION.

Section I. Volition in general.

1. *Acts of Volition.*

600. Will, volition, free will, spontaneity, spontaneousness.

Pleasure, wish, mind, breast, mood, bosom, heart, discretion, accord.

Determination, *see* 604; intention, *see* 620.

V. To will, list, think fit, think proper, determine, &c., 604, settle, 609, to take upon one's self, to volunteer, to have one's will; to do as one likes, wishes, or chooses; to use or exercise one's own discretion, *see* Freedom, 748.

Adj. Voluntary, willing, content, minded, spontaneous, free, left to one's self, unconstrained, unfettered, unbidden, unasked, uncompelled, of one's own accord, gratuitous, prepense, advised, express, designed, intended, calculated, premeditated, preconcerted, predetermined, 611.

Adv. At will, at pleasure, spontaneously, freely, of one's own accord, voluntarily, advisedly, designedly, intentionally, purposely, knowingly, determinately, deliberately, expressly, pointedly, in earnest, in good earnest, studiously, purposely.

601. Necessity, instinct, blind impulse, necessitation, fate, destiny, doom, 152, foredoom, destination, election, predestination, preordination, compulsion, 774, subjection, 749.

The fates, the stars, the planets, astral influence.

V. To lie under a necessity, to be fated, doomed, destined, &c., 152, to need be.

To necessitate, destine, doom, foredoom, predestine, preordain.

To compel, force, constrain, &c., cast a spell, &c., 992.

Adj. Necessitated, fated, destined, doomed, elect, spellbound.

Compelled, forced, &c., inevitable, unavoidable, irresistible, irrevocable, inexorable.

Compulsory, involuntary, unintentional, undesigned, unintended, instinctive, automatic, blind, mechanical, impulsive, unwitting, unaware.

Adv. Necessarily, of necessity, perforce, forcibly, compulsorily; on or by compulsion or force, involuntarily, &c., impulsively 612, unwittingly, 491.

602. Willingness, voluntariness, disposition, inclination,

603. Unwillingness, involuntariness, indisposition, indis-

leaning, humor, mood, vein, bent, bias, propensity, proclivity, aptitude, predisposition, predilection, proneness, docility, assent, 488.

V. To be willing, &c., to incline to, lean to, mind, *see* Desire, 865, to have lief, to propend.

Adj. Willing, fain, disposed, inclined, minded, bent upon, set upon, forward, predisposed, hearty, cordial, genial, prepense, docile.

Free, spontaneous, unforced, unasked, unbiased, unsolicited, undriven, 600.

Adv. Willingly, freely, heartily, genially, 600, certainly, be it so, 488.

---

posedness, backwardness, disinclination, averseness, aversion, reluctance, repugnance, demur, remissness, slackness, indifference.

Dislike, 867, scrupulousness, scrupulosity, delicacy, demur, scruple, qualm, hesitation, shrinking, recoil, suspense.

A recusant.

V. To be unwilling, &c.

To demur, stick at, hesitate, 605, waver, hang in suspense, scruple, stickle, boggle, falter; to hang back; to hang fire.

Decline, reject, refuse, 764, refrain, keep from, abstain, recoil, shrink, swerve.

Adj. Unwilling, unconsenting, disinclined, indisposed, averse, reluctant, not content, laggard, backward, remiss, slack, indifferent, frigid, scrupulous, repugnant, disliking, 867.

Demurring, wavering, &c., refusing, 764.

Adv. Unwillingly, &c., perforce.

604. Resolution, determination, decision, resolvedness, fixedness, steadiness, constancy, unchangeableness, inflexibility, firmness, doggedness, tenacity of purpose, solidity, perseverance.

Energy, manliness, vigor, spirit, spiritedness, pluck, bottom; self-reliance; mastery over one's self; self-control.

A devotee, zealot, enthusiast.

V. To be resolved, &c., to have resolution, &c., to resolve, determine, conclude, make up one's mind; to stand, keep, or remain firm, &c., to come to a determination; to form a resolution; to take one's stand; to stand by, hold by, hold fast, stick to, abide by, adhere to, keep one's ground, persevere, keep one's course, hold on, not to fail.

To insist upon; to make a point of.

Adj. Resolved, resolute, firm, steady, steadfast, stanch, stable, constant.

605. Irresolution, indecision, (want of decision or determination,) indetermination, demur, hesitation, suspense, hesitancy, vacillation, unsteadiness, inconstancy, wavering, fluctuation, flickering, changeableness, mutability, fickleness, levity, trimming, softness, weakness.

A weathercock, a shuttlecock, a butterfly, a harlequin.

V. To be irresolute, &c., to hesitate, hang in suspense, debate, demur, waver, balance, vacillate, quaver, fluctuate, shuffle, blink, boggle, flicker, falter, palter, hang fire, dally with.

Adj. Irresolute, undecided, unresolved, undetermined, vacillating, wavering, hesitating, faltering, blinking, shuffling, &c.

Unsteady, unstable, unsteadfast, wavering, fickle, changing, changeable, versatile, variable, inconstant, mutable, fluctuating, unsettled, unfixed.

Weak, feeble-minded, frail,

Decided, determinate, definitive determined, fixed, unmoved, unshaken, unbending, unyielding, unflinching, stiff, inflexible, unwavering, unswerving, unfaltering, unshrinking, undiverted, immovable, not to be moved, unhesitating, *see* Obstinate, 606.

Peremptory, indomitable, strenuous, persevering, bent upon, set upon, intent upon, proof against, steeled, staid, serious, irrevocable, irreversible.

Adv. Resolutely, &c., without fail.

soft, pliant, giddy, volatile, fitful, freakish, lightminded.

In suspense, in doubt, *see* 485

Revocable, reversible.

---

606. Obstinacy, obstinateness, wilfulness, self-will, pertinacity, pertinaciousness, tenacity, tenaciousness, inflexibility, doggedness, stubbornness, headiness, *see* Resolution, 604, restiveness, contumacy, obduracy, obduration, obdurateness, unruliness.

Intolerance, dogmatism, bigotry, opiniativeness, zealotry, infatuation, monomania, indocility, intractableness.

An opinionist, opinionatist, stickler, zealot, dogmatist, fanatic.

A fixed idea, rooted prejudice, blind side, &c., 481.

V. To be obstinate, &c., to persist, hold out, stickle.

Adj. Obstinate, opinionative, opinionated, opinioned, self-opinioned, prejudiced, 481, wilful, self-willed, positive, tenacious.

Stiff, stubborn, obdurate, starch, rigid, stiffnecked, pertinacious, dogged, restive, pervicacious, dogmatic, unpersuadable, inexorable, mulish, unmoved, uninfluenced, unyielding, wayward, intractable, haggard, headstrong, hairbrained, refractory, unruly, infatuated, heady, crossgrained, contumacious, fanatical.

Adv. Obstinately, &c., headlong; at any rate, risk, hazard, price, cost, or sacrifice.

607. Change of mind, intention, purpose, &c.

Tergiversation, retractation, recantation, revocation, reversal, renunciation, abjuration, abjurement, relinquishment, 624, repentance, 950, vacillation, &c., 605.

Going over, apostasy.

A renegade, apostate, backslider, trimmer, timeserver, deserter, weathercock, &c., 605.

V. To change one's mind, &c., to retract, recant, revoke, abjure, renounce, apostatize, relinquish, trim, veer round, change sides; go over, pass, change, or skip from one side to another; swerve, flinch.

Adj. Changeful, changeable, versatile, mobile, unsteady, 605, trimming, doublefaced, double-minded, timeserving.

Fugacious, fugitive, revocatory.

608. Caprice, fancy, humor, whim, crotchet, quirk, freak, vagary, whimsey, prank, fit, freakishness, skittishness, volatility, fancifulness, whimsicality, giddiness, inconsistency.

V. To be capricious, &c.

Adj. Capricious, inconsistent, fanciful, fantastic, whimsical, full of whims, &c., erratic, crotchety, perverse, humorsome, wayward, captious, contrary, skittish, restive, fitful.

609. CHOICE, option, election, adoption, selection, gleaning, eclecticism, preference, predilection.

Decision, determination, award, adjudication, vote, suffrage, ballot, verdict, voice.

Alternative, dilemma.

Persuasion, seduction, bringing over, *see* 615.

Thing chosen, 650.

V. To choose, decide, determine, elect, list, think fit, use one's discretion, fancy, shape one's course, prefer, take one's choice, adopt, select, fix upon, pitch upon, pick out, single out, pick up, take up, catch at, cull, glean, pick, winnow.

To persuade, overcome, seduce, entice, *see* 615.

Adj. Optional, discretional, eclectic, choosing, &c., chosen, &c., decided, &c.

Adv. Discretionally, at pleasure, at will.

Decidedly, &c., rather, in preference, before; once for all, either the one or the other.

610. Absence of choice, *see* Necessity, 601.

REJECTION, refusal, *see* 764; declining, repudiation, exclusion.

Indifference, indecision, 605.

V. To reject, refuse, &c., decline, give up, repudiate, exclude, lay aside, to refrain, spare.

Adj. Rejecting, &c., rejected, cast out, &c., not chosen, &c.

Having no choice, indifferent, undecided, 605.

Adv. Neither; neither the one nor the other.

611. PREDETERMINATION, premeditation, predeliberation, having no alternative, compulsory choice.

V. To predetermine, premeditate, resolve (beforehand.)

Adj. Prepense, premeditated, predetermined, advised, predesigned, preconcerted.

612. IMPULSE, sudden thought, inspiration, flash.

V. To flash on the mind.

Adj. Extemporaneous, impulsive, unmeditated, unpremeditated, unprompted, spontaneous, natural, unguarded, unconducted.

613. HABIT, habitude, wont, rule, routine.

Custom, use, usage, practice, run, way, prevalence, observance, fashion, 852, etiquette, vogue.

Seasoning, training, hardening, &c., 673.

A second nature, taking root, radication.

V. To be habitual, &c., to be in the habit of, be wont, be accustomed to, &c.

To follow, observe, conform to, obey, bend to, comply with, accommodate one's self to, adapt one's self to; fall into a habit, custom, or usage; to addict one's self to.

614. DESUETUDE, disuse, want of habit or of practice.

Non-observance, infraction, violation, infringement.

V. To be unaccustomed, &c., to be new to; to leave off, cast off, wean one's self of break off, break through, infringe, violate, &c., a habit, usage, &c., to disuse, to wear off.

Adj. Unaccustomed, unused, unusual, unwonted, uncustomary, unfashionable, non-observant, disused, weaned.

Unseasoned, uninured, unhabituated, untrained, unhackneyed.

To become a habit, to take root.

To habituate, inure, harden, season, form, train, accustom, naturalize, acclimatize.

To acquire a habit, to get into the way of, to learn, &c.

Adj. Habitual, accustomed, habituated, &c.; in the habit, &c., of; used to, given to, addicted to, attuned to, wedded to, usual, wonted, customary, hackneyed, fixed, rooted, permanent, inveterate, besetting, ingrained, running in the blood, hereditary, congenital, innate, inborn, natural, instinctive, &c., 5.

Fashionable, in fashion, in vogue, according to use, routine, &c.

2. *Causes of Volition.*

615. Motive, reason, ground, principle, mainspring, account, score, sake, consideration, calculation.

Inducement, recommendation, encouragement, attraction, temptation, enticement, bait, allurement, witchery, bewitchery.

Persuasibility, persuasibleness, (susceptibility, impressibility,) softness.

Influence, prompting, dictate, instance, impulse, impulsion, incitement, incitation, press, instigation, excitement, provocation, invitation, solicitation, suasion, persuasion, hortation, exhortation, seduction, cajolery, tantalization, seducement, bewitchment, inspiration.

Incentive, stimulus, spur, goad, provocative.

Bribe, lure, decoy, charm, spell, loadstone, the golden apple, the voice of the tempter, the song of the Sirens.

Prompter, tempter, seducer, Siren, Circe, instigator, firebrand, incendiary.

V. To induce, move, lead, draw, draw on, draw over, carry, bring; to influence, to weigh with; bias, sway; to operate, work upon, engage, incline, dispose, predispose, prompt, call upon, recom-

616. Absence of motive, see Caprice, 608.

Dissuasion, dehortation, discouragement, (counter influence.)

Cohibition, check, restraint, curb, bridle, rein, stay, damper, remonstrance, expostulation.

Scruple, qualm, demur, 867.

V. To dissuade, discourage disincline, indispose, dispirit, damp, dishearten, disenchant deter, keep back, render averse, &c.

To withhold, restrain, hold, check, bridle, curb, rein in, keep in, cohibit, inhibit, repel, 751.

To cool, blunt, calm, quiet, quench, shake, stagger, remonstrate, expostulate, warn.

To scruple, refrain, abstain, &c., 603.

Adj. Dissuading, &c., dissuasive, dehortatory.

Dissuaded, discouraged, &c., uninduced, unmoved, unactuated, uninfluenced, unbiased, unincited, unimpelled, unurged, unswayed, unprovoked, uninspired, untempted, unattracted.

Repugnant, averse, scrupulous, &c., 867, (immovable.)

---

mend, encourage, invite, solicit, press, enjoin, entreat, 765, court, plead, advocate, exhort, enforce, dictate, seduce, overpersuade, entice, allure, decoy, charm, conciliate, wheedle, coax, cajole, inveigle, persuade, prevail upon, get to do, bring over, enlist, procure.

To act upon, to impel, excite, suscitate, stimulate, exsuscitate, incite, animate, instigate, provoke, set on, urge, pique, spirit, inspirit, inspire, awaken, light up, kindle, enkindle, rekindle, whet, quicken, goad, spur, hurry on, stir up, work up, fan, fire, inflame, set on fire, fan the flame, blow the coals, stir the embers, put on one's mettle, set on, force, rouse, arouse.

Adj. Impulsive, motive, persuasive, hortatory, seductive, suasory, suasive, honey-tongued, tempting, alluring, provocative, exciting, piquant, tantalizing, &c.

Persuadable, persuasible, suasible, soft, yielding, facile, easily persuaded, &c.

Induced, moved, disposed, led, persuaded, &c., spellbound, instinct with.

Adv. Because, for, since, on account of, out of, from; by reason of.

As, forasmuch as, therefore, hence, why, wherefore.

617. Ostensible motive, or reason assigned.

Plea, allegation, pretext, pretence, excuse, apology, cue, color gloss, loophole, handle, shift, quirk, guise, makeshift, special pleading, claptrap.

V. To make a pretext, &c., of; to use as a plea, &c.; to plead, allege, pretend, excuse, make a handle, &c., of; to shelter one's self under the plea of.

Adj. Ostensible, colorable, pretended, alleged, &c.

3. *Objects of Volition.*

618. Good, benefit, advantage, service, interest, weal, boot, gain, profit, good turn, blessing; behoof, behalf.

Luck, good fortune, piece of luck, windfall, godsend, bonus; prize.

Cause of good, *see* Utility, 644, Goodness, 648, and Remedy, 662.

Adv. Aright, well, favorably.

In behalf of, in favor of.

---

619. Evil, harm, injury, wrong, curse, detriment, hurt, damage, disservice, ill turn, grievance, prejudice, loss, mischief, disadvantage, drawback, trouble, annoyance, nuisance, molestation, oppression, persecution, plague, corruption, 659.

Blow, bruise, scratch, wound, mutilation, outrage, spoliation, plunder, pillage, rapine, destruction, dilapidation, havoc, ravage, devastation, inroad, sweep, sack, forray, 716, desolation.

Misfortune, mishap, mischance, reverse.

Affliction, woe, visitation, disaster, calamity, catastrophe, downfall, ruin, prostration, blight, blast.
Cause of evil, *see* Bane, 663.
Production of evil, 649.
Adv. Amiss, wrong, evil.

Section II. Prospective Volition.*

1. *Conceptional Volition.*

620. Intention, intent, intentionality, purpose, design, purport, mind, meaning, view, proposal, study, bent, turn.

Final cause, object, aim, end, scope, drift, destination, mark, point, butt, goal, target, prey, quarry, game.

Decision, determination, resolve, resolution, 604, predetermination, 611; set purpose.

A hobby, ambition, wish; *see* Desire, 865.

V. To intend, purpose, design, mean, propose to one's self, have in view, have in one's eye, have an eye to.

To be at, aim at, drive at, be after, point at, level at, take aim, aspire at or after, endeavor after.

To meditate, think of, dream of, premeditate, 611, contemplate, study, destine, destinate.

To propose, project, devise, take into one's head, take upon one's self, to have to do; to see one's way.

Adj. Intended, &c., intentional, minded, earnest, express, prepense, set upon, bent upon, intent upon, in view, in prospect.

Adv. Intentionally, &c., expressly, designedly, purposely, on purpose, studiously, for, with a view to, for the purpose of, with the view of, in order to, to the end

621. Absence of purpose in the succession of events.

Chance,† fortune, accident, hazard, haphazard, lot, chance-medley, hit, casualty, contingency, fate, adventure, random shot, lottery, &c., 156.

A godsend, luck, a run of luck, a windfall, &c., 618.

Drawing lots.

Wager, bet, betting, gambling.

V. To chance, turn up; to stand a chance.

To take one's chance, try one's luck, bet, wager, lay a wager, gamble, raffle, toss up, cast lots, draw lots.

To risk, venture, hazard, stake, incur or run the risk; stand the hazard.

Adj. Casual, fortuitous, accidental, contingent, random, adventitious, incidental.

Unintentional, aimless, driftless, designless, undesigned, undirected; purposeless, causeless, without purpose, &c., unmeditated, unpremeditated, unpurposed

Indiscriminate, promiscuous.

Adv. Casually, &c., by chance by accident, accidentally, &c.. a haphazard.

---

* That is, volition having reference to a future object.
† See note on 156.

that, on account of, in pursuance of, pursuant to, with the intent, &c.

622. Purpose in action.

PURSUIT, undertaking, enterprise, adventure, game, endeavor, *see* 676.

Prosecution, search, angling, chase, hunt, race, scramble, course, direction.

V. To pursue, undertake, engage in, take in hand, carry on, prosecute, endeavor.

To court, seek, angle, chase, give chase, course, dog, hunt, track, follow, run after, prowl, hound, bid for, aim at, take aim, make a leap at, rush upon, jump at.

To take or hold a course; to tread a path; to shape one's course; to direct or bend one's steps or course; to run a race, rush headlong, rush headforemost, make a plunge, snatch at, &c., to start game.

Adj. Pursuing, &c.

Adv. In order to, for the purpose of, with a view to, &c., 620.

623. Absence of pursuit.

AVOIDANCE, forbearance, abstinence, sparing, refraining, 681

Flight, &c., evasion, elusion

V. To avoid, refrain, abstain, not to attempt; to spare, hold, shun, fly, flee, eschew, run away from, get out of the way, shrink, hold back, draw back, *see* 286, recoil from, flinch, blench, shy, elude, evade, parry.

Adj. Avoiding, &c., elusive, evasive, flying, fugitive, &c., unsought, unattempted.

Adv. Lest; with a view to prevent.

624. RELINQUISHMENT, dereliction, abandonment, renunciation, desertion, *see* 607, discontinuance.

Dispensation, riddance.

V. To relinquish, give up, give over, leave off, desist, 681; put away; set, put, or lay aside, discard, dismiss; to leave, quit, drop, desert, forsake, abandon, renounce, forswear; to depart from, swerve from, *see* 279.

Adj. Relinquishing, &c., relinquished, &c., unpursued.

625. BUSINESS, affair, concern, task, work, job, errand, commission, office, charge, care, part, duty.

Province, department, function, mission, vocation, calling, avocation, profession, cloth, faculty, trade, craft, mystery, walk, beat, race, career, walk of life.

Place, post, orbit, sphere, capacity, employment, engagement, exercise, occupation; situation, undertaking, 676.

V. To carry on a business, trade, &c.

Adj. Business-like, official, functional, professional, in hand.

Adv. On hand, on foot, afoot, afloat, going.

626. PLAN, scheme, device, design, project, proposal, proposition.

Line of conduct, game, card, course, tactics, strategy, policy, polity, 692, craft, practice, campaign.

Measure, step, precaution, proceeding, procedure, process, system, economy, organization, expedient, contrivance, artifice, shift, stop gap, manœuvre, stratagem, fetch, trick, 702, stroke, stroke of policy masterstroke.

Intrigue cabal, plot, conspiracy, complot, machination.

Alternative, loophole, counterplot, counterproject, side wind, underplot.

Sketch, outline, programme, draught, rough draught, skeleton forecast, prospectus.

Aftercourse, aftergame.

A projector, designer, schemer, contriver, artist, schematist.

V. To plan, scheme, devise, imagine, design, frame, contrive, forecast, project, plot, invent, fall upon, hit upon, strike out, chalk out, sketch, lay out, lay down, cut out, cast, recast, arrange, mature, organize, concoct, digest, pack, prepare, hatch; to counterplot, countermine.

Adj. Planned, &c., strategic; planning, scheming, &c.

Well-laid, deep-laid, cunning, well-devised, &c., maturely considered, well-weighed, prepared, organized, &c.

Adv. In course of preparation, on the anvil, on the stocks, on the tapis.

627. Method, way, manner, wise, gait, form, path, road, route, channel, walk, access, course, pass, ford, ferry, passage, line of way, orbit, track, avenue, approach, beaten track, turnpike road, high road, highway, roadway, causeway, pathway, footpath, railway, thoroughfare, gateway, street, lane, alley, gangway, hatchway, aisle, crossroad, crossway, cut, short cut, royal road, cross cut.

Bridge, stepping stone, stair, corridor, staircase, flight of stairs, ladder, steps, scaffold, scaffolding.

Indirect way; by-path, by-way, by-walk, by-road, back door, back stairs.

Inlet, gate, door, gateway, portal, porch, doorway, conduit, tunnel, 350.

Adv. How, in what way, in what manner, by what mode.

By the way, by the by.

628. Mid Course, middle course, mean, *see* Middle, 68, and Mean, 29.

Direct, straight, straightforward course, path, &c.

V. To keep in a middle course.

Adj. Undeviating, direct, straight, straightforward.

629. Circuit, roundabout way, zigzag, *see* 311, wandering, deviation, 279, divergence, 291.

V. To perform a circuit, &c., to deviate, wander, go round about, meander, &c., 279.

Adj. Circuitous, indirect, roundabout, zigzag, &c.

Adv. By a side wind, by an indirect course, in a roundabout way.

630. Requirement, requisition, need, lack, wants, necessities, desideratum, exigency, pinch, the very thing,

Needfulness, essentiality, necessity, indispensability, urgency, call for.

V. To require, need, want, have occasion for, stand in need of, lack, desire, be at a loss for, desiderate, not to be able to do without or dispense with.

To render necessary, to necessitate, to create a necessity for, to call for.

Adj. Requisite, required, &c., needful, necessary, urgent, exigent, essential, indispensable, prerequisite; that cannot be spared or dispensed with.

2. *Subservience to Ends.*

1. *Actual Subservience.*

631 INSTRUMENTALITY, medium, intermedium, intervention mediation, dint, *see* Agency, 170.

Key, master key, pass key, passport.

Adj. Instrumental, intervening, intermediate, subservient, (ancillary.)

Adv. Through, by, with, by means of, along with, thereby, through the medium, &c., cf, wherewith.

632. MEANS, resources, appliances, ways and means, appointments, expedients, steps, measures, 626, aid, 707, intermedium; dernier resort.

Machinery, mechanism, mechanics, engineering, mechanical powers, scaffold, ladder, mainstay.

Adj. Instrumental, subservient, ministerial, mechanical.

Adv. How, by what means, by all means, any how, 627, by the aid of, by dint of, by the power or agency of.

633. INSTRUMENT, tool, implement, apparatus, utensil, craft, machine, engine.

Weapon, arms, armory, battery.

Equipment, gear, tackle, tackling, rigging, harness, paraphernalia, equipage.

A wheel, jack, mill, clockwork, wheelwork, pulley, spring, screw, wedge, flywheel, lever, pinion, crank, winch, crane, capstan, windlass, hammer, mallet, mattock, mall, bat, sledge hammer, mace, club, truncheon, pole, staff, bill, crow, crowbar, poleaxe, handspike, crutch, boom, bar.

Organ, limb, arm, hand, finger, fist, claw, paw, talons, tentacle, wing, oar, paddle, pincer, plier, forceps.

Handle, hilt, haft, shaft, heft, trigger, tiller, helm, treadle, pummel, peg, 215.

Edge tool, *see* 253, axis, *see* 312.

634. SUBSTITUTE, shift, makeshift, *see* Substitution, 147, and Deputy, 759.

635. MATERIALS, stuff, raw material, pabulum, fuel, grist, provender, provisions, food, 298, aliment, fodder, forage, prog, pasture, pasturage.

Supplies, munition, ammunition, reënforcement, relay.

Baggage, luggage, bag and baggage, effects, goods, chattels, household stuff, equipage, paraphernalia, stock in trade, pelf, cargo, lading.

636. STORE, stock, fund, supply, reserve, relay, budget, quiver reserved fund, mine, quarry, vein, fountain.

Collection, accumulation, heap, 72, hoard, magazine, pile, rick, savings, bank, 802, treasury, reservoir, repository, repertory, depository, depot, thesaurus, museum, storehouse, reservatory, conservatory, menagerie, receptacle, warehouse, dock, larder, garner, granary, storeroom, cistern, well, tank, armory, arsenal, coffer, &c., 191.

V. To store, stock, treasure up, lay in, lay by, set by, lay up, fund, garner, save, reserve, keep back, husband, hoard, deposit, accumulate, 72.

Adj. Stored, &c., in store, in reserve.

637. PROVISION, supply, providing, supplying, &c., purveyance, purveying, reënforcement, husbanding, commissariat, victualling

Forage, pasture, food, &c., 299.

A purveyor, commissary, quartermaster, feeder.

V. To provide, supply, furnish, purvey, replenish, fill up, feed, stock with, recruit, cater, find, keep, lay in, lay in store, store, forage, husband, *see* 636.

638. WASTE, consumption, (squandering,) expenditure, exhaustion, drain, leakage, wear and tear, dispersion, 73, ebb, *see* Prodigality, 819.

V. To waste, spend, (squander, to be lavish,) expend, use, consume, spill, leak, run out, run to waste, disperse, 73, ebb, dry up impoverish, drain, empty, exhaust; to throw away, cast away, fritter away.

Adj. Wasted, spent, &c., at a low ebb.

639. SUFFICIENCY, adequacy, (full supply,) competence; satiety, enough.

Fulness, plenitude, plenty, abundance, copiousness, amplitude, richness, fertility, luxuriance, uberty, cornucopia.

Impletion, repletion, saturation.

Riches, 803, mine, store, fund, 636.

A flood, draught, shower, rain, 347, stream, tide, springtide, flush.

Moderation, *see* Mediocrity, 651.

V. To be sufficient, &c., to suffice, to do, satisfy, saturate, make up, (to meet the case, to supply the want.)

To abound, teem, stream, flow, rain, shower down, pour, swarm.

To render sufficient, &c., to make up, to fill, replenish, pour in.

Adj. Sufficient, enough, adequate, commensurate, (what is requisite or necessary.)

640. INSUFFICIENCY, inadequacy, inadequateness, incompetence.

Deficiency, scantiness, (insufficient supply or store,) defect, defectiveness, defalcation, default, deficit, shortcoming, falling short, 304, what will not do, scantiness, slenderness, &c., 32.

Scarcity, dearth, want, need, lack, exigency, inanition, indigence, poverty, penury, 804, destitution, dole, pittance, short allowance, starvation, famine, drought, emptiness, vacancy, flaccidity.

V. To be insufficient, &c., not to suffice, &c., to come short of, to fall short of, fail, stop short, to want, lack, need, require, 630.

To render insufficient, &c., to stint, grudge, hold back, withhold, starve, pinch, famish, (to put on short allowance.)

To empty, drain, &c., *see* 638.

Adj. Insufficient, inadequate, incompetent, not enough, &c

Moderate, measured.

Full, ample, plenty, copious, plentiful, plentious, plenary, abundant, abounding, replete, laden, full-laden, charged, fraught; well stocked or provided, liberal, lavish, unstinted, to spare, unsparing, unmeasured.

Brimful, to the brim, choke-full, saturated, crammed, rich, luxuriant, heavy-laden.

Unexhausted, unwasted, exhaustless, inexhaustible.

scant, scanty, deficient, defective, ill-furnished, ill-provided, ill stored, in default, scarce, empty, devoid, short of, wanting, &c.

Destitute, dry, drained, unprovided, unsupplied, unfurnished unreplenished, unfed, unstored untreasured, bare, meagre, poor thin, spare, stinted, starved, famished, pinched, starveling, jejune, without resources.

---

641. Redundance, superabundance, superfluity, superfluence, exuberance, profuseness, profusion, plethora, congestion, glut, surfeit, load, turgidity, turgescence, 192, pleonasm.

Excess, an overdose, oversupply, overplus, surplusage, overmeasure, overflow, inundation, deluge, extravagance, prodigality, 818, exorbitance, lavishment.

V. To overabound, (superabound,) run over, overflow, flow over; roll in; wallow in, swarm.

To overstock, overdose, overlay, gorge, glut, load, overload, surcharge, overrun, drench, inundate, deluge, whelm.

Adj. Redundant, superfluous, exuberant, superabundant, excessive, in excess, overmuch, too much, needless, over and above, 40, more than enough, running to waste, overflowing, running over.

Turgid, gorged, plethoric, profuse, lavish, prodigal, extra, supernumerary, expletive, surcharged, overcharged, overloaded, overladen, overburdened, overrun, overfed.

Adv. Over, over and above, too much, overmuch, over and enough, too far, without measure, without stint.

2. *Degree of Subservience.*

642. Importance, consequence, moment, weight, gravity, seriousness, concern, consideration, significance, import, influence, 175, pressure, urgency, stress, emphasis, preponderance, prominence, 250, greatness, 31.

The substance, essence, quintessence, gist, pith, marrow, soul.

The principal, prominent, or essential part; the corner stone.

V. To be important or of importance, &c., to signify, import, matter, boot, weigh, to be prominent, &c., to take the lead.

643. Unimportance, indifference, insignificance, triflingness, paltriness, emptiness, nothingness, inanity, lightness, levity, frivolity, vanity, frivolousness, puerility.

Poverty, meagerness, meanness shabbiness, &c., 804.

A trifle, small matter, bagatelle, cipher, molehill, joke, jest, bubble.

A straw, pin, fig, button, rush, feather, farthing, brass farthing, peppercorn, pebble, small fry.

Toy, plaything, knickknack, gimcrack, gewgaw, bawble.

tance to; to value, care for, &c., 897.

To over-estimate, &c., 482, to exaggerate, 549.

To mark, underline, score.

Adj. Important, of importance, &c., grave, serious, critical, material, weighty, influential, significant, emphatic, momentous, earnest, pressing, urgent, preponderating, pregnant, paramount, essential, vital.

Great, considerable, &c., *see* 31, first-rate, capital, leading, principal, superior, chief, main, prime, primary, cardinal, prominent, salient.

Signal, notable, memorable, remarkable, &c., grand, solemn, eventful, stirring; not to be despised or overlooked, &c., worth while.

Trumpery, trash, rubbish, stuff, frippery, froth, smoke, cobweb.

Refuse, lumber, litter, orts, tares, weeds, sweepings, scourings, offscourings; rubble, debris, dross, dregs, scum, dust, *see* Dirt, 653.

V. To be unimportant, to be of little or no importance, &c.; not to signify, not to deserve, merit, or be worthy of notice, regard, consideration, &c.

Adj. Unimportant, secondary, (subordinate,) inferior, immaterial, insignificant, unessential, non-essential, beneath notice, indifferent; of little or no account importance, consequence, moment, interest, &c., contemptible.

Trifling, trivial, slight, slender, flimsy, foolish, idle, puerile, childish, infantile, frothy, trashy, catchpenny, commonplace.

Vain, empty, inane, poor, sorry, mean, meagre, shabby, vile, miserable, scrubby, beggarly, pitiful, pitiable, despicable, ridiculous, farcical, finical.

Adv. Meagrely, pitifully, vainly, &c.

644. Utility, service, use, function, office, sphere, capacity, part, task, work.

Usefulness, worth, stead, avail, advantageousness, profitableness, serviceableness, merit, applicability, adequacy, subservience, subserviency, efficacy, efficiency, help. Productiveness, 168.

V. To be useful, &c.

To avail, serve, subserve, help, 707, conduce, serve one's turn, stand instead, profit, advantage, benefit, accrue.

To render useful, to use, 677, to turn to account.

To serve an office, act a part, perform a function, serve a purpose, serve a turn.

Adj. Useful, beneficial, advantageous, serviceable, helping, gainful, profitable, prolific.

Subservient, conducive, appli-

645. Inutility, uselessness, unsubservience, inefficacy, inefficiency, ineptness, inadequacy, inaptitude, fruitlessness, worthlessness, unproductiveness, barrenness, sterility, vanity, futility, triviality, paltriness, unprofitableness, unfruitfulness, rustiness, obsoleteness, supererogation.

Litter, rubbish, lumber, trash, orts, weeds, 643.

A waste, desert, wild, wilderness.

V. To be useless, &c., to be of no avail, use, &c., 644.

Adj. Useless, inefficient, inefficacious, unavailing, inoperative, bootless, inadequate, unprofitable, unproductive, sterile, barren.

Worthless, valueless, at a discount, gainless, fruitless, profitless, unserviceable, rusty, effete, washy, wasted, nugatory, futile,

cable, adequate, efficient, efficacious, effective, effectual, 168.

Adv. Usefully, &c.

inept, withered, wasteful, ill spent.

Unneeded, unnecessary, uncalled for, incommodious, discommodious.

Adv. Uselessly, &c.

646. Specific subservience.

Expedience, expediency, fitness, suitableness, aptness, aptitude, appropriateness, pertinence, seasonableness, 644, adaptation, congruity, consonance, 23, convenience, eligibility, applicability, seemliness.

V. To be expedient, &c.

To suit, fit, square with,(match,) adapt itself to, agree with, consort with, tally with, accord with, conform to.

Adj. Expedient, fit, fitting, suitable, applicable, eligible, apt, appropriate, adapted, proper, advisable, desirable, pertinent, congruous, seemly, consonant, becoming, meet, due, consentaneous, congenial, well-timed, seasonable, opportune, befitting, happy, felicitous, auspicious, acceptable, &c., convenient, commodious, *see* 23, 134.

647. Inexpedience, inexpediency, disadvantageousness, unserviceableness, disservice, unfitness, (unsuitableness,) inaptitude, ineligibility, inappropriateness, impropriety, unseemliness, incongruity, impertinence, inopportuneness, unseasonableness.

Inconvenience, incommodiousness, incommodity.

V. To be inexpedient, &c., to embarrass, cumber, lumber, &c.

Adj. Inexpedient, disadvantageous, unprofitable, unfit, unfitting, unsuitable, amiss, improper, unapt, inept, unadvisable, ineligible, objectionable, inadmissible, unseemly, inopportune, unseasonable, *see* 24, 135.

Inconvenient, incommodious, in the way, cumbrous, cumbersome, lumbering, unwieldy, unmanageable, awkward, clumsy.

648. Capability of producing good.

Goodness, excellence, value, worth, preciousness, estimation, rareness, exquisiteness, (good qualities.)

Superexcellence, superiority, supereminence, transcendence, perfection, 650.

Mediocrity, innocuousness, *see* 651.

V. To be good, &c.; to be superior, &c., to excel, transcend, top, vie, emulate, &c.

To be middling, (ordinary, or indifferent,) &c., 651; to pass.

To produce good, benefit, &c., to avail, to profit, to benefit, to be beneficial, &c., to confer a benefit, &c., to improve, 658.

649. Capability of producing evil.

Badness, hurtfulness, disserviceableness, injuriousness, banefulness, mischievousness, noxiousness, malignancy, venomousness, virulence, destructiveness, curse, bane, 663.

Vileness, foulness, rankness, depravedness, pestilence; deterioration, *see* 659.

V. To be bad, &c.

To cause, produce, or inflict evil; to harm, hurt, injure, mar, damage, endamage, scathe, prejudice.

To wrong, molest, annoy, grieve, aggrieve, trouble, oppress, persecute, weigh down, run down, overlay.

Adj. Harmless, innocuous, hurtless, unobnoxious.

Good, beneficial, valuable, estimable, serviceable, advantageous, precious, favorable, propitious.

Sound, sterling, standard, true, genuine, fresh, unfaded, unspoiled, unimpaired, uninjured, undemolished, undamaged, undecayed, natural, unsophisticated, unadulterated, unpolluted, unvitiated.

Choice, nice, fine, rare, felicitous, unexceptionable, excellent, admirable, first-rate, prime, cardinal, superlative, superfine, superexcellent, exquisite, high-wrought, inestimable, invaluable, priceless, incomparable, transcendent, matchless, peerless, inimitable, unrivalled, spotless, immaculate, perfect, 650.

Moderately good, 651.

To maltreat, abuse, ill use, ill treat, bruise, scratch, maul, strike, smite, scourge, 972, wound, lame, maim, scotch, cripple, mutilate, hamstring, hough, stab, pierce, &c., crush, crumble.

To corrupt, corrode, pollute, &c., 659.

To spoil, despoil, sweep, ravage, lay waste, devastate, dismantle, demolish, level, raze, consume, overrun, sack, plunder, destroy, 162.

Adj. Bad, evil, wrong, prejudicial, disserviceable, disadvantageous, unprofitable, unlucky, sinister, obnoxious, untoward, unadvisable, inauspicious.

Hurtful, injurious, grievous, detrimental, noxious, pernicious, mischievous, baneful, baleful.

Morbific, rank, peccant, malignant, corroding, corrosive, virulent, cankering, mephitic, narcotic.

Deleterious, poisonous, venomous, envenomed, pestilent, pestiferous, destructive, deadly, fatal, mortal, azotic.

Vile, sad, wretched, sorry, shabby, scurvy, shocking, horrid, horrible.

Hateful, abominable, villanous, dire, detestable, execrable, cursed, accursed, confounded, damnable, diabolic, devilish, demoniacal, infernal, hellish, satanic.

Adv. Wrong, wrongly, badly, &c.

650. PERFECTION, perfectness, indefectibility, impeccability, beau ideal, 210.

Masterpiece, model, pattern, mirror, phœnix, paragon, prime, flower, cream, nonesuch.

Gem, jewel, pearl, diamond, ruby, brilliant; bijoutry.

V. To be perfect, &c., to excel, transcend, overtop, &c.

To bring to perfection, to perfect, to ripen, mature, &c., 52, 729.

Adj. Perfect, best, faultless, finished, indeficient, indefective, indefectible, immaculate, spot-

651. IMPERFECTION, imperfectness, unsoundness, faultiness, deficiency, drawback, inadequacy, inadequateness.

Fault, defect, flaw, crack, twist, taint, peccancy.

Mediocrity, mean, 29, inferiority.

V. To be imperfect, middling, &c., to fail, to lie under a disadvantage.

Adj. Imperfect, deficient, defective, faulty, inadequate, unsound, unremedied, cracked, warped, frail, tottering, decrepit, rickety, battered, worn out, thread-

less, matchless, peerless, &c., *see* 648, inimitable, superlative, transcendent, superhuman, divine.

---

bare, wormeaten, used up, decayed, mutilated.

Indifferent, (ordinary,) middling, secondary, second-rate, second-best, second-hand.

Tolerable, passable, pretty well, well enough, rather good, admissible, not bad, not amiss, unobjectionable.

652. Cleanness, cleanliness, purity, neatness, tidiness, spotlessness, immaculateness.

Cleaning, purification, lustration, abstersion, depuration, expurgation, purgation.

Washing, ablution, clarification, defecation, colation, filtration.

Fumigation, ventilation, disinfection.

Scavenger; brush, broom, besom, sieve, riddle, screen, filter.

V. To be clean, &c.

To render clean, &c., to clean, cleanse, wipe, mop, sponge, scour, swab, scrub, brush, sweep, brush up.

To wash, lave, absterge, deterge, clear, purify, depurate, defecate, lixiviate, edulcorate, clarify, rack, filter, filtrate.

To disinfect, fumigate, ventilate, purge, emasculate.

To sift, winnow, pick, weed.

Adj. Clean, pure, spotless, unspotted, immaculate, unstained, stainless, unsoiled, unsullied, taintless, untainted, uninfected.

Spruce, tidy, washed, swept, &c., cleaned, purified, &c.

---

653. Uncleanness, (filthiness,) uncleanliness, soiliness, foulness, impurity, pollution, nastiness, offensiveness, beastliness, defilement, contamination, abomination, taint, tainture; *see* 659.

Slovenliness, untidiness, sluttishness, coarseness, grossness.

Dirt, filth, soil, slop, dust, cobweb, flue, smoke, soot, smut.

Dregs, grounds, sediment, lees, settlement, dross, drossiness, precipitate, slag, scum, sweepings, offscourings, scurf, scurfiness, dandriff, vermin.

Mud, mire, quagmire, slough, alluvium, slime, spawn, offal, recrement, fæces, excrement, ordure, dung, guano, manure, compost, dunghill, sink, cess, cesspool, sewer, bilge-water.

Sty, pigsty, dusthole; lair, den.

Rottenness, corruption, decay, putrefaction, putrescence, putridity, purulence, feculence, rankness, rancidity, moulding, mustiness, mould, mother, must, mildew, dryrot; *see* Fœtor, 401.

V. To be unclean, dirty, &c. to rot, putrefy, mould, moulder fester, &c.

To render unclean, &c., to dirt, dirty, soil, begrime, smear, besmear, spatter, bespatter, splash, bedraggle, daub, bedaub, beslime, to cover with dust, &c.

To foul, befoul, pollute, defile, debase, contaminate, taint, corrupt, deflower, rot, &c.

Adj. Unclean, dirty, soiled, &c., dusty, dirtied, &c., sooty, smoky, turbid, dreggy.

Slovenly, untidy, sluttish, unkempt, unscoured, unswept, unwiped, unwashed, unstrained, unpurified.

Nasty, foul, impure, offensive, abominable, beastly.

Mouldy, musty, mildewed, rusty, mouldering, effete, rotten,

rotting, tainted, flyblown, maggoty, putrescent, putrid, putrefied, festering, purulent, feculent, excrementitious.

654. Health, sanity, soundness, heartiness, haleness, vigor, freshness, bloom, healthfulness, incorruption, incorruptibility.

V. To be in health, &c., to bloom, to flourish.

To return to health, to recruit, to recover, to get the better of.

To restore to health, to cure, recall to life.

Adj. Healthy, in health, well, sound, healthful, hearty, hale, fresh, whole, florid, stanch, flush, hardy, vigorous, weatherproof.

Unscathed, uuinjured, unmaimed, unmarred, untainted.

655. Disease, illness, sickness, ailment, ailing, indisposition, complaint, disorder, malady, distemper, (delicate health, feebleness, weak, feeble or delicate constitution.)

Sickliness. sickishness, infirmity, diseasedness, invalidation, witheredness, atrophy, marasmus, incurableness, incurability.

Taint, pollution, infection, epidemic, endemic, murrain, plague, pestilence, virus, pox.

A sore, ulcer, abscess, fester, canker, cancer, gangrene, leprosy.

A valetudinarian, an invalid, a patient, a cripple, a martyr to disease.

Science of disease: Pathology, Nosology.

V. To be ill, &c., to ail, suffer, be affected with, &c., to complain of, droop, flag, languish, halt, gasp.

Adj. Diseased, ill, taken ill, seized, indisposed, unwell, sick, ailing, suffering, affected with illness, laid up, confined, bedridden.

Unsound, sickly, poorly, weakly, infirm, drooping, flagging, withered, decayed, decrepit, lame, crippled, battered, halting, worn out, used up, motheaten, wormeaten.

Morbid, tainted, vitiated, peccant, contaminated, mangy, poisoned, immedicable; cureless, gasping, 360.

656. Salubrity, healthiness, wholesomeness, innoxiousness.

Preservation of health; hygiene.

V. To be salubrious, &c., to agree with.

Adj. Salubrious, wholesome, healthy, salutary, salutiferous, healthful, sanitary.

Innoxious, innocuous, harmless, uninjurious, innocent, uninfectious.

Remedial, restorative, sanative, see 662.

657. Insalubrity, unhealthiness, unwholesomeness, deadliness, fatality, malaria, &c., 663.

Adj. Insalubrious, unhealthy, ungenial, uncongenial, innutritious, indigestible, unwholesome, morbific, deleterious, pestilent, pestiferous, pestilential, virulent, poisonous, contagious, infectious, epidemic, deadly, mortiferous.

658. Improvement, melioration, amelioration, betterment, emendation, advance, advancement, progress, elevation, prefer-

659. Deterioration, wane, ebb, debasement, degeneracy, degeneration, degradation, degenerateness.

ment, convalescence, recovery, curableness.

Repair, reparation, cicatrization, correction, reform, reformation, epuration, purification, &c., 652, refinement, relief, redress.

Reformer, radical.

V. To be, become, or get better, &c., to improve, mend, advance, progress, 282, to get on, make progress, gain ground, make way, pick up, rally, recover, get the better of, get well.

To render better, improve, mend, amend, better, meliorate, ameliorate.

To repair, refit, retouch, botch, vamp, tinker, cobble, patch up, touch up, cicatrize, darn, rub up, furbish, polish, bolster up, prune, calk, careen, to stop up a gap, to stanch.

To correct, rectify, redress, reform, restore, 660.

To purify, depurate, 652, defecate, strain, filter, rack, refine, disinfect.

To advance, forward, enhance.

To relieve, refresh, restore, renew, redintegrate, heal, &c., *see* 660; to palliate, mitigate.

Adj. Improving, &c., improved, &c., progressive, corrective, reparatory, emendatory, sanatory.

Curable, corrigible.

Impairment, injury, vitiation, debasement, alloy, perversion, corruption, prostitution, pollution, poisoning, venenation.

Decline, declension, declination, falling off, going down hill, recession, retrogression, retrogradation, 283, caducity, decrepitude, decadency.

Decay, disorganization, wear and tear, falling to pieces, mouldiness, rottenness, moth and rust, dryrot, blight, marasmus.

Incurableness, remedilessness, *see* Hopelessness, 859.

V. To be or become deteriorated, to deteriorate, wane, ebb, degenerate, fall off, decline, sink, lapse, droop, be the worse for, recede, retrograde, fall into decay, fade, break down, fall to pieces, wither, moulder, rot, rust, crumble, totter, shake, tumble, fall, topple, perish, die, 360.

To render less good; to deteriorate, injure, impair, vitiate, debase, alloy, pervert.

To spoil, defile, taint, infect, contaminate, sophisticate, poison, impoison, canker, corrupt, pollute, deprave, denaturalize, leaven, envenom, debauch, prostitute, defile, adulterate, stain, spatter, bespatter, soil, tarnish.

To corrode, wear away, wear out, gnaw, gnaw at the root of, sap, mine, undermine, shake, break up, disorganize, dismantle, dismast, lay waste, ruin.

To imbitter, acerbate, aggravate.

To injure, harm, hurt, damage, endamage, &c., 649.

Adj. Deteriorated, become worse, impaired, &c., degenerate, on the decline, deciduous, unimproved, unrecovered, unrestored.

Remediless, hopeless, past cure, past mending, irreparable, irremediable, cureless, incurable, irremedicable, irrecoverable, irretrievable, irreclaimable, irreversible.

Decayed, &c., motheaten, wormeaten, mildewed, rusty timeworn, mossgrown, effete, wasted, worn, crumbling.

660 RESTORATION, reinstatement, replacement, restoral, instauration, reestablishment, rectification, redintegration, refection, cure, refitting, recruiting, redress, retrieval, &c., refreshment, 689.

Renovation, reanimation, recovery, resuscitation, revival, rejuvenescence, regeneration, regeneracy, regenerateness, redemption, 672; a phœnix.

V. To return to the original state, to right itself.

To restore, replace, reëstablish, reinstate, reconstitute, rebuild, redintegrate, set right, set to rights, rectify, redress, reclaim, redeem, recover, come to, retrieve.

To refit, recruit, refresh, rehabilitate, reconvert, reconstitute, renovate, revive, regenerate, resuscitate, reanimate, recall to life, set on one's legs, reseat.

To cure, heal, cicatrize, remedy, physic, medicate.

Adj. Restoring, &c., restored, &c.

Restorable, sanable, remediable, retrievable, (recoverable.)

661. RELAPSE, lapse, falling back, retrogression, retrogradation, &c., 659.

Return to, or recurrence of a bad state.

V. To relapse, lapse, fall back, slide back, sink back, return, retrograde, &c.

---

662. REMEDY, help, redress, cure, antidote, counter-poison, corrective, restorative, sedative.

Physic, medicine, drug, medicament, nostrum, prescription, catholicon.

Panacea, elixir, balm, balsam, cordial.

Salve, ointment, plaster, embrocation, cataplasm, poultice, vulnerary, cosmetic, &c.; sanativeness.

Pharmacy, Pharmacology, Materia Medica, Therapeutics, Dietetics, Dietary, Regimen, Chirurgery, Surgery.

A hospital, infirmary, pest-house, lazaretto.

Adj. Remedial, medical, medicinal, therapeutic, chirurgical, sanatory, sanative, salutary, salutiferous, healing, restorative, tonic, balsamic, anodyne, sedative, lenitive, demulcent, emollient, detersive, detergent, abstersive, disinfectant, corrective.

Dietetic.

663. BANE, rod, scourge, curse, scathe, sting, thorn; gall and wormwood.

Poison, leaven, virus, venom, miasm, malaria, azote, pest, rust, canker, cancer, canker worm,

Hemlock, hellebore, nightshade, henbane, aconite.

A viper, adder, serpent, rattlesnake, cockatrice, scorpion, wireworm, torpedo, hornet, vulture, vampire, &c.; Demon, &c., 980; Fury, *see* 913.

Science of poisons, Toxicology.

---

3. *Contingent Subservience.*

664. SAFETY, security, surety, impregnability, invulnerability, invulnerableness.

Safeguard, guard, guardianship, protection tutelage, ward-

665. DANGER, peril, insecurity, jeopardy, risk, hazard, venture, precariousness, slipperiness, *see* 667.

Liability, exposure. 177, vul-

ship. wardenship, safe conduct, escort, convoy, garrison.

Watch, watch and ward, sentinel, scout, watchman, patrol, picket, bivouac, watchdog.

Protector, guardian, guard, defender, warden, warder, preserver, tutelary saint, guardian angel; *see* Defence, 717.

Custody, safekeeping, 751.

Precaution, quarantine.

V. To be safe, &c.

To render safe, &c., to protect, guard, mount guard, shield, shelter, flank, cover, screen, shroud, ensconce, ward, secure, fence, hedge in, intrench, house.

To defend, forfend, escort, convoy, garrison.

Adj. Safe, in safety, in security, secure, sure, protected, guarded, &c., snug, fireproof.

Defencible, tenable, invulnerable, unassailable, impregnable, inexpugnable.

Protecting, &c., guardian, tutelary.

Unthreatened, unmolested, unharmed, harmless, scathless, unhazarded.

666. Means of safety.

REFUGE, asylum, sanctuary, fastness, retreat, hiding-place.

Roadstead, anchorage, breakwater, mole, port, haven, harbor, harbor of refuge, pier.

Fort, citadel, fortification, &c., shield, &c., *see* Defence, 717.

Screen, covert, wing, fence, rail, railing, wall, dike, ditch, &c., 232.

nerability, vulnerable point, the heel of Achilles.

Hopelessness, 859, forlorn hope, alarm, *see* Fear, 860, defencelessness.

V. To be in danger, &c., to be exposed to, to run, incur or encounter danger, run a risk.

To place or put in danger, &c., to endanger, expose to danger, imperil, jeopardize, compromise, adventure, risk, hazard, venture, stake.

To insnare, entrap, entangle,

Adj. In danger, peril, jeopardy, &c., unsafe, insecure, unguarded, unscreened, unsheltered, unprotected, helpless, exposed, defenceless, at bay.

Unwarned, unadmonished, unadvised.

Dangerous, perilous, hazardous, fraught with danger, adventurous, precarious, slippery, unsteady shaky, tottering, topheavy.

Threatening, alarming, minatory, minacious, 909.

667. Source of danger.

PITFALL, rocks, reefs, sunken rocks, snags, sands, quicksands, breakers, shoals, shallows, bank, shelf, flat, lee shore, precipice.

Trap, snare, gin, springe, toils, noose, net, spring net, spring gun, masked battery, mine.

———

Anchor, sheet anchor, prop, stay, mainstay, jury mast lifeboat, plank, (life preserver,) stepping stone.

668. WARNING, caution, notice, premonition, premonishment lesson, dehortation, admonition, *see* 864.

Beacon, lighthouse, pharos, watchtower, signal post, &c.,

Sentinel, sentry, watch, watchman, patrol, &c., 664.

V. To warn, caution, forewarn, premonish, give notice, give warning, admonish, dehort.

To take warning, to beware, to be on one's guard, 864.

Adj. Warning, &c., premonitory, dehortatory, admonitory.
Warned, &c., careful, on one's guard, 459.

669. Indication of danger.
ALARM, alarum, larum, alarm bell, tocsin, signal of distress, blue lights, &c., warning voice.
False alarm, cry of wolf, bugbear.
V. To give, raise, or sound an alarm, to alarm, warn, ring the tocsin, to cry wolf.
Adj. Alarming, &c.

670. PRESERVATION, conservation, conservatism, maintenance, support, sustentation, deliverance, salvation, rescue, redemption.
Means of preservation, preservative, preserver. Superstitious remedies, *see* 993.
V. To preserve, maintain, support, save, rescue.
To embalm, dry, cure, salt, pickle, season, bottle.
Adj. Preserving, conservative, preservatory.
Preserved, unimpaired, uninjured, unhurt, unsinged, unmarred.

671. ESCAPE, evasion, retreat, reprieve, reprieval, deliverance, redemption, rescue.
Narrow escape, hairbreadth scape.
Means of escape; bridge, drawbridge, loophole, ladder, plank, stepping stone, &c., 666.
V. To escape, elude, evade, wriggle out of, make or effect one's escape, make off, march off, pack off, slip away, steal away, slink away, flit, decamp, run away, abscond, fly, flee, bolt, elope, break loose, play truant.
Adj. Escaping, &c., escaped, &c., fugitive, runaway.

672. DELIVERANCE, extrication, rescue, redemption, salvation, riddance, redeemableness.
V. To deliver, extricate, rescue, save, redeem, bring off, to get rid of, to rid.
Adj. Delivered, saved, &c., scot free, scathless.
Extricable, redeemable, rescuable.

3. *Precursory Measures.*

673. PREPARATION, making ready, providing, provision, providence, anticipation, precaution, laying foundations, ploughing, sowing, brewing, digestion, gestation, hatching, incubation, concoction, maturation, elaboration, predisposition.
Preparation of men; training, drill, drilling, discipline, exercise, exercitation, gymnasium, prenticeship, apprenticeship, qualification, inurement, education, novitiate, *see* Teaching,
Putting or setting in order, put-

674. NON-PREPARATION, want or absence of preparation, improvidence.
Immaturity, crudeness, crudity, greenness, rawness, disqualification.
Absence of art, nature.
An embryo, skeleton, rough copy, germ, &c., rudiment, 153.
V. To be unprepared, &c., to want or lack preparation.
To render unprepared, &c., to dismantle, dismount, dismast, disqualify, disable, unrig, undress, 226.

ting to rights, clearance, arrangement, disposal, organization, adjustment, adaptation, disposition, accommodation, putting in tune, tuning, putting in trim, dressing, putting in harness, outfit, equipment, accoutrement, &c.

Groundwork, basis, foundation, pedestal, &c., *see* 215, first stone, scaffold, scaffolding.

State of being prepared, preparedness, ripeness, maturity, readiness, mellowness.

Preparer, pioneer.

V. To prepare, get ready, make ready, get up, anticipate, forecast, preëstablish, preconcert, settle preliminaries, to found.

To arrange, set or put in order, set or put to rights, organize, dispose, cast the parts, adjust, adapt, accommodate, trim, betrim, fit, predispose, inure, elaborate, mature, ripen, nurture, hatch, cook, brew, tune, put in tune, attune, set, temper.

To provide, provide against, make provision, keep on foot, take precautions, make sure; to lie in wait for, 507.

To equip, arm, man, fit out, fit up, furnish, rig, dress, dress up, furbish up, accoutre, array, vamp up.

To prepare one's self; lay one's self out for, get into harness, gird up one's loins, buckle on one's armor.

To train, drill, discipline, break in, cradle, inure, habituate, harden, season, acclimatize, qualify, educate, teach, &c.

Adj. Preparing, &c., in preparation, in course of preparation, in agitation, brewing, forthcoming, in embryo, afoot, afloat, on the anvil, on the carpet, on the tapis, on the stocks, provisional.

Prepared, trained, drilled, &c., forearmed, ready, in readiiness, ripe, mature, mellow, fledged, ready to one's hand, ready-made, cut and dried, concocted.

Adv. In preparation, in anticipation of, &c., against.

Adj. Unprepared, rudimental, immature, unripe, raw, green, crude, rough, roughcast, roughhewn, unhewn, unformed, unhatched, unfledged, unnurtured, uneducated, in a state of nature, unwrought, unconcocted, undigested, indigested, unfashioned, fallow, uncultivated, untrained, undrilled, unexercised, unseasoned, disqualified.

Unbegun, unready, unarranged, unorganized, unfurnished, unprovided, unequipped, undressed, in dishabille, dismantled, untrimmed.

Shiftless, improvident, thoughtless, unthrifty.

Unpremeditated, offhand, 612, from hand to mouth, extempore.

---

675. Essay, trial, experiment, 463, probation, endeavor, attempt, venture, adventure, random shot.

V. To try, essay, make trial of, experiment, make an experiment; attempt, make an attempt; to grope, feel one's way, pick one's way; to venture, adventure.

To endeavor, strive, use one's endeavors.

Adj. Essaying, &c., experimental, tentative, empirical, on trial probative, probatory, probationary; attempting, endeavoring, &c.

Adv. Experimentally, &c., at a venture.

676. UNDERTAKING, enterprise, move, first move, the initiative, first step, *see* Beginning, 66, debut, embarkation.

V. To undertake, take in hand, set about, go about, set to, fall to, set to work, engage in, launch into, embark in, plunge into, volunteer.

To begin, set on foot, set a-going, take the first step, take the initiative; to break ground, break the ice.

Adv. Undertaking, &c.

677. USE, employment, employ, application, appliance, disposal, exercise, agency, *see* 170.

Recourse, resort, avail, service, wear, conversion to use.

V. To use, make use of, employ, 134, apply, dispose of, work, wield, put to use; turn or convert to use; avail one's self of, resort to, have recourse to, recur to, take up with; to betake one's self to.

To render useful, serviceable, available, &c.; draw, call forth, tax, task, try, exert, exercise, consume, absorb, expend.

To practise, put in action, set to work, set in motion, ply, put in practice.

To be useful, to serve one's turn, &c., *see* 644.

Adj. Used, employed, &c., applied, exercised, tried, &c.

678. DISUSE, forbearance, abstinence, dispensation, desuetude, dispensableness.

V. To disuse, not to use, to do without, to dispense with, to let alone, not to touch; to spare, wave.

To lay by; set, put, or lay aside; to discard, dismiss, cast off, throw off, turn off, turn out, turn away, throw away, do away with; to keep back.

To dismantle, dismast.

Adj. Disused, &c., not used, unemployed, unapplied, undisposed of, unspent, unexercised, kept back.

Unessayed, set aside, ungathered, untouched, unculled, untrodden.

---

679. MISUSE, misemployment, misapplication, misappropriation, abuse, profanation, prostitution, desecration.

Waste, wasting, spilling, exhaustion, 638.

V. To misuse, misemploy, misapply, misappropriate, desecrate, abuse, profane, prostitute.

To waste, spill, fritter away, exhaust.

Adj. Misused, &c.

Section III. VOLUNTARY ACTION.

1. *Simple Voluntary Action.*

680. ACTION, performance, work, operation, proceeding, procedure, process, handicraft, workmanship, transaction, job, doings; business, affair.

Deed, act, overt act, move, stroke, blow, feat, exploit, passage, stroke of policy.

681. INACTION, abstinence from action, *see* Inactivity, 683.

V. Not to do, to let be, abstain from doing; let or leave alone, refrain, desist, stop, leave off, keep one's self from doing; let pass, lie by, wait.

To undo, take down, take or

V. To act, do, work, perform, operate, commit, perpetrate, inflict; exercise, practise; to strike a blow.

To labor, drudge, toil, ply, dabble; to set to work, go about, serve, officiate.

pull to pieces, do away with; *see* 163.

Ad. Not doing, not done, let alone, undone, &c.

Adj. Acting, &c., in action, in operation, &c., on foot, at work, operative, in harness, in exercise, in play; on duty.

682. Activity, briskness, (liveliness,) quickness, promptness, promptitude, readiness, alertness, smartness, sharpness, nimbleness, agility.

Spirit, vivacity, eagerness, alacrity, zeal, energy, 171, vigor, intentness.

Movement, bustle, stir, fuss, ado, fidget, restlessness.

Wakefulness, vigilance, sleeplessness, 459.

Industry, assiduity, assiduousness, sedulity, sedulousness, diligence; perseverance, persistence, plodding, painstaking, drudgery, indefatigability, indefatigableness, patience, habits of business.

Dabbling, meddling, interference, interposition, intermeddling, tampering with, intrigue, supererogation, superfluence.

V. To be active, busy, stirring, &c., to busy one's self in, stir, bestir one's self, bustle, fuss, make a fuss, speed, hasten, push, make a push, go ahead.

To plod, drudge, keep on, hold on, persist, take pains; to take or spend time in; to make progress.

To meddle, intermeddle, interfere, interpose, tamper with, agitate, intrigue.

To overact, overdo, overlay, outdo.

Adj. Active, brisk, quick, prompt, alert, on the alert, stirring, spry, sharp, smart, quick, nimble, agile lightfooted, tripping, ready

683. Inactivity, inaction, lull, idleness, sloth, laziness, indolence, inertness, lumpishness, supineness, sluggishness, languor, torpor, listlessness, remissness, want of occupation.

Dilatoriness, procrastination, 133, relaxation, dronishness, truantship, lagging, dawdling, rust, rustiness.

Somnolence, drowsiness, doziness, nodding, oscitation, sleepiness.

Sleep, nap, doze, slumber, lethargy, hybernation.

An idler, laggard, truant, sluggard, slumberer, drone, lounger.

Cause of inactivity, *see* 174, torpedo.

V. To be inactive, &c., to do nothing, to let alone, lie by, lie idle, keep quiet, relax, lag, lounge, loiter; to waste, lose, idle away, kill, trifle away, fritter away time.

To sleep, slumber, nod, close the eyes, close the eyelids, doze, fall asleep, to drop asleep, hybernate, yawn.

To render idle, &c.

Adj. Inactive, unoccupied, unemployed, unbusied, doing nothing, at leisure, 685.

Indolent, lazy, slothful, idle, slack, inert, torpid, sluggish, languid, supine, heavy, dull, lumpish, exanimate, soulless, listless.

Dilatory, laggard, lagging drawling, creeping, dawdling rusty.

Sleeping, asleep, fast asleep, in a sound sleep.

awake, alive, lively, vivacious, frisky, forward, eager, strenuous zealous, enterprising, spirited, in earnest.

Working, on duty, at work, hard at work, intent, industrious, assiduous, diligent, sedulous, notable, painstaking, business-like, operose, plodding, toiling, hard-working, busy, bustling, restless.

Persevering, indefatigable, untiring, unflagging, unremitting, unweared, never-tiring, undrooping, unintermitting, unflinching.

Meddling, meddlesome, pushing, intermeddling, tampering, &c., officious, over-officious, intriguing, (managing.)

Adv. Actively, &c., *see* 684.

Sleepy, drowsy, somnolent, dormant, asleep, lethargic, napping sleepful, somniferous, soporific, somnific, unwakened.

---

684. HASTE, despatch, precipitancy, precipitation, precipitousness, impetuosity, posthaste, acceleration.

Hurry, flurry, bustle, fuss, scramble, fidget, fidgettiness, 682.

V. To haste, hasten, make haste, urge, press on, push on, bustle, hurry, precipitate, accelerate, bustle, scramble, plunge, dash on.

Adj. Hasty, hurried, precipitate, scrambling, &c., headlong, boisterous, impetuous, cursory.

Adv. Hastily, &c., headlong, in haste, amain, hurryskurry, by fits and starts; all at once, at short notice, *see* 113.

685. LEISURE, spare time, spare hours, breathing time, holiday, vacation, recess, repose.

V. To have leisure, take one's leisure, repose, 687, pause.

Adj. Leisurely, undisturbed, quiet, deliberate, calm, reposing, &c.

Adv. Leisurely, &c., at leisure.

---

686. EXERTION, labor, work, toil, exercise, travail, duty, trouble, pains, ado, drudgery, fagging, slavery.

Effort, tug, stress, struggle, &c.

V. To labor, work, exert one's self, toil, strive, use exertion, drudge, take pains, take trouble, trouble one's self, bestir one's self, fall to work.

Adj. Laboring, &c., laborious, toilsome, troublesome, operose, strained, herculean, gymnastic, palestric.

Hardworking, painstaking, strenuous, *see* 682.

Adv. Laboriously, &c.

687. REPOSE, rest, halt, pause, relaxation, breathing time, respite, *see* Leisure, 685.

V. To repose, rest, relax, unbend, take rest, breathe, take breath, take one's ease, respire, pause, halt, lie by, lie fallow, recline, lie down, &c., unbend.

Adj. Reposing, resting, &c., unstrained.

---

688. FATIGUE, lassitude, weariness, 841, yawning, exhaustion, sweat, collapse, swoon, prostration, faintness, fainting.

689. REFRESHMENT, recovery of strength, recruiting, repair, refection, relief, bracing, regalement, restoration, revival.

V. To be fatigued, &c., to droop, sink, flag, lose breath, gasp, pant, puff, blow, yawn, swoon, faint, succumb.

To fatigue, tire, weary, fag, jade, harass, exhaust, knock up, wear out, strain, overtask, overwork, overburden, overtax, overstrain.

V. To refresh, recruit, repair give tone, restore.

To recover, regain, renew, &c., one's strength.

Adj. Refreshing, &c., refreshed, &c., untired, unwearied, &c.

Adj. Fatigued, tired, unrefreshed, unrestored, weary, wearied, jaded, wayworn.

Breathless, out of breath.

Drooping, flagging, faint, fainting, exhausted, sinking, prostrate, spent, overspent, over-fatigued, &c.

Fatiguing, &c., tiresome, irksome, weary, wearisome, trying.

690. Agent, doer, performer, operator, hand, executor, maker. Artist, workman, worker, artisan, artificer, architect, handicraftsman, mechanic, machinist, manufacturer, practitioner, operative, journeyman, laborer, smith, wright, day laborer, co-worker.

691. Workshop, laboratory, manufactory, mill, factory, cabinet, studio, (counting room,) workhouse.

Crucible, alembic, caldron.

2. *Complex Voluntary Action.*

692. Conduct, course of action, practice, procedure, transaction, doings, dealing, business, ways, tactics, policy, polity, generalship, statesmanship, economy, husbandry, seamanship, housekeeping, housewifery.

Execution, manipulation, treatment, process, course, campaign, career, race.

Behavior, deportment, carriage, demeanor, bearing, manner, observance.

V. To conduct, carry on, transact, execute, carry out, work out, carry through, go through, despatch, treat, deal with, proceed with, officiate, acquit one's self, discharge.

To behave, acquit one's self, demean one's self.

Adj. Conducting, &c.

693. Direction, management, government, (administration,) statesmanship, conduct, 692, regulation, charge, agency, ministry, ministration, guidance, steerage, pilotage, superintendence, stewardship, proctorship, supervision, (control.)

Board, board of control, committee, council, &c., 696.

V. To direct, manage, govern, guide, conduct, regulate, steer, pilot, have or take the direction, preside, take the helm, have the charge of, superintend, overlook, supervise, control.

To head, lead, show the way, &c.

Adj. Directing, &c.

694. Director, manager, master, 745, head, minister, premier, governor, comptroller, superintendent, intendent, supervisor, supercargo, president, inspector, visitor, monitor, overseer, taskmaster, official, officer, 726.

Conductor, steersman, pilot, guide, cicerone, guard, driver, charioteer, coachman, postilion, carman.

Steward, factor, foreman, proctor, procurator, housekeeper.

695. ADVICE, counsel, suggestion, recommendation, hortation, dehortation, instruction, charge, monition, admonition, caution, warning, expostulation, injunction, persuasion.

Guidance, helm, cynosure, rudder, guide, hand book, manual, itinerary, reference.

An adviser, counsellor, counsel, monitor, Mentor, guide, teacher 540.

Referee, arbiter, arbitrator, referendary.

V. To advise, counsel, give advice, admonish, caution, warn, forewarn, *see* 668.

To persuade, 615, to dehort, exhort, enjoin, expostulate, charge, instruct.

To deliberate, consult together, hold a council, &c., confer, call in, refer to, take advice, be closeted with.

Adj. Monitory, admonitory, recommendatory, (hortatory,) dehortatory, warning, &c.

696. COUNCIL, conclave, court, chamber, cabinet, house, committee, sub-committee, board, meeting.

Senate, (house of representatives,) parliament, synod, convocation, congress, consistory, diet, cortes, divan, Areopagus, sanhedrim, directory, &c.

A meeting, assembly, sitting, session.

697. PRECEPT, direction, instruction, prescript, prescription, order, *see* 741.

Rule, canon code, formula, formulary, maxim, apothegm, &c., 496.

698. SKILL, skilfulness, cleverness, ability, talent, ingenuity, capacity, calibre, shrewdness, sagacity, parts, genius, faculty, gift, forte, turn, invention; cunning, 702.

Address, dexterity, adroitness, dexterousness, facility, knack, expertness, aptitude, aptness, quickness, sharpness, readiness, excellence, felicity.

Qualification, proficiency, accomplishment, acquirement, craft, mastership.

Tact, knowledge of the world, discretion.

Prudence discretion, *see* Caution, 864.

699. UNSKILFULNESS, inability, incompetence, incompetency, infelicity, inexpertness, unaptness, awkwardness, maladroitness, clumsiness, slovenliness, greenness, rawness, inexperience, disqualification.

Bungling, blundering, fumbling, floundering, stumbling, dulness, unteachableness.

Indiscretion, imprudence, 863, folly, thoughtlessness, giddiness, wildness, mismanagement, misconduct, maladministration, misrule, misgovernment, misapplication; misdirection.

V. To be unskilled, unskilful, &c.

Art, management, tactics, manœuvering, sleight, policy.

A master-stroke, a masterpiece, a bold stroke.

V. To be skilful, skilled, &c., to excel in, be master of.

Adj. Skilled, skilful, &c., clever, able, accomplished, ingenious, inventive, gifted, sagacious.

Expert, dexterous, adroit, apt, sharp, handy, ready, quick, smart, nimble.

Conversant, versed, proficient, knowing, competent, qualified, good at, master of, at home in.

Experienced, practised, hackneyed, trained, initiated, prepared, primed, finished, thorough-bred.

Technical, artistic, workman-like, masterly, statesman-like.

To mismanage, misconduct, bungle, blunder, botch, boggle, mistake, misapply, missend, misdirect.

Adj. Unskilled, &c., unskilful, bungling, &c., awkward, clumsy, unhandy, maladroit.

Unapt, unqualified, incompetent, disqualified, ill qualified, inapt.

Unaccustomed, unused, unhackneyed, unexercised, untrained, unpractised, undisciplined, uneducated, undrilled, uninitiated, unschooled, unconversant, unversed, inexperienced, unstatesman-like.

Unadvised, misadvised, ill devised, ill imagined, ill judged, ill advised, unguided, misguided, ill conducted, misconducted, foolish, wild.

Discreet, politic, surefooted, felicitous.

Adv. Skilfully, &c., aright, artistically, &c., with consummate skill.

700. PROFICIENT, adept, genius, master, masterhand, tactician, politician, marksman, veteran, picked man, conjuror, wizard, &c., 994.

701. BUNGLER, greenhorn, novice, no conjuror, flat.

702. CUNNING, cunningness, craft, artfulness, subtlety, shrewdness, archness, insidiousness, shyness, artificialness, artificiality. Artifice, device, manœuvre, stratagem, wile, finesse, trick, ruse, diplomacy, politics.

Duplicity, guile, circumvention, chicane, chicanery, Machiavelism, legerdemain, trickery, &c., 545.

Net, toils, trap, &c., 667.

V. To be cunning, &c., to contrive, design, manœuvre, intrigue, circumvent.

703. ARTLESSNESS, nature, naturalness, simplicity, ingenuousness, frankness, openness, candor, sincerity, straightforwardness, honesty, 939.

V. To be artless, &c.

Adj. Artless, natural, native, plain, simple-minded, ingenuous, candid, naive, sincere, frank, open, open hearted, above board, downright, guileless, inartificial, undesigning, single-minded, honest.

Adj. Cunning, crafty, artful, wily, sly, subtle, arch, designing, intriguing, contriving, insidious, deceitful, 545, tricky, artificial, crooked, deep, profound, diplomatic, Machiavelian, timeserving.

Section IV. Antagonism.

1. *Conditional Antagonism.*

704. Difficulty, delicacy, troublesomeness, encumbrance, laboriousness.

Impracticability, infeasibleness, intractability, toughness, perverseness, *see* Impossibility, 462.

Embarrassment, awkwardness, perplexity, intricacy, intricateness, inextricableness, entanglement, knot, Gordian knot, labyrinth, net, meshes, maze, &c., 248.

Dilemma, nice point, delicate point, knotty point, poser, puzzle; nonplus, quandary, strait, pass, critical situation, crisis, trial, rub, emergency, exigency.

Scrape, lurch, slough, quagmire, hot water, stew, mess, ado, false position.

V. To be difficult, &c.

To meet with, experience, labor under, get into, plunge into, be surrounded by, be encompassed with, be entangled by; to struggle, contend against, or grapple with difficulties.

To come to a stand, to stick fast, to be set fast, to boggle, flounder.

To render difficult, &c., to embarrass, perplex, put one out, pose, puzzle, nonplus, ravel, entangle, gravel, run hard.

Adj. Difficult, not easy, hard, troublesome, laborious, onerous, operose, awkward, unwieldy, beset with or full of difficulties.

Unmanageable, tough, stubborn, hard to deal with, ill-conditioned, refractory, perverse, crabbed, intractable.

Embarrassing, perplexing, delicate, ticklish, intricate, thorny, knotty, pathless, trackless, labyrinthic, labyrinthine.

Impracticable, not possible, impossible, 471, not practica-

705. Facility, practicability, feasibility, practicableness, *see* Possibility, 470.

Ease, easiness, child's play, smoothness, tractableness, ductility, flexibility, malleability, tractility, capability, disencumbrance, disentanglement.

Plain sailing, smooth water, smooth sailing, fair wind, freedom, full play, a clear coast, advantage, vantage ground.

V. To be easy, &c., to flow, swim, or drift with the tide or stream.

To render easy, &c., to facilitate, smooth, ease, lighten, free, clear, disencumber, disembarrass, clear the way, smooth the way, *see* 673, disentangle, unclog, disengage, extricate, unravel, disburdon, exonerate, emancipate, free from.

Adj. Easy, facile, attainable, accessible, practicable, feasible, achievable, performable, possible, 470, superable, surmountable.

Easily managed or accomplished, &c., tractable, manageable, smooth, pliant, yielding, malleable, plastic, ductile, tractile, flexible, submissive.

At ease, free, light, easy, unburdened, unencumbered, unloaded, disburdened, disencumbered, disembarrassed, exonerated, unrestrained, unobstructed, at home.

Adv. Easily, &c.

---

ble, not feasible, infeasible, unachievable, inaccessible, inextricable, impassable, innavigable, desperate, insuperable, insurmountable.

In difficulty, at a loss, perplexed, &c., beset, put to it, hard put to it, run hard, hard pressed, adrift, at fault.

Stranded, aground, stuck fast, at bay.

Adv. With difficulty, hardly, &c., uphill.

2. *Active Antagonism.*

706. HINDERANCE, prevention, preclusion, retardment, retardation, embarrassment, interruption, obstruction, stoppage, interception, interclusion, coarctation, restraint, inhibition, embargo.

Interference, interposition, obtrusion, discouragement, discountenance.

An impediment, hinderance, obstacle, knot, obstruction; stumbling stone or block; check, bar, barrier, barricade, wall, dead wall, bulkhead, portcullis, &c., 717, dam, wear, boom.

Drawback, objection.

An encumbrance, clog, drag weight, dead weight, lumber, pack, incubus; trammel, &c., 752.

A hinderer, an interloper; an opponent, 710.

V. To hinder, impede, prevent, preclude, retard, slacken, obviate, forefend, avert, turn aside, ward off, draw off, cut off, incommode, discommode, undermine.

To obstruct, stop, stay, bar, lock, debar, inhibit, cramp, clog, restrain, check, discourage, discountenance, foreclose.

To thwart, traverse, contravene, interrupt, intercept, interclude, frustrate, defeat, disconcert, undo, intercept; to balk, cushion, spoil, mar.

To interpose, interfere, intermeddle, obtrude, 682.

To hamper, clog, cumber, encumber, saddle with, load with,

707. AID, assistance, help, succor, (helping hand,) support, relief, advance, furtherance, promotion.

Patronage, championship, countenance, favor.

Sustentation, alimentation, nutrition, nourishment; ministration, ministry, accommodation.

Supplies, reënforcements, succors, recruits; physical support, *see* 215.

V. To aid, assist, help, succor, support, promote, further, abet, advance, foster; foment; to give, bring, furnish, afford or supply support, &c., to reënforce, nourish, nurture.

To favor, countenance, befriend, cherish, encourage, patronize, make interest for.

To second, stand by, back, take part with, side with, to come or pass over to; to join, to rally round.

To serve, do service, minister to, tender to, oblige, accommodate, work for, administer to, pander to; to tend, attend, take care of, wait on, nurse, entertain.

To speed, expedite, forward, quicken, hasten, set forward.

Adj. Aiding, helping, assisting, &c., auxiliary, adjuvant, coadjutant, ancillary, accessory, subsidiary.

Friendly, amicable, favorable, propitious.

Adv. On or in behalf of; in the service of; hand in hand.

———

overload, overlay, lumber, block up, incommode; to curb, shackle, fetter.

Adj. Hindering, &c., (repugnant,) in the way of, inimical, unfavorable, onerous, burdensome.

Hindered, &c., windbound.

708. Opposition, antagonism, counteraction, 179, contravention, control, clashing, collision, competition, rivalry, emulation.

Absence of aid, &c., counterplot, 719.

V. To oppose, withstand, antagonize, cross, counteract, control, contravene, countervail, counterwork, stultify, thwart, overthwart, countermine, run counter, go against, clash, rival, emulate, pit against, militate against, beat against, stem, breast, encounter, compete with.

Adj. Opposing, &c., adverse, antagonistic, opposed, pitted against, contrary, conflicting, unfavorable, unfriendly.

Unaided, unassisted, unhelped, unsustained, unseconded, &c., unsupported, unbefriended.

Adv. Against, counter to, against the stream, tide, wind, &c., in the way of, in spite of, in despite of, in the teeth of, in the face of.

Across, athwart.

Though, although, 179, even

709. Coöperation, concert, collusion, coefficiency, *see* Concurrence, 178.

Alliance, colleagueship, joint stock, copartnership, coalition, federation, confederation, 712.

V. To coöperate, concur, conspire, concert; draw or pull together, to join with, unite one's efforts, club together, fraternize, be in league, &c., with, be a party to.

Adj. Coöperating, &c., in coöperation, &c., in concert, allied, &c.

Unopposed, unobstructed.

---

710. Opponent, antagonist, adversary, adverse party, rival, competitor, enemy, foe, 891, assailant.

---

711. Auxiliary, assistant, adjuvant, adjunct, adjutant, help, helper, helpmate, colleague, partner, coadjutor, coöperator, ally; votary.

Friend, confidant, champion, partisan, sectary; adherent, abetter, confederate, accomplice, accessory; servant, *see* 746.

712. Party, partnership, fraternity, company, society, firm, house, body, corporation, corporate body, guild, joint concern.

Fellowship, brotherhood, sisterhood, communion, clan, clanship club, clique, junto, coterie, faction, cabal, league, alliance, confederacy, confederation, federation; side, partisanship, party spirit.

Band, staff, crew, set, posse, phalanx.

V. To unite, join, club together, join forces, coöperate, befriend, aid, &c., 707, cement, form a party, league, &c.

Adj. In partnership, alliance, &c., banded, linked, cemented, &c. together.

713. Discord, variance, difference, dissent, misunderstanding,

714. Concord, accord, agreement, 23, unison, unity, union,

dissension, jar, jarring, clashing, odds; disunion schism, breach, falling out, rupture, disruption, open rupture, feud, faction, contentiousness, litigiousness, strife, contention. 720.

Dispute, controversy, polemics, quarrel, altercation, bickering, chicanery, squabble, row, brawl.

Litigation, words, war of words, logomachy, wrangling, jangle, *see* Warfare, 722.

Subject of dispute; ground of quarrel, disputed point; the bone of contention; the apple of discord.

V. To be discordant, &c., to differ, dissent, disagree, clash, jar.

To fall out, dispute, controvert, litigate; to quarrel, wrangle, bicker, spar, jangle; to break with; to split; to declare war.

To embroil, entangle, disunite, set against, pit against

Adj. Discordant, disagreeing, differing, disunited, clashing, jarring, dissentient, at variance, controversial.

Quarrelsome, disputatious, litigious, litigant, factious, gladiatorial, pettyfogging, polemic, schismatic; unpacified, unreconciled.

good understanding, quiet, peace, 721, unanimity, 488, harmony, amity, alliance.

V. To agree, accord, be in unison, &c., to harmonize with, fraternize.

Adj. Concordant, agreeing, &c., united, in unison, &c., harmonious, allied, cemented, friendly, amicable, fraternal, at peace, peaceful, pacific, tranquil.

---

715. Defiance, challenge, daring.

V. To defy, challenge, dare, beard.

Adj. Defying, &c.

Adv. In defiance of; with arms akimbo.

716. Attack, aggression, offence, assault, charge, onset, onslaught, brunt, thrust, pass, sally, inroad, invasion, irruption, sortie, storm, storming, boarding, forray, dragonade, *see* 619, siege, investment.

Fire, volley, cannonade, broadside, bombardment, raking fire.

An assailant, aggressor.

V. To attack, assault, assail, impugn, fall upon, close with, charge, bear down upon, set on, strike at, fly at, butt, tilt at, make a pass at, thrust at, cut and thrust, buffet, beat, *see* 972, pelt; to march upon, march against, advance against.

To shoot at, fire at, fire upon, shoot, open fire, bombard, pour a broadside into, fire a volley.

717. Defence, self-defence, self-preservation, protection, ward, guard, guardianship, shielding, &c., *see* Resistance, 718, and Safety, 664.

Fence, wall, parapet, dike, &c., 232, boom, picket, mound, mole, outwork, intrenchment, fortification, embankment, bulwark, barbican, battlement, stockade, abattis, muniment, vallum, circumvallation, contravallation, buttress, abutment, breastwork, portcullis, glacis, bastion, redoubt, rampart.

Hold, stronghold, fastness, keep, fort, fortress, citadel, tower, castle, capitol. asylum, 666.

Shield, buckler, ægis, breastplate, coat of mail, cuirass, hawberk, habergeon, screen, &c., 666, helmet. casque; panoply.

To beset, besiege, lay siege to, invest, beleaguer, open the trenches, invade, storm, board, scale the walls.

To press one hard, be hard upon, drive one hard.

Adj. Attacking, &c., aggressive, offensive, up in arms

———

Defender, protector, guardian, *see* 664, champion, knight errant.

V. To defend, shield, fend, fence, guard, 644, keep off, keep at bay, ward off, beat off, parry, repel, bear the brunt of, put to flight.

To fall back upon, to stand or act on the defensive, to maintain one's ground.

Adj. Defending, &c., defensive, defended, &c., armed, armed cap-à-pie, armed to the teeth.

Adv. Defensively, on the defence, on the defensive, at bay.

718. Retaliation, reprisal, retort, counterstroke, reciprocation, retribution, counterplot, counter-project, *see* Revenge, 919, and Compensation, 30.

V. To retaliate, retort, be even with one, pay off.

Adj. Retaliating, retaliatory, retaliative.

———

719. Resistance, stand, front, repulse, rebuff, &c., *see* Disobedience, 742, recalcitration.

Strike, meeting, tumult, riot.

Revolt, rising, insurrection, rebellion.

V. To resist, not to submit, &c., to withstand, stand or strive against, stand firm, make a stand, confront, reluctate.

To kick, kick against, recalcitrate, lift the hand against, *see* Attack, 716, to repel, repulse, rise, revolt, mutiny.

Adj. Resisting, &c., resistive, refractory, mutinous, repulsive, recalcitrant, up in arms, *see* Disobedient, 742.

Unyielding, unconquered, indomitable.

720. Contention, strife, contest, struggle, contestation, debate, logomachy, high words, rivalry, competition, race, heat, bickering.

Wrestling, pugilism, boxing, fisticuffs, spar, prize fighting, set-to, round, row, outbreak, clash, collision, shock, breach of the peace.

Conflict, skirmish, rencounter, scuffle, encounter, digladiation, broil, fray, affray, affair, brush, fight, battle, combat, action, engagement, running fight, joust, tournament, tournay, pitched battle, death struggle.

Naval engagement, (sea fight.)

Duel, satisfaction, monomachy.

V. To contend, contest, struggle, vie with, outvie, battle with, strive, cope with, compete, close with, enter the lists, take up arms, take the field, encounter struggle with, grapple with, engage with, fal [illegible], enc[illegible]unter

721. Peace, amity, truce, harmony, *see* Concord, 714, tranquillity.

V. To be at peace, &c., to keep the peace, &c., 714.

Adj. Pacific, peaceable, peaceful, tranquil, untroubled.

———

722. WARFARE, war, hostilities, fighting, &c., open war war to the knife.

Battle array, campaign, crusade.

The art of war, tactics, strategy, military evolutions, arms, service, &c.

War cry, fire-cross, trumpet, clarion, bugle, war-whoop, beat of drum, to arms.

V. To fight, set to, spar, justle, skirmish, stave, fence, engage, combat.

Adj. Contending, &c., unpeaceful, contentious, belligerent, bellicose, martial, warlike, military, militant, gladiatorial, chivalrous, in arms, embattled.

723. PACIFICATION, reconciliation, accommodation, arrangement, adjustment.

Peace offering, olive branch, preliminaries of peace.

Truce, armistice, suspension of arms, of hostilities, &c., convention.

Flag of truce, cartel.

V. To make peace, pacify, make it up, settle, arrange, accommodate matters, tranquillize, compose, hush up, settle differences, restore harmony, heal the breach.

Adj. Pacified, &c.

---

724. MEDIATION, intervention, interposition, interference, intermeddling, intercession, parley, negotiation, arbitration, mediatorship, good offices, diplomacy, peace offering.

A mediator, intercessor, peacemaker, makepeace, negotiator, bottle holder.

V. To mediate, intercede, interpose, interfere, negotiate, arbitrate *see* Compromise, 774.

725. SUBMISSION, surrender, non-resistance, yielding, capitulation, cession.

V. To surrender, succumb, submit, yield, give in, bend, capitulate; lay down or deliver up one's arms, retreat, give way.

Adj. Surrendering, &c., non-resisting, submissive.

Undefended, untenable, indefensible.

726. COMBATANT, armigerent, champion, disputant, litigant, competitor, rival, assailant, bully, fighter, duellist, pugilist, boxer, gladiator, athlete; swordsman, wrestler.

Warrior, soldier, man at arms, foot soldier, trooper, dragoon, hussar, light horseman, (or hussar,) grenadier, fusileer, guardsman, lifeguard, lancer, cuirassier, spearman, musketeer, carabineer, rifleman, sharpshooter; ensign, standard bearer, halberdier; private subaltern, conscript.

Artilleryman, gunner, cannonier, bombardier.

Marine, jolly.

Armed force, the army, the military, soldiery, infantry, cavalry horse artillery.

Militia, trainband, legion, phalanx, levy, squadron, troop, cohort, regiment, corps, platoon, battalion, company, 72, column, detachment, brigade, garrison, battle array.

Man-of-war, war ship, privateer, &c., 273.

727. ARMS, armament, armor, armory, quiver, arsenal.

Mail, lorication; ammunition, powder, gunpowder, cartridge, 635

Artillery, park, ordnance piece, gun, cannon, swivel, howitzer, carronade, culverin, fieldpiece, basilisk, mortar, grenade, petronel, petard, falconet.

Firearms, sidearms, stand of arms, musketry, musket, fusil, firelock, matchlock, fowling piece, rifle, revolver, carabine, blunderbuss, pistol.

Bow, harquebuss, crossbow, ballister, sling, catapult.

Missile, projectile, shot, ball, grape, grapeshot, chainshot, bullet, shell, bomb, rocket.

Pike, lance, spear, spontoon, javelin, dart, arrow, reed, shaft.

Bayonet, sword, sabre, broadsword, cutlass, falchion, cimeter, rapier, claymore, dagger, dirk, poniard, stiletto, dudgeon, axe, bill, poleaxe, battleaxe, halberd, tomahawk, bowieknife.

Club, mace, truncheon, staff, bludgeon, cudgel.

Catapult, battering ram.

728. Arena, field, walk, battle field, field of battle, lists, palæstra, course, stage, boards, racecourse, turf, circus, ring, scene of action, theatre of war, the enemy's camp, amphitheatre, hippodrome, coliseum.

Section V. Results of Voluntary Action.

729. Completion, accomplishment, performance, fulfilment, execution, achievement, despatch, work done, superstructure, finish, termination, consummation, winding up, the keystone, the last stroke, finishing stroke, last finish, final touch, crowning touch, *see* End, 67, Arrival, 292, and Completeness, 52.

V. To complete, effect, perform, do, execute, go through, accomplish, fulfil, discharge, achieve, compass, effectuate, despatch, close, terminate, conclude, finish, end, 67, consummate, bring about, bring to bear, bring to pass, go through, carry through, bring through, work out, make good, carry out, wind up, bring to a close, termination, conclusion, &c.

To perfect, bring to perfection, stamp, crown.

To reach, arrive, 292, touch, reach, attain the goal; to run one's race.

Adj. Completing, final, concluding, conclusive, crowning, &c., done, completed, wrought, high-wrought, &c., out of hand.

Adv. Completely, &c., 62, effectually, with a witness, with a vengeance.

730. Non-completion, inexecution, shortcoming, 304, non-performance, neglect; incompleteness, 53.

V. Not to complete, perform, &c., to fall short off, leave unfinished, &c., neglect, leave undone, &c.

Adj. Not completed, &c., uncompleted, incomplete, unfinished, left undone, 53, short, unaccomplished, unperformed, unexecuted, (still in progress, going on, or in hand.)

---

731. SUCCESS, successfulness, speed, thrift, advance, luck, good fortune, 734, godsend, prize, hit; lucky or fortunate hit; bold stroke, masterstroke, checkmate; *see* Skill, 698, time well spent.

Continued success, run of luck, tide, flood, high tide.

Advantage over, the upper hand, ascendency, mastery, conquest, subdual, victory, subjugation, triumph, exultation, &c., 884.

A conqueror, victor.

V. To succeed, to be successful, to come off successful, to be crowned with success, to come off well; to thrive, speed, prosper, bloom, blossom, flourish, go on well, be well off.

To gain, attain, carry, secure, or win a point or object; to triumph, be triumphant, &c.; to surmount, overcome, conquer, master, or get over a difficulty or obstacle.

To advance, 282, get on, gain ground, make one's way, to find one's way, make progress, progress; to strive to some purpose, to gain an advantage.

To bring to bear, to bring about, to effect, accomplish, complete, 729, make sure; to reap, gather, &c., the benefit of.

To master, get the better of, to get the upper hand; conquer, subdue, subjugate, reduce, overthrow, overpower, vanquish; get or gain the ascendency, obtain a victory; beat, floor, put down, checkmate, nonsuit, capsize, shipwreck, victimize, put to flight, &c.

To baffle, disconcert, frustrate, foil, outgeneral, outmanœuvre, outwit, overreach, balk, outvote, circumvent.

To answer, succeed, work well, run smoothly, take a favorable turn, turn out well.

Adj. Succeeding, &c., success-

732. FAILURE, want of success, non-fulfilment, disappointment, blow, frustration, abortion, miscarriage, lost trouble; vain, ineffectual, or abortive attempt or effort.

A mistake, error, blunder, fault, miss, oversight, slip, trip, stumble, false step, wrong step, botch, sad work, bad job, want of skill, *see* 699.

Mischance, mishap, misfortune, misadventure, disaster.

Repulse, rebuff, defeat, fall, downfall, rout, discomfiture, wreck, perdition, shipwreck, ruin, subjugation, overthrow, deathblow, destruction, &c.

A victim, bankrupt, insolvent, 808.

V. To fail, to be unsuccessful, &c., to come off ill, go on ill, go amiss, go wrong, turn out ill, work ill, lose ground, recede, 283, to fall short of, 304.

To miss, miss one's aim; to labor, toil, &c., in vain; to lose one's labor, flounder, miscarry; to make vain, ineffectual, or abortive efforts; to make a slip; to make or commit a mistake, fault, or blunder; to botch, make a botch of.

To be defeated, overthrown, foiled, worsted, &c.; to break down, (slump through,) sink, drown, founder, go to ruin, &c., fall, slip, stumble, falter, be capsized, &c., run aground.

Adj. Unsuccessful, failing, &c., uncompleted, 730, unfortunate, in a bad way, unlucky, luckless, ill-fated, ill-starred, disastrous.

Unavailing, abortive, addle, still-born, fruitless, bootless, ineffectual, unattained, lame, hobbling.

Aground, grounded, swamped, stranded, cast away, wrecked, foundered, shipwrecked, &c., 731.

ful, prosperous, felicitous, blooming, &c., set up, triumphant.

Unfoiled, unbeaten, unsubdued, &c.

Adv. Successfully, &c., triumphantly, with flying colors, in triumph, to good purpose.

Defeated, overcome, overthrown, overpowered, mastered, worsted, vanquished, conquered, &c., *see* 731, subjugated, routed, silenced, distanced, foiled, unhorsed, baffled, unhinged, stultified, undone, ruined, circumvented.

Adv. Unsuccessfully, &c., in vain, to no purpose.

733. Trophy, laurel, palm, crown, bays, wreath, chaplet, civic crown, medal, prize, triumphal arch, ovation, triumph, 883, flourish of trumpets, flying colors.

734. Prosperity, *see* Success, 731, thrift, good fortune, welfare, well being, luck, good luck, palmy days, halcyon days, Saturnian age.

An upstart, mushroom.

V. To prosper, thrive, flourish, be well off; to flower, blow, blossom, bloom, fructify.

Adj. Prosperous, fortunate, lucky, well off, thriving, prospering, &c., blooming, palmy, halcyon.

Auspicious, propitious, in a fair way.

735. Adversity, bad, ill, evil, adverse, &c., fortune, luck, reverse, broken fortunes, falling or going down in the world, hard times, the pressure of the times.

Fall, ruin, ruinousness, undoing, disaster, calamity, catastrophe, a hard life, evil star, evil genius.

V. To be ill off; to decay sink, fall, decline, go down in the world; to go hard with.

Adj. Unfortunate, unlucky, luckless, untoward, badly off, decayed, ill-fated, ill-starred, unprosperous, adverse, untoward.

Disastrous, calamitous, ruinous, dire, deplorable, &c.

736. Mediocrity, the golden mean, moderate circumstances.

Division II. INTERSOCIAL VOLITION.*

Section I General Intersocial Volition.

737. Authority, influence, patronage, credit, power, prerogative, control, authoritativeness, absoluteness, despotism, absolutism.

Command, empire, sway, rule,

738. Absence of authority.

Laxity, laxness, license, licentiousness, relaxation, looseness, loosening, slackness, toleration, remission.

Misrule, anarchy, interregnum

* Implying the action of the will of one mind over the will of another

dominion domination, supremacy, lordship, seigniory, mastery, government, empire, body politic.

Acquisition of authority, accession, inauguration, installation, see 755.

Hold, grasp, gripe, grip, reach, fang, clutches, talons, helm, reins.

Reign, directorship, proconsulship, prefecture, caliphate, seneschalship, electorate, magistrature, magistracy, presidency, presidentship.

Empire, monarchy, dynasty, royalty, regality, kingcraft, aristocracy, oligarchy, democracy, military, dictatorship, protectorate, protectorship.

Vicarious authority, *see* 755 and 759.

V. To have, hold, possess, or exercise authority, &c.; to be in office; to fill an office; to hold or occupy a post.

To be master, &c.; to have the control, &c.; to overrule, overawe.

To rule, govern, sway, command, control, direct, administer, lead, preside over; to dictate, reign, hold the reins; to possess or be seated on the throne; to ascend or mount the throne; to sway or wield the sceptre.

Adj. Ruling, &c., dominant, authoritative, executive, official, imperative, peremptory, overruling.

Imperial, regal, sovereign, royal, monarchical, princely, aristocratic, &c.

Adv. In the name of, by the authority of, in virtue of.

Deprivation of power, dethronement.

V. To be lax, &c., to hold a loose rein, tolerate, to relax, to misrule.

To dethrone.

Adj. Lax, loose, slack, remiss, relaxed, licensed, reinless, unbridled, anarchical.

Unauthorized, 925.

---

739. Severity, strictness, rigor, rigidness, sternness, stringency, austerity, harshness, stiffness, rigorousness, inexorableness.

Arbitrary power, absolutism, despotism, dictatorship, autocracy, domineering, tyranny, iron rule.

Assumption, usurpation, arrogance, see 885.

V. To be severe, &c.; to assume, usurp, arrogate, take liberties; to dictate; to domineer, tyrannize, inflict, wreak.

Adj. Severe, strict, rigid, stern, stiff, straitlaced, rigorous, stringent, peremptory, absolute, positive, uncompromising, harsh, inclement, austere, haughty, arrogant, dictatorial, imperious, domineering, tyrannical, extortionate, obdurate, inflexible, inexorable; Draconian.

Adv Severely, &c.; with a high hand; with a strong, tight, or heavy hand.

740. Lenity, mildness, lenience, gentleness, indulgency, clemency, mercy.

V. To be lenient, &c., to tolerate, indulge, to allow one to have his own way.

Adj. Lenient, mild, gentle, soft, indulgent, tolerant, clement, 914.

---

741. Command, order, act, bidding, behest, call, beck, nod, message, direction, injunction, charge, appointment, demand, exaction, imposition, requisition, requirement, claim.

Dictation, dictate, mandate, decree, enactment, precept, prescript, writ, rescript, law, ordinance, ordination, bull, regulation, prescription, brevet, warrant, passport, summons.

V. To command, to issue a command, order, give order, bid, require, enjoin, appoint, charge, claim, call for, demand, exact, insist on, make a point of, impose, set, tax, prescribe, direct, dictate, ordain, decree, enact; to issue a decree, &c.

To cite, summon, call for, send for.

Adj. Commanding, &c., authoritative, peremptory, &c., *see* 737, decretory, decretive, decretal.

742. Disobedience, non-compliance, inobservance, contumacy, insubordination, defection, infringement, infraction, violation.

See Defiance, 715, Resistance, 719, and Non-observance, 773.

Rising, insurrection, revolt, rebellion, strike, riot, riotousness, mutinousness, mutiny, tumult, sedition, treason.

An insurgent, mutineer, rebel, revolter, rioter, traitor.

V. To disobey, resist, 719, defy, 715, turn restive, mutiny, rise, rebel, lift the hand against, turn out.

Adj. Disobedient, resisting, unruly, unsubmissive, uncomplying, uncompliant, restive, insubordinate, mutinous, riotous, seditious, refractory, contumacious.

743. Obedience, submission, non-resistance, passiveness, resignation, cession, compliance, surrender, 725, subordination, deference, allegiance, obeisance, homage, fealty, prostration, kneeling, genuflection, submissiveness, obsequiousness, *see* 886, subjection, 740.

V. To be obedient, &c.; to obey, submit, succumb, give in, knock under, cringe, yield, 725, comply, surrender, follow, give up, give way, resign, bend to, bear obedience to.

To kneel, fall on one's knees, bend the knee, bow, pay homage to.

To attend upon, tend; to be under the orders of, to serve.

Adj. Obedient, submissive, resigned, passive, complying, compliant, yielding, unresisting; restrainable, unresisted.

---

744. Compulsion, coercion, coaction, force, constraint, enforcement, press, conscription, brute force, main force, the sword.

V. To compel, force, drive, coerce, constrain, enforce, put in force, oblige, force upon, press, extort, put down, bind, bind over.

Adj. Compelling, &c., compulsory, forcible, coercive, peremptory, rigorous, stringent, inexorable, &c., *see* 739, being fain to do.

Adv. (Forcibly,) by force, perforce, by compulsion, &c.

745. Master, lord, chief, leader, captain, head, chieftain, commander, commandant, director, 694, governor, ruler, lord paramount, potentate, dictator, liege, sovereign, monarch, autocrat,

746. Servant, servitor, subaltern, retainer, vassal, dependant, pensioner, hanger on, puppet, emissary, *see* 886.

Retinue, staff, court.

An attendant, squire, chamber

despot, tyrant, pacha, demagogue, ringleader.

Emperor, king, majesty, tetrach, regent, vice king, protector, president, stadtholder; empress, queen.

Princess, duchess, margravine, &c.

Nobility, *see* 875.

Military authorities, marshal, field marshal, generalissimo, commodore, commander-in-chief, admiral, general, colonel, officer, captain, major, lieutenant, adjutant, aid-de-camp, ensign, cornet, cadet, subaltern, non-commissioned officers, sergeant, corporal, centurion.

Civil authorities, mayor, prefect, chancellor, provost, magistrate, burgomaster, alderman, warden, constable, beadle.

Statesman, politician, statist, legislator, lawgiver.

President, chairman, speaker, moderator, vice president, comptroller, director, 694.

lain, follower, usher, page, domestic, footman, lackey, scout, flunkey, valet, waiter, equerry, groom, livery servant, underling, menial, understrapper, journeyman, bailiff, seneschal, cupbearer.

Serf, slave, helot, bondsman.

A maid, handmaid, waiting maid, nurse, scullion, &c.

Badge of slavery, bonds, chains, &c., *see* 752.

V. To serve, attend upon, wait upon, squire.

---

747. Ensign, badge, or insignia of authority.

SCEPTRE, regalia, regality, crown, coronet, rod of empire, mace, wand, truncheon, staff.

Helm, bit, curb, reins, leading strings.

A throne, chair, woolsack.

Diadem, tiara, ermine, signet, seals, robes of state.

748. FREEDOM, independence, liberty, scope, range, latitude, play, swing, free play, full play, elbow room, margin.

Franchise, immunity, exemption, emancipation, 750, denization.

Free land, allodium, *see* 780.

A freeman, freedman.

V. To be free, to have scope, &c.

To render free, &c., to free, to emancipate, enfranchise, affranchise, manumit, to denizen.

Adj. Free, independent, at large, loose, unconstrained, unrestrained, unchecked, unprevented, unobstructed, unconfined, unbound, uncontrolled, ungoverned, unenslaved, unchained, unshackled, unfettered, uncurbed, unbridled, unrestricted, unmuzzled, unin-

749. SUBJECTION, dependence, subordination, thrall, thraldom, subjugation, bondage, serfdom, servitude, slavery, vassalage, villanage, service, clientship, liability, 177, enslavement.

Yoke, harness, collar, 751.

V. To be subject, dependent, &c., to fall under, obey, serve, 743.

To subject, inthrall, enslave, keep under, control, &c., 751, to reduce to slavery.

Adj. Subject, dependent, subjected, subordinate, in subjection to, feudatory, feudal, a slave to, at the mercy of, stipendiary, in leading strings, inthralled, controlled, constrained, &c., *see* 751, the puppet, sport, plaything of, &c.

Being a puppet, or football.

---

thralled, unforced, uncompelled, unhindered, uncaught, unclaimed.

Free and easy, at ease, wanton, rampant, irrepressible, unprevented, unvanquished, exempt, enfranchised, emancipated, released, disengaged, &c., *see* 750.

750. Liberation, disengagement, release, enlargement, emancipation, mancipation, enfranchisement, manumission, discharge, dismissal.

Escape, 671, deliverance, 672, redemption, extrication, acquittance, absolution, 970.

License, toleration.

V. To gain, obtain, acquire, &c., one's liberty, freedom, &c., to deliver one's self from, to cast off trammels.

To break loose, escape, slip away, make one's escape, &c., 671.

To liberate, free, set free, set at liberty, emancipate, disinthrall, release, loose, let loose, loosen, relax, unloose, untie, unbind, unchain, unshackle, unfetter, unclog, disengage, unharness, &c., *see* 44.

To enlarge, set clear, let go, let out, disincarcerate, unbar, unbolt, uncage, unclose, uncork, discharge, dismiss, deliver, extricate, let slip, *see* 748.

To clear, acquit, redeem, ransom.

751. Restraint, constraint, coercion, discipline.

Confinement, durance, duress, imprisonment, incarceration, prisonment, captivity.

Arrest, custody, keep, care, charge, ward, restringency.

Curb, &c., *see* 752.

V. To restrain, constrain, coerce, curb, cramp, keep under, inthrall, put under restraint, debar; to chain, enchain, fasten, tie up, 43, picket, fetter, shackle, trammel, entrammel, bridle, muzzle, gag, pinion, tether.

To confine, shut up, shut in, lock up, cage, incage, impound, hem in, enclose, imprison, incarcerate, immure, intomb.

To take charge of, lead captive, send or commit to prison, give in charge or in custody, arrest, commit.

Adj. Restrained, under restraint, coerced, confined, &c.

Stiff, restringent, straitlaced.

Adj. Liberated, freed, emancipated, &c.

752. Means of restraint.

Prison, jail, prison house, cage, cell, stronghold, fortress, keep, dungeon, bastile, bridewell, penitentiary, guard room, hold, roundhouse, station, enclosure, pen, fold, pound, stocks.

Fetter, shackle, trammel, bond, chain, iron, collar, pinion, gyve, fetlock, manacle, handcuff, strait waistcoat.

Bolt, bar, lock, padlock, rail, wall, paling, palisade, 232, fence, barricade.

753. Keeper, custodian, warder, jailer, castellan, guard, watch, watchman, watch and ward, sentry, sentinel, escort.

754. Prisoner, captive.

Adv. In custody, in charge.

755. Vicarious authority.

Commission, delegation, con-

756. Abrogation, annulment, cancel, revocation, repeal, rescis

signment, assignment, deputation, legation, mission, embassy, agency, clerkship, agentship; errand, charge, diploma.

Appointment, nomination, return, ordination, installation, inauguration, investiture, coronation.

Vicegerency, regency, regentship.

V. To commission, delegate, depute, send out, consign, charge.

To appoint, name, nominate, return, ordain, install, induct, enroll. inaugurate, invest, crown.

sion, rescinding, deposal, dismissal.

Abolition, abolishment, counter order, countermand, repudiation, nullification, recantation, retraction, *see* 607.

V. To abrogate, annul, cancel, revoke, repeal, rescind, overrule, abolish, disannul, dissolve, quash, repudiate, nullify, retract, recant, recall, countermand, counterorder, break off, disclaim, declare null and void, ignore, set aside, do away with.

To dismiss, send off, send away, discard, turn away, cashier, oust, unseat, unthrone, dethrone, depose, send back.

---

757. Resignation, retirement, abdication, renunciation, abjuration.

V. To resign, give up, throw up, retire, abdicate, lay down, abjure, renounce, forego, disclaim, retract, &c., *see* 756.

758. Consignee, delegate, commissary, commissioner, vicegerent, legate, ambassador, consul, representative, secondary, nominee, surrogate, functionary, plenipotentiary, emissary, nuncio, internuncio.

Agent, factor, attorney, broker, bailiff, clerk, man of business, go between, middleman, curator, placeman.

759. Deputy, substitute, vice, proxy, delegate.

Regent, viceroy, vicegerent, minister, premier, commissioner, chancellor, prefect, provost, warden, lieutenant, consul, legate, surrogate.

V. To be deputy, &c., for; to appear for.

Section II. Special Intersocial Volition.

760. Permission, leave, allowance, sufferance, tolerance, toleration, liberty, law, license, concession, grant, authorization, accordance, admission, favor, dispensation, exemption, connivance.

A permit, warrant, precept, authority, pass, passport, furlough, license.

V. To permit; give leave or permission; to let, allow, admit, suffer, tolerate, concede, accord, vouchsafe, humor, indulge, to leave it to one; to grant, em-

761. Prohibition, inhibition, veto, disallowance, interdiction, hinderance, 706, restriction, restraints, 751, embargo, an interdict, ban, proscription.

V. To prohibit, forbid, inhibit, disallow, bar, debar, interdict. taboo, keep in, hinder, restrain, 751, cohibit, restrict, withhold, limit, circumscribe, keep within bounds.

To exclude, shut out, proscribe.

Adj. Prohibitive, restrictive, exclusive, prohibitory, forbidding, &c.

power, license, authorize, warrant.

To let off, absolve, dispense with, favor, wink, connive at.

Not permitted, prohibited, &c. unlicensed, &c.

To take a liberty; to use a freedom.

Adj. Permitting, &c., permissive, conceding, &c.

Unconditional, unforbid, unforbidden.

762. Consent, compliance, acquiescence, assent, 488, agreement concession, acknowledgment, settlement, ratification, confirmation.

V. To consent, give consent, assent, comply with, acquiesce, agree to, accede, accept.

To concede, yield, satisfy, grant, settle, acknowledge, confirm, ratify, deign, vouchsafe.

Adj. Consenting, having no objection, &c., unconditional, *see* Assent, 488.

763. Offer, proffer, tender; overture, proposition, motion, proposal, invitation, present, presentation, offering, bribe.

V. To offer, proffer, tender, present, invite, volunteer, propose, move, make a motion, hold out.

Adj. Offering, &c.

764. Refusal, rejection, declining, non-compliance, declension, dissent, denial, repulse, rebuff, discountenance; *see* 489.

Disclaimer, recusancy, abnegation, protest.

Revocation, violation, abrogation, 756, flat refusal, peremptory denial.

V. To refuse, reject, deny, decline, disclaim, protest, resist, repel, refuse or withhold one's assent, to negative.

To discard, set aside, rescind, revoke, discountenance.

Adj. Refusing, &c., recusant, uncomplying, unconsenting, ungranted, being out of the question.

Adv. No, by no means, 489; on no account; not for the world.

765. Request, asking, petition, demand, suit, solicitation, craving, entreaty, begging, solicitation, canvass, prayer, supplication, imploration, importunity, application, address, appeal, motion, overture, invocation, imprecation.

Claim, reclamation.

V. To request, ask, beg, crave, pray, petition, solicit, demand, prefer a request or petition, apply to, make application, invite, beg leave, put up a prayer.

To beg hard, entreat, beseech, supplicate, implore, conjure invoke, imprecate, appeal to, address, press, urge, beset, importune, dun, besiege.

To bespeak, canvass, make interest, court.

To claim, reclaim, sue.

766. Negative request.

Deprecation, expostulation, intercession.

V. To deprecate, protest, expostulate; to enter a protest; to intercede for.

Adj. Deprecating, &c., deprecatory, expostulatory, deprecated, protested.

Unsought, unbesought.

Adj. Requesting, asking, beseeching, &c., suppliant, supplicatory, importunate, &c., supplicant, postulant.

767. Petitioner, solicitor, applicant, suppliant, supplicant, mendicant, beggar, suitor, candidate.

Section III. Conditional Intersocial Volition.

768. Promise, word, word of honor, assurance, vow, oath.

Engagement, preëngagement, insurance, assurance, contract, 769, obligation, affiance, betrothment.

768. *a*. Release from engagement, *see* Liberation, 750.

Adj. Absolute, unconditional

V. To promise, give a promise, assure; to give or pledge one's word, honor, credit, &c.; to swear, vow, take oath; to attest.

To engage; to enter on, make or form an engagement; to bind or pledge one's self; to contract an obligation; to be bound; to undertake.

To answer for, be answerable for, secure, give security, 771.

Adj. Promising, &c., promised, pledged, sworn, &c.; votive.

769. Compact, contract, agreement, bargain, pact, paction, stipulation, covenant, settlement, charter, treaty, indenture.

Negotiation, transaction, bargaining, haggling, chaffering; diplomacy, diplomatics, embassy.

Ratification, settlement, signature, seal, signet, bond.

A negotiator, diplomatist, agent, attorney, broker, &c., 759.

V. To contract, covenant, bargain, agree for, engage, &c., *see* Promise, 768; to underwrite.

To treat, negotiate, bargain, stipulate, higgle, chaffer, insist upon, make a point of, compound for.

To conclude, close, confirm, ratify.

To subscribe, sign, seal, put the seal to.

770. Conditions, terms, articles, articles of agreement, clauses, provisions, convenant, stipulation.

V. To make it a condition, &c., to stipulate, insist upon, &c.

Adj. Conditional, provisional, guarded, &c.

Adv. Conditionally, with the understanding; provided, unless, *see* 469.

771. Security, surety, guaranty, mortgage, warranty, bond, pledge, hostage, sponsor, bail.

Deed, instrument, indenture, warrant, debenture, charter, cartel, protocol, recognizance; verification, acceptance, indorsement, signature, execution.

Stake, deposit, earnest.

772. Observance, performance, fulfilment, satisfaction, discharge, compliance, acquittance, acquittal, adhesion, acknowledgment, fidelity, 939, *see* Obedience, 743.

773. Non-observance, failure, neglect, infringement, infraction, violation, transgression.

Retraction, repudiation, nullification, protest, forfeiture.

V. To observe, perform, keep, fulfil, discharge, comply with, meet, satisfy, adhere to, be faithful to.

Adj. Observant, faithful, true, honorable, &c., 939, strict, rigid, punctilious.

Adv. Faithfully, &c., conscientiously, scrupulously, religiously, rigidly, literally; to the letter.

Informality, lawlessness, disobedience, bad faith, 742.

V. To break, violate, fail, neglect, omit, forfeit, infringe, transgress.

To retract, discard, protest, repudiate, nullify, ignore, cancel, &c., 552, palter, elude, evade.

Adj. Violating, &c., elusive, evasive, unfulfilled, &c.

774. Compromise, composition, middle term; bribe, hush money, *see* 29 and 30.

V. To compromise, compound, take the mean, split the difference, come to terms.

Section IV. Possessive Relations.*

1. *Property in general.*

775. Acquisition, gaining, earning, procuration, procuring, gathering, collecting; recovery.

Gain, profit, benefit, emolument, the main chance, pelf, lucre, produce, return, fruit.

Inheritance, bequest, legacy.

V. To acquire, get, gain, win, earn, realize, regain, receive, 785, take, 789, obtain, procure, derive, secure, collect, raise money, net, reap, inherit; recover, retrieve.

To profit, make profit, turn to profit, make money by, obtain a return, make a fortune.

To be profitable, to pay, to answer.

To fall to, come to, accrue.

776. Loss, forfeiture.

Privation, bereavement, deprivation, 789, dispossession, riddance.

V. To lose; to incur, experience, or meet with a loss; throw away, forfeit, 782, to waste, 638, 679.

Adj. Losing, &c., lost, &c.

Devoid of, not having, unblest with, long-lost.

Shorn of, deprived of, bereaved of, cut off, dispossessed, forfeited.

Irrecoverable, irretrievable, irremediable, irreparable, irredeemable.

Adj. Acquiring, acquired, &c., profitable, remunerative, paying.

777. Possession, ownership, proprietorship, occupancy, preoccupancy.

Exclusive possession, monopoly, inalienableness.

Future possession, heritage, inheritance.

V. To possess, have, hold, own, be master of, be in possession of, enjoy, occupy.

To engross, monopolize, forestall.

To be the property of, belong to, appertain to, pertain to, be in the hands of, be in the possession of.

* That is, relations which concern property

Adj. Possessing, &c., possessed of, worth, endowed with, instinct with, fraught, laden with, charged with.

Possessed, &c., on hand, in hand, unsold.

778. Joint possession.

PARTICIPATION, joint stock, common stock, partnership, copartnership, possession in common, community of possessions or goods, communism.

A partner, copartner, shareholder.

V. To participate, partake, share, go halves, to have or possess, &c., in common; to come in for a share.

Adj. Partaking, &c.

779. POSSESSOR, owner, holder, proprietor, proprietary, master, occupier, landlord, tenant; proprietress.

Future possessor, heir, inheritor.

780. PROPERTY, possession, ownership, occupancy.

Estate, effects, assets, stock, goods, chattels, fixtures, movables, furniture; patrimony.

Real property, land, landed estate, tenement, freehold, farm.

Ground, acres, field, (land.)

State, realm, empire, kingdom, principality.

Adj. Predial, manorial, allodial, freehold, leasehold, copyhold, &c.

781. RETENTION, holding, keeping, retaining, detention, custody, grasp; tenacity.

V. To retain, keep, keep in hand, detain, hold fast, grasp, clutch, clinch, gripe, hug, withhold, keep back, keep close.

Adj. Retaining, &c., retentive, tenacious.

Unforfeited, undeprived, undisposed, uncommunicated, incommunicable.

782. RELINQUISHMENT, cession, abandonment, renunciation, surrender, riddance, 776, resignation, 758.

V. To relinquish, give up, lay aside, resign, forego, renounce, surrender, part with, lay down, abandon, cede, yield, dispose of, divest one's self of, give away, throw away.

Adj. Relinquished, &c., left unculled, residuary, 40.

2. *Transfer of Property.*

783. TRANSFER, interchange, exchange, transmission, barter, 794, abalienation, demise.

V. To transfer, consign, make over, demise, pass, transmit, interchange, exchange, 148.

To change hands, change from one to another, alienate, devolve.

To dispossess, abalienate, disinherit.

784. GIVING, bestowal, donation, accordance to, presentation, presentment, delivery, granting.

Cession, concession, consignment, communication, dispensation.

Gift, donation, boon, present, benefaction, charity almsgiving,

785. RECEIVING, reception, acceptance, admission.

A recipient, (beneficiary,) stipendiary, beggar.

V. To receive, take, 789, accept, admit, take in.

Adj. Receiving, &c., recipient.

grant, offering, contribution, subscription, donative, meed, tribute, gratuity, bribe, free gift, favor, bounty, largess, subsidy, allowance, endowment, charity, alms, *see* Payment, 807.

Bequest, legacy, demise, dotation.

V. To give, bestow, accord, confer, grant, concede, present, give away, deliver, deliver over, make over, consign, render, impart, hand over, part with, communicate, yield, dispose of, put into the hands of, vest in, assign, put in possession, settle upon, endow, invest.

To bequeathe, leave, demise, devise.

To give out, dispense, deal, deal out, dole out, mete out.

To contribute, subscribe, pay, 807, spend.

To furnish, supply, afford, spare, accommodate with, indulge with, administer to.

To bribe, suborn.

Adj. Giving, &c., given, &c., charitable, eleemosynary, tributary.

Not given, unbestowed.

---

786. Apportionment, distribution, allotment, assignment, partition, division.

Dividend, portion, contingent, share, allotment, lot, measure, dole, meed, pittance, ration, ratio, proportion, mess, allowance, appropriation.

V. To apportion, divide, distribute, billet, allot, share, mete, parcel out, deal, partition, assign, appropriate.

Adj. Apportioning, &c.

787. Lending, loan, advance, mortgage, accommodation, pawn, investment.

Lender, pawnbroker.

V. To lend, advance, mortgage, invest, pawn, place or put out to interest, accommodate with.

Adj. Lending, &c., unborrowed.

Adv. In advance.

788. Borrowing, pledging, replevin.

Borrowed plumes, plagiarism, plagiary.

V. To borrow, raise money, desume.

Adj. Borrowing, &c., borrowed second-hand.

789. Taking, appropriation, capture, seizure, abduction, catching, seizing, &c.

Abstraction, subtraction, deduction, subduction

Dispossession, deprivation, deprivement, bereavement, divestment, sequestration, confiscation.

Resumption, reprisal.

Clutch, swoop, wrench.

V. To take, lay one's hands on; lay, take, or get hold of; to possess one's self of, take possession of, make sure of.

To appropriate, pocket put into one's pocket.

790. Restitution, return, rendition, restoration, reinvestment, reparation, atonement.

Redemption, recovery, recuperation, release, replevin.

V. To return, restore, give back, render up, bring back, render, refund, reimburse, repair, redeem, reinvest.

To let go, unclutch, disgorge.

Adj. Restoring, &c.

To pick up, gather, collect, absorb, 297, reap, glean, intercept.

To take away, carry away, carry off, bear off, pounce upon, run away with, abduct, kidnap.

To lay violent hands on, scramble for, fasten upon, catch, seize, snatch, grasp, clutch, wring, wrest, wrench, pluck, tear away.

To take from, deduct, 38, subtract, curtail, retrench, abridge, dispossess, take away from, abstract, deprive of, bereave, divest, despoil, strip, fleece, levy, distrain, confiscate, sequester, sequestrate, oust, extort, usurp, drain, exhaust.

Adj. Taking, &c., privative, predatory, rapacious, predial, parasitic, ravenous.

791. Stealing, theft, thieving, thievery, appropriation, plagiarism, depredation, pilfering, larceny, robbery, shoplifting, burglary.

Spoliation, plunder, pillage, sack, rapine, forray, marauding.

Peculation, embezzlement, swindling, 545, smuggling, thievishness.

License to plunder; letters of marque.

V. To steal, rob, abstract, appropriate, filch, pilfer, purloin.

To convey away, carry off, run off with, abduct, kidnap, seize, lay violent hands on, &c., 789.

To cabbage, sponge, swindle, peculate, embezzle, poach, smuggle.

To plunder, pillage, rifle, sack, spoil, spoliate, despoil, strip, fleece.

Adj. Stealing, &c., thievish, lightfingered, stolen, furtive, &c.

792. Thief, robber, spoiler, pickpocket, cutpurse, depredator, footpad, highwayman, burglar, housebreaker, shoplifter; the light-fingered gentry.

Swindler, smuggler, sharper, blackleg, shark, harpy, peculator, plagiarist.

Brigand, freebooter, bandit, pirate, corsair, buccaneer, marauder.

793. Booty, spoil, plunder, prey.

3. *Interchange of Property.*

794. Barter, exchange, interchange, commutation.

Traffic, trade, commerce, dealing, business, custom, jobbing, bargain, commercial enterprise, speculation, brokery.

V. To barter, exchange, interchange, commute, traffic, trade, speculate, transact or do business with, deal with, have dealings with; open or keep an account with; to carry on a trade.

To bargain; drive, make, or strike a bargain; negotiate, higgle, chaffer, cheapen, compound for, beat down, outbid.

Adj. Commercial, mercantile, interchangeable; wholesale, retail

795. Purchase, buying, purchasing; preëmption, coemption, bribery.

A buyer, purchaser, customer.

V. To buy, purchase, procure, hire, rent, farm, pay, fee, repur-

796. Sale, disposal, custom.

Auction.

Lease, mortgage.

Vendibility, vendibleness.

A vender, seller, &c., 797.

chase, keep in one's pay; to bribe, suborn.

Adj. Purchased, &c.

To sell, vend, dispose of, undersell, retail, dispense, hawk.

To let, lease, mortgage.

Adj. Unpurchased, unbought, on one's hands.

---

797. MERCHANT, trader, dealer, tradesman, buyer and seller, vender, monger, shopkeeper, shopman, salesman.

Retailer, chapman, hawker, huckster, peddler, sutler; auctioneer, broker, money broker, money changer, jobber, factor, go-between money lender.

House, firm, concern, partnership, company, guild.

Buyer, customer, purchaser.

798. MERCHANDISE, ware, commodity, effects, goods, article, stock, cargo, produce, freight, lading.

799. MART, market, change, exchange, market-place, fair.

Office, shop, counting house, counter, stall.

Warehouse, depot, store, 636, emporium.

4. *Monetary Relations.*

800. MONEY, money matters, finance; funds, treasure, capital, stock, proceeds, assets, cash. Sum, amount, balance.

Currency, circulating medium, specie, coin, hard cash; pounds, shillings, and pence, (dollars and cents.)

Gold, silver, copper, dollar, &c.

Pocket money, change, small coin.

Science of coins, Numismatics.

Paper money, note, bank note, note of hand, promissory note.

Bill, or draft, check, order, warrant, bill of exchange, liabilities, 806.

A drawer; a drawee.

False money, base coin.

V. To draw, draw upon, indorse.

Adj. Monetary, pecuniary, fiscal, financial, sumptuary; numismatical.

801. TREASURER, pursebearer, purser, bursar, banker, paymaster, cashier, teller, cashkeeper, bursary.

Chancellor of the Exchequer, financier.

802. TREASURY, bank, exchequer, coffer, chest, stocks, money box, money bag, strong box, purse, pocket.

803. WEALTH, fortune, riches, money, opulence, affluence, independence, solvency, competence, easy circumstances, command of money.

Means, provision, substance, property, revenue, income, alimony, dower, pension, annuity, livelihood, pelf, mammon, lucre.

A rich man; a moneyed man;

804. POVERTY, indigence, penury, pauperism, destitution, want, need, lack, necessity, privation, distress, an empty purse, bad circumstances, straits, insolvency, beggary, mendicancy, mendicity.

A poor man, pauper, mendicant, beggar, starveling.

V. To be poor, &c., to want, lack, starve.

To render poor, &c., to reduce,

a capitalist; a millionaire; a nabob, Crœsus, Dives.

V. To be rich, &c., to afford.

To raise money; to make money, see 775.

To enrich, fill one's coffers, &c.

Adj. Wealthy, rich, affluent, opulent, flush.

to impoverish, reduce to poverty ruin.

Adj. Poor, indigent, penniless moneyless, short of money, out of money, out of cash, out of pocket, needy, destitute, necessitous, distressed, in need, in want, in distress, pinched, reduced, insolvent, *see* 806, beggared, fleeced, stripped.

805. Credit, trust, tick, score.

Letter of credit, duplicate.

A creditor, (lender,) lessor, mortgagee; a usurer.

V. To keep an account with, to credit, accredit.

Adj. Crediting.

Adv. On credit, on account.

806. Debt, obligation, liability, debit, indebtedness, arrears, deficit, default, insolvency.

Interest, usance, usury.

A debtor, lessee, mortgager; a defaulter, 808.

V. To be in debt, to owe, to answer for, to incur a debt, *see* Borrow, 788.

Adj. In debt, indebted, owing, due, unpaid, in arrear, liable, answerable for, insolvent, outstanding, unrepaid, unrequited, unrewarded.

807. Payment, defrayment, discharge, quittance, acquittance, settlement, clearance, liquidation, satisfaction, reckoning, arrangement, acknowledgment, release receipt in full.

Repayment, reimbursement, retribution, reward, *see* 973.

Bill, check, cash, ready money, remittance, &c., 800.

V. To pay, cash, defray, discharge; settle; account or reckon with; clear, liquidate, release.

To repay, make repayment, refund, retribute, reimburse.

Adj. Paying, &c.; paid, owing nothing, out of debt.

808. Non-payment, default, defalcation, protest.

Insolvency, bankruptcy, repudiation.

Waste paper, bonds, dishonored or protested bills, &c.

A defaulter, a bankrupt, an insolvent debtor.

V. Not to pay, to fail, to break, to become insolvent or bankrupt.

To protest, dishonor, repudiate, nullify.

Adj. Not paying, in debt, insolvent, bankrupt, beggared, &c., 804.

809. Expenditure, expenses, disbursement, outlay.

Money paid; pay, payment, fee, hire, wages, perquisites, avails, allowance, stipend, salary, subsidy.

Remuneration, recompense reward, *see* 973, drink money, largess, mouchoun, bribe, hush money.

810. Receipt, income, revenue, rent, rental, return, proceeds, premium, bonus.

Pension, annuity, jointure, dower, dowry, alimony.

Emoluments, perquisites, recompense, &c., *see* 809, sinecure.

V. To receive, pocket, &c., *see* 785, 789, to draw from, derive from.

Pay in advance; earnest.

Contribution, donation, subscription, deposit, contingent, dole, quota.

Investment, purchase, &c., *see* 795, alms, *see* 784.

V. To expend, spend, pay, disburse, lay out; lay or pay down; to cash; make up a sum; to invest, sink money.

To bring in, yield, afford, pay accrue.

Adj. Receiving, &c., received, &c.

Gainful, profitable, remunerative, lucrative, advantageous, &c., 775.

Adj. Expending, &c., expended, &c., sumptuary.

811. Accounts, money matters, bills, score, balance sheet, books, account books, leger, day book, debtor and creditor accounts.

Bookkeeping, audit; double entry.

An accountant, auditor, actuary, bookkeeper.

V. To keep accounts, enter, post, credit, debit, carry over; balance, make up accounts, take stock, audit.

To falsify or garble accounts.

812. Price, cost, expense, charge, demand, damage, fare.

Dues, duty, toll, tax, levy, assessment, benevolence, custom, exactment, ransom, excise, tariff, brokerage.

Bill, account, score, reckoning.

Worth, rate, value, valuation, appraisement; money's worth, pennyworth.

813. Discount, abatement, reduction, allowance, drawback, percentage, rebate, setoff, salvage.

V. To discount, bate, abate, rebate, reduce, take off, allow, give, discount.

Adj. Discounting, &c.

Adv. At a discount.

V. To set or fix a price, appraise, assess, charge, demand, ask, require, exact, distrain.

To fetch, sell for, cost, bring in, yield.

814. Dearness, costliness, high price, expensiveness, rise in price, overcharge, extravagance, exorbitance.

V. To be dear, &c., to cost much, to overcharge.

Adj. Dear, high, high-priced, expensive, costly, dear-bought, unreasonable, extravagant, exorbitant, extortionate.

Adv. Dear, at great cost.

815. Cheapness, low price, bargain, gratuity, &c.

V. To be cheap, &c., to cost little, to come down or fall in price.

Adj. Cheap, low, moderate, reasonable, unexpensive, low-priced, worth the money, half-price.

Gratuitous, gratis, free, for nothing, free of cost, without charge, not charged, untaxed, scot-free, free of expense.

816. Liberality, generosity, bounty, munificence, bounteousness, bountifulness, charity, hospitality.

V. To be liberal, &c., spend freely.

817. Economy, frugality, thrift, thriftiness, care, husbandry, retrenchment, savings.

V. To be economical, &c., to save, economize, meet one's expenses, retrench; to lay by;

Adj. Liberal, free, generous, charitable, hospitable, bountiful, bounteous, unsparing, ungrudging, openhearted, freehearted, munificent, princely.

Overpaid.

818. PRODIGALITY, unthriftiness, waste, profusion, profuseness, extravagance, prodigality, squandering

A prodigal, spendthrift, squanderer.

V. To be prodigal, &c., to squander, lavish, waste, dissipate, exhaust, run out, misspend, throw away money, drain.

Adj. Prodigal, profuse, thriftless, unthrifty, wasteful, extravagant, lavish, over liberal.

to save money; to invest money.

Adj. Economical, frugal, thrifty, careful, saving, chary, sparing.

Adv. Sparingly, &c.

819. PARSIMONY, stint, stinginess, niggardliness, illiberality, closeness, penuriousness, avarice, covetousness, greediness, avidity, rapacity, venality, mercenariness, cupidity.

A miser, niggard, harpy.

V. To be parsimonious, &c., to grudge, stint, pinch.

Adj. Parsimonious, stingy, miserly, mean, shabby, niggardly, close, close-fisted, chary, grudging, illiberal, ungenerous, churlish, sordid, mercenary, venal, covetous, avaricious, greedy, rapacious.

CLASS VI.

WORDS RELATING TO THE SENTIENT AND MORAL POWERS.

SECTION I. AFFECTIONS IN GENERAL.

820. AFFECTIONS, character, qualities, disposition, nature, spirit, temper, temperament, idiosyncrasy; cast or frame of mind, or soul, turn, bent, bias, turn of mind, predisposition, proneness, proclivity, vein, humor, grain, mettle, nerve.

Soul, heart, breast, bosom, the inner man, inmost heart, heart's core, the heart of hearts.

Passion, pervading spirit, ruling passion, master passion; flow of soul, fulness of the heart, heyday of the blood, flesh and blood.

V. To have or possess affections, &c.; be of a character, &c.

Adj. Affected, characterized, formed, moulded, cast, tempered, attempered, framed, disposed, predisposed, prone, inclined, having a bias, &c., inbred, inborn, ingrained.

821. Feeling, endurance, experience, suffering, tolerance, sufferance, patience, content, 831.

Non-endurance, *see* 825.

Impression, sensation, affection, response, emotion, pathos, warmth, glow, vehemence, fervor, fervency, heartiness, cordiality, earnestness, ardor, zeal, eagerness, passion, enthusiasm.

Blush, suffusion, flush, hectic, thrill, turn, shock, agitation, 315, heaving, flutter, flurry, tremor, throb, throbbing, panting, palpitation, trepidation, perturbation, the heart swelling, throbbing, pulsating, melting, bursting, &c.

Passion, 825; transport, rapture, ecstasy, ravishment, *see* 827.

V. To feel, receive an impression, &c.; to be impressed with, affected with, moved with, touched with, &c.

To bear, suffer, endure, brook, tolerate, put up with, experience, taste, meet with, go through, prove; to harbor, cherish, support, abide, undergo.

To blush, tingle, throb, heave, pant, palpitate, agitate, thrill, tremble, shake, quiver, wince.

To swell, glow, warm, flush, catch the flame, catch the infection, respond.

To possess, pervade, penetrate, imbue, absorb, &c., the soul.

Adj. Feeling, suffering, enduring, &c.

Impressed, moved, touched, affected with, &c., penetrated.

Warm, quick, lively, smart, strong, sharp, keen, acute, cutting, piercing, pungent, racy, piquant, poignant.

Deep, profound, indelible, deepfelt, homefelt, heartfelt, warmhearted, hearty, cordial, swelling, thrilling, soul-stirring, electric.

Earnest, eager, glowing, fervent, fervid, ardent, burning, fiery, flaming, boiling, boiling over, zealous, pervading, penetrating, absorbing.

Wrought up, excited, passionate, enthusiastic, *see* 825.

822. Sensibility, impressiveness, impressibility, sensitiveness, susceptibleness, susceptibility, excitability, mobility, vivacity, vivaciousness, tenderness, softness.

Physical sensibility, *see* 375.

V. To be sensible, &c., shrink, &c.

Adj. Sensible, sensitive, impressible, susceptive, susceptible, excitable, tremblingly alive, lively, vivacious, mettlesome, tender, soft, sentimental, romantic, enthusiastic.

Adv. Sensibly, &c., to the quick.

---

823. Insensibility, inertness, insensibleness, impassibility, apathy, phlegm, dulness, hebetude, coolness, coldness, supineness, stoicism, indifference, lukewarmness, frigidity, cold blood, cold heart, deadness, torpor, torpidity

Lethargy, stupor, stupefaction, paralysis, palsy.

Physical insensibility, *see* 376.

V. To disregard, be insensible, not to be affected by, not to mind, not to care.

To render insensible, benumb, paralyze, deaden, render callous, sear, inure, harden, steel, stun, stupefy, brutalize.

Adj. Insensible, unconscious,

impassive, unsusceptible, impassible, unimpressible, dead to, passionless, spiritless, unfeeling, soulless, apathetic, phlegmatic, callous, obtuse, proof against, inured, steeled against, stoical, dull, frigid, cold, coldblooded, coldhearted, flat, maudlin, obtuse, inert, supine, sluggish, torpid, languid, tame, numb, numbed, sleepy, yawning, stupefied.

Indifferent, lukewarm, careless.

Unfelt, unaffected, unruffled, unimpressed, unmoved, uninspired, untouched, &c.; unshocked, unstruck, without being moved, &c.; Platonic, imperturbable, vegetative.

824. EXCITATION of feeling, excitement, stimulation, provocation, calling forth, infection, animation, agitation, perturbation, fascination, intoxication, enravishment, unction.

Repression of feeling, *see* 826.

V. To excite, affect, touch, move, stir, stir up, wake, awaken, arouse; fire, raise, raise up, evoke, call forth, call up, summon up, rake up.

To impress, strike, quicken, work upon; to warm, kindle, stimulate, whet, animate, inspire, impassion, inspirit, provoke, irritate, sting, rouse, work up, hurry on.

To agitate, ruffle, flutter, flush, mantle, swell, shake, thrill, penetrate, pierce, cut, work one's self up.

To soften, subdue, overcome, master, overpower, overwhelm.

To shock, stagger, stun, astound, electrify, give one a shock, petrify.

To madden, intoxicate, fascinate, transport, ravish, enrapture, enravish, entrance.

Adj. Excited, affected, &c., *see* 825, wrought up, worked up, fired, lost, wild, haggard, feverish, mantling.

Exciting, &c., impressive, warm, glowing, fervid, swelling.

825. Excess of sensitiveness.

EXCITABILITY, impatience, wincing, disquiet, disquietude, restlessness, fuss, hurry, agitation, flurry, flutter, irritability, 901.

Passion, excitement, vehemence, impetuosity, flush, heat, fever, flame, fume, wildness, turbulence, boisterousness, tumult, effervescence, ebullition, boiling, boiling over, gust, storm, tempest, breaking out, burst, fit, paroxysm.

Fierceness, rage, fury, raving, delirium, frenzy, intoxication.

Fascination, infatuation, fanaticism, infection.

V. To be (impatient, restive,) &c., not to bear, to bear ill, wince,

826. Absence of excitability.

INEXCITABILITY, dispassion, hebetude, patience.

Coolness, composure, calmness, imperturbation, collectedness, tranquilness, quiet, quietude, quietness, sedateness, soberness, gravity, staidness, placidity, sobriety, philosophy, equanimity, stoicism, demureness, meekness, gentleness, mildness.

Submission, resignation, sufferance, endurance, long-sufferance, forbearance, fortitude

Repression of feeling, (restraint, subdued feeling,) composure, &c.

V. To be composed, &c., to bear well, tolerate, put up with, take up with, bear with, take

chafe, fuss; not to be able to bear, (endure,) &c.

To break out, fly out, burst out, explode, run riot, boil, boil over, fly off, flare up, fire, take fire, fume, rage, rave, run mad.

Adj. Excitable, &c., excited, &c.

Impatient, feverish, unquiet, restless, irritable, mettlesome, skittish, chafing, wincing, &c.

Vehement, boisterous, impetuous, (violent,) fierce, fiery, flaming, boiling, over-zealous, passionate, impassioned, enthusiastic, rampant, mercurial, high-wrought, over-wrought, hotheaded, turbulent, furious, fuming, (maddening,) raging, raving, frantic, delirious, intoxicated, demoniacal.

Overpowering, overwhelming, soul-stirring, soul-subduing, uncontrolled, irrepressible, ungovernable, uncontrollable.

easily, make the best of, acquiesce, submit, yield, bow to, resign one's self, suffer, endure, support, go through, reconcile one's self to, bend under.

To brook, digest, eat, swallow, pocket, stomach, brave.

To be borne, endured, &c., to go down.

To allay, compose, calm, still, lull, allay, pacify, quiet, tranquillize, hush, smooth, appease, assuage, mitigate, soothe, soften, temper, alleviate, moderate, sober down, chasten, mollify, tame, blunt, dull, deaden, slacken, damp, repress, restrain, check, curb, bridle, rein in, smother, quell, lay, *see* 174.

Adj. Inexcitable, unexcited, calm, cool, temperate, composed, collected, placid, quiet, tranquil, undisturbed, unruffled, serene, demure, sedate, staid, sober, dispassionate, unimpassioned, philosophic, stoical, imperturbable, coldblooded.

Meek, tolerant, patient, submissive, unresenting, content, resigned, chastened, subdued, bearing with, long-suffering, gentle, mild, unpassionate, sober-minded, coolheaded.

SECTION II. PERSONAL AFFECTIONS.*

1. PASSIVE AFFECTIONS.

827. PLEASURE, gratification, enjoyment, fruition, relish, zest.

Well being, satisfaction, content, 831, comfort, bed of roses, bed of down, velvet.

Joy, gladness, delight, glee, cheer, sunshine.

Physical pleasure, *see* 377.

Treat, feast, luxury, voluptuousness, clover.

Happiness, felicity, bliss, beatitude, beatification, enchantment,

828. PAIN, suffering.

Physical pain, *see* 378.

Displeasure, dissatisfacion, discontent, discomfort.

Uneasiness, disquiet, inquietude, weariness, dejection, *see* 837.

Annoyance, irritation, infliction, plague, bore, bother.

Care, anxiety, mortification, vexation, chagrin, trouble, trial, solicitude.

* Or those which concern one's own state of feeling.

transport, rapture, ravishment, ecstasy, paradise, Eden, Elysium, 981.

Honeymoon, palmy days, halcyon days, golden age.

V. To be pleased, &c., to feel, receive, or derive pleasure, &c.; to take pleasure or delight in; to delight in, rejoice in, relish, like, enjoy, take in good part.

To indulge in, treat one's self, feast on, revel, luxuriate in, &c.; to enjoy one's self.

Adj. Pleased, enjoying, relishing, liking, gratified, glad, gladdened, rejoiced, charmed, delighted.

Cheered, enlivened, flattered, indulged, regaled, &c.

Comfortable, at ease, cosy, satisfied, content, 831, luxurious, &c., unalloyed, without alloy.

Happy, blest, blissful, overjoyed, enchanted, captivated, fascinated, transported, raptured, enraptured, in raptures, in ecstasies, in a transport, beatified, joyful, *see* 836.

Adv. Happily, &c.

Grief, sorrow, distress, affliction, woe, bitterness, heartache, a heavy heart, a bleeding heart, a broken heart, heavy affliction, &c.

Unhappiness, infelicity, misery, tribulation, wretchedness, desolation,

Ache, aching, hurt, smart, twinge, stitch, shoot, cramp, spasm, nightmare, convulsion, throe.

Pang, anguish, agony, torture, torment.

A sufferer, victim, prey, martyr.

V. To feel, suffer, or experience pain, &c.; to suffer, ache, smart, ail, tingle, wince, writhe.

To grieve, fret, pine, mourn, worry one's self, chafe, yearn, droop, sink, give way, despair, 859.

Adj. In pain; feeling, suffering, enduring, &c., pain; in a state of pain, of suffering, &c., sore, aching, suffering, ailing, &c., pained, hurt, stung, wounded, &c., *see* 830.

Displeased, annoyed, dissatisfied, discontented, weary, &c., 832, uneasy, uncomfortable, ill at ease.

Concerned, afflicted, in affliction, sorrowful, in sorrow, bathed in tears, 839.

Unhappy, unfortunate, hapless, comfortless, unblest, luckless, unlucky, ill-fated, ill-starred, wretched, miserable, careworn, disconsolate, inconsolable, woebegone, forlorn, a prey to grief, &c., despairing, in despair, 859, heart-broken, broken-hearted, doomed, devoted, undone.

829. Capability of giving pleasure.

PLEASURABLENESS, pleasantness, gratefulness, acceptableness, agreeableness, delectability, deliciousness, daintiness, sweetness, luxuriousness, lusciousness, voluptuousness.

Charm, attraction, attractiveness, fascination, loveliness.

V. To cause, produce, create,

830. Capability of giving pain.

PAINFULNESS, disagreeableness, unpleasantness, irksomeness, unacceptableness, bitterness, vexatiousness, troublesomeness.

Trouble, care, annoyance, burden, load, nuisance, plague, infliction.

Scourge, bitter pill, curse, gall and wormwood, sting, scorpi-

give, afford, procure, offer, present, yield, &c., pleasure, gratification, &c

To please, take, gratify, satisfy, indulge, flatter, humor, regale.

To charm, rejoice, cheer, gladden, delight, enliven, 836, to transport, bless, captivate, fascinate, enchant, entrance, bewitch, ravish, enrapture, enravish, beatify.

Adj. Causing or giving pleasure, &c., pleasing, agreeable, grateful, gratifying, pleasant, pleasurable, acceptable, welcome, glad, gladsome, refreshing, comfortable, cordial, genial.

Sweet, delectable, nice, palatable, dainty, delicate, delicious, dulcet, savory, luscious, luxurious, voluptuous.

Fair, lovely, favorite, attractive, engaging, winning, winsome, taking, prepossessing, inviting, captivating, bewitching, fascinating.

Charming, delightful, exquisite, enchanting, ravishing, rapturous, heartfelt, thrilling, heavenly, celestial, Elysian, seraphic.

Palmy, halcyon, Saturnian.

---

on, thorn, brier, bramble, hornet.

A mishap, misadventure, mischance, pressure, grievance, trial, hardship, blow, stroke, affliction, misfortune, reverse, infliction, dispensation, visitation, disaster, undoing, tragedy, calamity, catastrophe, adversity, 735.

Provocation, affront, indignity, outrage, *see* 900, 929.

V. To cause, produce, give, &c., pain, uneasiness, suffering, &c., to disquiet, &c.

To displease, annoy, incommode discompose, trouble, disquiet, grieve, cross, tease, tire, vex, worry, plague, bore, harass, importune.

To pain, hurt, wound, sting, grate upon, gall, chafe, lacerate, pierce, hurt one's feelings, shock, horrify.

To wring, harrow, torment, torture, rack, convulse, agonize.

To irritate, provoke, nettle, aggrieve, enrage.

To maltreat, bite, assail, persecute, prostrate.

To sicken, disgust, revolt, nauseate, repel, offend.

Adj. Causing, occasioning, giving, producing, creating, inflicting, &c., pain, &c., hurting, &c.

Painful, dolorous, unpleasant, unpleasing, displeasing, uncomfortable, unwelcome, unsatisfactory, disagreeable, distasteful, bitter, unpalatable, unacceptable, thankless, undesirable, untoward, unlucky, obnoxious.

Distressing, bitter, afflicting, afflictive, cheerless, joyless, depressing, depressive, mournful, dreary, melancholy, grievous, woful, disastrous, calamitous, tragical, deplorable, dreadful.

Irritating, provoking, stinging, biting, vexatious, annoying, unaccommodating, troublesome, tiresome, irksome, importunate, teasing, harassing, worrying, tormenting.

Intolerable, insufferable, insupportable, unendurable, shocking, frightful, terrific, grim, appalling, dire, heart-breaking, heart-rending, horrid, harrowing, horrifying, horrific.

Odious, hateful, execrable, unpopular, repulsive, offensive

nauseous, disgusting, sickening, revolting, shocking, vile, abominable, accursed.

Sharp, acute, sore, severe, grave, hard, harsh, bitter, cruel, biting, corroding, consuming, racking, excruciating, &c.

Adv. Painfully, &c.

831. CONTENT, contentment, contentedness, satisfaction, entire satisfaction, serenity, sereneness, ease, heart-ease.

Comfort, snugness, well being.

Moderation, patience, endurance, resignation, reconciliation.

V. To be content, &c.; to rest satisfied, to put up with; to take up with; to be reconciled to.

To render content, &c., to set at ease, to conciliate, reconcile, satisfy, indulge, slake, gratify, &c.

Adj. Content, contented, satisfied, at ease, snug, comfortable.

Patient, resigned to, reconciled to, unrepining.

Unafflicted, unvexed, unmolested, (undisturbed,) &c.

832. DISCONTENT, discontentment, dissatisfaction, disappointment, mortification.

Repining, inquietude, heart-burning, heart-grief, *see* Regret, 833.

V. To be discontented, &c., dissatisfied; to repine, regret, 833, grumble, 839.

To cause discontent, &c., to disappoint, dissatisfy, mortify.

Adj. Discontented, dissatisfied, unsatisfied, malcontent, mortified, disappointed.

Repining, grumbling, (complaining,) exacting.

Disappointing, unsatisfactory.

833. REGRET, bitterness, repining; lamentation, 839; *see* Penitence, 950.

V. To regret, deplore, lament, rue, repent, 950.

Adj. Regretting, &c., regretful.

834. RELIEF, easement, alleviation, mitigation, palliation, solace, consolation, comfort, encouragement, refreshment, 689, soothing.

Delivery from evil, &c.

Lenitive, balm, oil, restorative, (palliative,) cushion, pillow, bolster, bed, &c., 215.

835. AGGRAVATION, heightening, exacerbation, exasperation.

V. To aggravate, to render worse, heighten, imbitter, sour, envenom, exacerbate, exasperate.

Adj. Aggravating, &c., aggravated, &c., unrelieved.

V. To relieve, ease, alleviate, mitigate, palliate, soften, soothe, assuage, allay, cheer, comfort, console, encourage, bear up, refresh, restore, remedy, cure, 660.

Adj. Relieving, &c., consolatory, soothing, assuaging, assuasive; balmy, balsamic, lenitive, anodyne, &c., 662, remedial, curative.

836. CHEERFULNESS, gayety, cheer, good humor, spirits, high spirits, high glee, joyfulness, joyousness, hilarity, exhilaration, liveliness, sprightliness, briskness vivacity, jocundity levity,

837. DEJECTION, depression, low spirits; lowness or depression of spirits, dejectedness; weight or oppression on the spirits damp on the spirits, sadness.

Heaviness, dulness infestivity

sportiveness, sportfulness, jocularity, sprightfulness.

Mirth, merriment, merrymaking, laughter, *see* 838, amusement, *see* 840.

Gratulation, rejoicing, exultation, jubilation, jubilee, triumph, pæan, heyday.

V. To be cheerful, &c.; to be of good cheer, to cheer up, brighten up, light up; take heart, bear up.

To rejoice, make merry, exult, congratulate one's self, triumph.

To cheer, enliven, elate, exhilarate, inspire, entrance, &c.

Adj. Cheerful, gay, blithe, of good cheer, in spirits, in good or high spirits, buoyant, debonair, bright, lighthearted, hearty, free and easy, airy, canty, sprightly, lively, vivacious, sprightful.

Merry, joyous, joyful, jolly, jocund, winsome, bonny, buxom, playful, playsome, frisky, frolicsome, sportive, jocose, jocular.

Rejoicing, elated, exulting, jubilant, palmy, flushed.

Cheering, inspiring, exhilarating.

Adv. Cheerfully, cheerily, &c.

---

joylessness, gloom, darkness, dolefulness, weariness, 841, heaviness of heart, failure of heart.

Melancholy, melancholiness, the dismals, spleen, the horrors, hypochondria.

Despondency, despair, disconsolateness, prostration.

Demureness, seriousness, gravity, solemnity, solemness, sullenness, &c.

Cause of dejection; a damper.

V. To be dejected, sad, &c.; to grieve, to give way, droop, sink, look downcast, mope, brood over, fret, pine, *see* Despair, 859.

To refrain from laughter; to keep one's countenance.

To depress, discourage, dishearten, dispirit, dull, deject, lower, sink, dash, unman, prostrate.

Adj. Cheerless, uncheerful, joyless, dull, flat, dispirited, out of spirits, out of sorts, low-spirited, in low spirits, spiritless, lowering, frowning.

Grave, serious, sedate, staid, sober, solemn, demure, grim, grim-visaged, rueful, sullen, sulky.

Discouraged, disheartened, downcast, cast down, depressed, downhearted, desponding, crestfallen, dashed, drooping, sunk.

Dismal, melancholy, sombre, pensive, mournful, doleful, moping, splenetic, gloomy, lugubrious, funereal, forlorn, heartstruck; melancholic, hypochondriacal, bilious, jaundiced, saturnine.

Disconsolate, despairing, in despair, 859.

Depressing, preying upon the mind, &c.

838. Expression of pleasure.

Rejoicing, exultation, triumph, jubilation, jubilee, *see* 884, pæan, *see* 990.

Smile, simper, smirk, grin, broad grin.

Laughter, giggle, titter, chuckle, shout, hearty laugh; a shout, burst, fit, or peal of laughter.

839. Expression of pain.

Lamentation, complaint, murmur, mutter, plaint, lament, wail, sigh, heaving.

Cry, whine, whimper, sob, tear, moan, grumble, groan.

Outcry, scream, screech, howl, whoop, brawl, yell, roar.

Weeping, crying, &c.; a fit of

Derision, risibility, 856.

V. To rejoice, exult, triumph, 883, 884, to congratulate one's self.

To smile, simper, smirk, grin, mock; to laugh, giggle, titter; to burst out, shout.

To cause, create, occasion, raise, excite, or produce laughter, &c.

Adj. Laughing, &c.; jubilant, triumphant.

Laughable, risible, ludicrous.

---

crying, complaining, frown, scowl, sardonic grin or laugh.

Dirge, elegy, monody, jeremiade.

Plaintiveness, querimoniousness, languishment, querulousness.

Mourning, weeds, willow, cypress.

A grumbler, croaker, brawler.

V. To lament, complain, murmur, mutter, grumble, sigh; give, fetch, or heave a sigh.

To cry, weep, sob, blubber; snivel, whimper; to shed tears.

To grumble, groan, croak, whine, moan, bemoan, wail, bewail, frown, scowl; to make a wry face.

To cry out, growl, squeal, sing out, scream, screech, bawl, halloo, bellow, yell, roar; to cry out lustily.

Adj. Lamenting, complaining, &c.; lachrymose, plaintive, querulous, querimonious.

840. Amusement, diversion, entertainment, sport, divertisement, recreation, relaxation, pastime, holiday, red-letter day.

Fun, frolic, pleasantry, drollery, jocoseness, laughter, 838.

Play, game, gambol, romp, prank, heyday.

Dance, ball, (polka,) reel, cotillon, rigadoon, saraband, hornpipe, bolero, fandango, minuet, quadrille, waltz, gavot, &c.

Festivity, festival, jubilee, merrymaking, rejoicing, gala, revelry, revels, carnival, saturnalia.

Feast, banquet, entertainment, carousal, wassail; jollity, joviality, jovialness.

Buffoonery, mummery, tomfoolery, raree show, puppet show, masquerade.

Bonfire, fireworks.

Toy, plaything, bawble, &c., *see* 643.

A master of ceremonies or revels.

V. To amuse divert, entertain, rejoice, cheer, recreate, en-

841. Weariness, tedium, lassitude, fatigue, *see* 688, dejection, *see* 837.

Disgust, nausea, loathing, sickness, disgust of life.

Wearisomeness, irksomeness, tiresomeness, monotony.

A bore, a button holder, proser.

V. To tire, weary, fatigue, bore; send to sleep; to yawn.

To sicken, disgust, nauseate.

Adj. Wearying, &c., wearisome, tiresome, irksome, uninteresting, devoid of interest, monotonous, humdrum, flat, prosy, prosing, slow, soporific, somniferous.

Disgusting, sickening, nauseating.

Weary, tired, &c.; uninterested, flagging, used up, weary of life; drowsy, somnolent, sleepy &c., yawning.

Adv. Wearily, &c.

---

liven, solace to beguile or while away the time; to drown care.

To play, sport, disport, make merry, take one's pleasure, make holiday, keep holiday; to gambol, revel, frisk, frolic, romp; to dance, hop, jump, caper, cut capers, skip.

To treat, feast, regale, carouse, banquet.

Adj. Amusing, diverting, &c., amused, &c.

Sportive, jovial, festive, festal, jocund, jocose, romp-ish, &c.

842. Wit, humor, fancy, fun, pleasantry, drollery, whim, jocularity, facetiousness, waggery, waggishness, wittiness, atticism, attic wit, attic salt, smartness, banter, farce.

Jest, joke, conceit, quip, quirk, crank, witticism, repartee, flash of wit, sally, point, dry joke, epigram, pun, conundrum.

V. To joke, jest, retort; to cut jokes, crack a joke, perpetrate a joke or pun.

To laugh at, banter, jeer, to make fun of, make merry with.

Adj. Witty, facetious, humorous, pleasant, quick-witted, nimble-witted, smart, jocose, jocular, waggish.

Comic, comical, laughable, droll, ludicrous, funny, risible, farcical, roguish, sportive.

843. Dulness, heaviness, stolidity, stupidity, 499, flatness, gravity, 837, solemnity; prose, matter of fact.

V. To be dull, &c.

To render dull, &c., damp, depress.

Adj. Dull, prosaic, prosing, unentertaining, unlively, flat, pointless, slow, stolid, stupid, plodding, humdrum; Bœotian.

---

844. A humorist, wag, wit, reparteeist, epigrammatist, punster, jester.

A buffoon, merryandrew, tumbler, mountebank, charlatan, posture master, harlequin, punch, clown, gypsy, jackpudding.

2. Discriminative Affections.

845. Beauty, handsomeness, beauteousness, beautifulness.

Form, elegance, grace, symmetry.

Comeliness, seemliness, shapeliness, fairness, prettiness, neatness, spruceness, attractiveness, loveliness, polish, gloss.

Bloom, brilliancy, radiance, splendor, magnificence, sublimity.

Concinnity, delicacy, refinement.

V. To render beautiful, &c., to beautify, embellish, adorn, deck, bedeck, decorate, set out, set off,

846. Ugliness, deformity, inelegance, plainness, homeliness, uncomeliness, ungainliness, uncouthness, clumsiness, stiffness, disfigurement, distortion, contortion, malformation, monstrosity, misproportion, want of symmetry, roughness, repulsiveness, squalor, hideousness, unsightliness, odiousness.

An eyesore, a sight, fright, spectre, scarecrow, hag, monster.

V. To be ugly, &c.

To render ugly, &c., to deform, deface, distort, disfigure, misshape, blemish, spot, stain, dis-

ornament, *see* 847, array, garnish furbish, trick out, trim, emblazon

To polish, burnish, gild, varnish, japan, lacquer, &c.

Adj. Beautiful, handsome, fine, pretty, lovely, graceful, elegant, delicate, refined, fair, comely, seemly, well-favored, proper, shapely, well-made, well-formed, well-proportioned, symmetrical, becoming, goodly, neat, spruce, sleek, brighteyed, attractive, curious.

Blooming, brilliant, shining, beaming, splendid, resplendent, dazzling, gorgeous, superb, magnificent, sublime.

Picturesque, artistical.

Passable, not amiss, undeformed, undefaced, spotless, unspotted.

---

tain, soil, tarnish, sully, blot, daub, bedaub, begrime, blur, smear, besmear, bespatter, maculate.

Adj. Ugly, plain, homely, gross, inelegant, unsightly, ill-looking ordinary, unseemly, ill-favored, hard-featured, hard-visaged, ungainly, uncouth, slouching, ungraceful, clumsy, graceless, rude, rough, rugged, homespun, gaunt, rawboned, haggard.

Misshapen, shapeless, misproportioned, ill-proportioned, deformed, ill-made, ill-shaped, grotesque, disfigured, distorted, unshapen, humpbacked, hunchbacked, crooked, bald, rickety.

Squalid, grim, grisly, grimfaced, grim-visaged, ghastly, ghostlike, deathlike, cadaverous, repulsive, forbidding.

Frightful, odious, hideous, horrid, shocking, monstrous.

Foul, soiled, tarnished, stained, distained, sullied, blurred, blotted, spotted, maculated, spotty, splashed, smeared, begrimed, spattered, bedaubed, besmeared.

847. Ornament, adornment, decoration, embellishment, ornature, ornateness, gaud, pride.

Garnish, polish, varnish, gilding, japanning, lacquer, &c.

Jewel, gem, brilliant, &c., 650, spangle, trinket, carcanet.

Embroidery, broidery, brocade, galloon, lace, fringe, aigulet, trapping, trimming, hanging.

Wreath, festoon, garland, chaplet, tassel, knot, shoulder knot, brooch, flower, &c., epaulet, frog, ermine.

Feather, plume.

Nosegay, bouquet, posy.

Tracery, moulding, arabesque.

Frippery, finery, gewgaw, tinsel, tawdriness, &c.

Flourish, flowers of rhetoric,

Excess of ornament, *see* 851.

V. To ornament, embellish, dec-

848. Blemish, disfigurement, eyesore, defect, flaw.

Stain, blot, spot, speck, blur, freckle, mole, blotch, speckle, spottiness, maculation; soil, tarnish, smut, soot, dirt, &c., 653.

Excrescence, pimple, &c., *see* 250.

V To disfigure, deface, &c., *see* 846.

849. Simplicity, plainness, undress, chastity; freedom from ornament or affectation, homeliness.

V. To be simple, &c., to render simple, &c., to simplify.

Adj. Simple, plain, homely chaste, homespun, unaffected, flat, dull.

Unadorned, unornamented, undecked, ungarnished, unarrayed, untrimmed; in dishabille.

orate, adorn, beautify, garnish, polish, gild, &c., bespangle, dizen, bedizen; embroider, &c., *see* 845.

Adj. Ornamented, &c., beautified, ornate, dedecked, showy, gaudy, gilt, begilt, gorgeous.

850. Good taste.

TASTE, delicacy, refinement, nicety, finesse, grace, polish, elegance; dilettanteism.

Science of taste, Æsthetics.

A man of taste, connoisseur, judge, critic, virtuoso, amateur, dilettante.

V. To appreciate, judge, discriminate, criticize, 465.

Adj. In good taste, tasty, (tasteful,) unaffected, pure, chaste, classical, attic, refined, elegant, æsthetic.

Adv. Elegantly, &c.

851. Bad taste.

VULGARITY, vulgarism, barbarism, Vandalism, Gothicism.

Coarseness, grossness, indecorum, lowness, homeliness, low life, clownishness, rusticity, boorishness, brutishness, brutality, awkwardness, want of tact.

A rough diamond, slattern, sloven, clown, &c., 876.

Excess of ornament, (gaudiness,) false ornament, tawdriness, finery, frippery, trickery, tinsel, gewgaw.

V. To be vulgar, &c.

Adj. In bad taste, vulgar, coarse, unrefined, gross, heavy, rude, unpolished, homely, homespun, homebred, uncouth, awkward, ungraceful, slovenly, slatternly, impolite, ill-mannered, uncivil, ungentlemanly, unladylike, unfeminine, unseemly, unpresentable, unkempt, uncombed.

Rustic, boorish, clownish, barbarous, barbaric, Gothic, unclassical, heathenish, outlandish, untamed, 876.

Obsolete, out of fashion, unfashionable, antiquated, old-fashioned, gone by.

New-fangled, odd, fantastic, grotesque, *see* ridiculous, 853, serio-comic, tragi-comic, affected, meretricious, extravagant, monstrous, shocking, horrid, revolting.

Gaudy, tawdry, bedizened, tricked out.

Adv. Out of fashion, &c.

852. FASHION, style, mode, vogue.

Manners, breeding, politeness, good behavior, gentility, decorum, punctilio, form, formality, etiquette, custom, demeanor, air, port, carriage, presence.

Show, equipage, &c., *see* 882.

The world, the fashionable world, high life, town, court, gentility, civilization, civilized life, *see* Nobility, 875.

V. To be fashionable, &c.

Adj. Fashionable, in fashion, in vogue, modish, stylish, courtly, genteel, well-bred, well-behaved, polished, gentlemanly, ladylike, well-spoken, civil, presentable, refined, thorough-bred, unembarrassed.

Adv. Fashionably, in fashion, &c.

853. RIDICULOUSNESS, ludicrousness, risibility.

Oddness, oddity, whimsicality, comicality, grotesqueness, fancifulness, quaintness, frippery, preposterousness, extravagance, monstrosity.

Bombast, bathos, fustian.

Adj. Ridiculous, extravagant, monstrous, preposterous.

Odd, whimsical, quaint, grotesque, fanciful, eccentric, strange, out of the way, fantastic.

Laughable, risible, ludicrous, comic, comical, funny, derisive farcical, burlesque, quizzical, bombastic, inflated.

Awkward, lumpish, uncouth, &c.

854. Fop, dandy, exquisite, coxcomb, beau, macaroni, blade blood, buck, man-milliner.

855. Affectation, mannerism, pretension, airs, conceit, foppery, dandyism, man-millinery, affectedness, charlatanism, quackery, foppishness, pedantry, acting a part.

Prudery, demureness, coquetry, stiffness, formality.

A pedant, mannerist.

V. To affect, to give one's self airs, to simper, mince, to act a part, overact.

Adj. Affected, conceited, pedantic, pragmatical, priggish, puritanical, prim, starch, stiff, formal, demure.

Foppish, namby-pamby, simpering, mincing.

Overwrought, overdone, overacted.

856. Ridicule, derision, mockery, quiz, banter, irony, raillery.

Jeer, gibe, taunt, satire, scurrility, scoffing.

A parody, burlesque, travesty, farce, comedy, tragi-comedy, doggerel.

Blunder, bull, slip of the tongue, bathos, anti-climax.

Buffoonery, vagary, antic, mummery, tomfoolery, grimace, prank

V. To ridicule, deride, laugh at, 929, scoff, mock, jeer, banter quiz, rally, taunt, point at, grin at; to play upon.

To parody, caricature, burlesque, travesty.

Adj. Derisory, scurrilous, burlesque, Hudibrastic.

857. Object and cause of ridicule.

Laughing stock, jesting stock, gazing stock, butt; an original, oddity, buffoon, jester, 844, mountebank.

3. Prospective Affections.

858. Hope, trust, confidence, reliance, faith, assurance, credit, security, expectation, affiance, promise, assumption, presumption.

Hopefulness, bright prospect, optimism, enthusiasm, &c., Utopia.

Anchor, mainstay, sheet anchor, staff, &c., *see* Support, 215.

V. To hope; to feel, entertain, harbor, cherish, feed, nourish, encourage, foster, &c., hope or confidence.

To trust, confide, rely on, feel or rest assured, confident secure, &c.; to flatter one's self, expect, presume.

To give or inspire hope; to

859. Absence, want, or loss of hope.

Hopelessness, despair, desperation, despondence, 837, forlornness, a forlorn hope.

V. To despair, to give over; to despond; to lose; give up, abandon, relinquish, &c., all hope; to yield to despair.

To inspire or drive to despair; to dash, crush, or destroy one's hopes.

Adj. Hopeless, having lost or given up hope, losing, &c., hope, past hope, forlorn, desperate, incurable, irremediable, remediless.

Inauspicious, unpropitious, unpromising, threatening, &c.

augur well, encourage, assure, promise, flatter, buoy up, reassure, embolden, raise expectations, &c.

Adj. Hoping, &c., in hopes, &c., hopeful, confident, secure, buoyant, buoyed up, sanguine, enthusiastic.

Fearless, unsuspecting, unsuspicious; free or exempt from fear, suspicion, distrust, &c., undespairing.

Auspicious, promising, propitious.

---

860. FEAR, timidity, diffidence, nervousness, restlessness, inquietude, disquietude, solicitude, anxiety, distrust, hesitation, misgiving, suspicion, qualm, want of confidence.

Apprehension, flutter, trepidation, tremor, shaking, trembling, palpitation, quivering, fearfulness, despondency.

Fright, affright, alarm, dread, awe, terror, horror, dismay, panic, consternation, despair, 859.

Intimidation, terrorism, reign of terror.

Object of fear; bugbear; scarecrow, goblin, &c., 980, nightmare.

V. To fear, be afraid, &c.; to distrust, hesitate, have qualms, misgivings, suspicions, &c.

To apprehend, take alarm, start, tremble, shake, quake, shudder, quail, turn pale, blench, flinch.

To excite fear, raise apprehensions, to give, raise, or sound an alarm, to startle, to intimidate, put in fear, frighten, affright, alarm, scare, haunt, strike terror, daunt, terrify, awe, horrify, dismay, petrify, appall.

To deter, overawe, abash, cow, browbeat, bully.

Adj. Fearing, timid, timorous, fearful, nervous, diffident, apprehensive, restless, haunted with the fear, apprehension, dread, &c., of.

Frightened, pale, alarmed, scared, terrified, petrified, aghast, awestruck, dismayed, horrorstruck, horrified, appalled, panicstruck.

Inspiring fear, alarming, formidable, redoubtable, portentous, perilous, 665, fearful, dreadful, dire, shocking, terrible, tremendous, horrid, horrible, horrific, ghastly, awful.

861. Absence of fear.

COURAGE, bravery, valor, valiantness, boldness, spirit, spiritedness, daring, gallantry, intrepidity, contempt of danger, defiance of danger, confidence, fearlessness, audacity.

Manhood, nerve, pluck, mettle, bottom, heart, hardihood, fortitude, firmness, resolution.

Prowess, heroism, chivalry.

V. To be courageous, &c., to dare, to face, front, confront, despise, brave, defy, &c., danger; to

862. Excess of fear.

COWARDICE, pusillanimity, cowardliness, timidity, fearfulness, faint-heartedness, softness, effeminacy.

Poltroonery, baseness, dastardness, dastardy, a faint heart.

A coward, poltroon, dastard, recreant; an alarmist.

A runaway, fugitive.

V. To quail, &c., 860, to flinch, run away.

Adj. Coward, cowardly, pusillanimous, shy, timid, skittish,

take courage, to muster, summon up, or pluck up courage.

To venture, make bold, face, defy, brave, beard, hold out, bear up against.

To give, infuse, or inspire courage; to encourage, embolden, inspirit.

Adj. Courageous, brave, valiant, valorous, gallant, intrepid.

Spirited, high-spirited, high-mettled, mettlesome, manly, manful, resolute, stout, stout-hearted, iron-hearted, heart of oak, firm, indomitable.

Bold, bold-spirited, daring, audacious, fearless, undaunted, unappalled, undismayed, unawed, unabashed, unalarmed, unflinching, unshrinking, unblenching, unblenched, unapprehensive.

Enterprising, venturous, adventurous, venturesome, dashing, doughty, chivalrous, heroic, fierce, savage.

Unfeared, undreaded, &c.

timorous, spiritless, faint-hearted, chicken-hearted.

Dastard, dastardly, base, craven, recreant, unwarlike.

---

863. Rashness, temerity, audacity, presumption, precipitancy, precipitation, recklessness, foolhardiness, desperation, Quixotism.

Imprudence, indiscretion.

A deperado, madcap, bully, bravo, Hotspur, Don Quixote, knight errant.

V. To be rash, incautious, &c.

Adj. Rash, headstrong, foolhardy, reckless, desperate, hotheaded, hairbrained, headlong, hotbrained, precipitate, Quixotic.

Imprudent, indiscreet, overconfident, overweening, venturesome, uncalculating, incautious, improvident.

864. Caution, cautiousness, discretion, prudence, wariness, heed, circumspection, calculation, deliberation, *see* 459.

Coolness, self-possession, presence of mind, self-command, steadiness.

V. To be cautious, &c., to take care, to have a care, take heed, to be on one's guard, to look about one.

Adj. Cautious, wary, careful, heedful, chary, circumspect, prudent, discreet.

Unenterprising, unadventurous, cool, steady, self-possessed.

865. Desire, wish, mind.

Inclination, leaning, bent, fancy, fantasy, partiality, predilection, liking, fondness, relish.

Want, need, exigency.

Longing, hankering, solicitude, eagerness, anxiety, yearning, coveting, aspiration, ambition, overanxiety.

Appetite, appetence, keenness, hunger, thirst, thirstiness, prurience, cupidity, lust, concupiscence.

Avidity, greediness, covetous-

866. Indifference, coldness, coolness, unconcern, inappetency, listlessness, lukewarmness, *see* Disdain, 930.

V. To be indifferent, &c., to have no desire, wish, taste, or relish for; not to care for; to disdain, spurn, 930.

Adj. Indifferent, undesirous, cool, cold, unconcerned, unsolicitous, unattracted, &c., lukewarm, listless, unambitious, unaspiring.

Unattractive, unalluring unde-

ness, craving, voracity, canine appetite, rapacity, rapaciousness.

Passion, rage, mania, inextinguishable desire, vaulting ambition, impetuosity.

A gourmand, glutton, cormorant, *see* 957.

An amateur, votary, devotee, aspirant, solicitant, candidate.

Object of desire; attraction, allurement, temptation, idol, magnet, hobby.

V. To desire, wish, long for, fancy, have a mind to, be glad of, want, miss, need, feel the want of, would fain have, to care for.

To hunger, thirst, crave, lust after, hanker after, burn for.

To desiderate, sigh, cry, pine, pant, languish, yearn for, aspire after.

To woo, court, solicit, &c.

To cause, create, raise, excite, or provoke desire; to allure, attract, solicit, tempt, hold out temptation or allurement, to tantalize.

To gratify desire, slake, satiate, 827.

Adj. Desirous, inclined, partial to, wishful, wishing, desiring, wanting, needing, hankering after; lickerish.

Craving, hungry, thirsty.

Greedy, over-eager, voracious, agog, covetous, ravenous, rapacious, unsated, unslacked, insatiable, insatiate.

Eager, bent on, intent on, aspiring, ambitious, vaulting, impetuous.

Desirable, desired, desiderated, &c., *see* Pleasing, 829.

---

866. [continued] ...sired, undesirable, &c., uncared for, unwished, unvalued.

Vapid, tasteless, insipid, mawhish, flat, stale, vain.

867. Dislike, distaste, disrelish, disinclination, reluctance, backwardness, demur.

Repugnance, disgust, nausea, loathing, averseness, aversion, abomination, antipathy, abhorrence, horror, hatred, detestation, *see* 898, hydrophobia.

V. To dislike, mislike, disrelish.

To shun, avoid, eschew, withdraw from, shrink from, recoil from, shudder at.

To loathe, nauseate, abominate, detest, abhor, *see* Hate, 898.

To cause or excite dislike; to disincline, repel, sicken, render sick, nauseate, disgust, shock.

Adj. Disliking, disrelishing, &c., averse from, adverse, shy of, disinclined.

Loathing, nauseating, sick of, abominating, abhorrent.

Disliked, disagreeable, unpalatable, unpopular, offensive, loathsome, sickening, heart-sickening, nauseous, nauseating, repulsive, disgusting, detestable, execrable, abhorred, 330.

Adv. Disagreeably, &c.

868. Fastidiousness, nicety, daintiness, squeamishness, niceness, difficulty in being pleased, epicurism.

Excess of delicacy, prudery.

V. To be fastidious, &c., to disdain.

Adj. Fastidious, nice, delicate, difficult, dainty, squeamish, difficult to please; querulous.

869. Satiety, repletion, glut, saturation, surfeit.

V. To sate, satiate, satisfy, saturate, quench, slake, pall, glut, gorge, surfeit.

Adj. Satiated, sated, sick of, heartsick, used up.

4. Contemplative Affections.

870. Wonder, surprise, marvel, astonishment, amazement, admiration, awe, bewilderment, stupefaction, fascination, &c.

V. To wonder, marvel, be surprised, admire, &c.; to stare, gape, start.

To surprise, astonish, amaze, astound, dumfounder, strike, startle, take by surprise, strike with wonder, &c., electrify, stun, petrify, confound, stagger belief, stupefy, bewilder, fascinate.

To be wonderful, &c.

Adj. Surprised, astonished, amazed, astounded, struck, startled, taken by surprise, struck dumb, awestruck, aghast, agape, dumfoundered, thunderstruck, stupefied, petrified.

Wonderful, wondrous, surprising, astonishing, amazing, stunning, astounding, startling, unexpected, unforseen, strange, uncommon, unheard of, unaccountable, incredible, inexplicable, indescribable, inexpressible, ineffable, unutterable, monstrous, prodigious, stupendous, beggaring description, miraculous, passing strange.

871. Absence of wonder.

Expectance, expectation, 507

V. To expect, not to be surprised, not to wonder, &c.

Adj. Expecting, &c.

Expected, &c., foreseen, unamazed, astonished at nothing, 841.

Common, ordinary, *see* 82.

---

872. Prodigy, phenomenon, wonder, marvel, miracle, monster, 83, phœnix, gazing stock, curiosity, lion, sight, spectacle, sign, portent, 512.

Thunderclap, thunderbolt, volcanic eruption.

5. Extrinsic Affections.*

873. Repute.

Distinction, note, name, repute, reputation, figure, notoriety, vogue, celebrity, fame, famousness, popularity, renown, memory, immortality.

Glory, honor, lustre, illustriousness, gloriousness, credit, account, regard, respect, reputableness, respectability, respectableness.

Dignity, stateliness, solemnity, grandeur, splendor, nobleness, lordliness, majesty, sublimity.

Rank, standing, station, place, order, degree.

874. Disrepute, discredit, ingloriousness, derogation, abasement, abjectness, degradation.

Dishonor, shame, disgrace, odium, slur, scandal, obloquy, opprobrium, ignominy, baseness, turpitude, vileness, infamy.

Tarnish, taint, defilement, pollution.

Stain, blot, spot, blur, stigma, brand, reproach, slur.

V. To be conscious of shame, to feel shame, to blush, to color up, to be ashamed, humiliated,

* Or personal affections derived from the opinions or feelings of others.

Greatness, highness, eminence supereminence.

Elevation, ascent, 305, exaltation, aggrandizement.

Dedication, consecration, enshrinement, glorification, posthumous fame.

A star, sun, constellation, galaxy, paragon, 650, honor, ornament, mirror.

V. To be conscious of glory, to glory in, to be proud of, *see* 878, to exult, &c., 884, to be vain of, 880.

To be glorious, distinguished, &c., to shine, to figure, to make or cut a figure, dash, to rival, outshine, to throw into the shade.

To live, flourish, glitter, flaunt.

To confer or reflect honor, &c., on, to honor; to do honor to; to redound to one's honor.

To pay or render honor, &c., to; to honor, dignify, glorify, ennoble, exalt, enthrone, signalize, immortalize.

To consecrate, dedicate to, devote to, to enshrine.

Adj. Distinguished, noted, notable, respectable, reputable, notorious, celebrated, famous, famed, far-famed, honored, renowned, popular; imperishable, deathless, immortal.

Illustrious, glorious, splendid, bright, brilliant, radiant, heroic.

Eminent, prominent, high, preëminent, peerless, signalized, exalted, dedicated, consecrated, enshrined.

Great, dignified, proud, noble, worshipful, lordly, grand, stately, august, princely, imposing, transcendent, majestic, sacred, sublime.

humbled, abashed, &c. *see* 879 and 881.

To be inglorious, abased, dishonored, &c., to incur disgrace, &c.

To cause shame, &c.; to shame, disgrace, put to shame, dishonor, throw, cast, fling or reflect shame, &c., upon, to derogate from.

To tarnish, stain, blot, sully, taint, discredit, degrade, debase, defile.

To impute shame to, to brand, post, stigmatize, vilify, defame, slur.

To abash, humiliate, humble, dishonor, discompose, disconcert, shame, put down, confuse, mortify; to obscure, eclipse, outshine.

Adj. Feeling shame, disgrace, &c., ashamed, abashed, &c., disgraced, &c., branded, tarnished, &c.

Inglorious, mean, base, &c., 940, shabby, nameless, renownless, unnoticed, unnoted, unhonored.

Shameful, disgraceful, despicable, discreditable, unbecoming, unworthy, disreputable, derogatory, abject, vile, ribald, dishonorable, scandalous, infamous.

---

875. Nobility, noblesse, aristocracy, peerage, gentry, gentility, quality, rank, blood, birth, fashionable world, &c., 852, distinction, &c.

A personage, man of distinction, rank, &c; a nobleman, noble, lord, peer, grandee, don, gen-

876. Commonalty, the lower or humbler classes or orders, the vulgar herd, the crowd, the people, the multitude, the populace, the million, the peasantry.

The mob, rabble; the scum or dregs of the people or of society low company.

tleman, squire, patrician, lordling.

Prince, duke marquis, earl, viscount, baron, baronet, knight, count, esquire, &c., *see* 745.

V. To be noble, &c.

Adj. Noble, exalted, princely, of rank, titled, patrician, aristocratic, high-born, well-born, genteel, gentlemanly, fashionable, &c., 852.

877. TITLE, honor, knighthood, &c.

Highness, excellency, grace, lordship, worship, reverence, esquire, sir, master, &c.; his honor.

Decoration, laurel, palm, wreath, medal, ribbon, blue ribbon, cross, star, garter, feather, crest, epaulet, colors, cockade, livery; order, arms, shield, scutcheon.

A commoner, one of the people; a peasant, countryman, boor, serf.

A swain, clown, lout, underling.

An upstart, snob, mushroom.

A beggar, tatterdemalion, caitiff, ragamuffin.

A Goth, Vandal, Hottentot, savage, barbarian.

V. To be ignoble, &c.

Adj. Ignoble, mean, low, plebeian, vulgar, untitled, homespun, subaltern, underling, homely.

Base, base-born, beggarly, rustic, cockney, menial, sorry, vile, uncivilized, boorish. rude brutish, barbarous, barbarian.

878. PRIDE, haughtiness, loftiness, stateliness, vainglory, superciliousness, assumption, lordliness, stiffness, primness, crest, arrogance.

A proud man, &c., a highflier.

V. To be proud, &c., to presume, assume, swagger, strut.

To pride one's self on, glory in, pique one's self, plume one's self, to stand upon.

Adj. Proud, haughty, lofty, high, mighty, high-flown, high-minded, puffed up, flushed, supercilious, disdainful, overweening, consequential, swollen, arrogant.

Stately, stiff, starch, prim, in buckram, strait-laced, vainglorious, lordly, magisterial, purse-proud.

Unabashed, unblushing, &c.

879. HUMILITY, humbleness, meekness, lowness, lowliness, affability, condescension, abasement, self-abasement, humiliation, submission, resignation, *see* Modesty, 881.

V. To be humble, &c.; to condescend, humble, or demean one's self; stoop, submit, knuckle to.

To render humble; to humble, humiliate, set down, abash, abase, take down.

Adj. Humble, lowly, meek, sober-minded, submissive, resigned, unoffended.

Humbled, humiliated, &c.

880. VANITY, conceit, conceitedness, self-conceit, self-complacency, self-confidence, self-sufficiency, self-esteem, self-approbation, self-praise, self-laudation, self-gratulation, self-admiration.

881. MODESTY, humility, 879, diffidence, timidity, bashfulness, shyness, coyness, sheepishness shamefacedness, blushing.

Reserve, constraint, demureness.

V. To be modest, humble &c.

Pretensions, mannerism, egotism, coxcombry, vainglory, 943.

A coxcomb, &c., see 858.

V. To be vain, &c., to pique one's self; to plume one's self.

To render vain, &c., to puff up, to inspire with vanity, &c.

Adj. Vain, conceited, overweening, forward, vainglorious, puffed up, high-flown, inflated, flushed.

Self-satisfied, self-confident, self-sufficient, self-flattering, self-admiring, self-applauding, self-opinioned.

Unabashed, unblushing, unconstrained, unceremonious, free and easy.

to retire, keep in the background, keep private.

Adj. Modest, diffident, humble, 879, timid, bashful, timorous, shy, skittish, coy, shamefaced, blushing, over-modest.

Unpretending, unobtrusive, unassuming, unostentatious, unboastful, unaspiring.

Abashed, ashamed, dashed, out of countenance, crestfallen.

Reserved, constrained, demure.

Adv. Humbly, &c., quietly, privately, unostentatiously

---

882. Ostentation, display, show, flourish, parade, pomp, state, solemnity, pageantry, dash, glitter, strut, magnificence, pomposity, pretensions, showing off.

Pageant, spectacle, procession, turn out, gala, regatta.

Ceremony, ceremonial, mummery, solemn mockery; formality, form, etiquette, punctilio, punctiliousness, frippery, court dress, &c.

V. To be ostentatious, &c.; to display, exhibit, show off, come forward, put one's self forward, flaunt, emblazon, glitter; make or cut a figure, dash, to figure.

To observe or stand on ceremony, etiquette, &c.

Adj. Ostentatious, showy, gaudy, gairish, dashing, flaunting, glittering, pompous, sumptuous, theatrical.

Pompous, solemn, stately, high-sounding, formal, stiff, ceremonious, punctilious.

883. Celebration, jubilee, commemoration, solemnization ovation, pæan, triumph.

Triumphal arch, bonfire, salute.

Inauguration, installation.

V. To celebrate, keep, signalize, do honor to, pledge, drink to, toast, commemorate, solemnize.

To inaugurate, install.

Adj. Celebrating, &c., in honor of, in commemoration of, &c.

884. Boasting, boast, vaunt, vaunting, brag, pretensions, puff, puffing, puffery, flourish, gasconade, bravado, vaporing, rhodomon· bombast, see Exaggeration, 549.

Exultation, triumph, jubilation.

A boaster, braggart, braggadocio, Gascon; a pretender.

V. To boast, make a boast of, brag, vaunt, puff, show off, flourish strut, swagger.

To exult, crow, chuckle, triumph.

Adj. Boasting, vaunting, &c., vainglorious, braggart.

Elated, flushed, jubilant.

885. Undue assumption of superiority.

INSOLENCE, haughtiness, arrogance, imperiousness, contumeliousness, superciliousness, swagger.

Impertinence, sauciness, pertness, flippancy, petulance.

Assumption, forwardness, presumption, impudence, assurance, front, face, brass, shamelessness, effrontery, audacity.

V. To be insolent, &c.; to bluster, vapor, swagger, swell, arrogate, assume.

To domineer, bully, beard, bear down, beat down, browbeat, trample on, tread under foot, outbrave.

Adj. Insolent, &c.; haughty, arrogant, imperious, dictatorial, contumelious, supercilious, overbearing, intolerant.

Flippant, pert, cavalier, saucy, forward, impertinent.

Blustering, swaggering, vaporing, bluff, assuming, impudent, brazen, brazen-faced, shameless, bold-faced, unblushing, unabashed.

887. BLUSTER, bully, swaggerer, vaporer.

886. SERVILITY, obsequiousness, suppleness, fawning, slavishness, abjectness, prostration genuflection, &c., 990.

Fawning, sycophancy, *see* Flattery, 833, and Humility, 879.

A sycophant, parasite, hanger-on, time-server, 941.

V. To cringe, bow, stoop kneel, fall on one's knees, &c.

To sneak, crawl, crouch, truckle to, grovel, fawn.

Adj. Servile, obsequious, supple, mean, cringing, fawning, slavish, grovelling, snivelling, beggarly, sycophantic, parasitical, abject.

SECTION III. SYMPATHETIC AFFECTIONS.

1. SOCIAL AFFECTIONS.

888. FRIENDSHIP, amity, amicableness, friendliness, brotherhood, fraternity, sodality, confraternity, fraternization, harmony, good understanding, concord, 714.

Acquaintance, introduction, intercourse, intimacy, familiarity, fellowship.

V. To be friends, to be friendly, &c., to fraternize, sympathize with, 897, to be well with, to befriend, 707.

To become friendly, to make friends with.

Adj. Friendly, amicable, brotherly, fraternal, harmonious, cordial, neighborly, on good terms; on a friendly, a familiar, or an intimate footing; on friendly, &c., terms; well-affected.

Acquainted, familiar, intimate.

889. ENMITY, *see* Hate, 898, and Discord, 713.

Unfriendliness, alienation, estrangement.

Animosity, umbrage, pique hostility.

V. To be inimical, &c., to estrange, to fall out, alienate.

Adj. Inimical, unfriendly, at variance, hostile.

Firm, stanch, intimate, familiar, cordial, tried, devoted, lasting, fast, warm, ardent.

Adv. Friendly, amicably, &c.; on good or friendly terms.

890. FRIEND, well-wisher, bosom friend, favorer, patron, tutelary saint, good genius, advocate, partisan, *see* 711.

Neighbor, acquaintance, associate, compeer, comrade, companion, boon companion, schoolfellow, playfellow, playmate, shipmate, compatriot, countryman, fellow-countryman.

Host; guest, visitor.

891. ENEMY, foe, opponent, *see* 710.

---

892. SOCIALITY, sociability, sociableness, companionship, companionableness, intercourse, intercommunity.

Conviviality, good fellowship, hospitality, heartiness, festivity, merrymaking.

Society, association, copartnership, fraternity, sodality, coterie, 712, circle, clique.

An entertainment, party, levee, soiree.

Interview, assignation, appointment, visit, visiting, reception, 588.

V. To be sociable, &c., to associate with, keep company with, to club together, sort with, consort; make acquaintance with; to fraternize; to have dealings with.

To visit, pay a visit, interchange visits or cards, call upon, leave a card, make advances.

To entertain, give a party, &c.; to keep open house; to receive.

Adj. Sociable, social, companionable, neighborly, conversible, &c., on visiting terms, hospitable, convivial, festive.

893. SECLUSION, privacy, retirement, recess, retiredness, rustication.

Solitude, singleness, estrangement from the world, loneliness, lonesomeness, isolation, *see* Convent, &c., 1000.

Wilderness, depopulation.

EXCLUSION, excommunication, banishment, exile, ostracism, cut, inhospitality, inhospitableness, dissociability.

A recluse, hermit, cenobite, anchoret.

V. To be secluded, &c., to retire, to live retired, secluded, &c.; to keep aloof; to shut one's self up.

To refuse to associate with or acknowledge; repel, excommunicate, exclude, banish, exile, ostracize.

To depopulate, dispeople.

Adj. Secluded, sequestered, retired, private, domestic.

Unsociable, unsocial, dissocial, isolated, inhospitable, cynical.

Solitary, lonesome, isolated, single, estranged, unfrequented.

Unvisited, uninvited, friendless, deserted, abandoned, forlorn.

894. COURTESY, good manners, good breeding, mannerliness, urbanity, comity, civilization, politeness, civility, amenity, suavity, good temper, easy temper, gentleness, affability, obliging manner, amiability, good humor.

Compliment, fair words, salutation, reception, presentation,

895. DISCOURTESY, ill-breeding; ill, bad, or ungainly manners; rusticity, impoliteness, uncourtliness, rudeness, incivility, barbarism, misbehavior, roughness, ruggedness.

Bad or ill temper, churlishness, crabbedness, tartness, peevishness, moroseness, sullenness

introduction, greeting, recognition, welcome respect.

Obeisance, salutation, reverence, bow, courtesy, shaking hands, embrace, salute, kiss.

Valediction, *see* 292, Condolence, *see* 915.

V. To be courteous, civil, &c., to show courtesy, civility, &c.

To visit, wait upon, present one's self, pay one's respects.

To receive, do the honors, greet, welcome; hold or stretch out the hand; shake, press, or squeeze the hand.

To salute, kiss, embrace, nod to, smile upon, bow, courtesy, &c.

To pay one's respects; to pay homage or obeisance, &c.

To render polite, &c., to polish, civilize, humanize.

Adj. Courteous, civilized, polite, (refined,) well-bred, well-mannered, mannerly, urbane, gentlemanly, ladylike.

Gracious, affable, familiar, bland, obliging, mild, obsequious.

---

sulkiness, acrimony, sternness austerity, moodishness, asperity captiousness, sharpness, perversity, irascibility, *see* 901.

A bear, brute, blackguard, beast

V. To be rude, &c., frown scowl, insult, &c.

To render rude, &c., to brutalize.

Adj. Discourteous, uncourteous, uncourtly, ill-bred, ill-mannered, ill-behaved, unmannerly, unmannered, impolite, unpolite, unpolished, ungenteel, ungentlemanly, unladylike, uncivilized.

Uncivil, rude, ungracious, cool, repulsive, uncomplaisant, unaccommodating, ungainly, unceremonious, ungentle, rough, rugged, bluff, blunt, gruff, churlish, bearish, brutal, stern, harsh, austere.

Ill-tempered, out of temper or humor, crusty, tart, sour, crabbed, sharp, short, snappish, pettish, testy, peevish, waspish, captious, snarling, caustic, acrimonious, petulent, pert.

Perverse, cross-grained, wayward, humorsome, restiff, intractable, sulky, morose, scowling, surly, sullen, spleeny, spleenish, moody, dogged.

896. Congratulation, felicitation, wishing joy.

V. To congratulate, felicitate, give or wish joy, tender or offer one's congratulations, &c. To congratulate one's self, *see* 838.

Adj. Congratulatory, &c.

897. Love, fondness, liking, inclination, regard, good graces, partiality, predilection, admiration.

Affection, sympathy, fellow-feeling, heart, affectionateness.

Attachment, yearning, amour, passion, tender passion, flame, devotion, enthusiasm, transport of love, enchantment, infatuation, adoration, idolatry.

Attractiveness, &c., popularity.

A lover, suitor, follower, admirer, adorer, wooer, beau, sweet-

898. Hate, hatred, disaffection, disfavor, alienation, estrangement, odium, *see* Dislike, 867, and Animosity, 900.

Umbrage, pique, grudge, dudgeon, spleen, bitterness, ill blood, acrimony, malice, 907, implacability.

Disgust, repugnance, aversion, loathing, abomination, horror, detestation, antipathy, abhorrence.

Object of hatred; an abomination, aversion, antipathy.

V. To hate, dislike, disrelish

heart, flame, love, truelove, paramour.

Betrothed, affianced.

V. To love, like, fancy, care for, regard, revere, cherish, admire, dote on, adore, idolize.

To bear love to; to be in love with; to be taken, smitten, &c., with; to have, entertain, harbor, cherish, &c., a liking, love, &c., for.

To excite love; to win, gain, secure, &c., the love, affections, heart, &c.; to take the fancy of; to attract, attach, endear, seduce, charm, fascinate, captivate, enamour, enrapture.

To get into favor; to ingratiate one's self, insinuate one's self.

Adj. Loving, liking, &c., attached to, fond of, taken with, struck with, sympathetic, sympathizing with, charmed, captivated, fascinated, bewitched, lovelorn.

Affectionate, tender, loving, amorous, amatory, erotic, uxorious, ardent, passionate, devoted.

Loved, beloved, &c., dear, darling, favorite, 899, pet, popular.

Lovely, sweet, dear, charming, engaging, amiable, winning, attractive, adorable, enchanting, captivating, fascinating, bewitching.

&c., 867, loathe, nauseate, detest, abominate, shudder at, shrink from, recoil at, abhor.

To excite or provoke hatred; estrange, alienate, set against, to be hateful, &c.

Adj. Hating, &c., abhorrent, averse from, set against.

Unloved, disliked, unlamented, undeplored, unmourned, unbeloved, uncared for, unendeared, unvalued.

Crossed in love, forsaken, rejected, lovelorn, jilted.

Obnoxious, hateful, odious, repulsive, offensive, shocking, loathsome, sickening, nauseous, disgusting, abominable, horrid.

Invidious, spiteful, malicious.

Insulting, irritating, provoking.

---

899. Favorite, pet, dear, darling, jewel, idol, spoiled child.

900. Resentment, anger, wrath, indignation.

Soreness, dudgeon, moodiness, acerbity, bitterness, asperity, spleen, gall, heartburning, rankling, animosity.

Excitement, irritation, warmth, bile, choler, ire, fume, passion, fit, burst, explosion, storm, rage, fury.

Temper, petulance, angry mood, pique, miff, pet, umbrage.

Cause of umbrage; affront, provocation, offence, indignity, insult, 929.

V. To resent, take amiss, take offence, take umbrage, frown, scowl, lower

To chafe, mantle, fume; kindle, get, fall, or fly into a passion, &c., rage, storm, foam.

To cause or raise anger; to affront, offend, give offence or umbrage; discompose, fret, ruffle, nettle, irritate, provoke, chafe, wound, sting, incense, inflame, enrage, aggravate, imbitter, exasperate

Adj. Angry, wrath, boiling, fuming, raging, &c., nettled, ruffled, chafed, &c.

Fierce, rageful, furious, infuriate, mad with rage, fiery, savage, rankling, bitter, set against.

Relentless, ruthless, implacable, unpitying, pitiless, 919, inexorable, remorseless.

901. IRASCIBILITY, susceptibility, excitability, temper, petulance, irritability, fretfulness, testiness, peevishness, snappishness, hastiness, tartness, acerbity, pugnacity, *see* 895.

A shrew, vixen, termagant, virago; a tartar.

V. To be irascible, &c.; to take fire, flare up, &c., *see* 900.

Adj. Irascible, susceptible, excitable, irritable, fretful, fidgety, peevish, hasty, warm, hot, touchy, testy, pettish, waspish, petulant, fiery, passionate, choleric.

Ill-tempered, cross, churlish, sour, crabbed, out of sorts, fractious, splenetic.

Quarrelsome, querulous, disputatious, sarcastic, resentful, resentive, vindictive, pugnacious.

902. Expression of affection or love.

ENDEARMENT, caress, blandishment, fondling, embrace, salute, kiss.

Courtship, wooing, suit, addresses, flirtation.

Love letter, valentine.

V. To caress, fondle, pet, dandle, nestle, clasp, embrace, kiss, salute.

To court, woo, flirt.

To win the heart, affections, love, &c., of.

Adj. Caressing, &c., caressed, &c.

903. MARRIAGE, matrimony, wedlock, union, match, intermarriage.

Wedding, nuptials, espousals; leading to the altar.

A married man, a husband, spouse, bridegroom, consort.

A married woman, a wife, bride, helpmate, better half.

Monogamy, bigamy, polygamy.

V. To marry, wed, espouse.

To marry, join, give away.

Adj. Matrimonial, conjugal, connubial, nuptial, hymeneal, spousal, bridal, marital.

904. Unlawful marriage; a left-handed marriage.

CELIBACY, singleness, single blessedness.

An unmarried man, bachelor Cœlebs.

An unmarried woman, a spinster, maid, maiden, virgin.

V. To live single.

905. DIVORCE, separation, divorcement; widowhood.

A widow, relict, widower, dowager.

V. To live separate, to divorce.

2. DIFFUSIVE SYMPATHETIC AFFECTIONS.

906. BENEVOLENCE, good will, good nature, kindness, kindliness, benignity, beneficence, charity, humanity, fellow-feeling, sympathy, good feeling, kind-heartedness, amiability.

Charitableness, bounty, boun-

907. MALEVOLENCE, ill will unkindness, ill nature, malignity malice, maliciousness, spite, spitefulness, despite, despitefulness.

Uncharitableness, venom, gall, rancor, rankling, bitterness, acerbity, harshness, mordacity.

teousness, bountifulness, almsgiving.

Acts of kindness, a good turn, kind offices, good treatment.

V. To be benevolent, &c., to do good to, to benefit, confer a benefit, be of use, aid, assist, 707, render a service, treat well, to sympathize with.

Adj. Benevolent, well-meaning, kind, obliging, accommodating, kind-hearted, tender-hearted, charitable, beneficent, humane, clement, benignant.

Good-natured, well-natured, sympathizing, sympathetic, complacent, complaisant, amiable, gracious.

Kindly, well-meant, well intentioned, brotherly, fraternal.

Adv. With a good intention, with the best intentions.

Cruelty, hardness of heart, cruelness, brutality, brutishness, savageness, ferocity, barbarity, bloodthirstiness, truculence.

An ill turn, a bad turn, affront, *see* 900.

V. To injure, hurt, harm, molest, disoblige, do harm to, ill treat, maltreat, do an ill office to.

To worry, harass, oppress, grind, persecute, hunt down, dragoon, wreak one's malice on, *see* 830.

To bear or harbor malice against.

Adj. Malevolent, ill-disposed, evil-minded, ill-intentioned, (malicious,) maleficent, malign, malignant.

Ill-natured, disobliging, unfriendly, unkind, uncandid, uncharitable, ungracious, unamiable, unfriendly.

Surly, churlish, 895, grim, spiteful, despiteful, foul-mouthed, mordacious.

Cold, coldblooded, coldhearted, hardhearted.

Pitiless, unpitying, uncompassionate, merciless, unmerciful, inexorable, relentless, unrelenting, virulent.

Cruel, brutal, savage, ferocious, untamed, inhuman, barbarous, fell, ruthless, bloody, sanguinary, bloodstained, bloodthirsty, bloody-minded, sanguinolent, truculent, *see* 919.

Fiendish, fiendlike, infernal, demoniacal, diabolical, hellish.

Adv. Malevolently, &c., with bad intent or intention, de spitefully.

908. Malediction, curse, imprecation, denunciation, execration, anathema, ban, proscription, excommunication, commination, 909, fulmination.

Cursing, scolding, railing, Billingsgate language.

V. To curse, accurse, imprecate, scold, rail, execrate.

To denounce, proscribe, excommunicate, fulminate.

Adj Cursing, &c., cursed, &c.

909. Threat, menace, defiance, 715, abuse, (commination,) intimidation.

V. To threaten, menace, defy, fulminate; to intimidate, 860.

Adj. Threatening, menacing, minatory, abusive.

910. Philanthropy, humanity, public spirit.

Patriotism, nationality, love of country

911. Misanthropy, egotism, moroseness, *see* Selfishness, 943.

A misanthrope, egotist, cynic, man-hater.

A philanthropist, utilitarian, cosmopolite, citizen of the world, patriot.

Adj. Philanthropic, utilitarian, patriotic, &c., public-spirited.

Adj. Misanthropic, selfish, egotistical, morose, unpatriotic.

912. Benefactor, savior, good genius, tutelary saint, guardian angel, good Samaritan.

913. Maleficent being.

Evil-doer, evil-worker, mischief-maker, anarchist, firebrand, incendiary, evil genius, 978.

Savage, brute, ruffian, barbarian, catiff, desperado.

Monster, demon, imp, devil.

Fiend, bloodhound, beldam, Jezebel.

3. Special Sympathetic Affections.

914. Pity, compassion, commiseration, sympathy, fellow-feeling, tenderness, yearning, forbearance, mercy, clemency, lenience, long-suffering, quarter.

914. *a.* Pitilessness, mercilessness, unmercifulness, &c., *see* 907.

V. To pity, commiserate, compassionate, sympathize, feel for, enter into the feelings of, have pity, &c.; show or have mercy; to forbear, relent, spare, relax, give quarter.

To excite pity, touch, soften, melt, propitiate.

To ask for pity, mercy, &c.; to supplicate, implore, deprecate, appeal to, to cry for quarter, &c., beg one's life, kneel, fall on one's knees, &c.

Adj. Pitying, commiserating, &c., pitiful, compassionate, tender, clement, merciful, lenient, relenting, exorable, &c.; sympathetic, tender, tender-hearted.

915. Condolence, lamentation, lament, *see* 839, sympathy, consolation.

V. To condole with, console, sympathize; express, testify, &c., pity; to afford or supply consolation, lament with, weep with, &c., 839.

4. Retrospective Sympathetic Affections.

916. Gratitude, thankfulness, feeling of obligation.

Acknowledgment, recognition, thanksgiving, giving thanks, benediction.

Thanks, praise, pæan, 990.

Requital, thank-offering.

V. To be grateful, &c.; to thank, to give, render, return, offer, tender thanks, acknowledgments, &c.; to acknowledge, requite.

917. Ingratitude, thanklessness, oblivion of benefits.

V. To be ungrateful, &c.; to forget benefits.

Adj. Ungrateful, unmindful, unthankful, thankless.

Forgotten, unacknowledged, unthanked, unrequited, ill-requited, unrewarded.

To lie under an obligation, to be obliged, beholden, &c.

Adj. Grateful, thankful, obliged, beholden, indebted to, under obligation, &c.

918. Forgiveness, pardon, grace, remission, absolution, amnesty, oblivion, indulgence, reprieve.

Reconcilement, reconciliation, pacification, 723.

Excuse, exoneration, quittance, acquittal, propitiation, exculpation.

Longanimity, placability.

V. To forgive, pardon, excuse, pass over, overlook, forgive and forget, absolve, remit, reprieve, exculpate, exonerate.

To allow for; to make allowance for.

To conciliate, propitiate, placate, make it up, reconcile.

Adj. Forgiving, &c., placable.

Forgiven, &c., unresented.

919. Revenge, vengeance, avengement, retaliation.

Rancor, vindictiveness, implacability, Nemesis.

V. To revenge, take revenge, avenge.

Adj. Revengeful, vindictive, vengeful, rancorous, unforgiving, pitiless, unrelenting, implacable, rigorous.

920. Jealousy, jealousness.

V. To be jealous, &c.; to view with jealousy.

Adj. Jealous, jaundiced, yellow-eyed, unrevenged, horn-mad.

921. Envy, rivalry.

V. To envy.

Adj. Envious, invidious.

Section IV. MORAL AFFECTIONS.

1. Moral Obligation.

922. Right, what ought to be, what should be.

Justice, equity, equitableness, fitness, fairness, fair play, impartiality, reasonableness, propriety.

Morality, morals, ethics, &c., *see* Duty, 926.

V. To be right, just, &c.

To deserve, merit; to be worthy of, to be entitled to, *see* 924.

Adj. Right, just, equitable, fair, equal, even-handed, legitimate, justifiable, rightful, fit, proper, becoming, &c., *see* Duty, 926.

Deserved, merited, condign, entitled to, 924.

Adv. Rightly, in justice, in equity, fairly, &c.

923. Wrong, what ought not to be, what should not be.

Injustice, unfairness, foul play, partiality, favor, favoritism, party spirit, 925, unreasonableness, unlawfulness, 964, encroachment, imposition, &c.

V. To be wrong, unjust, &c.; to favor, lean towards, to encroach, impose upon, &c.

Adj. Wrong, unjust, unfair, undue, inequitable, unequal, partial, unreasonable, unfit, immoral, *see* 945.

Unjustified, unjustifiable, unwarranted, unallowed, unauthorized, unallowable.

Adv. Wrongly, &c

924. Dueness, due.

Right, privilege, prerogative, title, claim, birthright, immunity, license, liberty, franchise.

Sanction, authority, warranty, tenure, bond, security, constitution, charter.

A claimant, appellant.

V. To be due, &c., to.

To have a right to, to be entitled to, to have a claim upon, a title to, &c.; to deserve, merit, be worthy of, to deserve richly.

To demand, claim, call upon, exact, insist on, challenge, make a point of, enforce, put in force, use a right.

To appertain to, belong to, &c., 777.

To lay claim to, assert, assume, arrogate, make good, vindicate a claim, &c.

To give or confer a right; to entitle, authorize, warrant, sanction, license, legalize, ordain, prescribe.

Adj. Having a right to, a claim to, &c.; entitled to; deserving, meriting.

Privileged, allowed, sanctioned, warranted, authorized, permitted, ordained, prescribed.

Prescriptive, presumptive, absolute, indefeasible, unalienable, inalienable, imprescriptible, inviolable.

Condign, merited, deserved.

Allowable, permissible, lawful, legitimate, legal, legalized, 963, constitutional, proper, equitable, unexceptionable, reasonable, 922.

925. Absence of right.

Undueness, unlawfulness, impropriety, unfitness.

Falseness, spuriousness, emptiness or invalidity of title, illegitimacy.

Loss of right, disfranchisement.

Usurpation, violation, breach, encroachment, stretch, relaxation.

V. Not to be due, &c., to; to be undue, &c.

To infringe, encroach, violate; to stretch or strain a point; to usurp.

To disfranchise, disentitle; to relax, to disqualify, invalidate.

To misbecome, misbehave, 945.

Adj. Undue, unlawful, unconstitutional.

Unauthorized, unwarranted, unentitled, disentitled, unqualified, unsanctioned, unjustified, unprivileged, unchartered, illegitimate, spurious, false, usurped, unchartered, unfulfilled.

Undeserved, unmerited, unearned.

Improper, unmeet, unbecoming, unfit, misbecoming, unseemly.

---

926. Duty, what ought to be done; moral obligation, accountableness, liability, responsibility, bounden duty; dueness.

Allegiance, fealty, tie, office, function, province, post, engagement.

Morality, morals, conscience, accountableness, conscientiousness

927. Dereliction of duty, guilt, &c., *see* 947.

Exemption, freedom, irresponsibility, immunity, liberty, license, release, exoneration, excuse, dispensation, absolution, franchise, renunciation, discharge.

Non-observance, non-performance, neglect, infraction, viola-

Dueness, propriety, fitness, seemliness.

The thing, the proper thing, a case of conscience.

Science of morals: Ethics, Moral or Ethical Philosophy, Casuistry.

Observance, fulfilment, discharge, performance, acquittal, satisfaction, redemption, good behavior.

V To be the duty of, to be due to; ought to be; to be incumbent on, to behoove, befit, become, beseem, belong to, pertain to, devolve on, to owe to one's self.

To be, or stand, or lie under the obligation, to be beholden or indebted to, to have to answer for, to be accountable for.

To impose a duty or obligation; to require, exact, saddle with, prescribe, assign, call upon, look to, oblige; must be.

tion, transgression, failure, evasion.

V. To be exempt, free, at liberty, released, excused, exonerated, absolved, &c.

To exempt, release, excuse, exonerate, absolve, give absolution, acquit, free, set at liberty, discharge, set aside, let off, license, dispense with; to give dispensation.

To violate, break through, break, infringe, set at nought, slight, neglect, trample on, evade, renounce, repudiate, escape, transgress, fail.

Adj. Exempt, free, released, at liberty, absolved, exonerated, excused, let off, discharged, licensed, acquitted, unencumbered, dispensed, scot free.

Irresponsible, unaccountable, unanswerable, unbound

To do one's duty, to enter upon a duty, to perform, observe, fulfil, discharge, adhere to; acquit one's self of, satisfy a duty, &c., to redeem one's pledge.

Adj. Obligatory, binding, behooving, incumbent on, chargeable on, meet, due to.

Being under obligation, obliged by, bound by, beholden to, tied by, saddled with, indebted to.

Amenable, liable, accountable, responsible, answerable.

Right, proper, fit, meet, due, seemly, fitting, befitting.

Moral, ethical, casuistical, conscientious.

2. Moral Sentiments.

928. Respect, deference, reverence, honor, esteem, veneration, decorum.

Homage, fealty, obeisance, genuflection, kneeling, presenting arms, &c., *see* 896, prostration, obsequiousness, devotion, worship, 990.

V. To respect, honor, reverence, defer to, pay respect, deference, &c., to render honor to, look up

929. Disrespect, irreverence, dishonor, diparagement, slight, neglect, disesteem, superciliousness, contumely, indignity, insult.

Ridicule, 856, derision, mockery, scoffing, sibilation.

A jeer, gibe, hiss, hoot, fling, flout, grin; *see* Contempt, 940.

V. To treat with disrespect, &c., to disparage, dishonor, slight.

to esteem, revere, to think much of, to think highly of, to venerate, hallow.

To pay homage to, kneel to, bend the knee to, present arms, fall down before, prostrate one's self.

Adj. Respectful, reverential, obsequious, ceremonious, cap in hand, &c.

Respected, honored, hallowed, &c.

disregard, make light of, hold in no esteem, esteem of no account, set at nought, speak slightingly of, set down, pass by, overlook, look down upon, *see* 930.

To deride, scoff, sneer at, laugh at, ridicule, 856, mock, jeer, taunt, hiss, hoot.

Adj. Disrespectful, slighting, disparaging, dishonoring, &c., scornful, 940, irreverent, supercilious, contumelious, deriding, derisive, aweless.

Unrespected, unworshipped, unregarded, disregarded.

Adv. Disrespectfully, cavalierly, &c.

930. Contempt, disdain, scorn, contumely, slight, sneer, fling, spurn; a byword.

Scornfulness, disdainfulness, haughtiness, contemptuousness.

V. To despise, contemn, scorn, disdain, scout, spurn, look down upon, disregard, slight, make light of, hold cheap, hold in contempt, hoot, trample upon.

Adj. Contemptuous, disdainful, scornful, derisive, supercilious.

Contemptible, despicable, poor, &c., *see* 643, unenvied.

931. Approbation, approval, esteem, admiration, estimation, good opinion, appreciation, regard, account, popularity.

Commendation, praise, good word; meed or tribute of praise, encomium, eulogium, eulogy, panegyric.

Laudation, applause, clapping of hands, acclamation; pæan, benediction, blessing.

V. To approve, think well of, think highly of, esteem, appreciate, value, admire, countenance.

To commend, speak well of; recommend, praise, laud, compliment, clap, applaud, cheer, panegyrize, eulogize, cry up, extol, glorify, magnify, exalt, bless.

To redound to the honor or praise of; to do credit to; to ring with the praises of.

To deserve praise, &c., to be praised, &c.

Adj. Approving, &c., commendatory, complimentary, laud-

932. Disapprobation, disapproval, blame, censure, odium, disesteem, depreciation, detraction, condemnation.

Reprobation, insinuation, animadversion, reflection, stricture, objection, exception, criticism, correction.

Satire, sneer, fling, taunt, sarcasm, lampoon, cavil, pasquinade, invective, castigation.

Remonstrance, reprehension, reproof, admonition, expostulation, reproach, rebuke, reprimand.

Evil speaking, hard words, cutting words, foul language.

Upbraiding, abuse, vituperation, scolding, objurgation, railing, reviling, contumely, execration, 908.

A set down, trimming, frown.

A lecture, curtain lecture, blow up, jeremiade, philippic; clamor outcry, hue and cry, hiss, hissing sibilation.

A scold, shrew, vixen.

atory, panegyrical, eulogistic, encomiastic.

Approved, praised, uncensured, unimpeached, admired, &c., deserving or worthy of praise, &c., praiseworthy, commendable, plausible.

V. To disapprove, dispraise, find fault with, criticize, insinuate, cut up, carp at, cavil, object to, take exception to, animadvert upon, protest against, frown upon.

To disparage, depreciate, speak ill of, decry, vilify, defame, detract, *see* 934, revile, satirize, lampoon, inveigh against.

To blame, lay or cast blame upon; to reflect upon; to censure; pass censure on; impugn, censure, brand, stigmatize, reprobate.

To reprehend, admonish, remonstrate, expostulate, reprove, lecture, pull up, take up, set down, twit, taunt, reprimand, reproach, load with reproaches, rebuke.

To chide, scold, rate, objurgate, upbraid, vituperate, abuse; exclaim against, rail at, revile, blow up; castigate, chastise, lash.

To cry out against, cry down, run down, clamor, hiss, hoot, to accuse, *see* 938, to find guilty.

To incur blame; to excite disapprobation; to scandalize, shock, revolt.

To take blame; to stand corrected.

Adj. Disapproving, &c., condemnatory, damnatory, reproachful, abusive, objurgatory, clamorous, vituperative.

Censorious, critical, carping, satirical, sarcastic, cynical, hypercritical, captious, sharp, cutting, biting, severe, squeamish, fastidious, straightlaced, &c., 868.

Disapproved, &c., unapproved, unblest, unlamented, unbewailed, &c.

Worthy of blame, (blameworthy,) uncommendable, exceptionable, *see* 649, 945.

933. Flattery, adulation, sycophancy, blandishment, cajolery, fawning, wheedling, coaxing, blandiloquence.

Incense, honeyed words, flummery.

V. To flatter, wheedle, cajole, fawn upon, coax, humor, court, pay court to.

Adj. Flattering, adulatory, oily, smooth, unctuous, fair spoken, servile, sycophantic, fulsome; courtierly, courtier-like.

935. Flatterer, eulogist, encomiast, sycophant, hanger on, courtier, parasite.

934. Detraction, obloquy scurrility, scandal, defamation aspersion, traducement, slander, calumny, backbiting; criticism.

Libel, lampoon, sarcasm.

V. To detract, asperse, depreciate, run down, blacken, defame brand, malign, backbite, libel lampoon, traduce, slander, calumniate.

Adj. Detracting, &c., libellous scurrilous, scurrile, sarcastic, cynical, &c., *see* 932, foul-tongued, foul-mouthed, slanderous, defamatory, calumnious.

936. Detractor, critic, censor, caviller, carper, defamer backbiter, slanderer, traducer, libeller, calumniator.

937. VINDICATION, reply, justification, exoneration, exculpation, acquittal.

Extenuation, palliation, softening.

Plea, excuse, apology, defence, gloss, varnish, salvo, 617.

V. To vindicate, justify, exculpate, acquit, clear, set right, exonerate.

To extenuate, palliate, excuse, apologize, varnish, slur, gloss over.

To plead, advocate, defend, speak for, make good, vindicate, say in defence, contend for.

Adj. Vindicatory, exculpatory; vindicating, &c.

Excusable, defensible, pardonable, venial, specious, plausible, justifiable.

938. ACCUSATION, charge, imputation, inculpation, crimination, recrimination, invective, &c., 932.

Denunciation, denouncement, challenge, indictment, libel, delation, citation, arraignment, impeachment, bill of indictment.

V. To accuse, charge, tax, impute, taunt with, slur, reproach, criminate, inculpate, implicate, &c., *see* 932.

To inform against; to indict, denounce, arraign, impeach, challenge, show up, cite, summons.

Adj. Accusing, &c., accusatory, accusative, imputative, criminatory, accusable, imputable.

Indefensible, inexcusable, unpardonable, unjustifiable.

3. MORAL CONDITIONS.

939. PROBITY, integrity, uprightness, honesty, faith, good faith, fairness, honor, fair play, justice, equity, equitableness, impartiality, principle, fidelity, incorruptibility.

Trustworthiness, trustiness, uncorruptedness, truth, candor, veracity, 545, straightforwardness, singleness of heart.

Conscientiousness, punctiliousness, nicety, scrupulosity, punctuality.

Dignity, reputableness, *see* 873.

A man of honor, a gentleman, a man of his word.

V. To be honorable, &c.; to keep one's word; to deal honorably, impartially, fairly, &c.

Adj. Upright, honest, honorable, fair, right, just, equitable, impartial, even-handed, square, loyal, *see* 944.

Trustworthy, trusty, uncorrupt, true, straightforward, ingenuous, frank, open-hearted.

940. IMPROBITY, bad faith, unfairness, infidelity, faithlessness, want of faith, dishonesty, disloyalty, onesidedness, disingenuousness, shabbiness, littleness, meanness, baseness, vileness, abjection, turpitude, insidiousness, knavery, knavishness, fraud, &c., 545.

Disgrace, ignominy, infamy, tarnish, blot, stain, spot, pollution, derogation, degradation, &c., *see* Dishonor, 874.

Perfidy, perfidiousness, treason, high treason, perjury, apostasy, backsliding, breach of faith, defection, disloyalty, foul play, double dealing.

V. To be of bad faith, dishonest, &c.; to play false, break one's word, faith, &c., betray, forswear, shuffle, 545.

To disgrace one's self, dishonor one's self, stoop, demean one's self, lose caste.

Adj. Dishonest, unfair, fraudu

Conscientious, high-principled, high-minded, scrupulous, nice, punctilious, over-scrupulous, punctual, inviolable, inviolate, unviolated, unbroken, unbetrayed.

Chivalrous, unbought, unbribed, unstained, stainless, untarnished, unsullied, untainted, unperjured,

---

lent, knavish, false, faithless, unfaithful, foul, slippery, double, crooked, unscrupulous, insidious, treacherous, perfidious, false-hearted, perjured.

Base, vile, grovelling, dirty, scurvy, low, mean, paltry, pitiful, beggarly, inglorious, disgraceful, dishonorable, derogatory, disreputable, unhandsome, unbecoming, unbefitting, ungentlemanly, unmanly, undignified, base-minded, recreant, abject, low-minded, blackguard.

941. Knave, truant, trimmer, time-server, time-pleaser, turncoat. Apostate, renegade, traitor, arch-traitor, recreant, miscreant.

942. Disinterestedness, nobleness, generosity, high-mindedness, elevation, liberality, greatness, loftiness, exaltation, magnanimity, chivalry, chivalrous spirit, heroism, sublimity.

Self-denial, self-abnegation, self-sacrifice, devotion, stoicism.

Adj. Disinterested, generous, unselfish, handsome, liberal, noble, great, high, high-minded, elevated, lofty, exalted, spirited, stoical, self-devoted, magnanimous, chivalrous, heroic, sublime.

Unbought, unbribed, pure, uncorrupted, incorruptible.

943. Selfishness, egotism, egoism, self-love, self-indulgence, self-worship, self-interest.

Illiberality, meanness, baseness.

A time-server, fortune-hunter, jobber.

V. To be selfish, &c., narrow-minded.

Adj. Selfish, egotistical, egoistical, self-seeking, illiberal, mean, ungenerous, narrow-minded, mercenary, 819.

Worldly, earthly, mundane, time-serving, worldly-minded.

944. Virtue, goodness, righteousness, morality, morals, rectitude, correctness, dutifulness, conscientiousness, integrity, probity, 939, uprightness, nobleness.

Merit, worth, worthiness, desert, excellence, credit, self-control, self-conquest, self-government.

Well doing, good actions, good behavior, the discharge, fulfilment, or performance of duty; a well-spent life.

V. To be virtuous, &c.; to act well; to do, fulfil, perform, or discharge one's duty, to acquit one's self, to practise virtue; to command or master one's passions, *see* 926.

945. Vice, wickedness, sin, iniquity, unrighteousness, demerit, unworthiness, worthlessness.

Immorality, incorrectness, impropriety, indecorum, laxity, looseness of morals, want of principle, obliquity, demoralization, depravity, obduracy, hardness of heart, brutality, corruption, pollution, dissoluteness, grossness, baseness, knavery, roguery, rascality, villany, profligacy, flagrancy, atrocity.

Criminality, &c., *see* Guilt, 947.

Infirmity, weakness, feebleness, frailty, imperfection, error, weak side, blind side, foible, failing, failure, defect, deficiency, indiscretion, peccability.

Adj. Virtuous, good, meritorious, deserving worthy, correct, dutiful, duteous, moral, righteous &c., *see* 939, laudable, well-intentioned, praiseworthy, excellent, admirable, sterling, pure, noble.

Exemplary, matchless, peerless, saintly, saint-like, heaven-born, angelic, seraphic, godlike.

V. To be vicious, &c., to sin, commit sin, do amiss, err, transgress, go astray, misdemean or misconduct one's self, misbehave; to fall, lapse, slip, trip, offend, trespass.

*Adj.** Vicious, sinful, wicked, immoral, unprincipled, demoralized, unconscionable, worthless, unworthy, good for nothing, graceless, heartless, virtueless, unduteous.

Wrong, culpable, guilty, naughty, incorrect, criminal, dissolute, corrupt, profligate, depraved, abandoned, graceless, shameless, recreant, villanous, sunk, lost, obdurate, incorrigible, irreclaimable.

Weak, frail, lax, infirm, imperfect, indiscreet, erring, transgressing, sinning, &c. peccable.

Blamable, blameworthy, uncommendable, discreditable disreputable, exceptionable.

Indecorous, unseemly, sinister, base, scurvy, foul, vile, felonious, nefarious, scandalous, infamous, villanous, heinous, grave, flagrant, atrocious, satanic, diabolic, hellish, infernal, fiend-like, demoniacal.

Unpardonable, indefensible, inexcusable, irremissible, inexpiable.

Adv. Wrong, &c.; without excuse.

946. Innocence, guiltlessness, blamelessness, sinlessness, harmlessness, innocuousness, incorruption, impeccability.

A lamb.

V. To be innocent, &c.

Adj. Innocent, guiltless, faultless, sinless, clear, spotless, stainless, immaculate, unspotted, innocuous, unblemished, untarnished, unsullied, undefiled.

Inculpable, unculpable, unblamed, blameless, irreproachable, irreprovable, irreprehensible, unreproached, unimpeachable, unimpeached, unexceptionable, unerring.

Harmless, inoffensive, dove-like, lamb-like, pure, uncorrupt, uncorrupted, undefiled, undepraved, undebauched, unhardened, unreproved.

947. Guilt, guiltiness, culpability, criminality, sinfulness.

Misconduct, misbehavior, misdoing, malpractice, deviation from rectitude, dereliction.

Indiscretion, lapse, slip, trip, fault, error, flaw, blot, omission, failure.

Misdeed, offence, trespass, transgression, misdemeanor, delinquency, felony, sin, crime, enormity, atrocity.

---

* Most of these adjectives are applicable both to the act and to the agent.

Adv. Innocently, &c., with clean hands, with a clear conscience.

948. Saint, lamb, worthy, example, pattern, mirror, model, paragon, phœnix, hero, demigod, seraph, angel, *see* Perfection, 650.

949. Sinner, evil-doer, culprit, delinquent, criminal, malefactor, wrong-doer, outlaw, felon, convict, outcast.

Knave, rogue, rascal, scoundrel, scapegrace, varlet, blackguard, vagabond, recreant, outlaw, *see* 940.

Villain, ruffian, miscreant, caitiff, wretch, monster, reptile, urchin, imp, demon, cutthroat, incendiary.

950. Penitence, contrition, compunction, regret, 833, repentance, remorse.

Self-reproach, self-reproof, self-accusation, self-condemnation, qualms or prickings of conscience.

Confession, acknowledgment, apology.

V. To repent, regret, rue, repine, deplore.

To confess, acknowledge, apologize, humble one's self, to reclaim, to turn from sin.

Adj. Penitent, repentant, contrite, repenting, &c., self-accusing; self-convicted.

Not hardened, unhardened, reclaimed.

951. Impenitence, obduracy, recusance, hardness of heart, a seared conscience, induration.

V. To be impenitent, &c.; to steel or harden the heart.

Adj. Impenitent, uncontrite, obdurate, hard, hardened, seared, recusant, relentless, unrepentant, graceless, lost, incorrigible, irreclaimable, unatoned, unreclaimed, unreformed, unrepented.

952. Atonement, reparation, compromise, composition, compensation, 30, quittance; propitiation, expiation, redemption.

Amends, apology, satisfaction, peace-offering, sin-offering, scapegoat, sacrifice.

Penance, fasting, maceration, sackcloth and ashes, lustration, purgation.

V. To atone, expiate, propitiate, make amends, redeem, make good, absolve, do penance, apologize, purge.

Adj. Propitiatory, piacular, expiatory.

4. Moral Practice.

953. Temperance, moderation, forbearance, abnegation, self-denial, self-conquest, self-control, sobriety, frugality.

Abstinence, abstemiousness.

V. To be temperate, &c; to abstain, forbear, refrain, deny one's self, spare.

954. Intemperance, epicurism, sensuality, luxury, animalism, pleasure, effeminacy; the lap of pleasure or luxury; indulgence, self-indulgence, voluptuousness.

Excess, dissipation, licentiousness, debauchery, dissoluteness,

Adj. Temperate, moderate, sober, frugal, sparing, abstemious, abstinent, Pythagorean, vegetarian.

———

brutishness, revels, debauch, orgies.

V. To be intemperate, sensual, &c.

To indulge, exceed, revel; give a loose to indulgence, sensuality, &c., to wallow in voluptuousness, luxury, &c.; to plunge into dissipation.

To pamper, pander, slake.

Adj. Intemperate, sensual, pampered, self-indulgent, licentious, wild, dissolute, rakish, debauched, brutish, epicurean, voluptuous, swinish.

Indulged, pampered.

A debauchee, free-liver, a man of pleasure, voluptuary, rake, a votary of Epicurus, *see* 962.

955. Asceticism, austerity, mortification, maceration, sackcloth and ashes, flagellation, &c., martyrdom.

An ascetic, anchoret, martyr; a recluse, hermit, &c., 893.

Adj. Ascetic, puritanical.

956. Fasting, fast, spare diet, Lent, famishment, starvation.

V. To fast, starve.

Adj. Fasting, lenten, &c., unfed.

957. Gluttony, epicurism, greediness, good cheer, high living, voracity.

A glutton, epicure, cormorant, gormand.

V. To gormandize, gorge, stuff, overeat, pamper.

Adj. Gluttonous, greedy, gormandizing, swinish, pampered, over-fed.

958. Sobriety, teetotalism, hydropathy.

A water drinker teetotaler, or teetotalist, hydropathist.

V. To take the pledge.

———

959. Drunkenness, ebriety, inebriety, inebriation, intoxication, drinking, toping, tippling, sottishness, bacchanals, compotation.

A drunkard, sot, toper, tippler, bibber, wine-bibber, dram-drinker, reveller, carouser, bacchanal, bacchanalian.

V. To drink, tipple, tope; to guzzle, swill, carouse, get drunk, &c.; to take to drinking, &c.

To inebriate, intoxicate.

Adj. Drunk, drunken, tipsy, intoxicated, in liquor, inebriated, mellow, overcome, overtaken, dead-drunk, disguised.

Sottish, bacchanal, bacchanalian.

960. Purity, modesty, decency, decorum, delicacy, continence, chastity, pudicity.

Adj. Pure, modest, delicate, decent, decorous.

961. Impurity, immodesty, grossness, coarseness, indelicacy, indecency, obscenity, ribaldry, smut, obsceneness, smuttiness, bawdiness, bawdry.

Chaste, continent, Platonic, honest.

Concupiscence, lust, carnality, lewdness, pruriency, lechery, lasciviousness, voluptuousness, lubricity.

Incontinence, intrigue, gallantry, debauchery, libertinism, fornication.

Seduction, defloration, violation, rape, adultery, incest, stupration.

A seraglio, harem, brothel, bagnio, stew.

V. To intrigue, to debauch, &c.

Adj. Impure, immodest, indecorous, indelicate, indecent, loose, coarse, gross, equivocal, ribald, obscene.

Concupiscent, prurient, lickerish, rampant, lustful, lascivious, lecherous, libidinous, erotic.

Unchaste, light, wanton, debauched, dissolute, incontinent, meretricious, rakish, gallant, dissipated, adulterous, incestuous.

962. A LIBERTINE, voluptuary, man of pleasure, rake, debauchee, gallant, seducer, fornicator, adulterer.

A courtesan, strumpet, harlot, woman of the town, street walker, Cyprian.

Concubine, mistress, doxy.

Pimp, pander, bawd, procuress.

5. INSTITUTIONS.

963. LEGALITY, legitimateness, legitimacy.

Law, code, constitution, pandect, enactment, edict, statute, rule, order, ordinance, injunction, precept, regulation, decree.

Legal process, form, formula, formality, rite.

Science of law: Jurisprudence, Legislation, Codification.

Equity, common law, law of nations, international law, civil law, canon law, statute law, ecclesiastical law.

V. To enact, ordain, enjoin, prescribe, order, decree; to pass a law, issue an edict or decree; to legislate, codify.

Adj. Legal, according to law, legitimate, constitutional.

Legislative, statutory.

Adv. Legally, &c.

964. Absence or violation of law.

ILLEGALITY, arbitrariness, violence, brute force, despotism.

Mob law, lynch law, club law.

Informality, unlawfulness, illegitimacy.

Smuggling, poaching.

V. To smuggle, run, poach.

Adj. Illegal, unlawful, illicit, illegitimate, injudicial, unofficial, unauthorized, unchartered, unconstitutional, informal, contraband.

Arbitrary, extrajudicial, despotic, irresponsible, unanswerable unaccountable.

965. JURISDICTION, judicature, administration of justice.

The executive; municipality, magistracy, police, police

Sheriff, officer, constable, beadle.

Adj. Juridical, judicial, forensic, municipal, executive,

966. TRIBUNAL, court, bench, judicatory, senate house court of law, court of justice.

Assize, sessions, court martial.

967. JUDGE, justice, justiciary, chancellor, magistrate arbiter, arbitrator, umpire, referee.

Prosecutor, plaintiff, accuser, appellant.

Defendant, panel, prisoner, the accused.

968. LAWYER, the bar, advocate, counsellor, counsel, pleader, special pleader, conveyancer, civilian, barrister, jurist, jurisconsult, notary, notary public, attorney, solicitor.

969. LAWSUIT, suit, action, cause, trial, litigation, 713.

Denunciation, citation, arraignment, persecution, indictment, impeachment, apprehension, arrest, committal, imprisonment, *see* 751.

Pleadings, writ, summons, plea, bill, affidavit, &c.

Verdict, sentence, judgment, finding, decree, arbitrament, adjudication, award.

V. To go to law; to take the law of; to appeal to the law; to join issue; file a bill, file a claim.

To denounce, cite, apprehend, arraign, sue, prosecute, bring to trial, indict, attach, distrain, to commit, give in charge or custody, throw into prison.

To try, hear a cause, sit in judgment.

To pronounce, find, judge, sentence, give judgment; bring in a verdict; doom, to arbitrate, adjudicate, award, report.

970. ACQUITTAL, absolution, *see* Pardon, 918, clearance, discharge, release, reprieve, respite.

Exemption from punishment; impunity.

V. To acquit, absolve, clear, discharge, release, reprieve, respite.

Adj. Acquitted, &c.

Uncondemned, unpunished, unchastised.

971. CONDEMNATION, conviction, proscription; death warrant.

Attainder, attainment.

V. To condemn, convict, cast, find guilty, proscribe.

Adj. Condemnatory, &c.

972. PUNISHMENT, chastisement, castigation, correction, chastening, discipline, infliction.

Retribution, requital, reward, 973.

Imprisonment, 751, transportation, exile, 297, the tread mill, galleys; penal settlement.

Beating, lash, flagellation, flogging, &c., pillory, running the gantlet.

Execution, hanging, beheading, decollation, guillotine, crucifixion, impalement, &c., martyrdom.

V. To punish, chastise, castigate, chasten, correct, inflict punishment.

To execute, hang, behead, decapitate, decollate, guillotine, shoot, gibbet, hang, draw and quarter; break on the wheel; torture, &c.

Adj. Punishing, &c., penal, punitory, punitive, inflictive.

973. Reward, recompense, remuneration, meed, premium, indemnity, indemnification, compensation, reparation, requital, retribution, quittance, acknowledgement, amends, atonement, redress, consideration, return, tribute.

Crown, laurel, bays, cross, medal, ribbon, decoration, &c.

V. To reward, recompense, requite, remunerate, compensate, make amends, atone, satisfy, acknowledge, acquit one's self.

Adj. Remunerative, compensatory, retributive, reparatory.

974. Penalty, pain, penance. Fine, mulct, amercement, forfeit, forfeiture, damages, sequestration, confiscation.

V. To fine, mulct, amerce, confiscate, sequestrate.

975. Instrument of punishment.

Scourge, rod, cane, stick, ratan, cane, switch, ferule, birch, cudgel.

Whip, lash, strap, thong, cowhide.

Pillory, stocks, whipping-post.

Rack, wheel, stake, tree, block, scaffold, gallows, gibbet, axe, guillotine, halter.

Executioner, hangman, headsman.

Section V. RELIGIOUS AFFECTIONS.

1. Superhuman Beings and Regions.

976. Deity, Divinity, Godhead, (the Divine Nature or Existence,) Omnipotence, Providence.

Quality of being divine; divineness, divinity.

God, Lord, Jehovah, The Almighty; The Supreme Being; The First Cause; The Author, &c., of all things, The Infinite, The Eternal.

Attributes and Perfections; Infinite Power, Wisdom, Goodness, Justice, Truth, Mercy, Omnipotence, Omniscience, Omnipresence, Unity, Immutability, Holiness, Glory, Majesty, Sovereignty, Infinity, Eternity.

The Trinity, The Holy Trinity.

God the Father, The Maker, The Creator, The Preserver.

(Functions.) Creation, Preservation, Divine Government, Theocracy, Providence, the ways, the dispensations, the visitations of Providence.

The Son of God, Christ, Jesus, The Messiah, The Savior, The Redeemer, The Mediator, The Intercessor, The Advocate, The Judge, The Anointed, The Son of Man, The Lamb of God, The Word, Immanuel.

The Incarnation, The Hypostatic Union.

(Functions.) Salvation, Redemption, Atonement, Propitiation, Mediation, Intercession, Judgment.

THE HOLY GHOST, The Holy Spirit, Paraclete, The Comforter, The Spirit of Truth, The Dove.

(Functions.) Inspiration, Unction, Regeneration, Sanctification Consolation.

V. To create, uphold, preserve, govern, &c.

To atone, redeem, save, propitiate, mediate, &c.

To predestinate, elect, call, ordain, bless, justify, sanctify, glorify, &c.

Adj. Almighty, &c., holy, hallowed, sacred, divine, heavenly, celestial.

Superhuman, ghostly, spiritual, supernatural, theocratic.

977. Beneficent spirits.

ANGEL, archangel.

The heavenly host, the host of heaven, the sons of God.

Seraphim, cherubim, ministering spirits, morning stars.

Adj. Angelic, seraphic.

978. Maleficent spirits.

SATAN, the devil.

The tempter, the evil one, the author of evil, the wicked one, the old serpent, the prince of darkness; the foul fiend, the arch-fiend.

Fallen angels, unclean spirits, devils.

Adj. Satanic, diabolic, devilish.

Mythological and other fabulous Deities and Powers.

979. JUPITER, Jove, &c. &c.

Good genius, demiurge, fairy, fay, sylph.

Adj. Fairy-like, sylph-like, sylphid.

980. DEMON, evil genius, fiend.

Fury, harpy, siren, satyr, &c.

Vampire, imp, elf, dwarf, urchin, sprite, &c.

Ghost, spectre, apparition, spirit, shade, vision, goblin, hobgoblin.

Adj. Supernatural, ghostly, elfish; unearthly, spectral, ghost-like, fiendish, fiend-like, impish; demoniacal; haunted.

981. HEAVEN, the kingdom of heaven; the kingdom of God, the heavenly kingdom; the throne of God, the presence of God.

Paradise, Eden, the abode of the blessed; celestial bliss, glory, &c.

Mythological heaven, Olympus, mythological paradise, Elysium.

Resurrection, 163, translation, apotheosis.

982. HELL, bottomless pit, place of torment; the habitation of fallen angels, Pandemonium.

Hell fire, everlasting fire.

Purgatory, limbo, abyss.

Mythological hell; Tartarus, Hades, Pluto, Avernus.

The infernal regions, the shades below, the realms of Pluto.

Adj. Hellish, infernal, stygian.

Adj. Heavenly, celestial, supernal, unearthly, from on high, paradisiacal.

2. Religious Doctrines.

983. Religious knowledge.

Theology, (natural and revealed,) divinity, religion, monotheism.

Creed, belief, faith, persuasion, tenet, dogma, articles of faith, declaration, profession or confession of faith.

983. *a.* Orthodoxy, true faith, Christianity, Christendom; (supernaturalism, theism.)

A theologian, a divine.

The Church, the Catholic or Universal Church; the Church of Christ, the disciples or followers of Christ, the Christian community.

Adj. Theological, divine, religious.

Orthodox, sound, faithful, true, scriptural, Christian.

984. Heterodoxy, heresy, schism, latitudinarianism, (liberalism, rationalism, naturalism,) recusancy, backsliding, apostasy. Atheism, *see* 988.

Bigotry, fanaticism, superstition, credulity, 486, idolatry.

Dissent 489, sectarianism, sectarism.

(The Papacy, Romanism, Protestantism, Pelagianism, Arianism, Calvinism.)

Paganism, heathenism, mythology, polytheism, dualism, tritheism, pantheism.

Judaism, Mahometanism, Islamism, &c., &c.

A heretic, pagan, heathen, pantheist, idolater, schismatic, bigot, fanatic.

A nonconformist, separatist, dissenter, sectarian, sectary.

Adj. Heterodox, heretical, schismatic.

Sectarian, dissenting, dissident.

Bigoted, fanatical, superstitious, idolatrous.

Pagan, heathen, gentile, pantheistic.

985. Revelation, Word, Word of God, inspiration, Scripture, the Scriptures, Holy Writ, the Bible.

Old Testament; Septuagint, Vulgate, Pentateuch, the Apocrypha, &c.

New Testament; the Gospels, the Evangelists, the Epistles, the Apocalypse, the Revelation.

Talmud, Mishna, Masora.

A prophet, evangelist, apostle, disciple, saint; the fathers, the apostolical fathers.

Adj. Scriptural, biblical, sacred, prophetic, evangelical, apostolic, apostolical.

986. Pseudo-Revelation. The Koran, (or Alcoran,) Shaster, Vedas, Zendavesta, &c.

False prophets and religious founders: Buddha, Zoroaster, Confucius, Mahomet, &c.

3. Religious Sentiments.

987. Piety, religion, (spirituality,) faith, religiousness, godliness, reverence, humility, veneration, devoutness, devotion, grace, unction, edification; holiness, sanctity, sacredness, consecration.

Regeneration, conversion, justification, sanctification, salvation, inspiration.

A believer, Theist, Christian, saint, devotee.

V. To be pious, &c., to believe, have faith; to convert, edify, sanctify, regenerate, inspire; to consecrate, to enshrine.

Adj. Pious, religious, devout, reverent, godly, heavenly-minded, pure, holy, spiritual, saintly, saint-like.

Believing, faithful, Christian, catholic, &c.

988. Irreligion, ungodliness, unholiness.

Scepticism, doubt, unbelief, disbelief, incredulity, incredulousness, 485, 487.

Atheism, deism, (materialism,) infidelity, freethinking.

An atheist, sceptic, unbeliever, deist, freethinker, infidel.

V. To be irreligious, disbelieve doubt, question, &c.

Adj. Irreligious, indevout, undevout, ungodly, unholy, unsanctified.

Sceptical, unbelieving, freethinking, incredulous, unconverted.

Deistical, anti-Christian, unchristian, worldly-minded, mundane, carnal, earthly-minded.

989. Impiety, irreverence, profaneness, profanity, blasphemy, desecration, sacrilegiousness; reviling, scoffing.

Assumed piety; hypocrisy, pietism, (mysticism), formalism, austerity, sanctimony, sanctimoniousness, pharisaism.

A scoffer, hyprocrite, pietist, religionist, formalist.

A bigot, enthusiast, fanatic, Pharisee.

V. To be impious, &c.

To profane, desecrate, blaspheme, revile, scoff.

Adj. Impious, profane, irreverent, sacrilegious, desecrating, blasphemous, unhallowed, unsanctified, hardened, reprobate.

Hypocritical, pietistical, sanctimonious, pharisaical, over-righteous.

Bigoted, priest-ridden, fanatical, enthusiastic.

4. Acts of Religion.

990. Worship, adoration, devotion, homage, service, humiliation, kneeling, genuflection, prostration.

Prayer, invocation, supplication, petition, orison, &c., 765, litany, the Lord's prayer, paternoster, collect.

Thanksgiving, giving or returning thanks, grace, praise, benediction, doxology, hosanna, hallelujah.

Psalmody, psalm, hymn, chant, antiphon, response, anthem.

Oblation, sacrifice, incense, libation, burnt-offering.

Discipline, self-discipline, self-examination, self-denial, fasting.

V. To worship, adore, do service, pay homage, humble one's self, kneel, bend the knee, prostrate one's self.

To pray, invoke, supplicate, petition, put up prayers or petitions; to ask, implore, beseech, &c., 765.

To return or give thanks; to say grace, to bless, praise, glorify, magnify, sing praises, give benediction.

To propitiate, offer sacrifice, fast, deny one's self; vow, offer vows, give alms.

Adj. Worshipping, &c., devout, solemn, reverent, pure, fervid, heartfelt, &c.

991. Idolatry, idle worship, devil worship, fetichism.

Deification, apotheosis, canonization.

Sacrifices, hecatomb, holocaust; human sacrifices, immolation, infanticide, self-immolation.

V. To worship idols, pictures, relics, &c., to deify, to canonize.

Adj. Idolatrous.

992. Sorcery, magic, the black art, necromancy, theurgy, thaumaturgy, witchcraft, fetichism, sortilege, conjuration, fascination, mesmerism, clairvoyance, second sight, (spiritual rappings,) divination, enchantment, hocus-pocus, 545, ordeal.

V. To practise sorcery, &c.; to conjure, exorcise, charm, enchant, bewitch, entrance, mesmerize, fascinate; to taboo, wave a wand, cast a spell, call up spirits, (to be a spiritual medium.)

Adj. Magic, magical, cabalistic, talismanic, incantatory, charmed, exorcised, &c.

993. Spell, charm, incantation, exorcism.

Talisman, amulet.

Wand, caduceus, rod, divining rod.

994. Sorcerer, magician, conjurer, necromancer, seer, wizard, witch, weird, charmer, exorcist, soothsayer, 513.

5. Religious Institutions.

995. Churchdom, ministry, apostleship, priesthood, prelacy, hierarchy, church government, church:—(in a bad sense) priestcraft.

Monachism, monasticism.

Ecclesiastical offices and dignities; pontificate, primacy, archbishopric, bishopric, episcopate, episcopacy, see, diocese; deanery, stall, canonry, canonicate, prebend, prebendaryship; benefice, in cumbency, living, cure, rectorship, vicarship, vicariate, deaconry, deaconship, curacy, chaplaincy, chaplainship.

Holy orders, ordination, institution, consecration, induction, preferment.

Council, conclave, convocation, (association, consecration, presbyery, conference,) synod, consistory, chapter, vestry, 696.

V. To call, ordain, induct, prefer.

Adj. Ecclesiastical, clerical, sacerdotal, priestly, prelatical, pastoral, ministerial.

Pontifical, episcopal, canonical; monastic, monkish.

996. CLERGY, ministers, the ministry, priesthood, presbytery.

A clergyman, divine, ecclesiastic, churchman, priest, presbyter, pastor, shepherd, minister.

Dignitaries of the church; primate, archbishop, bishop, prelate, diocesan, suffragan; dean, subdean, archdeacon, prebendary, canon; rector, vicar, incumbent, parson, chaplain, curate, deacon, preacher.

997. LAITY, flock, fold, congregation, assembly, brethren, people.

Temporality, secularization.

A layman, parishioner.

V. To secularize.

Adj. Secular, lay, civil, temporal, profane.

Church warden; clerk, precentor, choir, almoner, beadle, sexton.

Roman Catholic priesthood; pope, pontiff, high priest, cardinal; confessor, spiritual director, &c.

Cenobite, conventual, abbot, prior, monk, friar; lay brother; mendicant, Franciscan, (or Gray Friars,) Capuchin, Dominican, (or Black Friars,) Carmelite, Augustin, (or Austin Friars.)

Abbess, prioress, canoness, nun, novice, scribe.

998. RITE, ceremony, ordinance, observance, formulary, ceremonial, solemnity, sacrament.

Liturgy, ritual, book of common prayer, litany, &c.; rubric.

Service, duty, ministration, &c., *see* 990; preaching; sermon, homily, lecture.

Baptism, christening.

Confirmation, imposition, or laying on of hands.

The Eucharist, the Lord's supper, the communion, the sacrament.

Roman Catholic rites and ceremonies; mass, high mass; matins, vespers; the seven sacraments, auricular confession, flagellation, &c., breviary, missal, &c.

Relics, rosary, beads, reliquary, pyx, host, crucifix, &c.

V. To perform service, do duty, minister, officiate; to baptize, dip, sprinkle, &c.; to confirm, lay hands on, &c.; to give or administer the sacrament.

To preach, sermonize, lecture.

Adj. Ritual, ceremonial, &c.

999. CANONICALS; robe, gown, pallium, surplice, cassock, scapulary, stole, tonsure, cowl, hood, bands, &c.

Mitre, tiara, triple crown, crosier.

1000. Place of worship, house of God.

TEMPLE, cathedral, minster, church, chapel, meeting house, tabernacle.

Parsonage, rectory, vicarage, manse, deanery, bishop's palace

Altar, shrine, sanctuary, sacristy, communion table; baptistery, font

Chancel, choir, nave, aisle, transept, vestry, crypt, stall, pew, pulpit, ambo, reading desk, confessional.

Monastery, priory, abbey, convent, nunnery, cloister.

Adj. Claustral, monastic, conventual

INDEX.

N. B. — The numbers refer to the headings under which the words occur. When the same word may be used in various senses, the several headings under which it will be found, according to those meanings, are indicated by the words printed in Italics. These words in Italics are not intended to explain the meanings of the word to which they are annexed, but only to assist in the required reference.

INDEX

INDEX.

INDEX.

INDEX.

INDEX.

INDEX.

INDEX

INDEX.

INDEX.

INDEX.

B.

INDEX.

INDEX.

INDEX.

INDEX.

INDEX.

INDEX.

INDEX

INDEX.

INDEX.

INDEX.

INDEX.

INDEX.

INDEX.

INDEX.

INDEX.

INDEX.

INDEX.

INDEX.

INDEX.

INDEX.

INDEX.

INDEX.

INDEX

E.

INDEX.

INDEX

F.

INDEX.

INDEX.

INDEX.

INDEX.

INDEX.

INDEX.

INDEX.

H.

INDEX.

INDEX.

I.

INDEX.

INDEX.

INDEX.

INDEX.

INDEX.

INDEX.

K.

L.

INDEX

INDEX.

INDEX.

INDEX.

INDEX.

N.

INDEX.

O.

INDEX.

P.

INDEX.

INDEX

INDEX.

INDEX.

INDEX.

INDEX.

INDEX.

INDEX.

Q.

INDEX

INDEX.

S.

INDEX.

INDEX.

INDEX.

INDEX.

INDEX.

INDEX.

INDEX.

INDEX.

T.

INDEX.

INDEX.

INDEX.

INDEX.

INDEX.

U.

INDEX.

INDEX.

INDEX.

INDEX.

INDEX.

W.

INDEX.

X.

Y.

Z.

NOTES

NOTES

NOTES

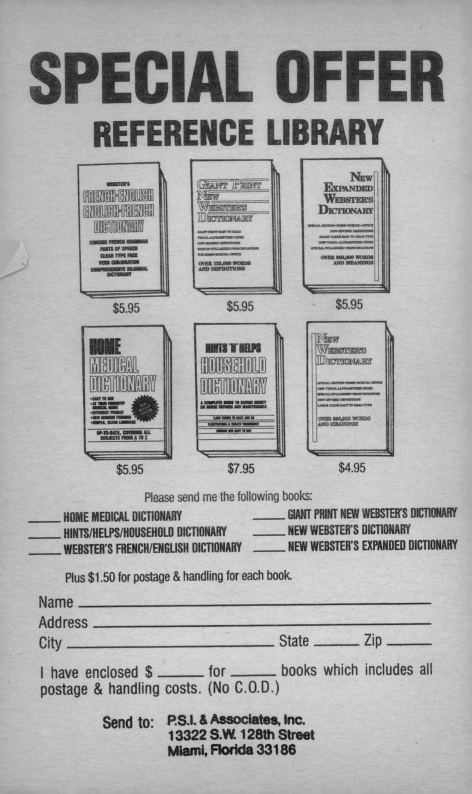